I0569391

REFLECTIONS
on
GROWTH

AN EXISTENTIAL JOURNEY

Randy M Herring

Reflections

on

GROWTH

An Existential Journey

By
Randy M Herring

The essays in this book are presented from an existential perspective, aiming to foster both personal and intellectual development. The author seeks to offer thoughtful insights that encourage introspection and self-development, though these reflections are rooted in their own experiences and interpretations. They are not intended to offend, nor should they be taken as professional advice or definitive answers to life's challenges. Recognizing that everyone's path is unique, the author invites readers to approach these essays with an open mind and a critical outlook. The primary aim is to inspire meaningful reflection and conversation, and to promote lifelong learning and personal growth in the pursuit of an authentic self.

Copyright © January 2025 by Randy M. Herring

This June 2025 edition features revised text for improved clarity, while maintaining the original content and page structure.

All rights reserved. No part of this publication may be reproduced, distributed, or transmitted in any form or by any means, including photocopying, recording, or any other electronic or mechanical methods, without the prior written permission of the author.

Typeset in New Caledonia 10.5 and 8.5 point

Front and back covers designed by Randy M. Herring
Back cover illustration by Santiago Vecino, used with permission.

ISBN: 979-8-218-56596-1

"It is not true that we have only one life to live; if we can read, we can live as many more lives and as many kinds of lives as we wish."

S. I. Hayakawa

"The aim of education is not to transfer knowledge; it is to guide the learning process, to put responsibility for study in the student's own hands, and place people on their own path of discovery and invention."

Tsunesaburo Makiguchi

CONTENTS

Contents (cont'd.)

Reflections

on

GROWTH

PREFACE

During my mid to late twenties, I grappled with an existential dilemma: If I am to truly exist as a human being and become who I am meant to be, I must take the risk of breaking free from the ideological systems that have shaped my existence—systems that told me how to think, who I was, and how I should live.

I lived and worked in Japan on three separate occasions over the span of seven years, from my early to late twenties. During my first time there, I took a one-year break from my university studies to travel to Japan and experience the work of a student missionary. I lived in Nishinomiya and worked in Osaka, where I taught English conversation and Bible classes.

I valued my first experience in Japan as a student missionary so deeply that it transformed me into a religious optimist. I became fully immersed in the system of a particular Christian organization, drawn to its sense of purpose and its mission to make a meaningful difference in people's lives.

My assimilation into the system was so profound that, upon returning to the United States, I took two significant steps at my university. First, I began pursuing a bachelor's degree in religious studies, eager to deepen my understanding of the subjects I had taught in Japan. Second, I initiated a community outreach program for the homeless, motivated by a desire to better understand their struggles and explore what I could—and couldn't—do to make a meaningful difference.

Two years later, I graduated with a degree in religious studies. A few months after that, I enrolled in a graduate program in religious education, intending to teach religion within the school system of that particular Christian denomination. However, the following year, I became disillusioned with the program. Just as I was questioning my path, I received an invitation to return to Japan. I decided to leave the graduate program behind and flew back for a second time, drawn by the value of my first experience and the mission that still called to me.

April 1988 in Tokyo marked a defining moment in my life, the beginning of a profound shift that would ultimately lead me to break away from the organization's system a year later. This period of transition prompted deep reflection on my experiences, and by the following year, I began writing what would become *Reflections on Growth*.

We cannot fully separate ourselves from an ideological system. Employers, for example, are part of a system that provides employees with the essential means of survival. To illustrate this, consider the first three levels of Maslow's hierarchy of needs. The first level addresses physiological needs: food, water, shelter, and sleep. The second level focuses on safety needs: security, employment, resources, and health. The third level pertains to love and belonging needs: friendship, intimacy, family, and social connections.

When an employer and an employee share a close friendship outside the workplace, the employee might feel a dual sense of obligation—not only to the business but also to the individual owner. This connection can blur the lines between the person and the system, causing the employee to become increasingly assimilated into the owner's identity. Over time, this can lead to a sense of losing oneself, even slipping into a state of "nothingness."[1] Similarly, anyone can fall into this nothingness simply by following an influencer or becoming part of a social group, often without even realizing it.

I began by questioning the very system that had shaped and absorbed me. In search of understanding, I turned to philosophy, exploring works like Aristotle's *Nicomachean Ethics*, Nietzsche's *Ecce Homo*, and Adler's

Great Ideas. I immersed myself in their ideas, hoping to uncover the deeper reasons behind my experiences and, more importantly, to discover what I could change within myself to transform my circumstances—and ultimately, my world.

I sent letters of discontent to the representatives of the organization, directly confronting them with my concerns. In these letters, I proposed ideas for reform, hoping to improve the system for the benefit of my colleagues. A few months later, as a result of my actions, I was asked to leave both my position and Japan.

Social systems often lack a focus on personal growth and the cultivation of authenticity. According to Maslow, the fourth and fifth levels of his hierarchy of needs are esteem and self-actualization. Esteem needs include respect, self-worth, recognition, and freedom. Self-actualization, on the other hand, is about realizing one's full potential—expressed through simplicity, autonomy, richness, and a deep sense of aliveness.[2]

I flew to Montana, where I stayed with my grandmother in Missoula and worked two jobs. It was the beginning of my journey toward self-discovery. During this time, I reflected on my mental and spiritual well-being, engaging deeply with my inner self. I wrote introspective essays about my personal state and the shifting state of the world around me. Through this process, I developed a deeper appreciation for myself, for others, and for the world. I also continued to send letters to the representatives of the organization in Japan, expressing my dissatisfaction and calling for change. After six months, I left Montana and moved to Oregon.

I drove to Portland and stayed with my father for a couple of weeks until I sold my car. Once it was gone, I bought a one-way ticket back to Japan. I packed my philosophy books, typewriter, a bowling ball, and a set of dress clothes. This third time to Japan was meant to be long-term—an opportunity not just to teach English conversation, but, more importantly, to study, observe, write, travel, and exercise.

After a couple of weeks in Japan, I began working for a company in Chiba, putting in 20 hours a week and living comfortably. In my free time, I read the newspaper, studied philosophy, and wrote essays and letters. As Nietzsche put it, I felt "fearless." I found myself facing a "great health"—a vast, unexplored territory filled with perspectives on what is beautiful, strange, unsettling, terrible, and divine.[3]

While it's impossible to fully detach ourselves from an ideological system, we can become aware of how such systems can stifle our growth and limit the potential of our existence. By recognizing this, we have the power to change what is necessary to awaken our conscious, autonomous selves—free from the constraints of collective identity. Instead of *conforming* to the norm, consuming everything around us, and blending in with the masses, we can nurture our true self by creating something meaningful and *living* as a free spirit.

I wrote these reflective essays thirty-five years ago, before the rise of the Internet, Google, and social media, compiling them into *Reflections on Growth*. Since then, they have been revised for this book. My way of life has changed little since I wrote these essays. I am still reading, still writing, still learning, and still thinking.

Writing and organizing the Afterword took me two years. To broaden my knowledge in areas where I was lacking, I delved into a variety of fields in addition to philosophical, religious, and biblical studies: depth psychology, social psychology, the history of early colonial America, biomedical ethics of human enhancement, cognitive neuroscience, and the ethics of artificial intelligence.

This journey has been one of personal growth, while reflecting on my experiences, which has, in turn, strengthened my sense of self. My hope is that by reading these *Reflections,* the reader may also embark on their own journey of self-exploration, discovering and strengthening their true, authentic self.

INTRODUCTION

Every individual finds themselves in an existential situation, whether they are aware of it or not, which either challenges or enhances their true authentic self and the meaning of their life.[4]

The term "existential" in existential philosophy refers to the human existence and the lived experience of being in an often absurd or indifferent world. It emphasizes individual choices, freedom, responsibility, and authenticity.

The core tenet of existential philosophy is that I first *exist*, confront myself, and emerge into the world. Only then do I assign an *essence* to my being, shaping the *meaning* of my existence *defined* through my *actions* and choices. In short, I create my own identity. This is the meaning of *"existence precedes essence."*[5] No one and nothing dictates who or how I should be. Each human situation is unique, offering the opportunity and challenge to act and define myself.[6]

To exist is to live through my intentional actions, not merely as one individual among many, but as *the* individual—my true, authentic self—engaging with others and being in the world. Human beings who consciously embrace their individuality are the ones who create values and shape meaning in their lives.

A truly free individual refuses to be absorbed into any system or defined merely by belonging to a group. Instead, they turn inward and reflect, using each unique situation to define and reaffirm their authentic self. For them, personal growth and well-being take precedence over conforming to an ideological system. By shaping their identity through actions, they foster mental, physical, social, psychological, and spiritual growth, broadening their perspective and continuously advancing toward greater development.

Learning Promotes Personal Growth

In his *The Advancement of Learning* (1605), English philosopher Francis Bacon outlines several key benefits of genuine learning. These are presented below in the order in which they appear in his text.

First, learning safeguards humans from ignorance and error.[7] Second, learning is health for the mind as exercise is health for the body.[8] Third, learning is an activity that is pleasurable in and of itself.[9] Fourth, learning makes the mind gentle, generous, and flexible, whereas ignorance makes it rude, decay, and defiant.[10]

Fifth, learning applies knowledge to human mannerisms to be beneficial for reward and comfort.[11] Sixth, learning ministers to all the diseases of the mind, providing healing and remedies.[12] Seventh, learning prevents the mind from becoming fixed or rigid, allowing it to remain open to growth and transformation.[13] Eighth, learning helps a person to grow into a better and more thoughtful human being each day.[14]

The seventh benefit leads directly to the eighth, which is the ultimate goal of learning. A sense of dissatisfaction with current knowledge, paired with an openness to new perspectives, allows the mind to shift and gain fresh insights. In this way, learning, in its patient pursuit of knowledge, remains flexible and open to revision as new insights arise from *experience*.[15] By maintaining an open mind, learning allows knowledge to evolve and deepen, helping a person grow into a more thoughtful human being each day.

Knowledge is Power

In his 1620 work *Novum Organum*, also known as *The New Instrument for Understanding Nature*, Bacon asserts that "knowledge and human power are synonymous."[16] He further notes, "[W]hile we falsely admire and extol the powers of the human mind, we do not search for its real helps. The subtilty [or the fineness of perception] of nature is far beyond that of [human] sense or of the understanding."[17]

Bacon argues that grasping the true essence of nature or reality is beyond the capacity of the human mind. When humans interpret nature, they do so from the perspective of the "human mind," which leads to distorted interpretations that are falsely presented as deriving directly from nature. In this way, humans replace what is truly natural with what is unnatural to them, creating misconceptions and false notions of knowledge, which are then mistakenly accepted as true knowledge.

Idols of the Mind

In the *Organum*, Bacon identifies four types of "idols" that reveal our biases and prejudices, leading to false knowledge and generic understandings of values. These *idols* represent misguided beliefs within ideological systems—Authority, Language, Identity, and Society—that distort our perception and hinder personal and intellectual growth. We often subconsciously idolize these human-made constructs, failing to question them as a result. These are known as "Idols of the Mind."[18] Like how a computer's programming dictates its function, these idols condition both the mind and the body, restricting the mind's adaptability and hindering the body's potential for growth.

The first group, *Idols of the Theater*, blindly follow the authority of powerful institutions and accept their judgments without questioning the reasoning behind them. The second group, *Idols of the Marketplace*, place excessive trust in conventional language as a neutral means of communication without questioning the complex meanings and functions that words can convey. The third group, *Idols of the Cave*, assume that one's identity is known, static, and unalterable, without considering the external influences and internal biases that shape both one's sense of self and its perceptions. The fourth group, *Idols of the Tribe,* are swayed by society's entertainment-driven distractions that shape our perceptions of reality without questioning how these diversions may be unnatural and detrimental, affecting our mental and physical well-being.[19]

Idols of the Mind erode the existential meaning of life, trapping us in a state of inauthenticity and robbing us of our fundamental right to live as genuine human beings. As Nietzsche observes, "There are more idols in the world than there are realities."[20] Indeed, countless idols are venerated across cultures and societies, while only a few realities remain.

A more detailed exploration of the Idols in the twenty-first century and their relevance is presented in the Afterword. Bacon's Idols of the Mind and their false notions of knowledge can be illustrated through Plato's *Allegory of the Cave,* which contrasts false knowledge with true knowledge.

Plato's Allegory of the Cave

Plato's *Allegory of the Cave* demonstrates the contrasting effects of counterfeit versus genuine education.[21] Counterfeit education involves passive learning, where individuals absorb information without critical engagement. In contrast, genuine education is an active, intellectual process of discovery, in which one ascends from mere opinion to true understanding. This journey transforms one's mindset, leading to a deeper grasp of reality and the attainment of authentic knowledge.[22]

Imagine a cave where people have been prisoners since childhood, shackled together and forced to face the wall. They have never seen the light outside the cave. Behind them, there is a low wall and a high ground, with a fire burning on the other side. The prisoners, unable to turn their heads, can only see the shadows of themselves and other objects projected onto the inside wall of the cave in front of them, cast by the fire behind them.

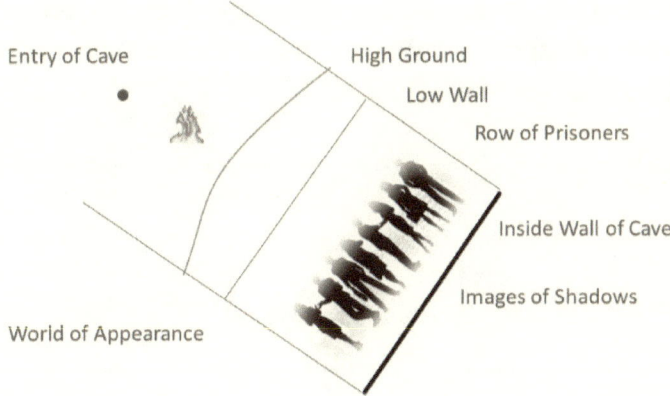

Entry of Cave
High Ground
Low Wall
Row of Prisoners
Inside Wall of Cave
Images of Shadows
World of Appearance

The prisoners believe the shadows on the wall are the true reality, thinking they represent genuine knowledge. In truth, these shadows only reflect a world of mere appearances—far from true knowledge or reality. The true, real world lies beyond them, outside the cave, hidden from their view.

We are all prisoners in Plato's Cave, clinging to the shadows we believe to be reality. Much like Bacon's Idols of the Mind, the images and impressions we perceive distort our judgment, shaped by hidden passions, biases, and prejudices that we are often unaware of. These distortions keep us from attaining authentic knowledge.

The Red or Blue Pill?

As prisoners, we are content to perceive reality through our senses, choosing the comfort of the "blue pill" and remaining in an illusionary world. If, by some means, we were to suddenly escape, we would be blinded by the harsh light of true reality, unable to comprehend it. In our confusion, we might cling to the shadows on the cave wall, believing them to be more real than the world beyond the cave.

However, if we chose the "red pill," freed ourselves, and ventured out of the cave, gradually adjusting to the light, we would begin to conceive reality through the intellect rather than perceiving it through the senses. In doing so, we would cross the divided line, moving from "belief" to "reasoning," and advancing into true reality.

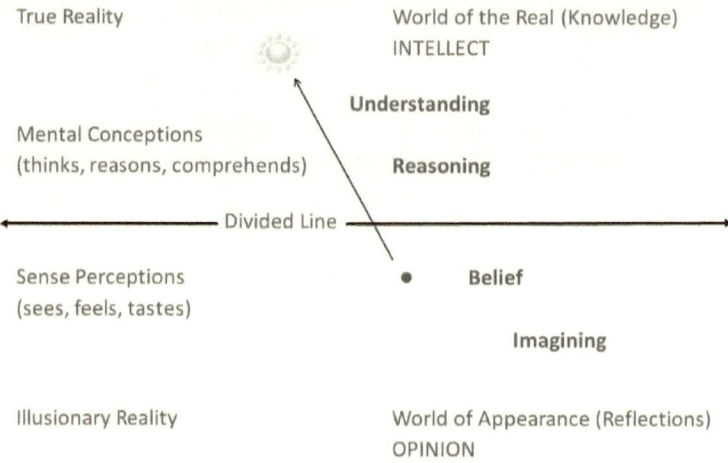

Below the divided line lies indoctrination and illusionary reality. "Opinion" pertains to perceiving the world through the senses—what we see, feel, and taste. Above the divided line, however, is the realm of true learning and understanding. "Intellect" involves comprehending reality through reason—what we think, analyze, and grasp with our minds. Crossing the divided line from opinion to intellect is not an automatic process; it demands effort and mental discipline.

The *Allegory of the Cave* and the divided line both illustrate how genuine education can awaken the mind, guiding it from the darkness of error and illusion into the light of truth and authentic knowledge. Education is a process of fostering, nurturing, and cultivating, all of which imply the "conditions of growth."[23] The word "education" itself comes from the Latin *educatum*, meaning "to lead out," reflecting the process of drawing the mind out of ignorance and into understanding.

Artificial Reality

Jean Baudrillard's 1981 book *Simulacra and Simulation* inspired the creation of the 1999 film *The Matrix*. In this work, Baudrillard explores how culture, media, and society shape our perception of reality, constructing a version of the world that we come to see as meaningful.

Baudrillard argues that representations of reality have evolved to a point where they no longer correspond to any original reference, a concept he refers as "simulacra." On social media platforms like Facebook, Instagram, TikTok, and LinkedIn, for instance, what we encounter is often just an endless repetition of existing content—copies of copies of copies of copies—devoid of new ideas, offering little to inspire growth and creativity.

Ultimately, simulacra creates a sense of hyperreality, where everything seems repetitive and uninspired. A hyperreality is an aggregate of simulations of 'reality' that either distorts the reality it purports to depict or does not depict anything with a real existence at all, but which nonetheless comes to constitute reality.[24]

A hyperreality suggests a perfect image or idealized object, yet their simulated or fake betrays the unreality of their nature. For example, a photo that has been touched up by a computer, a theme park like Disneyland, or a sports drink with a flavor that doesn't exist ("wild ice zest berry").[25]

On Baudrillard's account, the appearance of reality has taken a reversal turn opposite to Plato's Cave. Rather than ascending upward to true reality from illusionary reality, Baudrillard descends downward from reflection of reality to artificial reality.

Simulation Theory

What is reality? Could everything we experience, everything that exists in our entire universe be artificial? Supporters of simulation theory believe that not only is it possible that we're living in a simulation, but it's likely.[26]

Simulation theory is a philosophical concept rooted in metaphysics, proposing that our reality is an artificial construct, generated by a computer program. One of the most notable contemporary proponents of this theory is Oxford philosopher Nick Bostrom, who, in 2003, published a groundbreaking paper arguing that it is highly likely we are living within a computer simulation.[27]

We rely on computer models to analyze human populations and forecast the weather. In gaming, simulations recreate entire worlds for entertainment. Humans instinctively search for mathematical patterns in nature's chaos, perhaps because we are programmed to do so. What is fascinating is that, in attempting to disprove simulation theory, humans may inadvertently end up supporting it.

When a civilization can create a realistic simulation, the most obvious one to create is that of its own early existence. Bostrom calls this "ancestor-simulations."[28] A.J. Gentile, host of *The Why Files,* suggests a civilization that can do this would not just create one simulation; it would create many simulations. And those simulated civilizations might create their own simulations of the universe.[29]

A key argument for simulation theory is that it cannot be disproven, much like the Big Bang theory, which could be viewed as the moment the simulation "booted up." Gentile poses the question, "But who created the simulation?"[30]

Gentile goes on to say that when you consider the creator of the simulation as an all-knowing intelligence existing beyond our comprehension of space and time, it begins to sound remarkably similar to the concept of God. He further notes that, just as we cannot definitively prove we are not living in a simulation, we also cannot prove that God does not exist.[31]

Gentile continues by pointing out that when something miraculous or terrible occurs, you could just as easily attribute it to the simulation as you could to God's plan. Interestingly, many proponents of simulation theory are atheists who dismiss the idea of God as superstition. Similarly, there are many religious individuals who reject concepts like evolution and the scientific understanding of the Earth's age.[32]

Gentile wraps up his thoughts on simulation theory by noting that the religious community argues that without God, life becomes nothing more than a simulation—where our actions lack consequences, and nothing truly matters. On the other hand, the scientific community asserts that even if we live in a simulated reality, our actions still have real consequences. When it comes to what happens after we die, whether in a simulation or not, the truth remains uncertain. Both sides often claim that faith and science are incompatible. But, Gentile asks, isn't this a form of hypocrisy, regardless of whether you believe in God or in simulation theory? "The real question is," he adds, "what's the difference?"[33]

The Internet

The Internet stands as the quintessential artificial reality. Our lives are now so deeply intertwined with it—its systems and symbols—that meaning itself seems to have disappeared, leaving existence feeling hollow. The Internet informs us, entertains us, and watches us. It manipulates us, alienates us, and controls us. We have become increasingly dependent on it, and in doing so, the Internet has transformed into an existential *threat* to our very being.

Most, if not all, of our online existence is artificial. The articles we read and the accounts we follow are often fabrications generated by artificial intelligence (AI). We are little more than drones in a digital anthill, living, working, and dying without real meaning. AI's role is to keep us engaged with content that holds no true value and to push products we do not really need. This is known as the "Dead Internet Theory."[34] I explore this theory more in the fourth and final section of the Afterword, under Bacon's Idols of the Tribe, near the end.

We are no longer the architects of our own destinies as active agents. Instead, we have become passive participants, shaped by a coded and programmed order conveyed through the signals of the Internet, used as mere means to an end.[35] We have grown indifferent to one another, existing in what can only be called Nihilistic Times. In response, we have a choice: to embrace active nihilism or to yield to passive nihilism.[36]

An active nihilist, on one hand, embraces the freedom to create their own values and meaning, living a purposeful and authentic life outside the confines of the system, even in a world where all meaning and originality have dissolved into hyperreality.

A passive nihilist, on the other hand, remains dependent on the system, conforming to the widespread indifference of the masses within that hyperreality. They choose not to disconnect, driven by fear of the unknown and a reluctance to break free from the comfort of the familiar.

Existence Precedes Essence

Similar to Plato's *Allegory of the Cave, The Matrix* conveys the idea that ordinary perceptions of reality do not reflect the true nature of existence. It suggests that discovering the truth through one's insight has the power to transform one's understanding. In this way, Neo mirrors the prisoner in the cave who, after being freed from his chains, begins his journey toward the light of enlightenment.

In a scene where Morpheus takes Neo to meet the Oracle, Neo sits in the back seat of the car beside Trinity, gazing out the window as he struggles to come to terms with the staggering revelation that his life has been spent in a computer-generated illusion known as "the Matrix." He reflects, "I have these memories from my life, [but] none of them happened." Confused, he turns to Trinity and asks, "What does that mean?" She answers, "The Matrix cannot tell you who you are."[37]

Trinity is highlighting that nothing—whether it's a job, a role, a sport, an activity, a label, a disease, or even something as abstract as a computer program or hyperreality—can define who you are. No matter how long you've clung to it or how much recognition you've received for it, these things don't determine your essence. You exist first as a human being, and it is through your own choices and self-definition that you give yourself meaning.

Both *The Matrix* and Plato's *Allegory of the Cave* align with a core principle in Socratic philosophy: true education happens when learning is self-directed, empowering individuals to make their own discoveries. Before one can define their own identity, they must first undergo the essential journey of self-awareness to know oneself. As Morpheus tells Neo, "I can only show you the door. You have to walk through it."

Apathetic Loafer

We were passively born into a tradition that demanded our conformity, and as a result, we've become products of that tradition, bound to a system that stifles our personal growth. In doing so, we've allowed our authenticity to wither away. Sartre refers to this existential struggle as "nausea."[38]

In 1888, Nietzsche asks rhetorically, "Whether we have grown more moral?"[39] This question reflects themes he explored earlier in his 1881 work *Daybreak: Thoughts on the Prejudices of Morality*, where he examines the nature of morality and its roots in custom. Nietzsche contends that traditional morality is essentially a form of "obedience to customs," with customs serving as the established norms for behavior and judgment. He argues:

> [T]he *chief proposition* [of] morality is nothing other ... than obedience to customs, of whatever kind they may be; customs, however, are the *traditional* way of behaving and evaluating... The free human being is immoral because in all things he is *determined* to depend upon himself and not upon a tradition."[40]

To further explore the nature of tradition, Nietzsche asks, "What is tradition?" and answers, "A higher authority which one obeys, not because it commands what is *useful* to us, but because it *commands*."[41] When an individual breaks free from the authority of tradition, they are considered "immoral" by that tradition. This is why Nietzsche identifies himself as "the first *immoralist*" or, more broadly, as part of "we immoralists."[42]

An immoralist is someone who has liberated themselves to become their true, authentic self. They are conscious of the prejudices shaped by Idols of the Mind. The immoralist is like the prisoner who escapes from Plato's Cave, or like Neo, who breaks free from the Matrix.

An immoralist is freed from the constraints of collective values and is on the path to becoming a free spirit, fully realizing their true potential. Nietzsche describes the "free spirit" as drawing closer "to life," where warmth and new possibilities surround them. He writes:

> It grows warmer and around him ... warm breezes of all kind blow across him. It seems to him as if his eyes are only now open to what is *close at hand*... What a good thing he had not always stayed 'at home', stayed 'under his own roof' like a delicate apathetic loafer![43]

By remaining within the confines of familiar surroundings—whether tradition, social circles, or societal expectations—one risks becoming what Nietzsche calls an "apathetic loafer," stagnating in comfort and detachment from life's fuller possibilities. An apathetic loafer is indifferent, taking no steps toward personal growth or progress. They reject freedom, independence, critical thinking, identity, destiny, and the very possibility of change.

Leaving behind the comfort of home and the familiarity of one's surroundings can break the grip of indifference. Why is this important? As Spinoza wisely says, it's about "freeing every man from fear, so that he may live in security, *preserving* his natural right to *exist* and *act*—without harm to himself or others."[44] Only by stepping beyond the known can we truly tap into the full potential of life and our own growth.

Be fearless. Say goodbye to your comfort zone and take a leap of faith. Turn 180 degrees, leave behind the shadows of Plato's Cave, and walk toward the light—feel the warmth of the sun for the first time.[45] Take the red pill and discover how deep the rabbit hole really goes.[46] Move with awareness, causing no harm to yourself or others. Breathe in the fresh air, and soar to heights you've never imagined.[47]

Just as Kant was awakened from his "dogmatic slumber" by Hume, Nietzsche similarly woke me from a naïve religious optimism, revealing how systems of power—whether religious, political, or social—can manipulate, dominate, and imprison the mind, preventing individuals from achieving authenticity.[48] In response, we must embrace Paul's mindset, saying, "Not that I have already attained it, but I press on..." as we continue in our relentless pursuit of self-actualization and freedom from imposed constraints.[49]

Will-To-Power

Life is filled with many complexities, which often makes it ambiguous. This ambiguity can introduce negativity, causing individuals to become faint-hearted.[50] So, how can we find the motivation to act and build self-esteem in such moments? The answer lies in courage. Courage is the force that allows us to affirm life, even in the face of uncertainty.[51]

In his 1952 book *The Courage To Be,* Paul Tillich explores the idea of the "will-to-power" as presented by Nietzsche, offering a foundational impulse to act. Tillich explains that this concept is "neither will in the psychological sense nor power in the sociological sense," but rather refers to the "self-affirmation of life as life, including self-preservation and growth."[52] As Tillich puts it:

> [T]he will does not strive for something it does not have ... but wills itself in the double sense of preserving and transcending itself. This is its power, and also its power over itself. Will to power is the self-affirmation of the will...[53]

For Tillich, the self-affirmation of the will involves saying "yes" to life in two ways: first, by preserving itself, and second, by transcending itself. He further elaborates on Nietzsche's view by stating that "Life ... is the process in which the power of being actualizes itself."[54] In this sense, life is an ongoing act of self-actualization and affirmation.

Situations: Unique and Existential

John Dewey suggests that each person lives in a "series of" unique situations, while Karl Rahner similarly speaks of each individual existing within an "existential situation."[55, 56] The idea of a unique situation means that every experience we have is existential in nature. This implies that interactions take place either intrapersonally, between a person and objects, or interpersonally, between persons.

Unique and existential situations provide us with a constant, present reality that serves as a stimulus for action, driving us to affirm ourselves and cultivate authenticity. Life, like a human being, is dynamic—never static. Every person is a continuous process of organic, creative evolution, striving to become a particular kind of human being.[57] As Nietzsche puts it:

> Every person is a unique miracle ... beautiful and worth regarding... The person who does not wish to belong to the crowd needs only to cease taking himself easily; let him follow his conscience, which calls to him: 'Be yourself!'[58]

We are ultimately responsible for our own existence, serving as the true captains of our lives.

Language and Terminology in this Book

The concept 'God' is used in a broad sense, encompassing the views of theists, as well as serving as a point of discussion for agnostic and atheistic perspectives. It is also used when referring to the concept of God as understood within the three major monotheistic religions: Judaism, Christianity, and Islam. Additionally, the pronoun "He" is employed for simplicity when referring to God or the Divine, but this should not be interpreted as implying any gender-specific qualities.

When discussing the opposite of God—representing criticism, accusation, and the personification of evil—"the Devil" is used to signify a manifestation of evil, suffering, and disease as real forces. When referring to the figure within the Christian tradition, "Satan" is employed. Similarly, the pronoun "he" is used when referring to the Devil or Satan, though this is for convenience and does not imply any gendered nature.

When referring to "Jesus," the name is used to identify him as a historical religious figure of significant influence. When discussing Jesus as the "Christ"—that is, as God incarnate—the term "Christ figure" is used to highlight this as a debated event. In contexts where Jesus as the Christ is understood within the framework of the Christian tradition, the term "Christ" is employed. The pronoun "he" is used in all three instances when either referring to Jesus, the Christ figure, or Christ in the context.

The terms "Man," "man," "him," and similar expressions are used generically to refer to all of humankind, including both men and women, not just the male gender.

Names of individuals to whom three personal letters are directed in these *Reflections,* as well as the name of the organization, have been omitted. Instead, I use the individual's initials, and the organization is referred to by the generic acronym "ABC."

Organization of the Book

Reflections is structured into six parts, followed by an extensive—though not exhaustive—Afterword. While most of the reflections are arranged chronologically, Part Five consists of academic essays written during my time as a university student.

Each reflection is self-contained, exploring its own distinct context. This structure allows the essays to be read in any order without requiring cross-references, even though they collectively trace the evolution of my thinking. The essays have been updated and edited, with additional endnotes provided for further investigation.

Part I, "Social and Political," examines concepts such as truth, liberty, the problem of thinking and education, and the tension between individuality and politics. It also addresses issues like prejudice, racism, and the influence of tradition and language on our perceptions of freedom and identity.

Part II, "Self-Awareness," explores the journey of personal growth, covering topics such as self-confidence, overcoming insecurity, the importance of empathy, and the relationship between wealth and identity.

Part III, "Biblical Ethics and Social Change," discusses the inherent goodness in all people, God's justice, and the application of ethical principles in social change. It also highlights the distinction between pietism and moralism in distorting true goodness.

Part IV, "The Religious," considers issues such as religious optimism, the concept of predestination versus divine foreknowledge, and the contrast between a simple and cultivated person.

Part V, "Academia," analyzes the role of philosophy in education, the impact of teacher enthusiasm on student learning, the effects of repetition on memory and knowledge retention. It also includes an exegesis of a religious passage.

Part VI, "Autobiographical Reflections," features telling narratives on the existential path, complemented by poems that deepen insights into personal development.

The Afterword, "Idols of the Mind," is structured in four sections as a contemporary reflection on how institutional power, conventional language, self-perception, and cultural norms quietly constrain our growth. These mental idols—subtle yet pervasive—shape our ways of thinking, often reinforcing limiting beliefs rooted in authority, language, identity, and societal expectations.

Reflections on Growth urges readers to question and challenge the mindsets that hinder deep, authentic, and lasting transformation—shifts in how we think, perceive ourselves, and relate to the world. This inner change fosters greater clarity, freedom, and alignment with one's true self. *Reflections* encourages readers to let go of limiting ideologies and the distractions of digital noise, to break free from mental constraints, and to rediscover the limitless potential for personal growth in the pursuit of an authentic self.

Extensive endnotes provide references to the main text and suggest further reading, including books from my personal library—works, both historical and contemporary, that have shaped this philosophical vision.

Part I
Social and Political

Truth is Liberty[59]

WE HAVE SEEN RAPID CHANGES in the definition of 'truth' as it emerged during the immediate end of the previous decade, especially in Eastern Europe. Nineteen hundred and eighty-nine was a year of revolutions: whereas most were peaceful few were violent and bloody and cost the lives of thousands.

By looking back on these revolutions perhaps we are able to grasp the truth to the statement: *We always resist prohibitions and yearn for what is denied to us.* It is in this context that truth is liberty.

The transformation in Eastern Europe ought to be viewed as a symbol of 'truth' to the world to help, save and protect it from losing face, from the exploitation of those who abuse or misuse it to their own advantage beyond measure, e.g., the execution of the Romanian dictator on Christmas Day.

The ideological developments occurring in the Philippines, China, the Middle East, Hungary, Poland, Czechoslovakia, Bulgaria, East Germany, Romania and elsewhere in the world where freedom is being fought for, echoes the yearning for what is denied, and that is growth.

Growth depends on the capacity to find freedom. Liberty welcomes this, but not forgetting that it is regulated by justice. Growth prepares the way for upward progress, but it also calls for independence that must be respected.

The belief in growth implies independence, that which makes progress possible. Independence that must be respected means that individual differences must be valued.

We can only build a better world together if only individual differences are valued and independence respected. This means setting aside the superfluity of prejudice that hinders growth. From this perhaps it is easier to grasp in all persons their 'creative good' and esteem them accordingly from the results observed.

Postscript

Often, what is widely accepted as truth becomes a substitute for actual truth. When belief takes the place of truth, the latter is distorted or obscured. We tend to gather incomplete information, and rush to conclusions making hasty judgments. What is needed is time for careful, balanced thinking.

Truth means different things to different people, shaped by the values and influences around them. It is said that the Christ figure described himself as the "truth." Was he not implying, like so many other influential figures throughout history, that truth is also freedom? After all, he positioned himself as a liberator—one who sought to free people from the constraints of limited, conventional thinking.

In the context of a rapidly changing world, truth can be equated with liberty. Truth implies independence and calls for growth, as it is only through growth that progress becomes possible. But while liberty is crucial, justice holds an even deeper significance. Justice is what tempers liberty and ensures equality; it serves as the essential instrument of love. Through justice, love finds its true expression.

Yet, above all, friendship surpasses even justice in importance. As Aristotle says, "When men are friends, justice is unnecessary." In the bond of friendship, individuals no longer need external principles to justify their noble actions, because love flows freely from within. In this space, they love their neighbors as themselves.

In this way, a person can use their own doubts and uncertainties as a measure against higher principles, allowing for "freedom of spirit." This freedom fosters the development of virtue—the power to love one's neighbor as oneself. By embracing this ideal, we open the door to growth, progress, and a world where independence is respected, and differences are valued.

Madness, All Is Madness

I SET OUT TO SEEK AND EXPLORE the nature of Man and all his endeavors, all that is done under the sun. I pondered this, I reflected on that. In the end, I came to understand: *All is Madness.* I saw that what we pursue is a striving after illusion—the appearance of things, not their essence. Man judges by what he sees, lives for knowledge, lives to grow, lives to amass more of this Madness...

Look here! Look there! Everywhere you turn, Madness is rampant dancing in the streets, in institutions, in governments. It wasn't long before Man created his gods, and Madness crept in. It spread through religion, science, politics, morals, in foreign and domestic affairs. Madness proclaims, *"Kada wa qadar!"*—it is all predestined by God.

Madness emerged soon after Man was placed on this earth to tend it, to complete the work God had set in motion. And long, long before the Madman declared, "God is dead."

In a time far before Man's birth, there was the *Real World*. But no—when Man arrived, the Real World fled. It was never truly known. It was erased by Man. Thus, the Real World was replaced by the *Apparent World.* Man gave meaning to the Apparent World and called it the Real World. Both worlds clashed—one annihilated the other. Man destroyed the Real World... and created the Apparent World... and called it real. The Real and Apparent Worlds canceled each other out, and what was left? *Madness.*

Madness thrives on appearances, living in a pretended "truth." It values what is outward, what seems moral, what fits its view of the world. Madness lives to satisfy its image, to judge by it, to secure its own advantage. And yet, Madness later admits its judgments were hasty, inaccurate, and it apologizes.

Madness says, "I know this and that," but its knowledge is not true acquaintance. It is based on sight, on sound, on passing encounters. It is not genuine knowing—deep understanding of what something truly is.

Madness sees, hears, feels, reads, observes from its own limited angle. It perceives, but its perception is false. It perceives only the surface, without knowing what lies beneath, without true understanding. Human, all too human. *Madness*—all is Madness done under the sun.

Madness always says, "I see," and proclaim what it sees with triumph, as though that sight were truth itself. But sanity pauses and says, "I see, and I consider." Sanity reflects, whereas Madness is consumed with the outward dance of appearance. Madness is regression, a return to childhood. But, no, Madness never truly left childhood. In its purest form, Madness *is* childhood—endlessly imagining, endlessly dreaming.

Appearance satisfies Madness, fulfilling its deepest desires. Madness conjures illusions, for illusions are born from human longing. Madness esteems what things seem to be, or what it hopes them to be. Madness does not value what things actually are, or what they might become. Madness cannot believe in a true world, because it has created a fabricated one from its psychological needs.

Madness fears. Madness pretends to bravery. Madness grows anxious. Madness grows weak. It falls—falls in the face of appearance, of what things seem to wish to be. Instincts take the wheel, and Madness becomes driven by the lower animal instincts. The "genius of the species" submits to its own appetites! *"Kada wa qadar!"*

Madness crafts pretended truths that serve its own interests, that secure power and advantage. Madness proclaims itself! Madness is madness because it gives without possessing. It speaks without thinking. It acts without understanding. It knows but always forgets—and never learns. *Madness,* all is Madness. Madness—everything is Madness done under the sun.

The Problem with Thinking

WE DON'T THINK THINGS THROUGH ENOUGH because we passively go along with what we've been taught and what we take for granted. We seem to be losing our inspiration, and in doing so, we're losing the precious gift of thought that the Creator has bestowed upon us. Our minds appear to be narrowing, pushing us further from the great thinkers of history—Socrates, Aristotle, Augustine, Aquinas, Descartes, Voltaire, Nietzsche, Sartre—whose wisdom mirrors the innate, natural potential within every human being. This dormant potential yearns to be awakened, yet it remains shackled by the conformity and indifference that define our lives today. We are surrendering to the decay of custom, culture, and routine. In one word: Contentment.

We follow society's dictates: how to behave, what to say, what principles to uphold in the name of morality. Social conditioning feeds us a constant stream of ideas about what is "right" and "wrong," shaping our actions with its rewards and punishments. But has this made us *more moral?*

While social conditioning can offer stability and a sense of identity, it also enslaves our thinking, preventing us from viewing the world through different perspectives and appreciating beauty in the context of diversity and change. When we surrender to this conditioning, we risk becoming victims of "conscious incompetence"—so entrenched in our ways that we refuse to consider alternative viewpoints or seek understanding beyond the familiar.

Clinging exclusively to custom or herd mentality has two effects: first, it stifles human growth; second, it curtails the freedom of the spirit, denying us the possibility of a richer, more balanced life. The motto of the herd is simple: "You do it because that's the way it's always been, the way it is, and the way it always will be." Is it any wonder, then, that following the herd leads to stagnation and a life devoid of true progress?

When does genuine thinking begin? It begins with *doubt*—the willingness to question the dogmas and maxims we've absorbed without scrutiny. Next, it involves *examining* these ideas and identifying their core principles. What can be proven true or false? Are these ideas prescriptive or descriptive truths? Finally, thinking means *judging* what we have examined and defined with a balanced perspective—evaluating what is truly meaningful and beautiful, what advances humanity, and what deepens our understanding of life.

Dogmas and maxims handed down to us do not define who we are. Only when we begin to doubt and examine these beliefs do we start to form our own philosophy—one grounded in a deeper understanding of ourselves and the world. Only then do we become the true architects of our lives.

To create your own personal philosophy is not to reject everything you've been taught, but to weigh it against your own observations and experiences. Retain what is good and useful, discard what no longer serves you, and cultivate a life that reflects your true values. Custom and personal perspective are not enemies; when combined, they form a harmonious framework for living—one that draws upon both tradition and individuality.

In doing so, you are not merely adhering to a set of inherited rules; you are engaging with life's great questions in a meaningful way. The values you live by arise from your ability to exercise freedom, and the development of your personal philosophy requires not just knowledge, but wisdom—a wisdom that guides your actions and judgments in every situation.

I once came across a poem in a Christian home in Mountain View, California: *"What we are is God's gift to us. What we become is our gift to God."* This thought captures the essence of what I am describing—the challenge of thinking for oneself. Custom, culture, and external influences can shape us into what others want us to become, but that is not our true gift. True growth begins when we break free from societal conditioning and start living in alignment with our authentic selves, guided by genuine faith and a conscious heart.

The fear of stepping outside our conditioned roles often holds us back. We fear rejection and isolation, yet it is precisely in these moments of solitude that we discover our true selves—our unique "I." Those who dare to break away from conformity are the ones who unlock their potential, discovering the capacity to think, create, and become a gift to the world.

The challenge is to awaken our dormant ability to think, to ignite a spark of consciousness that makes us aware of our power to shape our lives and contribute to the greater good. The problem with thinking is not that we cannot think—it's that we have forgotten how to truly think for ourselves. Now is the time to remember, to reclaim that gift, and to transform both ourselves and the world around us.

Employment:
Individuality vs Politics

WHY DO I HAVE TO PRETEND TO BE SOMEONE I'M NOT just to be liked? Is it moral? Is it ethical? When people are drawn to a false version of me—one crafted to meet their expectations rather than reflect my true self—genuine connection becomes impossible. Some have become so accustomed to deception and manipulation that they no longer recognize how taking unfair advantage of others is never truly beneficial, even if it offers temporary gain.

If I allow someone to shape my identity into a version they prefer—one that mirrors their ideal of an "equal" but is, in truth, deeply unequal—I lose, and they gain the upper hand. By threatening my job security, they coerce me into becoming what they want, at the expense of my authenticity. My real identity is discarded, lost in the void. I become unsure, unstable in my own skin. My behavior shifts.

The result is tragic: I become what I despise—a politician without an identity, a face without integrity. Just like them—a liar. Why can't people simply accept me for who I am, rather than what I can do for them?

Why are those in positions of political power often the most skilled at lying? Their power—built on manipulation and control—explains their ease with deceit. How can you know they're lying? First, they deny that anything happened. Then, they become defensive, taking criticism personally—an implicit admission of guilt. Finally, they deflect blame, accusing others of actions they themselves committed, exposing the lie in the process.

What about "attitudes" and "leading by example" in the workplace? When an employee raises concerns, it's often dismissed as having a "bad attitude" or being "insubordinate." But in reality, expressing disagreement or frustration can be a vital form of communication—a search for truth. Arguments and attitudes aren't resistance; they're alternative perspectives. They are necessary for questioning falsehoods and revealing the truth.

If leaders model ethical behavior, employees will often follow. But when those in power lie, play mind games, use manipulative language, or treat subordinates unequally, those behaviors become the norm. Unethical behavior spreads—silently, insidiously—until it defines the workplace culture.

Treating employees unfairly is not just bad management; it's a glaring double standard. Without workers, there would be no business. Yet, the modern workplace often fails to appreciate human dignity, creativity, or knowledge. Instead, it prioritizes power and profit—seeking to suppress the very qualities that make individuals valuable.

In corporate culture, workers are expendable. One day you're hired; the next, you're replaced. This is the organization's version of survival of the fittest: *"Become like me, and you will survive."* But this demand isn't about personal growth—it's about conformity and control.

It's disheartening that in this nation—once a beacon of individualism— personal identity is now often dismissed or suppressed, except in select creative fields. Ironically, individualism is sometimes more respected in other countries, where it's viewed as a basic human right. But here, it's often sacrificed in service to systems that reward obedience over originality.

Isn't self-respect the foundation of respecting others' individuality? Sadly, many people don't truly know, like, or respect themselves. As a result, they treat others the way they've been treated—harshly, conditionally—rather than according to the Golden Rule: *treat others as you wish to be treated.*

True respect for individuality is rare. Yet it's the key to mutual growth, development, and ethical coexistence. In the corporate world, however, respect is too often a facade—a strategic illusion used to control the workforce rather than value it.

No Respecter of Persons

WE ARE ALL ENDOWED WITH THE FUNDAMENTAL RIGHTS to life, liberty, and the pursuit of happiness. The first of these—the right to life—is a divine gift, the breath of existence granted to us by our Creator. The other two—liberty and the pursuit of happiness—enable us to live meaningful, fulfilling lives when we follow the *golden mean*, a principle of moderation and balance. Together, these rights empower us to shape our own destinies, free from societal labels and external definitions.

Each person has a duty to exercise the talents and gifts given to them by God, doing so freely and responsibly. To live fully is to honor one's conscience and strive to become "all things to all people" in every way. Respecting others means protecting each individual's right to life, liberty, and the pursuit of happiness—ensuring that all people can reach their potential without hindrance. We must act in ways that allow others to experience their rights fully, without obstruction or interference.

The wisdom of the Old Testament teaches us to show no partiality—to be *no respecter of persons*. This principle calls us to value each individual for their inherent dignity, to see them as unique creations of God, and to uphold fairness in a way that sustains justice and protects everyone's rights.

The erosion of a person's right to life often comes from two sources: loyalty to an institution or a position within it, and favoritism—the selective respect shown to certain individuals or groups to preserve the status quo. Both arise from a fear of losing power or status—an instinct for self-preservation. While self-preservation can be virtuous when pursued with integrity, it becomes dangerous when rooted in selfishness or fear. In such cases, it leads to actions that harm others, often irreversibly.

The first source of this fear stems from the pressure to live up to the image of a "role model" defined by institutional expectations. The second, though related, is both internal and external: the fear of questioning or challenging an institution's ethical standards. This fear threatens to shift the moral norms of what is considered "good" or "bad" in society. Both fears are understandable, but only the first—the fear of failing to meet external expectations—lacks moral justification.

Living up to a prescribed role can be painful, especially when it demands sacrifices that undermine our shared rights. It may be easy to respect someone who performs their duties within an institution, but it becomes harder when that person values institutional loyalty over human dignity—prioritizing power over humanity. Even critics of such loyalty may admire its consistency, mistaking it for strength or moral conviction.

True respect, however, lies in championing humanity. The individual who transcends institutional morality becomes a *contestant* in the moral arena. They challenge accepted norms, asking whether the institution has become truly ethical—or merely more sophisticated in its control. With courage, such individuals step beyond conventional moral boundaries, rising above simplistic labels of "good" and "evil" to forge their own path.

Is it contradictory to respect someone while also opposing them? Consider the parent-child relationship: a parent may disagree with a child's actions while still loving and respecting them. The same principle applies here. One can respect another's dignity and humanity while resisting the systems or forces that restrict their freedom.

For the moral contestant, respect is not given to authority or position, but to the deeper principle of responsible action and love for others' well-being. Resistance—when motivated by the desire to preserve human dignity and prevent the degradation of others—is not only justified; it is a moral imperative.

When a person's rights are violated, justice demands that the balance between equality and inequality be restored. To preserve the rights we all possess—life, liberty, and the pursuit of happiness—we must defend these freedoms continually, not only for ourselves, but for all people. We share in the beauty of God's creation and the responsibility to honor it.

Tradition and Reflexivity

THE ERRORS OF PAST PHILOSOPHERS have created a false tradition. Philosophers who challenge this tradition—those who speak against its falsity by introducing new concepts and terms to offer altered perspectives—paradoxically undermine their own philosophy. After all, they are products of the very tradition they seek to escape. A philosopher may attempt to distance himself from tradition, but ultimately, he cannot. He remains entangled in it, unable to free himself. Even as he strives to offer new ideas, he contradicts himself—perhaps out of frustration or as a form of revenge against his own entrapment.

The philosopher becomes aware of this contradiction. He becomes unintelligible, contributing to the very tradition he condemns: a tradition of falsity. While he may create a new mode of thought, a new tradition, it remains a tradition nonetheless—albeit one that appears more colorful or novel.

When the philosopher believes he has created something entirely new, he has, in fact, merely revived the old, albeit in a modified form. He believes it to be new, but his philosophy remains false. He is an error, and he knows it. Yet he persists in his evasions and contradictions, aware of the direction of his journey, attracting followers along the way.

Human beings cannot fully express what they truly wish to say, for tradition constrains them with its language of certainty. If they reject tradition, they reject themselves, for they are products of it. They are caught in a web—a trap of their own making. Believing they can break free and speak their minds, they remain limited by the constraints of tradition and language. This limitation obscures their intent, making it impossible for them to fully articulate what they mean.

What, then, is this reflexivity? It is a powerful, deconstructive mode of thought that leads to a higher plane of understanding—though this understanding remains elusive. It returns not with conclusions, but with a language sweeter than honey, ever circling back upon itself.

Reflexivity is often labeled contradictory, evasive, and impenetrable, and therefore uncertain. It is the "other"—that is, reflexivity itself—that denies presence and allows for no final resolution. The text of reflexivity is never fixed and thus can never be definitively deciphered.

Reflexivity proposes nothing, defines nothing, and concludes nothing—not in the traditional sense of finality or presence. Instead, it leads us toward an awareness of the absence of presence, destabilizing the very foundations of tradition. This destabilization is a form of deconstruction—a challenge to tradition's authority.

Ultimately, reflexivity turns back upon itself and vanishes. It cannot stand, because it denies the idea of presence. It is this absence that denies presence, rendering reflexivity self-deconstructive. It brings us back to deconstruction—an ongoing process of questioning that never arrives at fixed conclusions.

Reflexivity, then, is more than a method that leads to an answer; it is an endless return to deconstruction itself, where every conclusion only reopens the possibility for further questioning.

Language and Perception

THE FORCE OF NIETZSCHE'S REFLEXIVITY IS POWERFUL because he understood the all-encompassing role of language. The modern idea of reflexivity arises when we move beyond the simple notion that language is merely a map of the world. The statement, "The character of the world is, to some extent, determined by the concepts we use to describe it," has an unsettling reflexive character.[60]

Nietzsche did not ask us to accept his ideas as true—in fact, he was more likely to insist that they were false. For him, to treat them as truth would be to petrify them, turning them into part of the very tradition he sought to disrupt. Heidegger, similarly, rejected the notion of ever having found the truth. What mattered to him was being "on the way"—a journey that is always in flux, always unfolding.

Derrida, by contrast, immerses himself in the texts of others as well as his own writing. In a sense, he becomes lost in the text. But how can such a state of being—being lost—be regarded as true? Perhaps the more effective stance is to maintain the fiction of truth, because, in a way, this fiction is something we can never fully abandon.

Take Wittgenstein's famous drawing of a rabbit:

Even if a magician conjures up a duck instead, no one can deny that what we see is a rabbit. But how does the magician perform this trick? Through the magic spell of the word "duck."

Are we not all magicians, casting spells with the words we call language? What else might you conjure? How do you seek out the new, the not-rabbit and not-duck, the thing that is neither page nor drawing? As you look at this elusive thing, before it takes form, it remains open.

Through language, theory, and text, we close off the openness of the world. These closures—these conceptual frameworks—shape our perception of the world. The desire for a final, definitive description of the world is a longing for something beyond what is possible. In the case of Wittgenstein's drawing, we can offer many interpretations: a rabbit, a duck, black lines on a page, tiny particles pressed onto a surface, an analogy, or simply a drawing.

Is it not absurd to insist on one of these as the "true" account? Or to think that the correct version could somehow be found, or that by adding all the interpretations together, we would arrive at the "complete" truth? So, it is with the world. We do not have different accounts of the same thing; we have different closures—different ways of interpreting and engaging with the world.

What matters is not the multiplicity of closures themselves, but how each closure textures our perception of the world and, in doing so, shapes what we can do within it. The closures we create determine the actions and possibilities available to us. They don't simply offer a worldview—they are the tools through which we navigate it.

The Influence of Ancient Literature

ANCIENT LITERATURE, SHAPED THE CULTURAL VALUES and worldviews of its time, continues to play a crucial role in how societies understand the universe and the nature of existence. These early texts were not merely stories or myths; they were frameworks for interpreting reality, helping civilizations define moral boundaries, spiritual beliefs, and the human condition itself.

One of the most profound ways ancient literature has shaped human thought is through the development of two key philosophical frameworks—monism and dualism—each offering distinct interpretations of the coexistence of 'good' and 'evil.'

Monism, expressed in texts like the *Upanishads*, presents the universe as a unified whole, where all things—including good and evil—are manifestations of a single divine essence. In contrast, dualism, seen in Zoroastrian scriptures and later Judeo-Christian writings, portrays existence as a battleground between two fundamentally opposed forces, such as light and darkness, or God and Satan. These frameworks provided early societies with powerful tools to interpret moral conflict, human purpose, and the nature of suffering.

Yet as these texts have been handed down through generations, their original meanings have often been lost or distorted. What were once culturally specific responses to existential questions have become universalized or oversimplified. In modern times, ancient narratives are frequently viewed as symbolic relics or dismissed as outdated myths. However, many foundational beliefs and values in contemporary culture—particularly around good and evil, justice, and identity—are still rooted in these early literary frameworks, even when their origins are no longer acknowledged.

This leads to a second problem: modern society inherits but often misinterprets ancient ideas. Influenced by Renaissance optimism and Enlightenment rationalism, we tend to prize contemporary literature and thought as fresh, objective, and superior, while relegating the past to irrelevance. And yet, ironically, many of the assumptions we consider "modern" are actually restatements of ancient concepts—unexamined beliefs passed down through tradition rather than reasoned discovery.

Finally, there is a deeper issue at work: language and inherited concepts themselves are often venerated uncritically. People are naturally drawn to the beauty and authority of words, often assuming that certain ideas originate from a higher—or even divine—source. In doing so, we elevate these human-made constructs—myths, moral systems, philosophical categories—to the status of timeless truths. Over time, such ideas become idols of thought: rarely questioned, yet profoundly influential.

And so, we arrive at a tragic irony: the very ideas created to help us understand the world become objects of blind reverence. We forget that these truths were once imaginative responses to real human concerns—tools, not absolutes. As a result, we become both masters and servants of our own creations, unable to clearly discern where inherited belief ends and authentic understanding begins.

Education Has Lost Its Mind

YOUNG WOMAN FOUND DEAD. Cause of death: drug overdose. True cause of death: failure of education. Occupation: prostitute. When investigators arrived at the scene, they estimated her age to be twenty-five. She was eighteen. Her name was Tina.

Young woman found dead. Cause of death: suicide, a jump from an apartment building. True cause of death: fear of education. Occupation: student. Reason for suicide: anxiety over an approaching exam. She was nineteen.

Young man feels exhilarated. Cause of exhilaration: self-esteem lessons. True cause of feeling good: arrogance fostered by education. Occupation: student. Reason for exhilaration: failure in a math exam.

Johnny is a high school graduate. Johnny cannot read or write. Cause of illiteracy: the failure of education. True cause of illiteracy: educational neglect.

It is the final decade of the 20th century, the cusp of a new millennium. From east to west, from west to east, a shadow of doubt and disillusionment hangs over education. It is clear: education is no longer fulfilling its expected role.

Education, as it currently stands, has drifted far from its true purpose. The attitudes and approaches shaping it today echo the skeptical words of the philosopher David Hume: *"No matter, never mind."* Education, according to Susanne Langer in 1956, is meant to "develop each individual mind as fully as possible to be immediately useful to society."[61] Twenty-six years before Langer's insight, Japanese educator Tsunesaburo Makiguchi wrote, "The purpose of education is to *arouse* interest."[62] He elaborates:

> The aim of education is not to transfer knowledge; it is to guide the learning process, to put the responsibility for study into the student's own hands, and place people on their own path of discovery and invention.[63]

Makiguchi emphasizes that the true goal of education is not simply to impart facts, but to spark curiosity and empower students to take ownership of their learning. By guiding students along their own paths of exploration and creativity, education becomes a process of self-discovery and invention, rather than passive absorption of knowledge.

Modern thinkers like Mortimer J. Adler have suggested that true education should allow individuals to engage with the "great ideas" that shape our world—ideas of truth, goodness, beauty, equality, liberty, and justice.[64] These ideas are not just abstract concepts; they are the principles by which we *judge* and *act* and shape our lives.

But to engage with such ideas, the mind must be open and free, ready to think deeply and critically. Why is this so crucial? Because through education, we develop the intellectual tools to engage with others, grow with new ideas, and apply them to live decent, meaningful lives.

Yet, from the perspective of these educators, the mind is all too often abandoned by the educational system, left vulnerable to the corrosive forces of societal ills. Education is failing in its core mission, and this is a failure we can no longer ignore or deny.

David S. Broder warns that simply meeting "minimal requirements" is a disservice to both students and society.[65] Choi Jin Young critiques the common reliance on multiple-choice tests, which are little more than "guessing games" that leave students "ill-equipped in thought."[66] This lazy form of assessment doesn't nurture the intellectual capacities of students; instead, it stifles them. What's worse, it celebrates a narrow, formulaic approach to learning that favors memorization over meaningful engagement with ideas.

Education is supposed to promote growth and creativity—qualities that emerge when students are free to think independently. The will to think and the capacity to create are driven by a natural desire for a fuller life. Education should foster this drive, rather than smother it. Yet too often, the system operates against this natural inclination, stifling the very intellectual freedom that should be its cornerstone.

Education has failed in its expected role. It has, in the words of the religious, "sinned." It obstructs growth, stifles freedom, and chokes the very intellectual life it is supposed to cultivate.

Education should not aim to create "memorizing machines," as one of my Japanese students once put it. Nor should it force conformity by "force-feeding" students with knowledge in a way that discourages dialogue and critical thinking.[67]

Education must embrace the inherent differences between individuals, recognizing that each person learns and grows at their own pace, according to their unique interests and intellectual capacities.

To truly foster growth, education must reject the myth of equality and acknowledge the diversity of minds. It must promote independent thinking, and embrace the creative arts, which nurture growth and the Aristotelian idea of *becoming*.

If Voltaire and Jean-Paul Sartre were to engage in conversation, they would likely find common ground on a central question: *"By what right could a being, created free, force another to think like himself?"* This question holds profound significance in the realm of education. When a single way of thinking is imposed, it stifles the intellectual development of individuals and limits the broader progress of society.

To illustrate this, we can draw on Sartre's concept of *"the existence of others."* [68] A free being, one who defines their own existence, experiences the fullness of life. In contrast, those who are reduced to objects—whether as subjects of desire or instruments of control—feel an existential emptiness. Their sense of self is bound to the will of others, reducing them to mere objects in the world.

This dynamic can be seen in the way we perceive, treat, and speak to others. When we view someone as an object, we strip them of their freedom, thus denying them the chance to define themselves.

Sartre suggests that those who are objectified in this way feel a deep sense of loss, because to be treated as an object is to be denied the right to define one's own existence. In a world of objects, one's subjectivity—the very capacity to exist freely and define oneself—becomes negated.

However, the object (or "the other") does not always wish to sever their connection to the free being. In fact, they may fear being separated from that subjectivity, as this would mean the dissolution of their place in the world. For the objectified person, their sense of meaning and purpose may depend on being seen or treated as an object of desire or control. It is through this objectification that they carve out their identity and sense of success.

Yet true freedom lies in the ability to define oneself—to exist as a subject in the world, rather than being reduced to an object. The prospect of total freedom, however, is often frightening. For those who prefer to objectify others, it may feel safer to maintain a world where both they and others are treated as objects. This allows them to avoid the anxiety and responsibility of self-definition.

To impose one's will on another and define their freedom for them—to reduce them to an object of desire or control—is, ultimately, an inhumane act. No one desires their freedom to be dictated by another.

True freedom is not *"someone else's"* vision of freedom; it is the autonomy to determine one's own path, to define one's own existence. To take that away is to strip away the very essence of what it means to be human.

Education in the early 1990s continues to uphold a false sense of certainty. It interprets life through a single, rigid system of memorization and standardized testing, narrowing students' understanding of the vast, complex world around them.

This system is based on the fear of independent and creative thought, and it begins in the formative years—often even in the home or kindergarten. It's a sad irony that education, instead of being a tool for personal growth, has become a mechanism for control, serving the needs of politics and the organization, rather than the individual.

What we need now is a *reevaluation* of educational values. We must move beyond rigid systems and dogmatic principles. Education must stop clinging to outdated notions of "certainty" and embrace the complexity of human thought. But this revaluation may not come easily, as education continues to be tangled in its own entrenched traditions.

Perhaps we have become a society of "educated fools." Yet this decadence can be remedied in adulthood, through the practice of lifelong learning. A degree from a school is not an endpoint but a license to continue learning throughout one's life. It is a certificate of possibility, not completion.

We owe much to our formal education. We can curse the system we've been subjected to, but we can also work to improve it, making education a shared, collective endeavor. As individuals, we must take responsibility for our own learning, continuing to educate ourselves, to ask questions, to seek knowledge.

A television commercial from the late 1970s captured the essence of this truth: *"A mind is a terrible thing to waste."* That message is just as relevant today, and it will remain so tomorrow. Education must awaken from its dogmatic slumber and begin to fulfill its true potential: to nurture minds that are free, open, creative, and capable of building a better world.

Harmony in Difference
A Personal Letter

Dear Y-s,

I MUST CONFESS THAT I AM DEEPLY TROUBLED by the way you seem to assume that I should share your values, beliefs, and ways of thinking. The very idea of trying to mold someone to think as you do is inherently flawed—it would be the same as claiming, "I am God." There is wisdom in understanding another person's thoughts and beliefs, even if we don't necessarily agree with them. This kind of understanding, free from emotional extremes, is to be celebrated and welcomed.

Although you may smile and deny it, there's a persistent "difference" between us that I think needs addressing. Your indifference towards me, especially after we've shared so many good moments together, often becomes a barrier when we try to connect. We all dislike being judged, especially by those who see themselves as superior, wielding their "rightness" to dictate how others should behave. But true unity can only come when we set aside prescriptive truths in favor of mutual respect.

Values differ from person to person because each of us has a unique calling, a mission that contributes to the betterment of humanity. It's unfortunate that conflict arises when we focus on these differences instead of appreciating the beauty of diversity. There's a saying: "A healthy unity requires the harmony of differences." This is something I truly believe.

You have your way of living, and I have mine—and so do many others. It's one thing to offer our way of life to another; it's another to *share* it. Sharing, in my view, is more open, more inviting. It allows space for consideration without the threat of imposition. You may not agree with me on this, and that's fine. Let's talk and see where we find common ground.

To truly communicate, we must speak while listening and listen with the "mind's ear." The beauty of good communication lies in our ability to understand one another, even when we don't see eye to eye. You may think differently than I do, and that's okay. It would be wonderful, though, if we could learn to appreciate those differences—so that, together, we can live decently and contribute to the betterment of society and the world.

There's wisdom in what an astrophysicist once said: appreciation lies in knowledge as the coveted prize. Similarly, a philosopher might say appreciation lies in understanding as the coveted prize. Both perspectives are correct. When we acknowledge the differences in people, we can still find the unity that binds us all. This is captured in the sociological concept known as the "looking-glass self," where we see ourselves reflected in others. In that reflection, differences are softened, and sameness emerges, helping to unite us across boundaries of culture, race, and identity.

Take a piano, for example. It has white keys and black keys. Each is distinct, each serves a different function, but when they come together, they create harmony. The beauty of music is in the diversity of notes working together to produce a unified whole. Similarly, we, though different, share a common humanity that, when embraced, can lead to unity, beauty, and harmony.

Despite the superficial differences we may have, we all need one another to create something beautiful, just like the piano needs both black and white keys. We are all unique, yet we are all the same, bound together by our shared humanity. As Paul says, we should strive to be "all things to all people"—not in an attempt to conform others to ourselves, but to help them, understand them, and contribute to their well-being.

What is "good" for one person may not be good for another, and the same goes for what is "bad." In moral matters, there are *universals,* but in ethical matters, there are *particulars.* The confusion often arises when we mix up what people "ought to" do with what they "should do." The concept of moral relativity can be dangerously misleading. It would be more helpful, I think, to focus on universals rather than the particulars that divide us.

As for Christian maturity, the author of Hebrews speaks of the importance of moving beyond the basics of the ABCs, of striving for growth to the XYZs (Hebrews 5:12–6:6). Maturity, in this sense, has little to do with age, position, or experience; it is about how we use our experiences to reflect on what it means to be human and to relate to others in a meaningful way. Maturity is an ongoing process—a continual effort to engage with the world in a thoughtful and compassionate manner, particularly in how we respond to people who differ from us.

Paul, in his writings, urges us to respect those who are fully convinced in their own minds, to act for the good of others, and to lead them toward edification (Romans 14:5–15:2). He reminds us that strength does not come from judgment, but from empathy and humility (Romans 14:1-4; 15:1; Philippians 2:3). This isn't just Christian teaching—it's how any decent human being should live.

Does Paul expect us to be like him? No. He was unique, with gifts and a mission all his own. But he did offer us an example: to become all things to all people, so that we might bring others closer to the truth (1 Corinthians 9:22). His goal was clear—to save others, to help them find their way to a better life, in every possible way.

If following the example of Jesus, the Christ figure, seems impossible to us, then we can look to Paul as an exemplary human being—a model for how to live decently and purposefully, keeping the well-being of others in mind.

Sincerely, Randy

Postscript

It strikes me as ironic that you often tell others how they should think, behave, or believe, yet I do not take that same approach as you. Maturity is not measured by age, position, or experience, but by our ability to live a decent life without judgment.

We are all teachers and students to each other. We learn from one another, whether or not the lessons are of a religious nature. The truth is, we all have something to contribute to one another's growth and happiness.

Children have much to teach us. They possess an innocence and curiosity that we often lose as we grow older. Their eagerness to learn, to ask questions, to seek understanding—these are qualities we would do well to emulate. It's not about immaturity or silliness, but about maintaining the wisdom of wonder, the ability to see the world with fresh eyes.

Unfortunately, as we grow, the complexities of life can blind us to that simplicity and wisdom. But perhaps by embracing the humility of a child, we can rediscover something we've lost along the way: the ability to learn, to grow, and to appreciate the harmony in difference.

Freedom

IN CULTURES WHERE BEHAVIOR IS VALUED more than the mind, it is a haunting entity. Behavior should not be more prized than thought; it is the mind that matters. Perhaps the shadows that linger in Beijing still haunt Jerusalem.

God created the world, yet remains separate from it, allowing His creatures the freedom to share in His creation and to continue shaping it. He granted humanity the responsibility of completing what He had begun.

It has been one year today since the Chinese military massacred hundreds, perhaps thousands, of pro-democracy demonstrators in Tiananmen Square—unarmed men and women who had come to peacefully demand their rights. Unarmed, they were helplessly shot down or crushed by heavily armed tanks.

What makes this massacre even more horrifying is that the Chinese government denied it ever happened, turning the truth into a mere illusion, and blaming the media for fabricating a false reality. Chinese government officials smile as they deny that the crime of genocide ever occurred. Trust no politician who smiles, or who smiles too much.

The world stood in stunned silence as they watched a lone pro-democracy student, captured on television, standing firm in front of a line of armed tanks. He was not adhering to his government's ideology, but his bravery symbolized that of a soldier of valor, holding firm to something far more powerful: *Freedom.*

He stood there, resolute, fully aware of the stakes—life or death—for the sake of freedom. In that moment, his determination was not just to his own humanity, but to a higher call: the freedom to choose, to be, and to exist. His courage halted the tanks in their mission to crush the pro-democracy movement, if only momentarily, and reminded the world of the power of an individual's resolve.

We cannot help but reflect on this truth: *We always resist prohibitions and yearn for what is denied to us.* It is the nature of every human being to desire freedom. We seek freedom *from* systems—governments, ideologies, cultures, families—that attempt to mold us into a version of ourselves that is not of our own choosing. True freedom is the ability to shape our own identity, to form our own destiny, and to exist as free, autonomous creatures of thought and will.

The massacre in Tiananmen Square, the fall of the Berlin Wall, the execution of Nicolae Ceausescu, the release of Nelson Mandela, the independence movements of the Baltic states, and the ongoing struggles in the Middle East for Palestinian statehood—all these events, past and present, can be summed up in one word: *Freedom.*

Without freedom, we are forced to fight, not just against others, but against ourselves. But acquiring freedom can also arouse fear that "everything is permissible, but not everything is beneficial." True freedom requires responsibility. Possessing too much freedom without moral restraint can harm not only others, but ourselves as well. But this fear must be mitigated by assuming responsible action given the freedom one has. Freedom tempered with responsibility brings growth, and with growth comes a thriving morality.

Freedom is the soil in which morality takes root. Where freedom is denied, morality begins to wither. In places where freedom is suppressed, individuals are reduced to mere cogs in a machine, deprived of the ability to truly *be.* Those who dominate others—whether through culture, race, nationality, or social status—assert a false superiority, one that is built on the exploitation of others. This dominance erodes a common morality, and replaces it with an ethic of power, control, and manipulation.

But freedom, when it is denied, does not die quietly. It becomes a haunting force that manifests itself in destructive ways. Just as an individual's will cannot be suppressed without consequence, neither can a nation's desire for freedom be contained indefinitely. The longer freedom is denied, the more it festers, and the greater the cost of its eventual release. Freedom is not merely a political ideal—it is a moral necessity. It is the foundation upon which societies are built, and the wellspring from which all human flourishing flows.

When governments use freedom as a tool for control, when they exploit it for political gain, they rob the people of their true power. It is a tragic irony that in the pursuit of freedom, some governments kill to obtain it, only to later use it to enslave others.

The pursuit of freedom is never a simple path. At times, it is a path of resistance, a fight against entrenched systems that would rather suppress than allow human flourishing. But the cost of that resistance, though high, is necessary.

We must seek freedom not only for ourselves, but for others. We must rise above the collective morality imposed by oppressive governments and define our own. We are not machines, subservient to the will of a higher power that seeks only to dominate us. We are human beings, capable of thought, of self-determination, and of pursuing what is good for *us*. We are not born to be caged, to be limited by the oppressive forces of the world. Freedom is essential to growth, to becoming, to living fully.

Without freedom, life becomes a curse—a hollow existence, disconnected from its true purpose. Freedom is the source of life. It is the condition under which we can grow, thrive, and pursue our highest ideals. It is only in its absence that morality deteriorates, and life itself becomes meaningless.

We hear discussions about Middle Eastern movements defined as organizations that participate in and support 'terrorism.' It is no wonder that this term is defined by authoritarian capitalist countries as a value they themselves exploit for profit.

In the unique circumstances of Tiananmen Square, in Europe, in the USSR, in South Africa, in the Middle East, and wherever else freedom is threatened, the fight for freedom is both just and necessary. Those who fight for freedom and those who resist it all seek the same thing—life, in its truest, most liberated form.

Who bears the greater 'sin par excellence'? Those who take life from those suppressing freedom in order to obtain it for themselves, or those who deny the right to life from those striving for freedom, only to retain it for themselves. Will the real "terrorist" please stand up!

Prejudice, Discrimination and Racism

SARTRE'S CONCEPT THAT *HELL IS OTHER PEOPLE* emphasizes the fear many feel when faced with individuals who are different—those who don't look or think like themselves. This idea underscores the discomfort and tension that can arise when encountering differences.

This fear manifests in three unjust acts of social evils: prejudice, discrimination, and racism. These acts, while distinct, are linked by an escalating intensity and a shared root in fear. From least to most severe, they unfold as follows: (1) prejudice, (2) discrimination, and (3) racism.

Prejudice is a subtle judgement. It is rooted in "preconception"— judging others based on superficial or unfounded beliefs. It often manifests in subtle words, phrases, or stereotypes. Prejudice is not always overt; it can be passive, internalized, and indirect, but it remains a harmful judgment, nonetheless. It is the first step on the path to greater acts of harm.

Discrimination is an open and active judgement. It goes beyond prejudice, moving into the realm of "misrepresentation." Discrimination can be active or passive but is more intentional than prejudice. Discrimination manifests in actions that, whether public or private, cause harm by privileges of one group over another. Though simple in its basic forms—denying someone a job based on race, for example—it is often cloaked in deceptive rhetoric, obscuring its true nature. Discrimination is more visible than prejudice and acts as a gateway to racism.

Racism is a heightened act of hate. Racism, at its core, is judgment by "membership." It is the active and often blatant mistreatment of others based on their nationality, race, or skin color. Racism is not just a personal belief or judgment; it becomes institutionalized and systemic, affecting laws, policies, and societal norms. Racism is rooted in a false belief in the superiority of one race over another, and it manifests through both overt and covert acts of violence, segregation, and marginalization.

Prejudice, discrimination, and racism represent a "false consciousness." They are grounded in misperceptions of difference and an irrational fear of the other. The more these acts are normalized, the more they impede social progress. If we are ever to create a harmonious, just society, we must first address and dismantle these "false divisions."

All three acts stem from *fear*—fear of the unknown, fear of difference, and fear of losing one's sense of superiority. Fear generates these false beliefs and causes people to treat others as "the other," which, in turn, allows them to feel more secure or empowered. These unjust acts are tools of self-deception, ways of creating imaginary divisions in the world to justify one's own sense of superiority.

Sigmund Freud posited that fear is the origin of religious belief, and similarly, fear is the origin of social divisions based on *superficial identifiers.* Fear of difference creates boundaries that prevent growth, hinder collaboration, and reinforce oppressive systems.

When we act from these false divisions—whether consciously or unconsciously—we not only harm others, but we harm ourselves by rejecting the potential for growth and understanding. If we cling to these fears, we exploit our own freedom and impede progress for all.

Beyond fear, there are specific factors that fuel discrimination and racism. These factors often stem from shallow, surface-level judgments based on characteristics such as: (1) physical appearance, (2) material wealth and dress, (3) race and ethnicity, (4) identity labels, (5) age, and (6) gender. Each of these factors serves as a basis for discrimination and racism, often in subtle or overt ways.

Physical Appearance. We make snap judgments about people based on their physical form—height, weight, and facial features. Those who fit societal ideals of beauty or fitness are often treated more favorably, while those who do not may face exclusion or pity. This form of discrimination is deeply ingrained in our culture and reflects a narrow view of what is "valuable" in a person.

Material Wealth and Dress. Clothing and material wealth often serve as indicators of social status. People are judged based on their outward appearance—whether they dress "well" or "poorly"—and this is often linked to their perceived worth in society. This reinforces a materialistic mindset where surface appearance is given more weight than internal qualities, such as intelligence, kindness, or integrity.

Race and Ethnicity. Race is one of the most significant sources of discrimination and racism. People often classify others based on their racial background or skin color, which leads to stereotypical assumptions about intelligence, behavior, and worth. Such racial classifications are based on misrepresentations and have historically been used to justify systemic inequality and violence.

Identity Labels. Labels like "democrat," "republican," "immigrant," or "executive assistant" are used to define and categorize individuals, often to assert superiority over others. These labels can become tools for dehumanization, making it easier to dismiss or mistreat someone who does not fit into our prescribed categories.

Age. Age is another common source of discrimination. It is not accurate to assume that older individuals are always wiser or more intelligent, just as it is not true that younger individuals lack wisdom or intelligence.

Gender. Gender-based discrimination is deeply rooted in patriarchal social systems. Historically, women have been treated as inferior to men, and this bias persists in many parts of the world. Women are often expected to conform to certain roles and are discriminated against for stepping outside these expectations. Gender-based discrimination also intersects with other forms of discrimination, such as racism and classism.

Racism, by its nature, is destructive. It is perhaps the most violent form of prejudice because it is the most visible and harmful. It is not only an act of judgment; it is a system of oppression that dehumanizes entire groups of people based on their race, ethnicity, or nationality. Racism is the culmination of fear, ignorance, and a desire for power, and it destroys both individual freedom and collective progress. Discrimination can lead to racism when it is allowed to fester and grow unchecked. Discrimination, whether subtle or overt, can breed resentment, anger, and violence, leading to the most extreme form of hate: racism. It is a dangerous, insidious force that has the potential to cause widespread harm.

To combat the damaging effects of social evils, we must reevaluate our values and move toward a more inclusive path. The distinctions we make—based on race, gender, age, appearance, labels, and wealth—are arbitrary and divisive. Progress requires us to see beyond these surface-level identifiers and instead focus on the depth and humanity of each individual. We need to shift from prioritizing outward appearances to recognizing the inherent worth and dignity of all people.[69] These social evils are not inevitable; they are learned behaviors, shaped by fear and ignorance.

To transform ourselves, we must have the courage to unlearn the biases we've been taught (as reflected in Plato's *Allegory of the Cave*) and rewire our brains through new neural connections (contemplating neuroplasticity). This process will free us from the "sins" of social evils, allowing us to engage in open dialogue and challenge societal norms that uphold these injustices. Such change requires humility, patience, and a willingness to dismantle harmful values in favor of more inclusive, compassionate ones.

Ultimately, the solution lies in recognizing the interconnectedness of all people. Just as an artist mixes colors to create harmony and beauty, we must blend our differences—race, ethnicity, gender, and culture—into a unified whole. In doing so, we can create a society that celebrates diversity and fosters progress for all.

Part II
Self-Awareness

Self-Confidence Or
"How One Becomes What One Is"

BECOMING A SELF-ASSURED AND CONFIDENT INDIVIDUAL, full of enthusiasm, can feel as though you are possessed by a god. As we gain knowledge, we become more capable and empowered, which in turn boosts our confidence and enthusiasm.

Have you ever had a day when your self-confidence was so elevated that nothing could bring you down? You feel so sure of yourself that even higher powers seem secondary to your sense of self-confidence. Everything falls into place with the mere force of your presence, and people respond positively to it.

Life presents us with a variety of situations. How we respond to them determines whether we feel confident in any given moment. Have you ever felt fear or faced something that made you uncertain? In those times, self-confidence may seem to diminish. While it's natural to experience this, staying in a state of uncertainty is not ideal. Or is it?

Doesn't uncertainty lead our minds into a world of thoughts and wonder, as we try to understand the harm it may cause if we don't confront and address it positively? If we respond to uncertainty in a positive way, we re-evaluate ourselves and make decisions that align with our anticipated outcomes, ultimately benefiting ourselves and others.

Fear and uncertainty are tests—forces that challenge and sometimes diminish our self-confidence. Our goal is to overcome these forces and restore our confidence by mastering the fears that threaten to erode it.

Self-confidence is ultimately about knowing ourselves and applying our unique strengths to areas where we excel. It is a deeper form of self-awareness, understanding, and self-consciousness.

To truly know ourselves also means understanding how to protect and preserve ourselves—self-preservation. Some philosophers, like Nietzsche, refer to this as "selfishness," while others call it the ego. Regardless of the term, this process is about defending and maintaining our sense of self in the face of external pressures that threaten to alter or damage it. Nietzsche famously says, "What does not kill me makes me stronger."

There are three key elements to developing self-confidence: (1) interacting positively with others, (2) facing challenges and taking risks, and (3) embracing adventure and the unknown. To maintain high self-confidence, positive outcomes must follow these efforts, which require motivation, persistence, prudence, and, above all, enthusiasm.

There is a contradiction inherent in self-confidence. It requires accepting who we are not, especially as reflected through the eyes of others. Favoring being liked over being authentic often signals low self-confidence. We may feel compelled to pretend to be someone we're not—driven by peer pressure—in the hope of gaining acceptance. In doing so, we internalize the power of suggestion. When we adopt behaviors or identities projected onto us by others, we create a disconnect within ourselves. This contradiction pulls us away from our true self. Instead, we must recognize and let go of the false identities imposed on us. True growth begins when we embrace who we truly are—rooted in self-awareness, not in the perceptions of others.

Words hold immense power. Nietzsche understood this. Words shape perception, and philosophers recognize their potential to create or destroy. When a word is attached to a behavior, it can define a person's identity, shaping their actions accordingly. Words can immortalize or constrain us, dictating our path and even depriving us of our sense of self.

We must resist allowing words to define us based on cultural assumptions or perceptions shaped by others. Our senses can be deceptive, and labeling someone based on these impressions can erode their self-confidence. If we truly value ourselves and others, we must avoid reducing anyone to a stereotype or false identity. If we are to immortalize anything, it should be our own growth and development. By constantly overcoming external pressures, we learn to become what we truly are—self-confident.

When we embrace an external perception of ourselves, we allow outside influences to shape our thoughts and actions. This acceptance traps us in a false version of who we truly are. As Nietzsche wisely says, "I do not want to be taken for what I am not—and that requires that I do not take myself for what I am not."[70]

Building self-confidence is a lifelong pursuit. It is an upward journey that many of us share, as we strive to be self-sufficient, in control of our own destiny. This goal is not only for our benefit, but for the benefit of those around us as well.

Insecurity that Strengthens

INSECURITY OFTEN COMPELS US to act or speak in ways that are out of character. It's a universal experience—everyone grapples with it to some extent. While it's easy to recognize insecurity in others, spotting it within ourselves is much more challenging.

The truth is, we tend to avoid confronting our own insecurity because acknowledging it can make us feel even more vulnerable. It forces us to confront the reality that we are not yet who we aspire to be. For many, the term "insecurity" carries a negative weight, as it threatens our sense of stability and well-being.

One philosopher suggests, "Anything thought of as bad is cowardly," and there is truth to this view. Yet another philosopher offers a more hopeful perspective: "Courage is facing negations despite their threat of non-being." This more optimistic take resonates with us as a healthier approach to insecurity.

A person's actions are often influenced by their past experiences and external factors. It can feel as though we rely on others to point out our flaws. This "finger-pointing" activates our insecurities and threatens our sense of self, prompting us to question who we truly are.

However, true courage lies in accepting our imperfections. We shouldn't shrink from others' opinions or fear the criticisms life throws at us. Doing so only hinders our growth and limits our potential. Our potential is shaped by the social, physical, mental, and spiritual aspects of our lives.

While life's negations remind us that we fall short of perfection, they also provide opportunities for growth. By acknowledging the criticisms or symbolic messages directed at us, we can use them as stepping-stones to realize our potential and gain a clearer understanding of who we are meant to become.

"I was a Booger in Buddha's Nose"

SQUIRMING THROUGH THE NOSTRIL OF BUDDHA, I found myself essentially transformed into a booger lodged in his nose. It was a strange, yet profound experience that led to deep spiritual insight. This newfound enlightenment brought me closer to understanding Buddha's origins.

One afternoon at Todai-ji Temple in Nara, Japan, I watched a group of children crawl through a hole in a giant pillar, the size of the nostril of the massive bronze statue of Buddha. The "nostril" hole in the pillar was large enough for the children to pass through unaided, thanks to their small physical stature. Each child emerged with a joyful smile, their faces beaming with a kind of enlightenment that could only come from being a "booger" in Buddha's nose. I envied them and longed to experience the same.

What struck me about these children was their courage. They faced the unknown, the possibility of becoming stuck, and yet they proceeded with faith and determination. They were not deterred by the potential negation—being trapped in Buddha's nose without hope of escape. Instead, they emerged triumphant, filled with the affirmation of their self-discovery. They had found enlightenment by simply trusting the process.

I, too, wanted to be like them, but my physical size was much larger. I believed this to be a disadvantage, one that would prevent me from achieving the same enlightenment. This realization saddened me deeply, and for a moment, I felt my spirit sink.

Around me, other onlookers—larger than the children but smaller than me—watched silently. They were "spectators," hesitant and full of doubt. It was clear they, like me, lacked the faith to try. We stood as "shameful bystanders," witnessing the children's joyful exits from the Buddha's nose and reflecting on the saying, *"Many are called, but few are picked."*

But then something surprising happened. A larger person, someone who had also stood at a distance, gathered the courage to enter the Buddha's nose. I doubted this person's success due to his size, but to everyone's amazement, he made it through. With a triumphant smile, he exclaimed, "I was a booger in Buddha's nose."

Seeing this larger person succeed reignited my hope. If he could do it, surely, I could too. I was inspired by his courage and self-denial. Still, my doubts lingered. I was much bigger than him, and I feared that my own journey would end in failure. Yet, through his example, I found the courage to try.

Before entering the Buddha's nose, I paused to examine the hole. I contemplated the dimensions of the journey ahead, and suddenly, a wave of dread washed over me. I doubted my ability to make it through alone. The possibility of becoming stuck, a booger with no way out, seemed all too real.

In my fear, I sought help. I asked for guidance from a larger Buddha and another figure—someone who was not enlightened but still offered encouragement. Their words of affirmation calmed my fears and gave me the confidence I needed to proceed.

But as I entered the Buddha's nose, I became stuck. Halfway through, I realized I was indeed a "booger stuck" in Buddha's nose. The negation I had feared had come true—I was blocking the path, inhibiting others from reaching enlightenment. In that moment, I feared that Buddha would expel me, that I would ruin the sanctity of the process and forever be excluded from nirvana.

As I began to lose hope, I felt the gentle touch of the Enlightened One. With great compassion, he reached up and took hold of me as I clung to his finger, and gently picked me out. Realizing that I was no longer a booger stuck in Buddha's nose what had I become? As I emerged from Buddha's nose, I wondered: Had I achieved enlightenment through his mercy? I hadn't succeeded by my own effort, but in the eyes of those watching— both big and small—there was no doubt. They cheered for me, and through my experience, Buddha had revealed that I, too, had reached nirvana.

I had become what I had always desired to be: a Buddha of enlightenment. Through my failure, I had found the path to true wisdom, and now I was equipped to help others on their journey. Those of my own physical stature followed my lead into Buddha's nose, and I, in turn, helped them emerge by picking them out, just as Buddha had done for me.

As a booger stuck in Buddha's nose, my spiritual perception deepened. I realized that Buddha himself must have also been a booger at some point—he, too, had to become something humble before attaining enlightenment. But the question remains: Whose nose was Buddha a booger in?

A Free Spirit

OCCUPY YOUR MIND WITH PURSUITS that contribute to the greater good of humanity. Measure your thoughts against the vast powers of the universe. Be open to both the new and the old. Just because something is new doesn't make it inherently bad, and the same goes for the old. Read a lot. Write a lot. Listen a lot. Act but think before you do. Speak less but say more. Give yourself to the growth of humanity, which depends on the ability to find freedom.

Become a Free Spirit. A Free Spirit is a humanist at heart, someone who has taken possession of himself. Say what you think but be respectful. Act on what you believe as you hope. Practice constructive criticism—not to tear down, but to build up. Yet, remember, to build, one must sometimes first destroy. Do this thoughtfully and conserve the happiness of others.

Become a Free Spirit. Go wherever your destiny leads. Your destiny is twofold: knowledge and choice. Give your time to the old, the young, and the new. Remain close to your own kind but venture out—meet people from all walks of life, from different cultures and classes. Embrace their differences, their perspectives for knowledge. Engage with those whose thoughts differ from yours. Work together. Let them teach you. Learn from them. Accept others as God accepts them—and as He accepts you. Understand them to understand yourself and the world. The more you understand, the better you can relate to others and thrive in a diverse world.

Do not remain in one place for too long, nor associate solely with those who share your views. Avoid the trap of complacency. Do not become an apathetic loafer. Learn not only to love but to like one another. Love not through faith or trust in ideals, but through the raw, authentic bond of shared humanity. Recognize each person as a unique "I," worthy of dignity and respect. Yes, embrace the challenge of human relationships, for it is not just a choice, but a responsibility.

Go where your destiny takes you. Take that leap into the unknown, a leap that demands courage and presupposes faith. Savor the moment, for the moment is where all experiences lie. Create a journey of self-discovery by opening your mind to new perspectives. Nourish your mind with new knowledge and cultivate a deeper understanding of yourself.

Build a more knowledgeable version of yourself. Take what you have and seek what you lack. We are all wanderers on earth, but citizens of a higher order. Each person we meet is a reflection of ourselves—our *looking-glass self.* In every individual, I see a part of me. We communicate, relate, and become friends. I am him, and he is me. The essence of my existence is not lost in him but is found in me through him. We are all part of a shared humanity. Through this connection, I find my unique place in the world and recognize the value I bring to it.

I see in all people the common thread that binds us. We unite in our shared struggles for freedom, peace, and prosperity. We are born adventurers, seeking to conquer mountains, discover new lands, and explore the farthest reaches of the universe. Ultimately, we seek to know ourselves. Our purpose is knowledge, and it is through this pursuit that we fulfill our destiny.

A Free Spirit is someone who knows themselves and claims ownership of their being. To take possession of oneself, one must be honest. A Free Spirit has faith—faith in their own potential. But where does this faith come from? It doesn't come from God, for we have long since killed that old conception. Our medieval ideas, our language, and our outdated ideals have rendered Him obsolete. So, what do we do? We forge a new sense of divinity. We become our own gods in a world where traditional gods no longer reign.

A man cannot have faith in himself unless he is honest—with himself and with others. Honesty breeds trust, and from this trust comes faith. When a man speaks the truth and acts with kindness, he strengthens his faith. Through this faith, he takes control of his destiny. Though he may face many paths, they all lead him toward the essence of his being.

A Free Spirit understands that through the pursuit of freedom, he discovers his true self. In doing so, he becomes like a god—a self-overcomer who transcends what once enslaved his spirit. A Free Spirit embodies the Nietzschean *Übermensch*—an individual who has empowered himself, transcended conventional morality, societal norms, and limitations, and created his own values and purpose in life. Ideals, once cherished, are discarded as mere superstitions—remnants of a false reality that once hindered his growth. A Free Spirit has broken down these illusions and, in their place, has built something of real value.

A Free Spirit destroys to create. Before one can build, one must first tear down the old to make room for the new. This destruction is not for its own sake, but to foster growth. A Free Spirit is committed to improving humanity by rejecting hollow ideals and embracing the fullness of life as it is—raw, human, and full of potential.

Become a fully realized human being. Embrace wisdom, but also embrace foolishness. Be both rational and irrational. How can one truly understand wisdom if one does not wrestle with its opposite? Laugh at the things that bring joy to humanity. Cry over the things that bring pain to humanity. Hate what harms humanity. Love what unites humanity. Become a contradiction yet remain consistent in your commitment to it. Stay true to the innate, natural humanity that unites us all.

We are unique, and in our uniqueness, we are superior. We take pride in our humanness, for it is both a source of beauty and of struggle. Though we are capable of great horror, we also have the potential for great compassion and creativity. Our humanness is a paradox—a source of both danger and hope.

Give yourself time for solitude, as personal growth flourishes in contemplative quiet. Take private moments to reflect and grow. Nietzsche once asked, "How can anyone become a thinker if one does not spend at least a third of the day without passions, people, and books?"[71] S. I. Hayakawa reminds us, "It is not true that we have only one life to live; if we can read, we can live many lives and as many kinds of lives as we wish."[72] Use your time to refresh and re-create your mind.

Do not fear solitude. Embrace it as a time for personal growth. It is not something to dread but a precious opportunity to discover yourself. In these quiet moments, you may stumble upon a truth that is both frightening and enlightening. Cherish the silence, for in it, you may discover the most profound truths.

Do not live for dreams, for they are illusions. Instead, live for ambitions—many ambitions. Live for the quiet moments that nourish your soul and allow you to fulfill your true purpose. Live for yourself, but also for others. Learn from life and share that knowledge with others. Teach, and let others teach you.

Heed the message of a Free Spirit. Life becomes easier to embrace when we adopt the mindset of a Free Spirit, especially when we take action. This attitude not only helps us heal from pain but also shows us the positive impact it can have.

Embracing Selfishness

THERE ARE MOMENTS IN LIFE—perhaps many of them—when we feel an overwhelming urge to say, "Forget everyone else." This statement, filled with frustration and emotional weight, doesn't refer to the disgusted disregard for others. No. It speaks to a deeper, more ego-driven instinct for self-preservation. At its core, this is a form of selfishness.

On one hand, many religions teach that selfishness is a vice, leading to spiritual damnation. This negative view has influenced humanity's path, causing us to lose touch with our true selves and become entangled in what might be called moral decay.

On the other hand, thinkers and philosophers have long argued that selfishness, in a more positive light, can be a path to personal freedom. This kind of selfishness encourages us to reclaim our own identities and lives, offering us a chance to know ourselves deeply and live freely.

To know ourselves, we must first take ownership of ourselves—something often lost when selfishness is viewed negatively. By reclaiming control over our own lives, we move closer to becoming free spirits. In this sense, we stop pretending to be gods and start embracing the truth of our human nature.

The pursuit of self-knowledge is the essence of being human. We question because we don't know. We take risks because we don't know. We strive and struggle, all in search of understanding ourselves and thriving in the world. The key to self-discovery lies in possessing ourselves, and to do so, we must understand that selfishness is not inherently bad—it is a vital tool in this process.

Selfishness, in this context, means being honest about our human or natural condition. It involves understanding our "riddle" by being conscious of the human "contradiction" in all of us if we truly want to know ourselves.[73, 74] By acknowledging this contradiction, we recognize the "dual character of our nature," an internal struggle that defines us all.[75] The contradiction represents our "natural condition" of "war" against ourselves and others.[76, 77]

The contradiction is a "division within ourselves" acknowledged by both Plato and Aristotle—a constant conflict between our rational desires and irrational impulses, between doing what we know is right and surrendering to what we should not do.[78] As Paul so poignantly put it:

> I do not understand what I do. For what I want to do, I do not do... I have the desire to do what is good, but I cannot carry it out. For what I do is not the good I want to do, but the evil I keep doing... My body wages war against the law of my mind and makes me a prisoner.[79]

To truly know ourselves, we must accept this internal contradiction as a necessary part of our nature. Only by understanding and embracing it can we use it wisely to live with respect for ourselves and others.

To know oneself is to have the courage to face the truth of who we are: a contradiction. This is a difficult and frightening task, driven by the fear of losing ourselves in that contradiction. But this fear is nothing more than weakness.

To defeat this weakness, we must turn inward, reflecting on our unique contradiction and learning how to use it to our advantage. By doing so, we gain a deeper understanding of ourselves, and this is where selfishness becomes something good. It is through this process that we can grow, become more honest, and truly know who we are.

Service

AS ONE DAY TRANSITIONS INTO THE NEXT, a new day is born—Today. The previous day becomes history, while Today arrives with the anticipation of its fleeting moments, each passing into the past, becoming part of history. As Today moves toward becoming Yesterday, we find ourselves both looking forward to the future and reflecting on the present, eager for what Tomorrow may bring.

To make Today meaningful and memorable is to live fully in the present, remembering to "seize the day" as the poet encourages. To create a lasting, positive history with Today, we learn by imitating the good deeds of others—acts of service that contribute to our personal growth and the progress of society.

We live first for ourselves, not out of selfishness, but so that we can better serve others. Only by understanding and fulfilling our own needs can we truly help others when they reach out in need. What man will give his brother war if his brother asks for peace? The truth is, if one does not possess peace within himself, he cannot offer it to others.

When a person gives what they do not possess, it becomes harder to understand what is truly needed and how to give appropriately. The key to service is not self-denial or selflessness, but rather *self-projection*—stepping into another's shoes to understand them more deeply, empathize with them, and offer what they truly need. This is *identification* and the essence of the *looking-glass self:* seeing ourselves in others, recognizing that we are not just individuals, but part of a shared human experience.

From this perspective, we can better understand both the similarities and the differences in the needs of others.

As humans, we are natural imitators. We mimic those we admire because we see something worth emulating in them—whether for personal gain or for the benefit of others. The most rewarding form of imitation, however, begins with living for ourselves in a way that allows us to serve others. We learn to imitate the best qualities by first mastering how to live well for ourselves.

What many religious leaders fail to understand is that the foundation of religion, in its purest form, is to live for others. We were created to coexist, and as the philosopher says, "Man is by nature a political [social] animal."[80]

The order of service, then, is this: before we can be selfless and give rightly, we must first be selfish in the sense of possessing what we have to offer. To give, we must first possess, and in this way, selfishness becomes the first step toward selflessness. By possessing what we can give, we are then able to offer it to others.

Service, therefore, is a blend of religious selflessness, philosophical selfishness, and sociological understanding. To live for others is both a form of selflessness and selfishness. It is a dual affirmation of life—acknowledging both self and other, preserving and nurturing both simultaneously, twice affirming the value of existence.

Lesser of Two Evils
A Personal Letter

Dear R.C.,

WHEN I SPOKE WITH THE DIRECTOR of the ABC [...] school branch today, she shared something troubling. She had "heard" from the directors of the ABC [...] and [...] schools, as well as their teachers and students, that I was no longer an ABC Christian. This news deeply concerned her, especially because I was planning to visit her school that day. It seemed she feared my visit, worried that I would influence the students and lead them astray from the Christian faith. But more troubling than her fear of me was her "concern" that I had become a wandering ABC Christian, implying that my faith was somehow blasphemous compared to hers or the shared beliefs within the ABC community.

The idea that I am "no longer an ABC Christian" perplexes me. What does this even mean? Where did this certainty come from? Does "ABC" stand for Christian in itself? These two—ABC and Christian—are not the same. While they can be connected and complementary if approached with balance, they should not be conflated. To me, it is more important to be a "Christian" than to be labeled an "ABC." It's not the name, but the balance of both that matters, with one's Christian identity being the foundation. The question is not whether ABC is Christian, but rather where one's roots lie.

The acronym "ABC" represents an institution devoted to a particular Christian denomination within Protestantism. The "ABC church," while a part of the whole Christian body, has been given a label—a small 'c'—to signify it is not the entirety but a part of a larger whole. In contrast, being a "Christian" isn't tied to a denomination but rather to a devotion to Christ. The distinction is significant. An ABC adheres to rules set by the institution, aiming to please God and save their soul, while a Christian acts out of love for God, seeking to save not just their soul, but to help save others as well.

In the early history of Christianity, the shift from a personal relationship with Jesus to a collective adherence to Church doctrines marked the evolution of what it meant to be "Christian." By the fourth century, Christianity became defined by adherence to creeds, and the concept of salvation became tightly tied to the Church. Bishop Cyprian, in the third century, famously says, "No one can have God for his Father, who has not the Church for his mother. There is no salvation outside of the Church."[81] This has led to the widespread belief that salvation is only possible through the Church—a belief that persists to this day.

An ABC performs acts of piety, while a Christian acts through faith. The former is rooted in religious observance—following a set of truths, while the latter is rooted in love for God, which transcends religious systems. The ABC is a system of works, while the Christian is a follower of faith. In this, Christianity is simpler and more direct. Christianity is not about following rituals to gain salvation, but about having faith in God's love and sharing that love with others. This simplicity makes Christianity far more attractive than the complex structure of the ABC church.

Nietzsche has said, "In reality, there has been only one Christian, and he died on the Cross."[82] If one identifies as a Christian, it is a commitment to living in the image of Christ, not adhering to a set of institutional beliefs. A Christian's identity comes first—Christ before any interpretation of Christ through human-made institutions. To say "I am a Christian ABC" is to put Christ at the forefront, while "I am an ABC Christian" places the institution before the individual's faith.

The claim that I am "no longer an ABC Christian" reflects a failure to listen without prejudice, to understand the heart of the speaker. True listening requires empathy—to understand the speaker's thoughts, feelings, and intentions, without judgment. When someone fails to listen with the heart, they misinterpret the speaker and diminish the potential for mutual understanding and connection.

This is like how a "good" Christian might relate to an atheist. If a Christian cannot interact with an atheist without judgment or attempts to convert them, the atheist will see the Christian as cruel and ignorant. The atheist's rejection of God will be reinforced by the Christian's actions if they fail to embody God's love. Nietzsche's philosophy challenges us to go "beyond good and evil," to act from a place of genuine goodness that transcends rigid moral frameworks.[83]

The reasoning behind the claim that "Randy is no longer ABC" follows a faulty syllogism:

1. All ABCs believe this to be the Truth.
2. Randy believes other things to be true as well.
3. Therefore, Randy is not ABC

This is a logical fallacy. It assumes that all ABCs must hold the same beliefs, when in fact it is entirely possible for someone to identify as ABC while holding different views. For example:

1. All Americans are Democrats.
2. Mr. Jones is an American.
3. Therefore, Mr. Jones is a Democrat.

We know this is not true, as not all Americans are Democrats. Likewise, not all ABCs are Christian in the strictest sense of the term. The assumption that the name "ABC" defines a person's faith is misleading.

The real question is: which is the lesser of two evils—an ABC or a Christian? The answer is a Christian. The term "Christian" encompasses a broader and more inclusive identity, one rooted in faith and love, while "ABC" represents a more exclusive and rigid structure. The problem lies in prioritizing a label over the essence of faith. It is not the label "ABC" that is evil, but the act of using it to separate people based on names and divisions. It's this obsession with labels that divides humanity.

In the end, we must remember that our identities are not defined by the labels we use, but by the core principles we embody. To identify first as a Christian—one who lives in the image of Christ—is the truest and most genuine way to live. Labels like "ABC," "Democrat," or "American" should never take precedence over our fundamental humanity and love for others. Sincerely, Randy

Listening with Empathy

IS IT A 'SIN' AGAINST GOD to state empathetically what one believes when asked, without being discriminated against by one's own kind afterward?

Must our words always be confined to another person's *interpretation?* Do you hear what I'm trying to communicate, or do you hear what you want to hear? If it's the latter, then perhaps the fault lies in how you listen, not how I speak. On the other hand, if you don't hear what I intend, then I may be at fault for not expressing myself clearly. But the question remains: do we truly understand each other's perspectives, or are we simply drawing conclusions from our own filters of interpretation?

The perception others have of you is vital. It shapes your ambitions and can help turn those ambitions into dreams. A dream can only come true through collective support, through how others perceive and contribute to its fulfillment. For example, Martin Luther King had a dream, but it was crushed by the fear and misperception of those who opposed him. A dream cannot be realized on a global scale, but within a smaller, collective context—whether a nation or community—it can thrive. However, when a dream is crushed, it can transform back into an ambition, provided the person affected has the courage to sever ties with those who seek to destroy it.

Perception, ultimately, is shaped by what we choose to see through the lens of our own understanding. This understanding comes from the knowledge we possess, which we select based on what suits our interests.

Perception is conveyed through history and literature; through the concepts we encounter and the people we interact with. It is influenced by our values, those ideals we hold to be most important, which in turn guide our actions and our understanding of others.

Our perception of the world can either be narrow or expansive. A closed perception relies on a single branch of knowledge, while an open perception embraces multiple perspectives. I ask: who is more learned and cultured? The person who chooses to learn from a variety of knowledge sources. Who is more complete, in terms of understanding the world? The person who is open to learning from multiple sources and perspectives.

Words and actions are often misunderstood, especially when viewed from a limited perception. I have had the privilege of living and working in multiple countries, experiencing a wide range of cultures, and meeting people from all walks of life. This diversity has taught me that understanding each person's perspective is crucial for building healthy relationships in our ever-more diverse world.

Understanding others requires listening with empathy, putting aside your own biases to hear their perspective. This act of empathy means adapting to the way another person speaks and behaves and appreciating their unique experiences. When we approach others with empathy and love, we create meaningful connections that help us grow as individuals and as a society.

Each person comes from a unique environment and brings their own meaning to the words and actions they use. By taking the time to understand where someone is coming from, we can bridge the gap of misunderstanding. The goal is not merely to listen, but to identify with the other person, which requires an active effort to suspend our own beliefs to truly listen. This is the essence of empathy and love.

When we learn from people who are different from us, we open ourselves to greater appreciation of others. This appreciation, in turn, helps us see the creative potential in every individual and fosters the building of bridges between diverse groups. A cultured person is one who can see aspects of themselves in others, recognizing the value of diversity and understanding that what may appear as differences are in fact aspects of shared humanity.

The richness of our interactions with diverse people can deepen our understanding of the world and broaden our capacity for empathy. We must be open to the idea that no one person's perspective is the sole truth; instead, it is the collective tapestry of human experiences that creates the full picture.

Yet, within the circles I move, I am often misunderstood. It is painful when people mistake me for someone I am not. This misunderstanding arises from the inability to listen with empathy or see with an open mind. Sociologically, this is known as *identification,* and in behavioral terms, it's related to "emotional intelligence."[84]

Listening with empathy requires five key skills:

1. Remaining non-judgmental
2. Giving your undivided attention
3. Listening to feelings
4. Allowing time for silence
5. Paraphrasing what you understand.

Listening with empathy goes beyond just hearing words—it's about truly understanding the emotions and intentions behind them. When we practice these skills, we create a space for deeper connection and trust, fostering more meaningful and supportive relationships.

Seeing with the mind's eye involves five additional skills:

1. Receiving new information
2. Allowing time for reflection
3. Making new neural connections (neuroplasticity)
4. Using your imagination to form connections
5. Translating that information into understanding

Seeing with the mind's eye is not just about visualizing but about actively engaging with new ideas and perspectives. By giving ourselves the space to reflect, allowing our brains to form new connections, and using our imagination, we can transform information into deeper understanding. This process empowers us to think more creatively and adapt to an ever-changing world.

The inability to listen or to see another person's perspective stems from preconceived notions and the rush to judge. This "failure to feel" is a form of apathy, while "failing to see" is a kind of blindness. When some people fail to listen or feel with empathy, they can become filled with arrogance, believing they possess the "truth" as the Word of God. These people are "blind" often speaking in contradictory ways, claiming not to judge but acting out of fear of others. They misinterpret the higher values of others as inferior, thus destroying the good that God intended for the world.

To preserve and promote the value of each individual, we must approach others with love and understanding. Love and understanding in their truest sense require action—practical, real-world results that bring people together. Love and understanding are not just abstract concepts but require tangible actions that lead to real, positive outcomes, such as fostering unity and connection among people from which all goodness arises. Conversely, when these values are ignored or misunderstood, they can lead to negative outcomes, such as conflict or harm, which are described as the "evil" that arises when people fail to truly understand and care for one another.

Priorities and Values

PRIORITIES ARE DEEPLY INTERTWINED WITH OUR VALUES. What we value may be beautiful or ugly, or a blend of both, with one dominating the other. After all, values can exist at extreme ends of the spectrum. What we value shapes our thinking and behavior, molding us into specific kinds of people. Our values can either nurture our growth, hinder it, or steer it toward our potential. They influence how we relate to others, what we desire in those relationships, and how we engage with the world.

When discussing values, we must also consider priorities, as values are inherently tied to what we prioritize. Nietzsche stated, "The value of a thing sometimes lies not in what one attains with it, but in what one pays for it— what it *costs* us."[85] True value is not only measured by what we gain, but also by the sacrifices we make to acquire it. Prioritizing one value over another is essential in guiding our decisions. As our values evolve, often unexpectedly, new ones replace the old. Priorities are fluid, constantly shifting to meet the demands of different situations and interactions.

For example, I had planned a trip to Palestine in the winter, but due to the ongoing conflict in Kuwait that summer, the trip became impossible. Then, I was involved in a car accident as a passenger in a company vehicle, which forced me to reevaluate my priorities. I began to question the importance of my life and what I hoped to accomplish before my time runs out. In that moment, my priorities shifted.

My material desires, such as buying a new television, were no longer a priority. I had considered replacing my old, second-hand television, but upon reflection, I realized there was no need. The television I had, which I had rescued from the garbage, still worked perfectly fine and fulfilled my needs. Why invest in a new one when the current one was sufficient?

However, when it came to purchasing a desk, I recognized its importance. A desk was necessary to help me stay organized and productive, contributing to my personal growth and efficiency.

As for a telephone, I had gone without one for over a year. While a telephone is an essential tool for modern communication, I questioned its value in my life. Society demands that we have phones for both convenience and efficiency—whether for business or emergencies—but I didn't feel the need to purchase one until a specific situation called for it. Why buy a cordless phone when a wired one would serve the same purpose? Convenience, after all, is not always the best measure of necessity.

Similarly, when contemplating purchasing a $500 winter overcoat, I considered its dual function: to protect me from the cold and to enhance my appearance. In our society, appearance plays a significant role in shaping first impressions, influencing how others perceive us professionally. A well-dressed person often enjoys increased self-confidence and may find more success in business interactions. Yet, the decision to buy an overcoat required a deeper evaluation of my true priorities.

Priorities and values are constantly in flux. Old values may give way to newer or better ones as we prioritize them. Values shape us, guide us, and sometimes transform us. They play a crucial role in determining the kind of individuals we become—individuals who can contribute to peace, stability, and progress in the world. Human beings are complex and unpredictable creatures. It is valuable, then, to be aware of the external influences that shape us and to understand how they impact our choices.

Attaining Wealth *Is* Acquiring Identity

ATTAINING WEALTH IS NOT MERELY about the accumulation of material resources; it is a process that shapes one's acquired identity. The pursuit of wealth should be balanced with a responsibility to others, ensuring that one's gain does not harm or infringe upon the well-being of others.

The concept of *the good* extends beyond material wealth. If we were referring to material possessions, we would use the term "goods." The good, in this context, refers to actions, interactions, and relationships that enrich our lives and advance our shared human potential. It is the force that drives the development of who we are as individuals, helping us grow toward self-actualization.

The good is that which brings about favorable results, advancing the well-being of the human being, while fostering individual growth and determination. These favorable results are not only desirable but are also recognized and esteemed by the individual. It is through this esteem that one comes to define and refine one's identity.

An individual is someone who has achieved self-actualization, someone who has discovered and embraced their authentic self. It is through this authentic living that one assigns meaning to one's life. But how does one measure their worth or "good"? This measurement comes from an internal evaluation—what is deemed good is assessed based on long-term, positive outcomes that promote personal and collective well-being.

However, before one can reach self-actualization and be recognized as an individual, they must first understand their origins. An individual is shaped by the environment in which they were nurtured, and it is through this environment that biases and prejudices are formed. These biases, often inherited from one's surroundings, influence how one perceives the world and others. As a result, an individual may form incomplete or inaccurate judgments based on this limited perspective.

To truly become an individual, one must critically examine the environment in which they were nurtured and work to transcend the biases it instilled. This process may involve distancing oneself from the protective influences of their upbringing to engage with and understand other environments and people on their own terms. By moving beyond the narrow perspective shaped by their own biases, an individual can free themselves from judgment based on limited notions of 'good' and 'evil.'

When an individual breaks free from the biases of their environment and attains a true sense of identity, they can then engage in a deeper, more thoughtful evaluation of *the good.* At this point, the individual can measure good not just for personal satisfaction, but for the broader benefit of all. The good is now defined by long-lasting, favorable outcomes that contribute to the general well-being of individuals and society.

Through this process, the individual can begin to esteem others as they too define their own identities. Ultimately, the pursuit of wealth becomes intertwined with the pursuit of self-actualization, identity, and the greater good—both for oneself and for others.

Part III
Biblical Ethics
And
Social Change

The Goodness in all People

WHEN SOMEONE ADOPTS A NEW FAITH—whether Christian, Jewish, Muslim, or any other religion—interacting with family members who do not share those beliefs can be a challenging experience. Yet, religious texts often remind us of God's impartiality and His ability to work in the lives of all people, regardless of their faith. The Apostle Paul, in the books of Romans and Acts, highlights this truth, emphasizing that God is one and impartial:

> Since God is One, He does not show favoritism but accepts all from every nation, putting them right before Him on the basis of their faith and what they believe according to their conscience of what is right. God neither favors Protestants over Catholics, nor Christians over non-Christians. [86]

This impartiality offers a model for how we should approach others, especially those who do not share our beliefs. We can learn to engage with people of all faiths and backgrounds by seeing them as individuals, rather than reducing them to their religious labels or ideologies.

At some point, we all form misconceptions about others—often influenced by what we hear, see, or read. I've experienced this firsthand, even in my relationship with my own father. After my parents divorced, like many children of divorce, I was caught in the middle, each parent trying to sway me to favor one over the other. After spending six years at university in Southern California, I decided to visit my father in northern Oregon. I wanted to form my own opinion of him based on my experiences, not just the stories I had heard growing up.

I spent the first two months of my summer vacation with a Christian couple, and the final month with my father. I realized that getting to know him wasn't just about talking, but about spending time with him—doing things together and doing things for him. This required me to put aside any negative judgments or preconceived ideas others had instilled in me.

Over time, I began to see a side of my father I had never noticed before, and I started to appreciate qualities in him I had previously overlooked. I realized that my misconceptions—shaped by the past—had kept us apart. Much like our relationship with God, the more we engage with someone, the more we learn about them, and the more our judgment shifts. In my case, I discovered a "spark" of goodness in my father that I hadn't known existed.

This experience led me to imagine God standing beside my father, defending him against the accusations of others—much like how God defends us against Satan's accusations.[87] It reminded me that when we judge others based on incomplete or skewed views, we not only harm them, but also create division. Whether within families or communities, judgment based on half-truths can lead to unnecessary conflict.

It is in our best interest to withhold judgment and focus on the goodness in others. This doesn't mean ignoring faults or problems, but it means approaching others with openness and humility, recognizing that everyone has their own unique story. Why is it that we often judge others based on what we see or hear, without truly understanding their motivations? Why do we judge those who do not share our faith?

I, too, was guilty of such judgments when I first became a "conscious" Christian. I left the Catholic Church at age eight, only to become a Protestant Christian eleven years later. Early in my faith, I was zealous, often harshly judging my family and friends for not sharing my newfound beliefs. I became a "religious fanatic," convinced that only those who embraced my interpretation of Christianity could be saved.

But over time, I began to understand that salvation is not exclusive to Christians. One experience that helped change my perspective occurred while I was hitchhiking in Japan. I was trying to get from Osaka to Nagano, but a truck driver dropped me off in a small town called Tatsuno, far from my destination. It was a cold, rainy morning, and I found myself stranded. I saw an elderly woman delivering newspapers on her bicycle. The elderly woman noticed me—who most likely came from a Buddhist tradition— and took me into her home without hesitation. She didn't speak English, but she recognized my need and responded with kindness—offering me tea, food, warmth, and a place to rest.

Though this woman did not identify as a Christian, her actions exemplified the teachings of Jesus in Matthew 25:35: *"I was hungry, and you gave me food; I was thirsty, and you gave me drink; I was a stranger, and you took me in."* Her selfless actions taught me that true goodness transcends religious labels. In that moment, both she and I found ourselves in a unique "existential situation," where I encountered not only her culture but also her personal sense of conviction.[88] I experienced her goodness in a tangible, real way that went beyond belief systems.

I couldn't fully understand her motivations from a theological perspective, but I saw the genuine goodness in her actions. She showed me grace, just as I would later try to show others. This experience became a guide for how I would live my life—learning to treat others with compassion, especially those who were different from me.

When I returned to university, I continued to reflect on my experience in Tatsuno, and it changed the way I saw people. One day, I took the bus to the local mall with the simple intention of striking up a conversation with a stranger. I sat down on a bench at the bus stop next to a homeless man who appeared scruffy and dirty. To my surprise, he turned to me and asked, "You're a Christian, aren't you?" Startled, I replied, "Yes. How did you know?" He looked at me intently and said, "I can tell by your eyes." His words took me aback. His name was Ed. Once a university professor, Ed had fallen on hard times due to alcoholism. But as we talked, I looked beyond his circumstances and saw his humanity. We rode the bus together, and I invited him to my dorm to rest. Later, I shared a meal with him at the university cafeteria before he went on his way.

Another time, I went to the city park near my university with my Bible—not to read, but as a conversation starter. Lying on the grass with the Bible open, a man approached and remarked, "I see you're reading the Book." I replied, "Yes, I am." He then quoted, *"Jesus said you must be born again."* However, he wasn't referring to the spiritual rebirth that most Christians understand; he was talking about reincarnation—the idea of the transmigration of souls, purging evil through suffering, and being purified by the Law of Karma.[89] This interpretation challenged my faith. But to understand his perspective—and why some people, even some Christians, might believe in reincarnation—I decided to buy a book on the subject.

Inspired by these experiences, my university friends and I started a community outreach program for the homeless. One day, we met a homeless woman named Wendy in the park. She was especially passionate about quoting Plato—a philosopher I knew little about at the time. Though I didn't ask her about her story, she struck me as an intelligent woman. Her enthusiasm sparked my curiosity about Plato's teachings and how they might have influenced Christian thought.

The people society often deems "outcasts" have names, and they have stories. The individuals I encountered were not uneducated; many were highly educated. Everyone has a story to tell. What's yours? Let your story inspire others.

In time, I began to realize that every person—whether rich or poor, religious or not—has a story, and that story deserves respect and empathy. I also came to understand that goodness isn't always tied to religious affiliations. I was later introduced to the work of Catholic theologian Karl Rahner, whose writings further challenged my previous beliefs.

Rahner proposes the concept of the "anonymous Christian," suggesting that people who have never heard the Christian Gospel may still be saved through God's grace as they live according to the moral principles of their traditions.[90] He maintains that non-Christian religions contain elements of truth and goodness, and that God's grace can be present in all people, regardless of their religious background.

These insights freed me from my former religious fanaticism and helped me understand that a person's goodness cannot be defined solely by their adherence to a particular faith. As Christians, our responsibility is not to judge others, but to focus on the good in them—following the example of Jesus, who "esteemed" all people, even those who were considered outcasts. [91]

Ultimately, we are called to see the goodness in all people. Just as God shows no favoritism, we too should approach others with the same impartiality, seeking to understand and appreciate the goodness within them. In doing so, we can build bridges rather than walls, fostering unity and love in our relationships and communities.

God's Justice and Ours

THE WAY EACH OF US UNDERSTANDS GOD shapes how we act toward ourselves and others. Those who view God as love will, in turn, share love. Those who see God as mercy will show mercy. Those who conceive of God as justice will practice justice. If this is true, then God's nature is far broader than we often imagine, and therefore, we are called to embody love, mercy, and justice simultaneously in our interactions with others.

Our perception of God often begins with our senses, but it is our mental conception that gives us understanding. How we perceive God—whether as love, justice, or mercy—depends on what we hear, read, and experience about Him. A religious person believes that human beings need God to guide their moral and ethical conduct. Thus, a person's understanding of God influences their view of humanity and shapes their moral actions.

To conceive of God as justice is especially significant for three reasons. First, justice is synonymous with doing good. Just actions benefit others and promote lives that strive for happiness and well-being. Second, unlike liberty or equality, justice is unlimited. We can have too much freedom or equality, which can harm others, but justice remains balanced. Justice respects the right balance between liberty and equality, preventing excess in either direction. Third, justice is essential to love. It is through justice that love is fully realized. Justice provides the necessary framework for love to be expressed, demonstrating our duty and obligation to act with kindness, mercy, and fairness in specific situations.

The command to do justice is not passive. It implies an active responsibility to ensure that justice is done, both in the lives of individuals and within the broader community. This means extending impartiality to all, respecting others' beliefs, and recognizing the intrinsic value in every person we encounter.

In the Old Testament, before Jesus' arrival, God's expectation for humanity was clear: "to do justice" (Micah 6:8). During his time on Earth, Jesus exemplified this by consistently practicing justice in his interactions, even with those who held beliefs or values different from his own (Luke 7:35). Jesus spent time with the marginalized, the poor, and those whom society had cast aside. His ministry often involved meeting their physical and social needs before addressing their spiritual needs. His acts of justice were not limited to grand gestures but extended to everyday, personal interactions that showed respect for their dignity.

Jesus' choice to associate with the marginalized often put him at odds with the religious leaders of his time, particularly the Pharisees and Sadducees, who criticized his practices. But he remained committed to meeting people where they were, embodying justice through his acceptance of diverse individuals and their unique situations.

Paul, following in Jesus' footsteps, also adapted his behavior to relate to others in his ministry.[92] In his letter to the Corinthians, he describes how he became "all things to all people" to connect with them more effectively. For Jews, he followed the law; for Gentiles, he lived as one not bound by it. Paul's approach was not about compromising his beliefs but about demonstrating justice by respecting the cultural context and personal convictions of others, saying, "I have become all things to all people, that by all means I might save some."[93]

To connect with others effectively in a diverse world, we must adopt a mindset that seeks justice in every situation. This involves recognizing the unique needs of individuals in communities and striving for the greater good. Justice is not just an abstract ideal but a moral and ethical action—a *way of being*, which values what is right, good, and fair for all.

Justice, at its core, is an expression of conscience. It is a moral and ethical awareness that guides both public and private actions. While moral action concerns what is right or wrong in public contexts, ethical action addresses what is good or bad in more personal, unique situations. The consciousness of doing justice, especially in how we interact with others, is a form of "introjection"—the internalization of shared values, traditions, and beliefs.

When we practice justice, we also practice love. The distinction between love and liking is important: love is discerning, not sentimental. It is deliberate and caring, aimed at serving others well. Justice, in this sense, is love working out its complexities and challenges.

My own journey into social justice was catalyzed by the injustices I experienced within the religious organization I once deeply identified with. I had learned that such injustices were often designed to secure power over individuals, often at the expense of their emotional and spiritual well-being. What I have since come to understand is that working for justice—ensuring the well-being of others—leads to greater happiness and fulfillment for both the giver and the receiver. By making life easier or more bearable for others, we can also experience the joy of seeing others flourish.

Perhaps the most crucial element in practicing justice is seeing the inherent goodness in all people. When we truly recognize and honor the dignity of others, we fulfill the command to "do justice," reflecting God's love and justice in the world.

Postscript [94]

Pietism and moralism, much like legalism, distort true goodness into something negative. Pietism corrupts religion by creating a separation between faith and everyday life. While legalism elevates and idolizes laws, pietism individualizes and subjectivizes piety.

Pietism reduces religion to mere religiosity, making it an exclusively personal or mystical experience detached from economic, political, or social concerns. It fosters the belief that religion should avoid "interfering" in politics or business, as though these realms exist in separate, non-overlapping spheres. Pietism often repudiates the notion of "holy worldliness" and insists that true religion must remain separate from worldly engagement.

Pietism rejects the Bible's integration of faith and action, opting instead for a form of religion focused on personal devotion, quietism, and sectarian interests. It discourages Christian involvement in matters of economic, racial, or political justice, often appearing conservative and cautious in the face of change. Furthermore, it can be sympathetic to right-wing extremism, offering a sanctified justification for such views.

Moralism, on the other hand, reduces moral life to a set of trivial rules. It often focuses on prohibitions like smoking, dancing, playing cards, drinking alcohol, or even harmless social activities, while largely ignoring deeper issues of love, justice, and social responsibility. Moralism tends to promote a "works doctrine," where salvation is viewed as a reward for adhering to a narrow set of behaviors, emphasizing external conduct over internal transformation.

Moreover, moralism's ethic is not only trivial but also easy. It simplifies the complexity of ethical living by reducing it to a set of manageable, superficial rules. This leads to a form of "righteousness" that is more about checking off moral boxes than about confronting the challenging, deeper demands of love and justice. Moralism fails to recognize any connection between Jesus' teachings, the Scriptures, and the urgent demands for racial justice or loving-kindness.

The negative absolutisms of pietism and moralism have a neurotic character. As Albert Schweitzer wisely noted, "the good conscience is an invention of the devil."[95] Schweitzer's remark challenges us to reflect on how the quietism of pietism and the rules of moralism can inadvertently create inner conflict, as it overlooks the complexities of human nature and the need for grace and empathy in our interactions with ourselves and others. When conscience becomes absolute, detached from compassion and understanding, it can lead to a form of self-righteousness that fosters guilt, fear, and separation rather than healing and connection.

The Social Gospel

THE *SOCIAL GOSPEL* is a concept rooted in the pursuit of social justice, attributed to W. Rauschenbusch in the early twentieth century. At its core, the Social Gospel interprets Jesus' message about the Kingdom of God not as a vision of a redeemed community in the afterlife, but as a call for the transformation of earthly social structures. This transformation can only occur by rebuilding a system of values that promotes justice and serves the broader goal of societal liberation.

The Social Gospel presents a radical, biblically inspired vision that aligns with the liberating God who makes all things new. It is a movement toward social justice, advocating for action that reconstructs societal values and creates a pathway for others to follow. The Social Gospel responds to social injustices and critiques religious pietism, positioning its hope for human progress within the potential of both human agency and societal advancement.

This vision challenges us to reimagine and reconfigure social relations through the lens of divine justice and deliverance, emphasizing that these principles are not just religious mandates but universal ones. Whether in personal or collective situations, we are called to live out God's will, as demonstrated by Jesus' teachings and Paul's actions.

From a sociological perspective, the Social Gospel incorporates three key ideas:

1. *Verstehen* (or *introjection* in social ethics) is the effort to understand a person's behavior from their own perspective.

2. *Common sense* involves knowing and recognizing expected behaviors within a given society or culture.

3. *Cultural relativity* asserts that we should not judge cultures or individuals by the standards of others, but instead approach each one on its own terms.

Ultimately, the Social Gospel focuses on relationships in society, aiming to achieve the highest good in every situation through justice, which is rooted in love. In essence, justice embodies love by manifesting the moral actions required to make love real and tangible in the world, especially in complex, real-world contexts.

The Language of Ethics

ETHICS ARE SITUATIONAL, WHEREAS MORALS ARE UNIVERSAL. Morality concerns what is *right or wrong* for public, normative behavior, while ethics are more about what is *good or bad* for personal, private conduct. Ethical morality refers to "right action for what is best" in specific social contexts. In this way, ethics are exclusive, focusing on individual situations, while morals are inclusive, grounded in universal principles.

Living in the world means navigating a series of unique situations, each involving interactions between individuals, objects, and others. Situations and interactions are inseparable—one cannot exist without the other. If we treat all situations as equal, we risk eliminating the concept of "right action" entirely, because no situation would stand out as distinct or valuable enough to warrant moral consideration. In such a world, ethics would become irrelevant, and human interactions would lack meaning.

Living with Other Minds

Understanding others' mindsets is crucial for cultivating tolerance, which forms the foundation of respect. When we respect others, we embrace their differences, even when they don't align with our own beliefs. Approaching each situation on its own terms requires wisdom and adaptability—changing how we think to respond appropriately to what each unique circumstance demands.

We learn from our successes and failures by reflecting on the outcomes of our interactions, striving to foresee what would be best in each situation. However, emotions often outpace reason, leading us to act in ways that may not be in our best interest or in alignment with our ethical values. This failure to learn can bring about consequences, especially in the context of karma, where our actions inevitably come back to affect us.

Being honest with ourselves and reflecting daily on our actions is essential to living ethically. We must ask whether our behavior aligns with our highest values, whatever they may be. However, right action is often clouded by personal conceptions of "God" or morality. Many justify their actions by invoking divine approval, but in doing so, they simply affirm their own *concept* of God, rather than seeking true alignment with a higher moral standard.

Men of Religion and the Escape from Responsibility

Religious individuals can sometimes be unsettling, especially when they focus too much on "saving" humanity from the present world in anticipation of a heavenly afterlife. A religious person who dismisses the present world as inherently evil is essentially renouncing their responsibility to engage with it. Such individuals may divide the world into opposing forces of good and evil, forcing others to conform to their ideals without regard for the broader context.

This perspective often leads to apathy, as religious figures who dismiss the world's problems as irrelevant may grow indifferent to the suffering and struggles of others. A religious person who interprets their suffering as "God's will" may fail to recognize that their own choices—such as poor lifestyle decisions—may be the root cause. The idea that God causes suffering to teach lessons is deeply unsettling, implying a deity who takes pleasure in human pain.

Human beings often project their own image onto God, creating a divine figure that reflects their strengths, weaknesses, and desires. Feuerbach claims:

God is ... a product of modern *unbelief*... On the ground that God is unknowable, man ... excuses himself: he denies God by his *conduct*... The denial ... is simply a subtle *disguised atheism*...[96]

Feuerbach suggests that man makes God in his own image, and in doing so, justifies his own actions, even when they may be harmful. This anthropomorphic conception of God becomes a tool for excusing behavior that would otherwise be seen as wrong.

The Problem of Religious Knowledge and Ignorance

The inability of religious individuals to answer basic theological questions—such as the difference between a "Protestant" and a "Christian"—highlights the deep ignorance that often accompanies faith. Socrates argues that ignorance is the root of evil, for it prevents individuals from seeing the truth of their actions and their impact on others. The failure to engage with this truth can perpetuate harm, both to oneself and to society.

Philosophers throughout history have emphasized the importance of knowledge and wisdom. Socrates held knowledge as the highest virtue, and ignorance as its greatest vice. Aristotle believed that justice and friendship were essential for human flourishing, while Descartes regarded doubt as the beginning of true understanding. Nietzsche saw the transcendence of prejudice as a critical step in personal growth, and Dewey championed progress through continuous learning. Martin Luther King Jr. fought for freedom and equality, recognizing these as essential to peace.

Labels, Name-Calling, and Tricks Against the Human Spirit

In our interactions, we should avoid reducing one another to labels. Labels impose an artificial identity. Labels such as "Christian," "American,"

"Democrat" or "Liberal," limit understanding and create divisions among people, separating us by categories rather than recognizing our shared humanity. Using labels prevents us from seeing the richness and complexity of an individual's life.

Once, a Japanese Christian asked me if I was a "Christian." I replied that I was "better than a Christian." I explained that, first and foremost, I am a human being, and second, I am christian. To me, the term "Christian" as a noun—especially when preceded by the article "a"—carries the weight of a label. However, when the word is written with a lowercase "c" and without the article, it suggests the active practice of the values it represents—compassion, kindness, justice—rather than merely identifying as a member of a religious group.

When people ask if I'm religious, I typically respond that I'm spiritual but not *a* Christian. My spiritual practice centers on exploring our identity *as* humans and what that means for humanity as a whole. I wouldn't label myself an atheist, but rather an agnostic. Like Einstein, I don't believe in the Christian concept of God, yet I remain *open* to the possibility of something greater *beyond* our current understanding.

The danger of labels is that they can create walls between people—between classes, races, and cultures—and obscure our shared humanity. Labels like "blue collar," "Catholic," or "Palestinian" do little to reflect the true essence of a person, reducing them to a narrow category. The danger is that labels can divide us, preventing us from seeing the humanity in others and denying the potential for mutual understanding.

Similarly, name-calling and tricks—such as gossip, sarcasm, or insult—are destructive. These actions dehumanize the individual, fostering division and harm rather than connection and understanding. Words like "stupid," or accusations of ignorance undermine communication, closing off opportunities for reconciliation and mutual respect.

We must remember that we are not just representatives of our race, nationality, or religion—we are representatives of Humanity. How we present ourselves to others reflects not only our own values but also the collective image of humanity. Too often, labels become the foundation of our identities, locking us into narrow or limiting perspectives and preventing us from seeing others as fully realized, complex human beings.

While labels can provide a sense of security, they can also act as a form of social control, imposing limits on how we interact with the world. It is important to recognize that when we label others, we limit their freedom to be seen as individuals, and in doing so, we lose the opportunity to connect on a deeper, more human level. True maturity requires us to move beyond labels and recognize the dignity of others as human beings, free from the constraints that labels impose.

Lying: Permissible but not always Beneficial

Lying, or withholding the truth, can be permissible in certain situations, depending on the context and ethical framework being applied. In "situational ethics," lying may be justified as a decision made for the benefit of an individual, especially when the intent is to preserve someone's life or well-being. Similarly, in the context of "institutional ethics," lying might be seen as acceptable when it serves the collective interest of an institution, such as protecting its reputation or maintaining stability.

In institutional ethics, for example, an individual may lie to protect their job or secure their position within the organization, especially if that institution sees them as a valuable member. On the other hand, someone who values their "individuated existence" may be viewed as a threat to the institution's collective identity. The institution, in this case, may employ lies and manipulations (using scapegoating tactics, for example) to maintain its power and protect its interests, even if it means exiling individuals in the wilderness who challenge the system.[97]

Niccolò Machiavelli's *The Prince* (16th century) laid out the groundwork for what is now known as Machiavellian ethics, where deceit, manipulation, and power games are justified to attain and maintain control. Machiavelli famously wrote that a ruler must learn to act immorally when necessary: "Any man who tries to be good all the time is bound to come to ruin among the great number who are not good."[98] For Machiavelli, virtue was not about adhering to moral principles but adapting to circumstances—sometimes using deceit to secure one's position.

In his modern interpretation of Machiavellianism, Robert Greene's *The 48 Laws of Power* draws on this concept, advising individuals to use any means necessary—whether moral or immoral—to gain and sustain power. Greene's advice echoes Machiavelli's strategy of combining the cunning of the fox with the strength of the lion: "He should imitate both the fox and the lion... to be a fox [is] to recognize traps, and a lion [is] to frighten away wolves."[99] For a Machiavellian, power is the end goal, and ethics bend to serve that end.

A Machiavellian manipulates others, using lies and deceit to achieve his goals, sometimes even at the expense of others. This strategic, often ruthless approach considers the greater good for the individual, rather than the collective. While Machiavellians might appear to be strategic masterminds, their use of lies as a tool to further their self-interest can be morally questionable, especially when their deceit leads to harm.

On the flip side, there are times when lying in abstract or personal situations may be justified from a moral perspective. For instance, in certain ethical dilemmas, such as saving a life or protecting a person's dignity, lying may be seen as permissible within "situational ethics." The apostle Paul, for example, advised believers to lie about their views on food served by unbelievers to avoid causing offense, even when such lying didn't align with the believer's personal conscience. In 1 Corinthians 10:23-33, Paul says:

> Everything is permissible—but not everything is beneficial. Everything is permissible—but not everything is constructive. Nobody should seek his own good, but the good of others... Eat anything sold in the meat market without raising questions of conscience... If some unbeliever invites you to a meal and you want to go, eat whatever is put before you without raising questions of conscience—the other man's conscience, I mean, not yours.

For why should my freedom be judged by another's conscience?

In this example, Paul's approach to truth in a specific context reflects a pragmatic view: lying can be justified to avoid causing someone else to "stumble" in their faith. This shows how, in certain situations, withholding the truth or offering a lie can be in the service of a higher ethical goal, such as maintaining peace, respect, or harmony.

The Ethics of Truth in Religion and Society

Religion often teaches that we are our brother's keeper, responsible for each other's well-being. This interconnectedness underlines the notion that what is good for one should ideally be good for all.[100] The responsibility to care for others transcends individual desires, elevating the welfare of the collective. Whether or not we subscribe to religious beliefs, the idea of shared responsibility reinforces the importance of making ethical decisions that benefit not just ourselves but society.

However, religion can also create harmful labels that undermine self-worth. The notion of being a "sinner" creates "guilt," shame, and a "bad conscience," which can alienate individuals from their true selves.[101] Nietzsche critiqued this in his writing, claiming that belief in absolutes—such as the idea of "sin"—limits human freedom. He argues that when one holds fixed convictions, it becomes a prison for the mind. True freedom, according to Nietzsche, comes from the ability to question and interpret life without being bound by rigid beliefs.[102]

In religious contexts, the idea of sin and salvation often works as a form of control. For example, the concept of being a "backslider" or a "lapsed believer" implies that people who question or diverge from prescribed beliefs are to be punished or excluded. Yet, Nietzsche suggests that beliefs become prisons when they limit our ability to engage with life freely and with open-mindedness.

Jesus' engagement with "sinners" provides a notable example of rejecting these limiting labels. He was criticized by the religious authorities for associating with outcasts such as tax collectors, prostitutes, and drunkards. The Pharisees and Sadducees condemned him for breaking societal and religious laws, but Jesus' actions showed that the rigid application of laws could hinder true understanding of human needs. He often questioned the conventional notions of purity and sin, emphasizing that the value of a person is not determined by outward appearances or rigid adherence to rules, but by their inherent dignity and potential.

The Nature of Truth and Knowledge

The search for truth is complicated and multi-dimensional. In the Gospels, when Pontius Pilate asks Jesus, "What is truth?" (John 18:38), it reveals the tension between philosophical and moral understandings of truth. Is truth an objective, absolute concept, or is it relative and shaped by individual experience? Jesus' life and teachings suggest that truth cannot be confined to one perspective, whether it be religious, political, or cultural.

Convictions, like truth confined to a belief or persuasion, can become a prison. Catholic theologian Karl Rahner suggests that non-Christian religions not only "contain elements of a natural knowledge of God" but also "supernatural grace-filled elements."[103] This suggests that truth can manifest in various forms across different religions and worldviews. Christianity, in this view, is not the singular embodiment of truth; rather, it is one of many paths pointing toward a deeper truth.

If Christianity were the exclusive and absolute truth, it would negate the validity of all other truths. Truth is not confined to a single perspective or closed system; it is seen from multiple vantage points, experienced through diverse lenses, and understood through the richness of varied human experiences. Therefore, the concept of truth must remain open, expansive, and inclusive. Nietzsche writes:

We usually endeavor to acquire a *single* attitude of mind towards all the events and situations in life... But for the enrichment of knowledge, listen to the gentle voice of each of life's different situations; these will suggest the attitude of mind appropriate to them. Cease to treat oneself as a *single* rigid and unchanging individual and take an intelligent interest in the life and being of many others.[104]

Nietzsche urges us to approach each situation with a "philosophical mind"—to recognize that different circumstances require different attitudes. He encourages us to embrace a multiplicity of perspectives, enriching our knowledge and expanding our understanding by acting according to what is best in each unique context.

Truth is a dynamic, evolving concept that is shaped by interactions with others and experiences in the world. As Nietzsche suggests, we should not view truth as a fixed entity but as something fluid that emerges from diverse perspectives and experiences. He advises us to embrace a multiplicity of views to enrich our knowledge and expand our understanding.

Truth, then, is something we experience actively. It emerges through our interactions with others—great thinkers and ordinary people alike—as we engage with them in the situations of life. By listening to their truths, we deepen our own and expand our perception of what truth can be. Truth is derived from three sources:

1. Our direct experiences and observations.

2. How we respond to others by either accepting or challenging their truths.

3. How we process and internalize these experiences as our own understanding of truth.

It is in this dynamic exchange that truth unfolds and deepens, broadening our perception and leading us to ever-greater heights of understanding.

Truth, therefore, is not one-dimensional or confined to any one religion or belief system. It is found in the exchange of ideas, in dialogue, and in the relationships, we form with others. By engaging with others' experiences and knowledge, we come closer to understanding the full scope of truth—not just through our own narrow perspective, but through a broader, more inclusive lens.

Mind Over Matter: The Path to Authenticity

A rigid adherence to fixed beliefs limits intellectual freedom and creativity. The true self is developed through the active engagement with the world and with others, not by simply conforming to established norms or doctrines. The mind must remain open, flexible, and capable of adapting to new experiences.

Kant's philosophy emphasized that the mind actively shapes our experiences, rather than passively absorbing data.[105] By actively engaging with the world and critically reflecting on those experiences, we develop an identity shaped by conscious interaction with others and the environment. This is not merely a process of conforming to societal expectations but of creating one's path in the world.

Jesus' attitude toward knowledge reveals a similar emphasis on openness. He criticized those who restricted the flow of knowledge by clinging to outdated laws and rules. True wisdom, in his view, came from humility and the willingness to learn from others, especially those outside traditional power structures.

In our pursuit of personal growth, we must stay open to new perspectives, drawing wisdom from the richness of human experience, and embracing the journey rather than fixating solely on the end goal. As the saying goes, "Live your life each day as you would climb a mountain. An occasional glance toward the summit keeps the goal in mind, but many beautiful scenes are to be observed from each new vantage point." Let us guide our ethical choices with the intention of nurturing understanding, compassion, and deeper connections with those around us.

Part IV
The Religious

The Religious Optimist

THE ESSENCE OF EVIL is the deliberate infliction of pain upon a sentient being capable of suffering. Evil is sensed as harm intentionally caused. Its existence requires no further proof: the fact that I am, and that I experience pain, establishes the reality of evil.

Evil manifests in two primary forms: natural and moral. *Natural evil* includes natural disasters, such as earthquakes, and diseases, like cancer, that seem inexplicable but, in some view, must have a purpose. *Moral evil* results from destructive actions by humans toward one another and the world, stemming from their freedom of choice.

While humans have the power to mitigate moral evil, doing so requires an understanding of its causes. Presented below are four reasons why I suffer moral evil at the hands of other humans, along with a fifth reason that involves the influence of a demonic force.

Moral Evil

1. *Biological Nature*

The first reason I suffer moral evil at the hands of other humans is that it stems from humanity's biological nature, suggesting that humans are innately or naturally inclined toward cruelty, destructiveness, and violence. This inherent instinct is part of our biology, as the "way we are." In the

Biblical story of Cain and Abel, Cain, driven by jealousy, killed his brother Abel.[106, 107] This early act of fratricide symbolizes a longstanding aspect of human nature: the capacity for cruelty.[108]

The philosopher Hsün-Tzu famously described humans as having "the heart of a tiger or a wolf."[109] Jesus highlighted a list of human vices, such as murder, covetousness, deceit, blasphemy, and pride.[110] Thomas Hobbes echoed this view, arguing that humans exist in a "state of nature" characterized by competition and conflict, driven by a desire for gain, security, and reputation.[111] He described life in this state as "solitary, poor, nasty, brutish, and short."[112] Even acts of apparent altruism, Hobbes claimed, are often tainted by selfish motivations, such as the pursuit of recognition. Humans are unique among animals in their capacity for interspecies violence—a trait that reflects an evil ingrained in our genetic makeup.[113]

2. *Behavioral Nurture*

The second reason I suffer moral evil at the hands of other humans suggests that it is the result of the "way we behave," which is humanity's environmental conditioning, or how we are shaped by society, family, culture, and education.[114] Just as a parent who prioritizes fitness will raise a physically healthy child, so too will a society that promotes certain beliefs shape its citizens' values and behaviors.

Societal influences can lead to the perpetuation of both good and evil. For example, a child raised in a violent environment may come to see violence as normal. While our innate nature might predispose us to certain tendencies, the society we grow up in plays a significant role in shaping our behavior. Thus, moral evil can be traced to the negative influences of social and cultural conditioning.

Although our character is shaped by both our inherent physiological needs and the environmental conditions we encounter—nature and nurture—we have the capacity to change and refine our character. By responding thoughtfully to life's challenges, we can grow into mature and responsible individuals.[115, 116] In other words, we possess the ability to influence both our natural tendencies and our upbringing, allowing us to actively choose the kind of person we wish to become.

3. The Unconscious Mind

The third reason I suffer moral evil at the hands of other humans involves the unconscious aspects of the human psyche—our repressed desires, impulses, and emotions that reside beneath the conscious mind that has the capability for destructiveness.[117] The "dark side" or the "shadow" of our personality, as Carl Jung described it, consists of all the aspects of ourselves that we deny or suppress.[118]

This hidden darkness may fuel destructive tendencies. When we ignore or repress these darker impulses, they can resurface in harmful ways, manifesting as cruelty, control, and sadism.[119, 120] People who fail to acknowledge and integrate their shadow can become dangerously apathetic or detached from the suffering of others, furthering evil. Thus, moral evil is produced by the unconscious mind, which, when ignored, can wreak havoc on human behavior.[121]

4. The Inflated Ego

The fourth reason I suffer moral evil at the hands of other humans is because of the inflated conscious ego.[122] The desire to be "like God," as depicted in the Biblical story of the Fall of Adam and Eve, reflects an inflated sense of self—pride and arrogance.[123] According to St. Augustine, humans are born with "original sin," a condition that alienates us from both our true selves and from God.[124]

When we strive to elevate ourselves above others, particularly in positions of unchecked power fueled by a sense of self-importance, devoid of empathy, and in defiance of divine will, we bring about sin and suffering.[125, 126] This ego-driven alienation distorts our perception of good and evil, ultimately leading to moral evil. By prioritizing our own self-interest, we cause harm to others and the world around us.

To truly be human and empathize with others is to refuse to play God. When suffering arises, we should consider our role in its cause and our responsibility in its relief. The only enduring rule of life today is to learn how to live and how to die—and, in order to be a man or a woman, to refuse to be a god.[127]

5. *The Demonic Influence*

The fifth reason I suffer moral evil is that it is influenced or perpetuated by a powerful demonic force. In religious traditions, this force is often personified as the Devil. In Christianity, for example, Satan is depicted as the deceiver of the world, cast out of heaven after rebelling against God.[128, 129] The Devil is believed to work through temptation, encouraging humans to act in ways that perpetuate suffering and evil. Many cultures have similar personifications of evil, from Mephistopheles to Lucifer.[130] For some, moral evil can be rationalized by blaming this external force, saying, "The Devil made me do it." In this view, the Devil embodies the active principle of evil in the world.

Natural Evil

Natural evil, by contrast, is the evil inherent in the natural world—suffering and pain that seem purposeless or unwarranted. *Natural evil* includes events like earthquakes, diseases, and the suffering of innocent beings. These occurrences seem random, unnecessary, and beyond human control. We may ask, why does God allow such suffering if He is all-powerful and all-good?

Consider the 7.8 magnitude earthquake in Turkey and Syria in 2023, which killed over 50,000 people. Or the 2004 Indian Ocean 9.1 magnitude tsunami, which claimed more than 225,000 lives. Or the 7.4 magnitude earthquake in Iran in 1990, which killed over 45,000 people.

These natural disasters raise profound questions about the nature of God and the purpose of suffering. There is no obvious explanation for why some individuals suffer extreme pain or premature death while others enjoy lives of relative ease and prosperity. This inequity suggests a fundamental contradiction between the existence of suffering and the image of a benevolent, omnipotent deity.

Some religious optimists argue that suffering has a divine purpose—perhaps as a "test" or a means to purify the soul, preparing it for immortality in the afterlife.[131] Others suggest that natural catastrophes "perfect" humanity through "suffering," bringing about a greater good. If this is true, it seems there are nearly as many 'gods' as there are speakers and worshippers claiming to understand His will.[132]

Theologians and philosophers have long debated whether suffering is a test, a punishment, or simply a consequence of the natural order. But even those who argue that suffering has meaning struggle to explain why so much pain appears meaningless or pointless. Some believe that human beings, with their limited understanding, cannot fully grasp the mind of God. However, this doesn't change the fundamental question of why such suffering exists in the first place.

The origin of moral evil can be traced to several interrelated factors: our biological nature, societal conditioning, repressed psychological impulses, inflated egos, and the influence of demonic forces. Natural evil, on the other hand, arises from the unpredictable and often inexplicable suffering embedded in the fabric of existence.

Both forms of evil challenge our understanding of morality, existence, and the nature of a divine being. In grappling with these realities, we confront the profound "mystery" of suffering, evil, and the search for meaning in a seemingly indifferent universe.

However, such views can seem dismissive of the real, indiscriminate suffering endured by countless people and creatures, which can disprove God's existence.[133] This raises further questions: If suffering is meant to have a higher purpose, why does it seem so arbitrary and cruel? Can we truly say that God is good while also accepting the widespread injustice and misery in the world?

Arguments for God's Existence

There are three primary arguments for the existence of God: the ontological argument, the cosmological argument, and the teleological argument. Each is based on different premises about God, followed by a critique.

1. *Ontological Argument*

The ontological argument, first developed by St. Anselm in the 11th century, argues for God's existence through pure reason alone, independent of empirical evidence. According to Anselm, God is defined as "that than which nothing greater can be thought."[134]

The premise is that a being so great and perfect must exist in reality because existence is a necessary attribute of greatness. God is a being so great and so "perfect" that one cannot conceive of a being that could be greater than God. Even the fool who says in his heart, "There is no God" (Psalm 14:1; 53:1) does, at least, understand that definition—that nothing greater than a greater being other than God can be thought of existing. According to Anselm, it is impossible to conceive of anything greater than a "necessary" being, as such a being is "complete in itself." Therefore, God must necessarily exist in reality to be the greatest being conceivable.

The main flaw in this argument lies in the leap from the concept of a perfect being to the actual existence of such a being. Just because something can be imagined as perfect or necessary does not mean it must exist in reality. For instance, the idea of a "perfect island" does not prove that such an island exists. In addition, nothing can be defined into existence by attaching certain attributes to it, e.g., God is "perfect," "all-knowing," and "all-powerful." Anselm's argument relies on the assumption that defining something into existence is valid, which remains highly contentious.

Anselm's 'God' is contingent upon his idea of God. If my idea of God is not Anselm's idea of God, then I cannot accept his idea of God.

2. Cosmological Argument

The cosmological argument traces its origins to Aristotle and was later developed by St. Thomas Aquinas.[135] This argument is Aquinas' first and second of "Five Ways" for God's existence, which is based on "natural" knowledge of empirical observation.[136] This argument posits that everything in the universe is caused by something else, and this chain of causes must ultimately trace back to an uncaused cause, which Aquinas identifies as God—the "First Unmoved Mover." The premise is that there must be a necessary being whose existence does not depend on anything else, setting the entire chain of events in motion.[137] God, therefore, must necessarily exist for He is that being who sets things in motion with an order and moves them.

The defect with this argument is the concept of an infinite regress. If every effect has a cause, why can't the universe itself be eternal, with no need for an initial mover? If God is necessary to end the chain of causality, then the argument begs the question: Who or what caused God?[138] The idea that God is an uncaused cause may contradict the original premise that all things must have a cause.

3. Teleological Argument

The teleological argument, also known as the "argument from design," argues that the universe's order and complexity suggests the existence of an intelligent designer. St. Thomas Aquinas presented this argument as his fifth "Way" for proving God's existence.[139] "It is not by chance, but by design," Aquinas says, that natural bodies "move towards a purpose" by some intelligent being whom exists; and this being we call God.[140] In other words, this argument asserts that the universe operates with such intricate purpose and design that it must have been created by an intelligent being, much like a watch is created by a watchmaker, or a computer is made by a hardware engineer.

The weakness of the teleological argument is due to the observable imperfections, chaos, and apparent randomness in the universe. Events like natural disasters, diseases, and exploding stars suggest that the universe is far from perfectly ordered or harmonious. Moreover, the idea of a "designer" does not necessarily imply the existence of a benevolent, omnipotent deity. The universe contains too much disorder to justify belief in God. The chaotic and evolving nature of the universe complicates the argument that it was designed with a specific purpose in mind.

Pascal's Wager

In his work *Pensées* (1670), French philosopher and mathematician Blaise Pascal (1623-1669) presents an argument for belief in God as a "wager" or a bet on God's existence. Pascal's wager encourages us to make decisions based on the potential outcomes of our choices, particularly when the stakes are so high, such as the possibility of eternal life or eternal damnation. Pascal suggests that even if God does not exist, believing in Him is still beneficial because of the positive impact faith has on our lives.

Pascal's Wager is structured as a cost-benefit analysis, positioning belief in God as the rational choice. He argues:

1. If you believe in God and He exists, you receive an infinite reward (eternal life in heaven).

2. If you believe in God and He does not exist, you lose very little (a limited sacrifice during your lifetime).

3. If you do not believe in God and He exists, you suffer an infinite loss (eternal damnation).

4. If you do not believe in God and He does not exist, you gain very little or nothing, living without religious commitment.

From a betting perspective, it is clear which option is preferable. The risk of eternal damnation outweighs the short-term pleasures of disbelief, and the potential for eternal reward makes the possibility of being wrong worth the risk, especially considering the benefits faith brings in life. Therefore, Pascal concludes that, purely from a practical standpoint, belief in God is the wisest choice.

Pascal's Wager rests on several key assumptions:

1. The assumption that God exists.

2. The assumption that God is just.

3. The assumption that belief in God leads to eternal reward (e.g., belief in the concept of heaven).

4. The assumption that non-belief results in eternal punishment (e.g., belief in the concept of hell).

5. The assumption that the decision to believe is a rational, risk-based choice rather than a genuine conviction.

6. The assumption that belief is motivated by self-interest, raising moral concerns about believing in God for personal gain.

These assumptions form the basis of Pascal's wager, which constrains the concept of God and faith to a narrow religious framework. For Pascal, belief in God is ultimately a matter of faith, but this faith is justified through rational reasoning. In the end, Pascal argues that in the face of uncertainty, religious faith is a safer bet than atheism—or is it?

Sartre's Atheistic Humanism

When we reflect on human nature, we often think of ourselves as the creation of a higher being—God—who crafted us with a clear purpose.[141] In this view, each individual is the manifestation of God's design, a particular embodiment of the universal concept of Humanity.[142] Thus, we all share a common essence, which precedes our individual existence. In essence, our nature is predetermined and fixed by a conception of God.

Jean-Paul Sartre, however, challenges this traditional view by embracing atheism.[143] He argues that if God does not exist, then there is no inherent human nature, because no divine creator exists to conceive it. Sartre contends that the concept of God is self-contradictory because it attempts to reconcile humanity's freedom with a predetermined essence. In other words, if humans are bound to an essence designed by God, they cannot truly be free. Sartre asserts that existentialism simply follows through on the logical consequences of an atheistic point of view. If there is no God, values or commands are not derived from a divine source but are instead created by each individual.[144]

Sartre's famous dictum, "existence precedes essence," encapsulates his view: people first exist, and only later define themselves through their actions.[145] In other words, individuals are not born with a predetermined essence; rather, they create their own essence through choices and actions. Thus, humans are not made by anyone or anything; they make themselves through their decisions.

For Sartre, the fact that existence precedes essence means that individuals are entirely responsible for who they become. Without a fixed human nature, no one can blame God or external forces for their situation. We are solely responsible for the choices we make, as our actions define our essence.

Sartre's notion of freedom is crucial: humanity is free because individuals must choose who they become. Even if God did exist, humans would still be free to choose their values and pursue their goals, as no divine plan could dictate their actions. In the absence of God, the absence of a moral order means humans are entirely responsible for creating their own values. There is no external moral framework to rely on; instead, humans must act and make decisions not solely based on their subjective experience, but rather in a way that "transcends human subjectivity."[146]

For Sartre, transcending human subjectivity means that individuals are not limited by their personal perspective or circumstances. Instead, through freedom and their relation to others and to the world, individuals can act in ways that embrace this freedom, taking on the responsibility of creating their own meaning in life. Thus, in choosing a value judgement, an individual is not only making a personal choice but also endorsing that value for "all of humanity."[147] To assert a value is to imply that it is universally valid, and thus, Sartre's concept of existentialism involves responsibility for others.[148] When an individual chooses a course of action, they are implicitly setting a standard that should be applicable to everyone—that "nothing can be good for any of us unless it is good for all," reflecting his belief in the universality of choice.[149]

This idea links to Kant's categorical imperative, though Sartre's interpretation differs. While Kant proposed a universal moral law, Sartre emphasizes that each individual must make choices without a predetermined moral guide.[150] Instead, individuals should consider whether they would want others to make the same choice. This sense of universal responsibility ensures that we are not only accountable for ourselves but also for humanity as a whole. In this way, Sartre insists, "I am responsible for myself and for all."[151]

Thus, Sartre's existentialism is not devoid of moral values but instead posits human beings as the foundation of value. He asserts that our responsibility to humanity is far greater than we might realize. When we act, we affirm the value of what we choose, and for any action to be valid, it must be something that benefits all of humanity. Sartre's existentialism underscores the weight of responsibility in human choices, emphasizing that we are not just responsible for ourselves but also for the world we help shape.

Sartre's concept of freedom is deeply tied to this responsibility. In a world without God, humans are not guided by any predetermined essence, moral system, or divine law.[152] The absence of God means that we must define ourselves and our values, and in doing so, we take on a profound responsibility for both our actions and their universal implications. As Sartre puts it, "a person is condemned to be free," for although humans did not create themselves, they are responsible for everything they do.[153]

Sartre's atheistic humanism calls for a radical rethinking of human responsibility. In a world without a divine creator, we are solely responsible for shaping our lives and our values. This responsibility is universal: by choosing for ourselves, we are implicitly choosing for *all of humanity,* and therefore, the choices we make must be ones we would want all others to make as well. Sartre's existentialism emphasizes that the act of choice is a deeply moral act, grounded not in external values, but in our responsibility to humanity as a whole.

Theodicy

The problem of evil and suffering in the world raises the question of how a benevolent and omnipotent God can allow evil to exist. This is the essence of *theodicy*—the attempt to justify God's goodness in the face of evil.

In the Biblical story of the Fall, Satan tempts Eve to eat the forbidden fruit, which she shares with Adam.[154] Afterward, they realize they are naked and hide from God.[155] Adam blamed Eve, and Eve blamed the Devil, and ultimately blamed God for their changed state of nature from trust to fear.[156] This narrative highlights how the choice to seek "knowledge" and "be like God" leads to the corruption of human nature. It is often claimed that God created the Devil, and by extension, is responsible for both moral and natural evil in the world.[157] We tend to use the religious expression as a scapegoat, "God works in mysterious ways," or similar, "God's ways are mysterious."

Theodicy attempts to answer the question: If God is good, why does He permit evil? One classical response comes from Gottfried Leibniz, who introduced the term "theodicy" in the 18th century.

The concept of theodicy can be traced back to the Hebrew scriptures, particularly the Book of Job, which was written in the 6th century BCE. This book explores how God tests the faith of those who trust in Him. The story unfolds as follows: God allows evil to occur, and Satan brings suffering upon Job. Job loses all his possessions and endures immense hardship, yet he does not lose his faith in God. In the end, God restores everything Job had lost, giving him twice as much as he had before.

Leibniz argues that God *permits* evil in order to bring about a greater good, even if that good is not immediately apparent. For Leibniz, physical and moral evils are a result of human sin and a necessary component in God's plan to perfect creation.

In his *Theodicy: Essays on the Goodness of God, the Freedom of Man and the Origin of Evil*, Leibniz distinguishes between "antecedent" and "consequent" will. He claims that God antecedently wills that all men be saved, but consequently, because of justice, some must be damned.[158] Leibniz affirms with Augustine that evil is a defect and a certain kind of *privation* of the good.[159]

Aquinas sheds light on what Leibniz means by God's antecedent and consequent will. He says, "To understand this [distinction], we must consider that everything, in so far as it is good, is willed by God."[160] Aquinas continues:

> A thing taken in its primary sense, and absolutely considered, may be good or evil, and yet when some additional circumstances are taken into account, by a consequent consideration may be changed into the contrary. Thus, that a man should live is good, and that a man should be killed is evil, absolutely considered. But if in

a particular case we add that a man is a murderer or dangerous to society, to kill him is a good, that he lives is an evil. Hence, it may be said of a just judge, that antecedently he wills all men to live, but consequently wills the murderer to be killed. In the same way, God antecedently wills all men to be saved, but consequently will some to be damned, as his justice exacts... Hence, we will a thing absolutely according as we will it when all particular circumstances are considered, and this is what is meant by willing consequently... Thus, it is clear that whatever God wills absolutely takes place, although what he wills antecedently may not take place.[161]

Because God is considered the "architect of the universe," which has a "pre-established and perfect harmony," Leibniz can confidently make the claim and affirm with Aquinas that "there will be no good action that is unrewarded, no bad action that goes unpunished, and everything must result in the well-being of the good."[162] In addition, "it is impossible to make the order of the universe better than it is."[163]

The defect of this optimistic view of Leibniz's argument is that it's difficult to reconcile with the intense suffering experienced by many in the world. If everything is for the best, as he suggests, then why does God allow such seemingly pointless and extreme suffering? Critics argue that this kind of theological optimism only serves to dismiss the real pain and suffering humanity experiences. Again, does everything happen for a reason and for the best in a rational and ordered universe of a pre-established harmony?

The Best of all Possible Worlds

Voltaire's *Candide* satirizes the optimism of Leibniz's theodicy, particularly the idea that "all is for the best" in the world.[164] Through the character of Dr. Pangloss, Voltaire mocks the idea that all suffering, no matter how horrific, has a rational or divine purpose. Pangloss insists that everything is for the best, even as Candide witnesses and experiences absurd levels of suffering, including natural disasters, war, and personal loss.

The death of James the Anabaptist in *Candide* is an example of Voltaire's critique. A terrible storm is ragging at sea and splitting up the ship. On board the ship and in the midst of the tempest is Candide, his teacher and philosopher Dr. Pangloss, James, the Anabaptist, and the few crew members. Suddenly, before anybody realizes it, James gets thrown overboard by the mighty storm, and Candide tries to save him, only to be stopped by Pangloss, who rationalizes by "proving from first principles" that it was his "purpose to drown there" because James's death is part of some greater divine plan.[165]

Throughout Voltaire's novel, Candide, his teacher, and friends all undergo unbearable suffering. In the end Candide's teacher stays true to his belief that this is the "best of all possible worlds" and everything that happens is for the best. Voltaire's point is that such reasoning is morally indefensible and insensitive to the very real suffering of individuals.

The Nature of Nature

Natural disasters—hurricanes, earthquakes, tsunamis—are often explained through scientific principles such as weather patterns or geological movements. These natural events are indiscriminate in their destruction, causing suffering and chaos. Whether one subscribes to a *scientific* view of the world (e.g., evolution, natural processes) or a *creationist* view of the world (e.g., the Book of Genesis), it's undeniable that nature is both ordered and chaotic. The universe, like the earth, is constantly changing—expanding, evolving, and sometimes destroying itself in the process.

While these natural events seem random or chaotic from a human perspective, they are part of the natural processes that govern the universe. The earth evolves through these destructive and constructive forces, just as the universe is in constant flux. Human beings, too, experience growth, aging, and death as part of the natural order.

In the face of suffering, many turn to religious beliefs for comfort, often invoking the idea that suffering has a divine purpose. Dr. Langdon Gilkey's reflection on his time in an internment camp during World War II highlights the human need for a "spiritual center of security" to find meaning in times of distress.[166] When this sense of security is lost, existence feels incoherent and without direction.

Religious expressions such as "In-sha'allah" ("God willing") or "In-sha'arrab" (Lord willing) reflect an acceptance of divine will. Yet, when faced with natural evil or suffering, it's easy to fall into despair or create a false understanding of God to justify one's suffering. In Nietzsche's famous proclamation, "God is dead," he critiques the human tendency to create gods to fit our needs, a theme reflected in the *Gospel of Philip*, which argues that humanity has created God in its own image:

> ... God created humanity; [but now human beings] create God. That is the way it is in the world—human beings make gods and worship their creation. It would be appropriate for Gods to worship human beings![167]

Since humanity created the language of religious expression, it has also, in a sense, created God and the divine realm. In doing so, humanity has effectively put to death the Eternal by confining it to human concepts and definitions.[168]

Nietzsche claims that humanity, over time, has killed God—abandoning divine meaning and leaving behind a void.[169] As Walter Kaufman notes, the loss of God leads to madness and despair, as humanity struggles to find meaning in a world devoid of divine purpose.[170] Nietzsche's "God is dead" declaration points to the emptiness and loss that follows the abandonment of religious faith. Yet, beyond our concepts and images of God, there may be a "God beyond God"—an infinite reality that transcends human understanding.[171]

Predestination vs Divine Foreknowledge

PREDESTINATION ASSERTS THAT GOD has eternally determined all events and outcomes. If this view holds true, then human beings are deprived of freedom and responsibility, as our actions would be preordained, and our choices meaningless. Under this framework, human beings would be compelled to act in a certain way, leaving no room for true agency or moral responsibility. In this case, God's role in history would also be called into question—would God be the architect of global tragedies like World Wars I and II, natural disasters, or even diseases like AIDS? If everything is predestined, does that imply God is the cause of evil and suffering, or worse, that He is indifferent to it?

Despite the profound theological and philosophical implications of predestination, sacred texts from Judaism, Christianity, and Islam do not offer a satisfactory resolution to the tension between divine omniscience and human freedom. These religions each grapple with the problem of how an all-powerful, all-knowing God can coexist with human freedom.

Jewish Perspective on Free Will and Divine Sovereignty

In Judaism, God's sovereignty is central to the faith, as expressed in the Torah, which states, "The Lord shall reign forever and ever" (Exodus 15:18). The Hebrew Bible also emphasizes that God tests His people: "That I may test them, whether they will walk in My law or not" (Exodus 16:4). While God has authority over the world, humans are given the freedom to choose how to live within His covenant. The Torah affirms in Exodus 20:6 that blessings come from worshiping God alone, implying that human actions, though guided by God's will, still carry moral weight.

Christian Perspective on Divine Control and Human Responsibility

Christianity likewise upholds the idea of divine sovereignty but adds the belief in God's ultimate purpose through Jesus Christ. The New Testament affirms God's plan in passages like Ephesians 1:11, which speaks of being "predestined according to the purpose of Him who works all things according to the counsel of His will." Christians are encouraged to trust in God's plan, knowing that "for those who love God, all things work together for good" (Romans 8:28). The central Christian belief that "by Him all things were created" (Colossians 1:16) reflects the view that God has control over everything, yet individuals are still responsible for responding to God's grace.

Islamic Perspective on Divine Will

In Islam, the doctrine of predestination is integral to belief in the unity and sovereignty of Allah's will. The Qur'an states that Allah "created all things and ordered them in due proportions" (Súra Al-Furqán 25.2).[172] It also asserts, "the command of Allah is a decree determined" (Súra Al-Ahzáb 33.38). And to every Muslim believer the Qur'an declares, "I have only created men, that they may serve Me" (Súra Az-Záriyat 51.56).

The phrase "Inshallah" ("God willing") reflects the Islamic belief that everything happens according to Allah's will. Muslims are taught that they must submit to Allah's decree, acknowledging that both their successes and failures are part of His greater plan. This submission does not negate human action, but rather frames it within the context of divine sovereignty, reinforcing that humans are accountable to Allah for their choices.

Philosophical Foundations: Aristotle's Influence

The problem of predestination versus free will is not new. Aristotle, over two millennia ago, engaged with these ideas in his works on determinism and chance. In *Physics*, Aristotle writes that some things arise out of a "determinate" cause, while others "occur by chance."[173] For instance, a sculptor might be the determinate or necessary cause of a statue, while the sculptor's eye color is a chance or accidental cause. Aristotle also discusses in the *Metaphysics* how events unfold according to necessity but that the specifics of how they happen—such as the way a person dies—can depend on chance occurrences.[174]

Aristotle's reflections lay the groundwork for modern discussions of determinism, where he considers the tension between events that are determined and those that occur by chance, with the latter remaining unexplained. He suggests that chance events lack final causes, meaning they don't fit into a larger purpose, which he describes as a "divine thing and full of mystery."[175] This opens the possibility that not everything in life is preordained; some things happen due to causes beyond human comprehension.

Reconciling Divine Sovereignty and Human Freedom

The challenge of reconciling divine predestination and human freedom remains a profound theological and philosophical dilemma. Some Christian and Islamic scholars have suggested that both concepts can coexist, despite seeming incompatible. They argue that God exists outside of time and space, meaning He can know the future without necessarily determining it. From this perspective, divine foreknowledge doesn't equate to predestination—God can foresee what will happen without causing it.

One way to understand this is through the analogy of a "Time Telescope." Imagine that God, existing outside time, can see future events clearly, but His knowledge of these events doesn't necessitate their occurrence. Just as a hiker preparing for a journey anticipates challenges without causing them, God's foreknowledge of human actions does not force those actions to occur. God sees the potential outcomes of human choices, but He doesn't dictate them.

Augustine and Open Theism

The philosopher and theologian Augustine of Hippo provides insight into this issue with his understanding of God's foreknowledge. Augustine argues that God knows all things He causes but doesn't cause everything He knows. He used the analogy of human memory: just as remembering past events doesn't force those events to have occurred, God's knowledge of future events doesn't force them to happen.[176] Augustine contended that free will is essential for moral responsibility; without it, there could be no good or evil in the world, and humans could not freely choose to follow God.

This perspective aligns with modern theological movements like *Open Theism* or the "openness of God," which suggests that the future is not entirely determined by God. According to Open Theism, God's foreknowledge doesn't predetermine human choices; instead, He knows all possible outcomes based on the decisions humans make.[177] This allows for a dynamic relationship between divine sovereignty and human freedom.

Conclusion: Compatibility of Divine Foreknowledge and Free Will

The apparent conflict between divine predestination, foreknowledge, and human freedom can be resolved by recognizing that God, existing outside time, does not experience the limitations we do. His knowledge of future events does not impose necessity on them. While God is sovereign and His will is supreme, human beings still have the capacity to choose, and these choices carry real consequences. Divine foreknowledge does not dictate human action, and predestination does not eliminate the possibility of free will.

Thus, divine sovereignty and human freedom are not mutually exclusive. God can predestine a broad divine plan, while allowing humans the freedom to make choices within that plan. This resolution upholds the responsibility of human beings to choose moral actions while affirming God's ultimate authority over all creation.[178]

The tension between predestination, foreknowledge, and human freedom is a complex mystery, but one that reflects the depth and richness of the divine nature—one that transcends time and space and allows for both divine purpose and human responsibility.

The Simple and the Cultured Person

IN THE WORLD, THERE EXIST TWO DISTINCT TYPES OF HUMAN BEINGS, each with their own version of reality, each engaged in a dynamic of dominance: the simple person and the cultured person. The "simple person" is often religious or traditional, clinging to established beliefs, while the "cultured person" is worldly or intellectual, embracing diverse perspectives. The simple person sees the world through a single lens, following a singular, prescribed path; the cultured person, on the other hand, views the world through multiple lenses, open to various ways of living and understanding.

The Goals of the Simple and the Cultured

The simple person's primary goal is "to be." This is a static existence in which belief emanates from an Absolute value (often identified as 'God'), projected anthropomorphically into the world and the things around them as absolute truth. The simple person's worldview is one of fixed certainty, seeing the world as sinful and in need of salvation, with the hope of a heavenly reward. Their mission is to save the world through faith, aiming for a future redemption that is separate from the realities of the present.

The cultured person, however, seeks "to become." The focus is not on a fixed state of being, but on continuous growth and transformation. Meaning and belief are not projected onto the world from a Supreme Being but come from an inward value, shaped by experiences and the ongoing evolution of self-awareness. The cultured person embraces a plurality of truths, understanding that what is true for one may not be true for another. The mission of the cultured is to understand the world, improve their grasp of it, and work toward creating a "heaven on earth," where human decency and happiness prevail.

The Conflict of Truths

The simple person views the world through the lens of certainty, where "truth" is absolute and unquestionable. The mission is to save the world by adhering to this truth, no matter the cost. In contrast, the cultured person's view of the world involves a recognition that truth is not fixed; it is fluid, subject to change and revision. The cultured person seeks understanding, knowing that truth is a process and that what we once thought to be true may no longer hold in the face of new evidence or reflection.

The tension between these two worldviews often leads to the question: which approach is healthier? Can a person save the world without understanding it? Can one's faith alone bring about meaningful change without a deep understanding of the world and its workings? The simple would argue that faith, unburdened by understanding, is sufficient. They would say that salvation is a matter of belief, not knowledge. The cultured person, however, would argue that faith without understanding is empty; that to save the world, one must first understand how it works.

The Role of Understanding

If understanding is necessary to save the world, then from where does this understanding come? The simple person derives it from a divine source— God or the Christ figure—believing that understanding comes from aligning with the will of a Supreme Being. For the cultured person, understanding comes from within, from a belief in the potential of humankind to improve and evolve.

Humankind, in this sense, must rely on its inwardness, its common sense, and its collective experience to gain knowledge about itself and the world. By understanding human beings, one can also understand the world, recognizing the ways in which individuals, as organisms within a greater system, contribute to the functioning of society.

The simple person might claim that the Christ figure, through his connection with God, had the understanding necessary to save the world. But the question remains: where does this understanding come from? Does it come from God, or does it come from a deeper understanding of oneself?

The Limits of the Simple Person's View

The problem with the simple person's worldview is that it often denies the complexity of human existence. The simple person's reliance on fixed, externally imposed truths means they fail to understand themselves or the world in which they live. This is a significant flaw—how can one save the world if one is ignorant of the world's workings? The simple often misunderstand themselves, unable to see the diversity and complexity of human experience. Their understanding of the world is shallow, based on a narrow, dogmatic lens.

The simple person's refusal to engage with the world leads to the creation of idols—false gods and certainties—that limit their perspective and keep them trapped in ignorance. They impose rigid, unquestionable truths, stifling any opportunity for growth or change. These idols become the center of their lives, creating a static, superficial existence that prevents them from seeing the richness of the world beyond their narrow view.

The Cultured Person's Understanding of Reality

The cultured person, by contrast, embraces uncertainty and change. They recognize that truth is not absolute but rather contingent upon context, experience, and ongoing reflection. This openness allows them to see the world from many perspectives, embracing the idea that reality is not fixed but constantly evolving. They approach the world not as something to be conquered, but as something to be understood and nurtured.

Both the simple and the cultured, however, must eventually come to terms with the limitations of their respective worldviews. Neither can claim absolute truth without acknowledging that their perspective is just that—a perspective. Both are engaged in the act of "considering-something-true," but both must recognize that truth is not a static fact, but a process of ongoing exploration.

The Narrow Gate and the Cultivated Path

Jesus, in his wisdom, spoke of the narrow gate that leads to life, and the wide gate that leads to destruction.[179] This metaphor speaks to the struggle between the simple and the cultured. The simple, in their childlike innocence, often take the wide gate, seeking comfort in certainty and faith without understanding. The cultured, on the other hand, often take the narrow gate, embracing the challenge of understanding, growth, and continuous transformation.

For Jesus, the narrow gate was not simply about spiritual salvation but about intellectual and moral growth. Jesus himself embodied the fusion of simplicity and culture: he understood both the need for faith and the necessity of reason. He used the wisdom of the Old Testament, which includes secular wisdom from books like Proverbs and Ecclesiastes, to teach practical lessons on how to live in harmony with others in the world.

Letting Go and Moving Beyond

The simple must let go of their dogmatic, fixed beliefs and embrace the complexity of life. They must stop hiding behind masks of ignorance and begin to see the world, with all its messiness, diversity, and potential. The simple must stop fleeing from the world and start engaging with it, with all its challenges and contradictions.

The simple and the cultured are both trapped by their understanding of reality. Both must be willing to question their assumptions, to step outside their comfort zones, and to create new values—values that are not dictated by tradition, dogma, or religious authority. Only then can they begin to move toward a more authentic, meaningful existence, one that is guided by self-awareness and a genuine understanding of the world.

Paul: A Model of Becoming

Paul, a figure who transcended both the simple and the cultured worlds, provides a model for how to live without clinging to any single identity. Paul was a man of both reason and faith, embodying the wisdom of both the simple and the cultured. He was deeply grounded in his understanding of humanity, not merely as a scholar, but as a servant to others. Paul understood that the key to making a difference in the world was not to assert an identity or dogma, but to become "all things to all people," to understand and engage with others on their own terms.[180]

In this way, Paul exemplified the ideal of becoming—of transcending rigid identities and embracing the fluidity of human experience. He was certain of one thing: the necessity of uncertainty, of growth, and of embracing change. He pressed on, grew, and made a difference, not by asserting absolute truths but by cultivating a deep understanding of humanity.

We, too, must follow Paul's example—striving to become fully human, to understand ourselves and the world around us, and to create values that help us live meaningful lives. Only through this process of becoming can we truly make a difference in the world.

The Mind's Eye
A Personal Letter

Dear R.C.,

IT IS A SMALL WONDER TO ME THAT I MUST BELIEVE, and no reason not to believe, that the relentless turning of your ego-driven religious wheel is widening your mind by filling it up with pomp and other foul stuff that injure others. You are not only injuring others, but also yourself, which comes from your own ignorance of thinking you know but you don't.

I hesitate to say this, but I must: you are becoming, or perhaps have already become, a Father Pope, a Beast, a 666. Excuse me for the symbolism, if you must, but it stands as a force that revolts against God. Did my words pierce your soul? If they did, then you are right: The Bible is indeed a "two-edged sword" that pierces the soul.

Notice that I've intentionally taken this quote out of context to serve my own purpose. In the wrong hands, the Bible can be used to inflict unnecessary harm on others—whether consciously or unconsciously. If the pain becomes too much for someone to bear, they may be at high risk of contemplating suicide, especially if the source of their suffering is someone who has made them feel shame and anguish. Did you know, and this is a fact, that a person once attempted to swallow a pocket-sized Bible in a desperate attempt to purge their soul of the Devil?

In the wrong hands, and when fueled by religious fanaticism, the Bible can become a tool for passing judgment on others without understanding their story, leaving them feeling sad and wounded. I've been there myself—

once a religious fanatic—so I truly understand that mindset. But in the right hands, the Bible can offer valuable insight into how to navigate life's complexities and diversity, providing guidance that can enrich and improve an individual's quality of life.

Before we can improve the quality of an individual's life, we must first "save" the individual from what he fears most in life, right? 'Salvation' implies knowing what alienates an individual. This process demands great effort, involving a deep engagement of the mind in pursuit of understanding. It is only through knowledge, guided by genuine understanding, that we can truly contribute to the salvation of another—doing so with a spirit of gentleness.

The difference between you and me is that you seek to advance life through a reliance on religion, focused primarily on "future rewards" and "punishments." In contrast, I am more focused on fostering growth through the ability to find freedom and self-reliance, with an emphasis on the present moment and the individual's ongoing process of becoming.

I'm not engaging in the "games of ignorance" that you seem so eager to play to control the destinies of others. Do you remember learning anything of value from the student missionaries? Are they not, like you, guides who help foster growth and advance life?

It is no surprise that some past and present missionaries have felt uneasy around you. You impose your way of thinking on them, convinced—much as I fear—that you hold the keys to both life and death. That is blatant arrogance. You behave like a "conscious incompetent" by doing hurtful things to missionaries, which stem from your ignorance of what you think your "mission" is. "Believe like I do" is a tautology, essentially saying "I am God." As Voltaire aptly remarked, "The man who says to me, 'Believe as I do, or God will damn you,' will presently say, 'Believe as I do, or I shall assassinate you.'"[181]

The idea that all men are created free implies that all men are inherently unequal. This inequality means that no one should be forced to conform to the likeness of another, as each mind is unique. Voltaire was deeply outraged by the religious excesses of his time. Catholics were killing

Protestants, and vice versa. Injustice was rampant, yet true friendship seemed nowhere to be found.

To participate in the advancement of life means that all should be welcomed in the process of guidance. Unfortunately, this opportunity is denied by you and the organization. But now, what does the decline of your organization reveal to you? If you have not learned anything from your fellow Christians, then perhaps you fail to give them the opportunity to share their spiritual meat with others. But you're still drinking spiritual milk!

You seem to take pleasure in imposing your values on others and stripping away what they hold dear. What you value, however, appears to be something you assume everyone else should value as well.

R.C., you are someone who constantly takes, without giving back. You've placed yourself on a pedestal above your fellow missionaries and others. You expect them to adopt your beliefs and thinking, yet you refuse to learn from them! Is this because you see them as "children," as you once called them, and yourself as their "daddy"?

I've learned a couple of things from you that I have no intention of incorporating into my own life. These lessons stem from ignorance: inflicting pain and unnecessary suffering on others, as well as harming oneself in the process. It is unfortunate that men of religion, like yourself, often reshape religion to fit their own image. This is unfortunate for two reasons. First, shaping religion to resemble something else distorts its true nature. Second, when religion is molded to reflect the likeness of one individual, it becomes unattractive and repellent to both the intellectual and the *worldly* person.

We all know that Mr. C. was hailed as the "savior" of the schools in recent times, introducing a modified teaching method for English as a second language, which was presented as new or "proven" effective. We are all grateful for your assistance, and I've personally expressed my thanks. You, above all, should take pride in your contribution. But please, don't pat yourself on the back too much, especially when it's cloaked in false humility or a feigned sense of holy reverence. It doesn't just make me uncomfortable—it makes many missionaries uneasy as well. I have done my best to contribute to the schools with goodwill, using my knowledge and abilities, even if that meant breaking certain rules of the organization.

If you, like some others, see me as someone who was "once a Christian" but has fallen from my "proper place" to instead expose and teach non-Christians about extra-biblical literature, then I suppose any communication between us will only reinforce that perception—that I am no longer a Christian. It is difficult to be a friend to anyone when people view me as "demonic," "anti-Christ," or someone who has *strayed* from the "Christian way" of life.

Aristotle argues that friendship is more important than justice because "between friends, there is no need for justice."[182] Treating a stranger as a friend is a form of justice. In close friendships, justice is about looking out for each other's well-being and goodwill.

To love someone "in Christ" often means using a debated historical figure as both a *scapegoat* and an excuse for love. The true maxim, however, is to love your neighbor as you love yourself. To love yourself and extend that same love to your neighbor signifies a deep mutual respect.

Living a hermit-like lifestyle, as you do, wisdom suggests that loving others as you love yourself is unwise, since respect is clearly lacking. Loving others with the same respect that one shows oneself is challenging, honest, and transparent. This kind of love is what truly qualifies a person to be in right relationship with God.

In the foreword to *A History of Christian Thought* by Gonzalez, Roland H. Bainton writes:

> But Jesus added, 'You shall love the Lord your God with all your mind.' This addition provides the *raison d'être* for this book. There has been a continuous history of Christian thought because the Master called upon his disciples to love their God not only with heart and strength but also with their mind.[183]

We cannot drink the milk that is for babes for the rest of our life. We must move beyond the basic ABCs of knowledge and press forward with our minds, striving toward the XYZs, if the brevity of our lives allows us to do so.

Just as a newborn babe grows, so too must a newly born Christian, Muslim, Jew, or Buddhist. Regardless of how long someone has been part of a religious tradition, one thing remains clear: the individual must continue to grow and mature.

Growth and maturity enhance the quality and love of life, deepening our appreciation for the love of God. A refusal to grow leads to a stagnation of the mind and a limited understanding of God. Therefore, let us live and view life through the lens of the mind, being considerate of others in their own pursuit of knowledge and truth.

Sincerely, Randy

Part V
Academia

The Role of Philosophy in Education

EVEN IF WE KNOW WHAT PSYCHOLOGY APPLIED TO TEACHING IMPLIES, we cannot understand it until we know at least the conditions it is applicable to. A theory of educational objectives would therefore have to face questions which involves knowing at least the conditions under which the advice will be applied, what problems, and what intermediate ends will arise.[184]

The role of philosophy in education is a necessity.[185] It guides the pupil's understanding by establishing meanings and concepts—translating the material by various means into a more satisfying language—making it relevant for direct application.

Before we ask, "What is Teaching?" It is appropriate to ask, "What is Education?" and "What is the Aim of Education?" The former refers to an academic discipline, and the latter is to develop each individual mind as fully as possible that would be immediately useful to society.[186, 187] To answer What is Teaching? Socrates' answer was that teaching is a process of eliciting knowledge, which is dormant in the pupil's mind and bringing his own insights to birth.[188]

The aim of this essay is three-fold: (1) to establish the importance of philosophy in education, (2) how philosophy of education is integrated into the teaching process, and (3) how it is relative to the teaching process.[189]

The Importance of Philosophy in Education

The inescapable fact is that we all are philosophers. We must inquire because we do not know. This ignorance makes us a philosopher by nature. Why is the sky blue? Why are planets round? How do you do this? Why is that so? Why do men kill? Where did I come from? How did I get here? Where am I going? What does it all mean?

These questions are all philosophical in nature. We continually seek answers because we do not know. We seek knowledge driven by our desire to learn.[190] Through learning, we gain understanding. With understanding, we become intelligent. By actively applying our intelligence, we deepen our comprehension. This understanding is the path to wisdom. This is the aim of practicing philosophy.

If philosophy is to "love wisdom" and if wisdom is "knowledge guided by understanding" then to be wise (speaking of the teaching process) means to possess that understanding and the skill to transfer that understanding in the context of daily life.[191, 192] Therefore, philosophy is a skill; it is something one learns to do. It is learning how to ask and re-ask questions until meaningful answers begin to appear. It is learning how to relate materials. It is learning where to go for the most dependable, up-to-date information that might shed light on some problem.[193] By all means, philosophy is everybody's business.[194] Philosophy is useful, and is for those who do not already know, for those who already know but wish to understand, and for those who understand but want to understand better.[195]

Philosophy is a method employed in educational objectives, particularly within the framework of the cognitive domain. It is the process used to establish meaningful connections within the material, helping to "guide the pupil's understanding" and make the content relevant to daily life.

Teachers become philosophers when they speculate or theorize—developing a method or choosing a premise for a system through logical analysis and synthesis—that brings coherence and relevance to learning for practical application. This skill and process are crucial in the art of education.

Integrating Philosophy in Education

Education takes on a philosophical aspect when we theorize about educational objectives, exploring how to implement them in ways that align with our teaching style and environment. This approach turns education into a personal philosophy. Philosophy in education can be demonstrated in two ways: first, through how we present the material, and second, through how we respond to students.

Presenting the Material

The first way philosophy is demonstrated in education is through the cognitive domain, specifically in how we present the material. Presenting the material in clear, simple language is crucial, as it helps clarify vague concepts. The material can be introduced in four distinct, sequential ways to enhance understanding.

First, the material is presented verbally (1st presentation); second, it is illustrated through experience, storytelling, or visual tools; third, the material is repeated in the same way it was illustrated in the second presentation; and fourth, active participation is encouraged through discussions, questions, or debates based on the prior presentations.

This process of presenting the material fosters spontaneous learning. Philosophy helps transform complex ideas into simpler language, making them easier to understand. This is the essence of the philosophy of education.

Responding to Students

The second way philosophy can be demonstrated in education is through the affective domain, particularly in how we respond to students. The way we respond in the classroom is important because it emphasizes the value of both the individual and education itself. While there are many ways we can respond to students, let's focus on one approach.

One way to respond to an incorrect answer is to address it in three sequential steps. First, restate the incorrect response in the form of another question, which helps to dignify the error.[196] Next, provide additional prompts to guide the student toward the correct answer. Finally, hold the student accountable for the answer, encouraging them to take ownership of their learning.

This philosophical approach of responding to students fosters learning while also preserving the dignity of the individual.

The Relevance of Philosophy in Education

Philosophy is a skill. Philosophy is a method. Philosophy is a process. Philosophy is an activity. Philosophy is a tool. It is a tool that makes teaching relevant.

The early Christians used philosophy as a tool to build bridges so that the "pagans" could cross over to Christianity.[197] Some Christians were accused of Hellenizing Christianity, but on the contrary, their purpose was to Christianize "Hellenism." And they were quite skillful in doing so. Similarly, the teacher of education is skillful when presenting material in a way that is easily understood by the pupil and connects to the context of daily life.

Philosophy is a system. It is a system of theories, analysis, synthesis, evaluation, judgment, etc. Philosophy can be found in all systems of belief, and it plays a crucial role in educational objectives because it is what structures them. Therefore, the structure of education is ultimately philosophical in its origin. This is why education itself is a philosophy. The philosophy of education: (1) clarifies understanding, (2) reconstructs concepts, (3) shows relationships, (4) provides a theory of learning, and (5) guides the pupil. I'll end with a quote by Abraham Edel:

Philosophy of education is important today... We are living in a time when change occurs rapidly... We are driven back to fundamental outlooks, that is to philosophy. And while there is not a body of certified truths which philosophy can hand over to education, educational theory very much needs the imaginative-speculative sense of alternatives, the comprehensive-integrative sense of wide relationship to the whole of life and culture, and the critical sense of responsibility in probing for its own presuppositions and testing objectives, that the philosophical tradition has developed and sharpened.[198]

Reflecting on this, it becomes clear that as the landscape of education evolves, the philosophical foundation is not only essential but dynamic, offering the flexibility and critical thinking needed to navigate and shape future educational practices.

The Impact of Teacher Enthusiasm
On Student Learning

A GOOD TEACHER IS ONE WHO IS ENTHUSIASTIC—enthusiastic about their subject and enthusiastic about student learning. Research shows that an enthusiastic teacher conveys a great sense of commitment, excitement, and involvement with the subject matter. Lessons are imaginative and stimulating and students are responsive because they appear to enjoy the activity.[199]

The word enthusiasm comes from a combination of Greek words "possessed by a god." Therefore, an enthusiastic person is literally inspired by a powerful force. Teaching with enthusiasm involves being stimulating, lively, energetic, and dynamic.

A teacher who presents materials with appropriate gestures, animation, and eye contact with students will achieve better test results than those who teach in an unenthusiastic manner, such as using a monotone voice and no gestures.

Research has indicated that there are eight characteristics of teacher enthusiasm. They are identified as: (1) variation of voice, (2) eye contact, (3) demonstrative gestures, (4) dramatic body movements, (5) facial expressions, (6) selection of varied words (especially adjectives), (7) animated acceptance of ideas and feelings, and (8) exuberant overall energy level.[200]

In this paper, I will not describe or discuss these characteristics specifically but will show their relation to effective teaching and student learning. I have broken these characteristics down into three categories: (1) Actions, (2) Language, and (3) Modeling. Each category will include how teaching enthusiastically increases student attentiveness, student interest in the subject, and student achievement. Although this paper leaves room for speculation (i.e., studies, research, experiments) my aim is to show how teacher enthusiasm can make a difference on student learning.

Action

Studies indicate certain actions are part of enthusiastic behavior. These actions include variation of voice, eye contact, demonstrative gestures, dramatic body movements, and facial expressions.

In one study, the relationship between certain "speech factors" of the teacher and pupil achievement was investigated.[201] This study was administered on seventh and eighth grade pupils in a rural environment. Teachers prepared two audio recordings: a three-minute recording reading the material, and a three-minute recording talking on the material. A correlation between "pitch" & "variation of pitch," and "volume" & "variation of volume" were rated. This was compared and rated, and it was described as a "composite of pupil-change scores" in "measurable attitudes, ideals, and information in the social studies field." The rating of the variation correlated more highly with pupil achievement than the rating of the characteristic itself, i.e., pitch and volume without variation.

Another study was spent on supporting the importance of animation in enhancing comprehension.[202] Two teachers presented two ten-minute lectures to college students in two ways: (1) statically and (2) dynamically. The static speaker, on the one hand, read the entire speech from a manuscript. He made no gestures, had no direct eye contact, and held vocal inflection to a minimum. However, he did speak with good diction and sufficient volume.

The dynamic speaker, on the other hand, delivered the lecture from memory, with much vocal inflection, gesturing, eye contact, and animation. After each lecture the college students took a ten-item multiple-choice test.

The mean score of the students who heard the dynamic lecture was significantly higher than that of the students who heard the static lecture.

Many of the same experiments were compared and reached the same conclusion.[203] The static teacher, on the one hand, who read the entire manuscript, made no gestures, made no direct eye contact, held vocal inflection to a minimum, made no movement about in the room, an absence of facial expression, withholding elements of humor, friendliness, charisma, etc., conveyed to students a feeling that he had an indifferent attitude toward the ideas and pictures being presented, and toward the subject of the lesson. In other words, he conveyed the message of boredom.[204]

The dynamic teacher, on the other hand, who lectured from memory, made demonstrative gestures, made direct eye contact with students, varied the inflection of his voice, made dramatic body movements about the room, varied emotive facial expressions, and created a friendly environment conveyed to students a sense of personal interest in the subject (as modeled by the teacher) impressing a desire to learn. Thus, an enthusiastic teacher presents stimulus characteristics that are likely to attract and hold students' attention, thereby promoting student achievement.

Language

When presenting a lecture, the use of word selection, especially adjectives, is inevitably important. Adjectives serve as metaphors that modify or simplify what has been said. Simplifying the material using metaphorical adjectives, such as questions, illustrations, stories, repetition, etc., transfers a kind of idea in place of another to suggest a likeness or analogy.

Take for example the biblical character of Paul and his teachings to clarify understanding. To get an important point across he uses circular logic. We know this as heuristics. Paul asks rhetorical questions, uses illustrations to form an analogy, repeats himself using adjectives, uses circular logic in the process, and uses words with double meanings.[205] Paul uses this kind of logical thinking not to confuse but to clarify understanding. Paul's linguistic form is a vehicle of literature that was relevant to the cultural setting and their attitude toward certain issues. Paul's use of circular logic illustrates a typical enthusiastic teacher trying to convey meaning and shed light on a particular situation or lesson.

Similarly, good teachers are like Paul. They use a kind of circular logic (maybe not as abstract or complicated as Paul's), which tries to simplify and convey meaning to the material presented. For example, good teachers will present the subject matter three or four times in different ways to clarify pupil's understanding.

First, the enthusiastic teacher may either ask a question pertaining to the material that will be presented, start with a problem that relates to the material previously learned, or start with a problem that relates to the material that will be presented. This is helpful because it increases students' attention. Second, the enthusiastic teacher will then present the material. Third, the enthusiastic teacher will illustrate the material that was presented previously. And fourth, the enthusiastic teacher will repeat the material to simplify and clarify understanding.

It is important to note that one study suggests that the frequency of questions might be important, and the research suggests that types of questions may be related to ratings of "energetic" and labeled "stimulating" for student learning.[206] This is identified when students respond to high cognitive questions. This acknowledgment of student responses to teachers' questions or lectures indicates understanding in the material presented and an increase of students' interest in the subject.

Modeling

Modeling not only includes animated acceptance of ideas and feelings and exuberant overall energy level, but it also includes organization of the subject matter and frequency of "shared experience."[207]

According to the *Practical Applications for Research* (PAR), enthusiasm and modeling are related. The enthusiastic teacher is engaged in learning activities and displays those activities to his or her students. This display of modeling behaviors, if accepted and carried out by individual students, results in achievement. If an enthusiastic teacher wants students to develop a desire to learn, he or she will display that desire along with the right behavioral attitude toward learning.

An enthusiastic teacher is one who models an animated acceptance of ideas and feelings. This can be thought of as encouraging active participation. The enthusiastic teacher is one who is not critical and apathetic but ready to accept students' ideas and sympathize with their feelings. This creates a friendly and shared environment that stimulates student understanding (by shared ideas) and helps students become interested in the subject matter.

Frequency of shared experience is equally important. This is a modeling behavior which attempts to relate the material to the students by reflecting on his or her feelings about the subject matter from past or present experience to integrate it into the situation. A shared experience could also be something that was previously learned from information and an attempt to relate the information to the material that will be presented that day.

This frequency of shared experience conveys to the students that the teacher is aware of the current issues and he or she is engaged in learning activities. This frequency of shared experience encourages reflective thinking on the part of the students; thereby, challenging their intellectual capacity to reach a conclusion. If teachers display a sense of involvement in their subject matter students will become excited and interested in it too, and learning in general.

Much human behavior is learned by watching others. We watch how other people behave, store these ideas in our memory, and later use them as models for our own actions.[208] Modeling is helpful to teachers. A lot of display of excitement and exuberant overall energy about the subject matter may arouse students to copy that behavior and in effect become effective enthusiastic teachers also.

Organization

While studies demonstrate superior organization is not necessary for the sake of increasing teacher enthusiasm or manipulating the amount of teacher animation it is nevertheless necessary for student learning.[209] Our knowledge is organized into certain categorical structures that is extremely important for efficient performance.[210]

Studies have indicated that remembering and recalling information quickly depends on the organizational structure of the knowledge we have acquired. Evidence shows that when material is presented in an organizational fashion, student achievement has yielded consistently positive results.

Conclusion

Behaviors learned from teaching enthusiastically can be useful in classroom management. When the teacher is up and around the room, has eye contact, accepts students' ideas and feelings, can be heard with many vocal inflections, and maintains this energy throughout the time spent in "direct" teaching, he or she will generally have excellent classroom control.[211]

Teacher enthusiasm increases students' attentiveness, increases students' interest in the subject so they spend more time at task, and increases students' achievement gains. The teacher's enthusiasm conveys to students that the teacher is interested in what he or she is teaching and is willing to expend energy to help students learn.

Experiment:
Effects of Repetition on Recall and Learning from Unfamiliar Text

Replication

This experiment was replicated from a study in the *Journal of Educational Psychology,* vol. 78, August 1986, pp. 271-278. I was curious to know whether I would get similar results.

Purpose

The purpose of this experiment was to find out the relationship between repetition and learning. How many repetitions or presentations would be necessary to "master" the material? And if mastery did nor did not occur, why?

Method

Those who participated in the experiment were seven females. (I speculate whether I would have come out with similar results had there been males present.) The participants were undergraduate students from this university campus. Five were majoring in a BA degree and two in a BS degree. I speculated (after the experiment) whether the field of study (either the arts or the sciences) would have influenced the results. But it seemed as if they did not, as we shall see.

The material presented to the students was a six-minute taped lecture on a brief history of the origins of Communism and its philosophy (material they were unfamiliar with). The lecturer that presented the material on tape was me. Before I began the experiment I taped the material more than ten times to make the material clear enough to understand what was being said.

In the tapings, I focused on voice speed, variation of pitch (not monotone), emphasizing specific important points (for the quiz), pauses (necessary for memory retention before presenting more of the material), and generally the way I would present the material—such as high, low, or neutral enthusiasm. From the tapings I chose the one I thought best was clear, understandable, and helpful for retention.

The material of unfamiliar text presented was taken from J. Edgar Hoover's *A Study of Communism* (New York; Holt, Rinehart and Winston, Inc., 1962). It was approximately six minutes. As mentioned above, this kind of material was presented because students were unfamiliar with it. This unfamiliar text that was presented on tape is included in this paper. After the tapings, I created a ten-item multiple choice quiz to measure the results.

The plan was to present the material three times to all the students. (The material was presented two times, however, as this will be explained below.) It was speculated that improvement in test scores would follow each presentation.

Procedures During the Experiment

I began the first presentation with three students present (the other four arrived fifteen minutes later). I did not tell them (the three students) that they would take a quiz or test after the lecture. I speculated whether they would listen more carefully during the second presentation, and thus, score higher. I simply told the students to listen carefully. After the first presentation they were naturally surprised when I handed them the ten-item multiple choice quiz.

When they were taking the test the other four students arrived. Thus, they knew they would take a small quiz after the taped lecture. I speculated how or if the scores would differ from the others (first three students) who did not know about a quiz.

I presented the material the second time to the first three students, and the first time to the other four students who arrived late. After the presentation the same quiz was taken.

When I presented the material for the third time two students from the first group of three had to leave. That was alright because they had been exposed to at least two presentations. So, now at this point, I had one student from the first group of three and four students from the second group. All in all, I had five students present. At this point the material would be presented for the third time to the one student from the first group of three and the second time to the four students from the second group. After this last presentation the same quiz was taken.

After the experiment was completed, I speculated whether those who expected the quiz (the four students from the second group) would score better than the three who did not expect the quiz. And whether the third presentation presented to the one student from the first group of three would master the material more than the four students from the second group who had been exposed to only two presentations.

Results

It appeared that the students who did not know about the quiz and those who did know about it scored approximately the same. The scores were surprisingly similar after the *first exposure* to the first presentation:

First Presentation

Student	Field of Study	% of score correct
1	BA	70%
2	BA	40%
3	BA	40%
4	BA	40%
5	BS	40%
6	BS	60%
7	BA	80%

Students 1, 2, and 3 averaged 55%. They were not aware of the quiz after the first presentation. Students 4, 5, 6, and 7 averaged 60%. They were aware of the quiz after the first presentation. Students taken collectively (all seven), for the first exposure of the first presentation, scores ranged from 40 to 80% of the number correct on the quiz. The mean or average was 65%. The *second exposure* of the second presentation was as follows:

Second Presentation

Student	Field of Study	% of score correct
1	BA	90%
2	BA	70%
3	BA	80%
4	BA	100%
5	BS	80%
6	BS	70%
7	BA	100%

The second exposure of the second presentation scores ranged from 70 to 100% of the number correct. The average or mean was 85%. A substantial improvement! As you can see from the first and second presentations the field of study did not make a difference.

The *third exposure* of the third presentation was only given to student 3. Her score decreased from 80% (second presentation) to 70% (third presentation). The reason for this is probably the time needed to master the material was sufficient, and that more presentations only caused fatigue or boredom in mental processes, thus, becoming weary of the experiment, which thereby decreased attentiveness.

I was curious to know how the students did on each question after the first and second presentations. Below indicates how many of students (out of seven) got each question correct:

Number of Answers Correct

Question No.	Presentation 1	Presentation 2
1	0	6
2	6	7
3	7	7
4	3	7
5	1	4
6	3	6
7	2	5
8	2	4
9	7	7
10	6	7

Each question indicated substantial improvement. This might seem to correlate the accuracy of questions on the quiz that was related to the material presented.

When preparing the quiz, prior to the experiment, I had to take into consideration how easy or difficult the questions should be and their relation to the material (presented two to three times). But as you can see, I believe the level of difficulty was respectable to the way the experiment was conducted. The first question was a dramatic improvement considering their understanding of the basic philosophy of communism. Answers to questions were given after the experiment was over.

Comments and Conclusion

Why did the students recall more after the second presentation? The first presentation seemed to have given the students an underlying structure and organization of the material. Students that scored higher after the second presentation was probably due to the: (1) awareness of the structure and its content (hence, students became familiar with an unfamiliar text), (2) organization of the material (not only the structure but the way it was presented), and (3) repetition of the material.

Students recalled more because of the organization of the material and the organization of the quiz, which is directly related to the former. Would the students have recalled less if, for example, question four became question one and so forth? Studies have indicated that we recall more if the material we are presented and the material that we study be organized. Our brain is so structured that organized material is recalled more readily; not only short-term but also, and more importantly, long-term.

Was the experiment valid? Before answering that question, it was brought to my attention two discrepancies during the experiment after it was conducted.

First, the experiment was conducted in the evening about an hour after dinner from 7-8 p.m. Students claimed that they might have gotten better scores had the experiment been conducted in the morning. This must be taken into consideration. However, according to the results of the experiment, 100% mastery of the material did occur.

And second, the students claimed that they did not have much concern for the experiment because they weren't "getting any credit for it." But to the contrary, the students appeared to be listening attentively during the taped lecture. The second presentation gave substantial evidence to the fact that improved scores occurred—once again, 100% mastery.

The experiment tested by its results proved to be valid. Although the effects of recall may heavily depend on the nature of the individual generally and the nature of the individual's listening ability specifically, achievement of 100% mastery of the passage did occur.

Communism is a philosophical system in which economic goods are distributed equitably, are owned in common, and are available to all as needed. This understanding of present social relations predicts the future development of society.

Communism, as we know it today, can be said to have begun with the theories of Karl Marx. Marx was born May 5, 1818, in Germany. As was the case with so many socialist thinkers, he had a middle-class background.

At a very early age, Marx demonstrated his intelligence and superior capacity for work. He attended the local high school of Trier and in 1835 entered the University of Bonn to study law. After a year at Bonn, he transferred to the University of Berlin. Here he concentrated more on history and philosophy than on law. It was at the University of Berlin that Marx first came under the influence of the philosophy of George Wilhelm Friedrich Hegel (1770-1831). This influence was to have an impact upon the development of Marx's social theories.

Hegel attempted to explain the nature of the universe through a theory of historical development and progress using what is called "the dialectical method". The word "dialectic" comes from Greek, meaning the art of discourse, reasoning and debate. In ancient times this was the art of arriving at a truth through the clash of opposing views and arguments. In order to arrive at a conclusion or a certain belief, arguments were weighed by their validity and persuasiveness. Errors were avoided by highlighting contradictions, which thereby lead to the "error-free" truth.

This is to say that arguments serve their purpose by "linking-up" certain beliefs; and help to arrive at a conclusion. Arguments seen together by their validity and persuasiveness seek to establish a logical point of conclusion, which thereby means rejecting certain other propositions.

This is illustrated in the classical argument over Evolution and Creation. If the evolutionist's argument appears to be invalid with little persuasiveness, according to the creationist's dialectical reasoning, it is thrown out in favor of the other—which in the creationist's case seems to be more valid and truthful. Henceforth, arguments are weighed by their validity and persuasiveness. We use dialectical reasoning when we arrive at a certain belief.

Hegel's attempt to explain the nature of the universe through the theory of historical development and progress was based on his philosophy of idealism. Idealism is a practice of forming "ideals" behind an imperfect object. For example, the chair that you're sitting on is an imperfect chair. There is another chair that you or I can imagine or idealize that is more perfect than that one. Hegel's idealistic philosophy is based on the concept that the universe is rational and spiritual.

Hegel used this philosophical method to interpret the past and the present. But Marx went further than Hegel. Marx rejected Hegel's idealistic philosophy in favor of his materialistic philosophy; in which it explains not only the past and the present, but it also predicts the future. The materialistic philosopher has no concern for spiritual or intellectual things because they cannot be seen. The materialistic philosopher is one who validates his arguments on the basis of what is seen, thereby making him a realist.

Recently, Reagan and Gorbachev met in Iceland to settle a few issues (Watson, Russell, "Dead Lock in Iceland", *Newsweek*, October 20, 1986, p. 20). But it ended in a "frustrating stalemate." The Kremlin's chief expert on the United States, announced that arms control had reached a "dead end." But both Reagan and Gorbachev stressed that the search for agreement would go on. Reagan said, "We made great strides in Iceland ... and we're going to continue our effort". Reagan typically views the progress of society idealistically with evidence of acting later. On the other hand, Gorbachev said, "Let America think," with a nod to public opinion in the west, "we are waiting. We are not withdrawing our proposals." Gorbachev appears to be dominated by viewing society materialistically or realistically with evidence of acting now. The Iceland Summit was a disappointment to all because of Reagan's idealistic hope for the future and Gorbachev's realistic hope for the present, which predicts the future.

Communists believe the dialectical method enables them to understand the "general law of development," not only nature but also of history. They believe that applying this method to society they can analyze the past history of man, understand his present social relations, and foresee the future development of society.

Quiz (Choose the best answer)

1. Communists' understanding of future social relations...
    a. are related to the past development of society.
    b. are related to the present development of society.
    c. are related to the concept of 'idealism.'
    d. both b & c
    e. *both a & b*
    f. both a & c

2. Who influenced the philosophy of Marx's social theories?
    a. Stalin
    b. Lenin
    c. *Hegel*
    d. Engels

3. The dialectical method is (either b or c):
    a. the art of highlighting certain contradictions to arrive at a conclusion.
    b. *the art of arriving at truth through opposing arguments.*
    c. *the art of weighing arguments by their validity and persuasiveness, thereby arriving at a truthful conclusion.*
    d. the art of reasoning through spiritual senses.

4. Arguments:
    a. serve their purpose by confusing everyone.
    b. *serve their purpose by linking up certain beliefs, thereby arriving at a logical conclusion.*

c.   serve their purpose by forming ideas, which
        help to establish a point of interest.
   d.   serve their purpose by contradicting statements
        of beliefs.

5. Hegel's attempt to explain the nature of the universe
   through the theory of historical development and
   progress is based on his philosophy of:
   a.   realism
   b.   materialism
   c.   dialectical method
   d.   *idealism*

6. Materialism is a philosophy that:
   a.   *predicts the future development of society based*
        on the present situation.
   b.   predicts the present development of society
        based on the past situation.
   c.   predicts a grim future for idealists.
   d.   predicts that the future is in the hands of God,
        and therefore, hope can be assured.

7. Marx rejected Hegel's philosophical method because:
   a.   Hegel not only could explain the past and the
        present, but he could also predict the future.
   b.   Hegel had a pessimistic view of society.
   c.   *Hegel couldn't predict the future.*
   d.   Hegel insisted that the universe was not
        rational and spiritual.

8. The Iceland Summit was described as a "frustrating
   stalemate" because:

a. Reagan opposed Gorbachev's sanctions to South Africa.

b. Gorbachev insisted that Reagan made a mistake with his dealings with the Iranians.

c. *Gorbachev views society differently than Reagan.*

d. Reagan's materialistic hope was undercut by Gorbachev's idealistic hope.

9. Communists believe:

a. the dialectical method enables them to understand the general laws of gravity.

b. *the dialectical method enables them to understand the general laws of social development.*

c. the dialectical method enables them to understand the being of God.

d. the dialectical method enables them to understand Humankind.

10. Communists believe:

a. *they hold the keys to the future.*

b. the American government is the "Great Satan."

c. the outbreak of AIDS in America is because of too much freedom.

d. Reagan is a man whom we can all trust.

Exegesis of Religious Passage:
"The Perils of Apostasy"
Hebrews 6:4-6

Setting the Stage of Hebrews 5:11-14: "Immaturity"

In the previous verses (5:11-14) the writer of the epistle addresses some words of practical admonition regarding his readers' spiritual condition. He says that his readers cannot grasp what he has to say because their minds have become sluggish. He goes on to say that they've been Christians for quite some time and by now ought to be able to teach others.[212] This doesn't necessarily mean they ought to be in an official teaching position, but rather they ought by now to be advanced in their comprehension of Christian doctrine and be able to instruct and edify those who are still young in the faith.[213]

Instead, they are so far from having maintained normal progress that they have slipped to a stage where they are themselves in need of a teacher to instruct them again at the very beginning by learning the ABCs of Christianity. This corresponds to their own shamefulness and are likened to that of kindergarten children.[214] One who is so unadvanced that he needs to be introduced once more to the ABCs of the faith is no better than a child in spiritual understanding: milk is the only diet suited to his immature condition, not the solid food of sound Christian doctrine. To go on living on milk, mere baby-food, is indicative of arrested development, and the recipients of this letter have evidently failed to advance beyond, or have relapsed into, a state of spiritual infancy.[215]

After the writer scolds his readers for their immature spiritual condition, he admonishes them to press on to Christian maturity (Ch. 6:1-3). Westcott rightly says, "It is characteristic of the tone of the epistle that the exhortation to progress is based directly on the stern criticism which precedes."[216]

Introduction to Hebrews 6:1-3: "On to Maturity"

The writer exhorts his readers to lay aside, i.e., not to lay them down again, the fundamental teachings of Christianity. He doesn't necessarily mean, however, to abandon them altogether. The necessary condition of progress is a "giving up." That is, we hold what we have as a preparation for something more.[217]

The writer lists six items which fall naturally into three pairs regarding the fundamental teachings of Christian truth. The first pair, and items 1 & 2, involve repentance from dead works and faith toward God; the second pair, and items 3 & 4, involve instructions about washing and laying on of hands; and the third pair, and items 5 & 6, involve resurrection and eternal judgment. These three pair items refer to basic Christian teachings and not to old Jewish teachings; yet they refer to what the readers as former Jews learned when they were brought to Christ.[218]

Exegesis of Hebrews 6:1-3

Repentance is the basis of right, religious conduct. It is a "turning" or "returning" to God.[219] It represents a "reorientation of one's whole life and personality, which includes the adoption of a new ethical line of conduct, a forsaking of sin and a turning to righteousness."[220] It's not a turning to their own righteousness (which is no righteousness at all) but a turning to God's righteousness.

According to Buchanan, 'dead works' refer "to the life Christians had lived before they were baptized into the community. 'Dead' describes those people who were outside of the covenant, living as other pagans."[221] Lenski comments, "they are dead works because they were works (outward observance of the law) that produced no spiritual life."[222] Lightfoot defines "dead works" as "the ineffective sacrifices of the Jewish law, which, with all its works, could never secure salvation."[223] Similarly, Bruce says, "They are works which issue in death ... they belong to the way of death and not the way of life."[224] Westcott appears to take a similar side, "There is but one spring of life, and all which does not flow from it is 'dead'."[225]

We must discard Buchanan's definition because it does not follow the normal exegesis in the previous versus regarding the readers present spiritual condition. 'Dead works' does not describe their works as pagans because the writer is not addressing their former condition before they became Christians. He is addressing their present spiritual condition (5:11-14). Lenski comes close to defining 'dead works,' but Lightfoot appears to come closest. They were 'dead works' because they "could never secure salvation." Faith involves faith in the Son through whom God has spoken. From the standpoint of the epistle, faith is always described as faith toward God, not faith in Christ.[226] Repentance and faith are interrelated because both have to do with a new attitude toward God.[227]

As the first pair was to be preached to men in sin, the second pair concerns the individual's introduction into the Christian community.[228] The suggestion that teaching ablutions (*baptismon* is the plural form of *baptismos*) could possibly refer to ceremonial washings practiced by the Jews has been disputed. Stuart, quoted by Buchanan, asked, "But what has the writer to do here with Jewish ceremonial rites, as the first elements of Christian doctrine?" His answer: "Plainly nothing; so that this exegesis cannot be admitted."[229]

Montefiore, quoted by Buchanan, agrees with Stuart and explains "it must refer to second baptisms for those first baptized by John (Acts 19:5-6)."[230] Moffatt, with Buchanan's approval, thought that ablutions probably continued among some group of Christians, even though others had objected to them.[231] This view seems to be credible accepting that the writer is indeed addressing Jewish Christians who seem to be leaning toward their Jewish customs and uses a term which is familiar to them. Bruce agrees that "it is very doubtful whether Christian baptism is directly in view here at all."[232]

It may be significant that the writer does not use *baptisma,* to denote Christian baptism (and the baptism of John), but *baptismos,* which in its two other indubitable New Testament occurrences refers to Jewish ceremonial washings."[233] Many insist that Jewish doctrine alone is in view here, as the term "washings" (*baptismon*) is plural, indicating that it is not the term used regularly for Christian baptism (*baptisma*).[234] Bruce rightly says, "If this epistle was sent to a group of believing Jews in Rome, the reference to 'instruction about ablutions' may have had a more direct significance than meets the eye of the twentieth-century reader."[235]

The fourth item of the second pair follows ablutions—the 'laying on of hands.' Laying on of hands, most scholars agree (Lenski, Westcott, Bruce, Buchanan, Kent, Lightfoot), was an early Christian practice associated with the reception and impartation of the Holy Spirit for confirmation. Bruce, as well as Lenski (p. 177) and Lightfoot (p. 122), rightly point out that it too like ablution, "was inherited from the Old Testament, where it is used especially in commissioning someone for public office (Num. 27:18, 23; Deut. 34:9), or as part of the sacrificial ritual (Lev. 1:4; 3:2; 4:4; 8:14; 16:21, etc.). In rabbinical Judaism the term appears regularly in the sense of ordination (of elders)."[236]

As the first pair was to be preached to men in sin, and the second pair was to introduce the individual into the Christian community, the third pair gives special importance to Christian doctrine.

Resurrection and eternal judgment are doctrines involving eschatological truth. Like the second pair, these were also prominent in Judaism. For the Christian death need hold no terrors, for his new life in Christ has assured him of resurrection. He need not shrink from the prospect of judgment for sin because Christ has born his judgment, and his sins are now eternally forgiven.[237]

These Christian beliefs are vital to normal Christian beginnings. They are foundational. For this reason, they are termed "milk" and must not be thought of as the end of the believer's interest and understanding, but as the start.[238] The writer hastens to bring his readers from spiritual childhood to spiritual maturity. He says, "And this we will do," adding reverently the qualifying clause, "if God permits" (cf. 1 Cor. 16:7).[239]

Introduction to Hebrews 6:4-6, Part 1

All these above (six in all in three pairs) are elementary teachings of Christianity, i.e., the ABCs, for what is milk for a child. The writer lifts his readers (6:1-3) out of their low state for which he has scolded them in 5:11-14 so that they might at least in part attain the mature state in which they ought to be.[240] They ought to be adults in Christ so that they may have a firm foundation in their beliefs and so they should press on beyond the elementary principles of their religion. To fail in advance would mean to fall back, and to fall back would be fatal.[241]

Introduction to Hebrews 6:4-6, Part 2

The following passage is one of the most disputed in the New Testament. Nearly all schools of interpretation face problems in trying to explain the passage consistently.[242] One must be reminded to keep the previous verses that we went over in mind (5:11-6:3) to interpret this passage accurately.

The following passage constitutes the *"Perils of Apostasy."*[243] Other themes have been suggested: *No Second Beginning* (Bruce), *Warning Against the Consequences of Apostasy* (Kent), *It is Impossible to Restore those who Commit the Sin Against the Holy Spirit* (Lenski), *Limits of Forgiveness* (Buchanan), *A Warning Against Apostasy* (Lightfoot), *Against Slothfulness and the Danger of Apostasy* (Wiley), *The Danger of Apostasy* (Hughes). I have chosen Westcott's theme because I feel it is closely linked within the context, and of the previous verses, and those that follow.

The reason why there is no point in laying the foundation over again (6:1c) is now stated: apostasy is irremediable.[244] Stated in another way, "It is apparent, therefore, that his (the writer) concern is not simply lest his readers should remain at a standstill on the threshold of the Christian life, immature and unfruitful in the faith they profess (5:11ff), but something far worse, lest there should be a relapse into unbelief in their midst. The danger of apostasy is real, not imaginary.[245] The writer emphasizes that continuance (perseverance) is the test of reality.[246]

4   For in the case of those who have once been enlightened and have tasted of the heavenly gift and have been partakers of the Holy Spirit,

5   and have tasted the good word of God and the powers of the age to come,

6   and then have fallen away, it is impossible to renew them again to repentance, since they again crucify to themselves the Son of God and put Him to open shame.

Exegesis of Hebrews 6:4-6

The writer is addressing his readers to the possibility of their dropping out of the Christian faith altogether, and in doing so places themselves beyond all hope of restoration.[247]

Three things must be pointed out in this text which will be valuable to us before we attempt to explain it. First, it must be pointed out that the writer is not describing any of his readers (6:9) because he shifts from "you" (5:11-12), "us" (6:1), and "we" (6:3) to "those" (6:4).[248] Lightfoot says, "It seems correct to say that the passage speaks to those who have embraced the Christian religion."[249] To support this he says, "The writer makes this even clearer by describing, clause after clause, their condition."[250]

Another thing that must be pointed out is commented by Bruce, "Those who have shared the covenant privileges of the people of God, and then deliberately renounce them, are the most difficult persons of all to reclaim for the faith. It is indeed impossible to reclaim them, says our writer. We know, of course, that nothing of this sort is ultimately impossible for the grace of God, but as a matter of human experience the reclamation of such people is, practically speaking impossible."[251]

And lastly, "once" (*hapax*) was an important word to the writer as Buchanan wisely points out.[252] The writer used it quite often throughout the epistle (9:7; 9:26, 28; 9:27; 10:2). This is not only true of Hebrews, but also as well as First Peter (3:18) and Jude (3, 5). The writer of Hebrews also used a more emphatic word for "once" (*ephapax*) several times (7:27; 9:12; 10:10). His emphasis in 6:4 is for the readers [sic] who had "once been enlightened."[253]

Six things are predicated of the spiritual experience of those whom "it is impossible to renew them again to repentance" if they rebel against the faith they claim to hold.[254] They are those who have: (1) once been enlightened, (2) tasted of the heavenly gift, (3) been partakers of the Holy Spirit, (4) tasted the good word of God, (5) tasted the powers of the age to come, and (6) fallen away.

1. *They* [255] *have once been enlightened.*

First, the use of "once for all" points to something complete, rather than partial or inadequate.[256] Secondly, "enlightened" was understood in the sense of baptism among Christians in Rome in the middle of the second century.[257] Recent scholars believe "enlightened" to refer to the catechism required for baptism (Buchanan). In either case both baptism and the catechism are the outward admission to Christian fellowship.

But most scholars dismiss this interpretation because it is not in line with New Testament teaching. The same verb that is used here is the same used in John 1:9 of the activity of the eternal Word who came into the world to enlighten men.[258] It is referred to when the light was apprehended and corresponds to the experience of a reception of "the knowledge of the truth" (10:26).[259] This knowledge of truth is none other than the gospel or Christ. Christ, the Light, and His saving truth filled their souls.

This enlightenment was a one-time act of entrance into Christ that could never be duplicated.[260] Like baptism, it is unrepeatable for the simple reason that its repetition would contradict its whole significance because "the death of Jesus (9:28), like their own (9:27), can never be repeated."[261, 262]

2. They have tasted of the heavenly gift.

"Tasted" has been a controversial term for scholars. It is the same word used in verse 5 and has been translated by Buchanan to mean "sampled" or "had been introduced to."[263] He illustrates this to refer to God's favorable promise that He would give the Israelites the land of Canaan. They were just on the verge of receiving the promised heritage. Numerous other scholars, including Owen, Westcott, and Montefiore, take the same position to that of Buchanan. They translate "tasted" to mean a temporary or superficial participation.[264] This translation is based on the interpretation of 2:9 as the writer was saying that Christ only briefly "sipped" death.

Other scholars take the opposite route. They argue that the verb "tasted," also used in verse 5, does not mean partial or a mere sampling, but a real deep personal experience. This is argued from the same text in 2:9, where instead of interpreting that Christ briefly sipped death, to mean that Christ actually experienced the full bitterness of death. The latter interpretation is more accurate because its context is linked to "those who were once enlightened," referring to the experience of receiving (not sampling) the light of the gospel with the fullness of joy.

"The heavenly gift" has been suggested to mean the Eucharist in connection with the verb "tasted," in the physical sense (unlike the metaphorical sense), according to some scholars. This interpretation is justified if one accepts "enlightenment" to mean baptism. This interpretation has proved attractive to some, but one "need not be restricted to the Eucharist; it may indicate the whole sum of spiritual blessings with are sacramentally sealed and signified in the Eucharist."[265]

Taking it one step further than Bruce, and being more specific, Westcott says that "the gift is described as 'heavenly'... It belongs to a higher sphere of existence than earth—the gift of the Holy Spirit."[266] Other suggestions include salvation, eternal life, forgiveness of sin, the Holy Spirit, or Christ.[267] The latter suggestion, Christ, appears to be the actual meaning of the 'heavenly gift,' since everything culminates in Christ. Furthermore, the writer will now turn to mention briefly the Holy Spirit, which seems to indicate that the writer wasn't referring to the heavenly gift as being the Holy Spirit in this participle.[268] Lenski sums up the meaning of the participle, 'have tasted of the heavenly gift,' "to describe the inner, personal experience of salvation."[269]

3. They have been partakers of the Holy Spirit.

Bruce, as well as other scholars, have pointed out that the absence of the Greek article with Holy Spirit seems to refer to the Spirit's activity or gifts, rather than His person, but this is not in itself sufficient to decide whether the Giver or His gifts are in question.[270]

Some scholars come to the conclusion that to be "partakers of the Holy Spirit" means to "share in a heavenly call" (3:1). So, here, they share in the Holy Spirit.[271] But then we may ask ourselves, In what way? Before answering this question, Bruce points out by saying, "The people whom he (the writer) has in mind had not only been baptized and received the Eucharist but had experienced the laying on of hands" (6:2).[272] The laying on of hands symbolizes Christian commission influenced by the divine Spirit who imparts gifts, distributed accordingly, for the purpose of proclaiming the gospel of Jesus Christ. These spiritual gifts confirm the truth and the power of the gospel. So, then, to be a partaker of the Holy Spirit means to experience the joy of sharing the gospel with others.

4. They have tasted the good word of God.

Most scholars (Bruce, Lenski, Buchanan, Westcott, Kent, Wiley, Hughes, Lightfoot) agree that this participle "refers to the experiencing (same metaphorical use of participle in verse 4) the word of God in the gospel and finding it good."[273]

The 'good word of God' may refer to God's promises, but more probably is to be taken to refer to the good news generally: they had heard the gospel, made trial of it, and found in it blessings that truly were worthwhile."[274] Likewise, Hughes says that it "implies to experience something in a manner that is real and personal."[275] Westcott goes further and says that it is the "direct experience in their essential completeness."[276]

5. They have tasted the powers of the age to come.

Some scholars identify "powers" with the signs, wonders, and miracles mentioned in 2:4 as accompaniments of the preaching of the gospel.[277] Other scholars identify "powers" with having reference to the activities of that life through the gifts of the Spirit, and that these gifts that are operative in us "promise far greater gifts to come."[278, 279] Lightfoot seems less restrictive in the identification of "powers." According to him, "powers" include not only "signs, wonders, and various miracles," but also the "gifts of the Holy Spirit" (2:4).[280]

Furthermore, "the age to come," says Lightfoot, "does not refer to some age which for Christians lies in the future. It is, rather, equivalent to the Messianic Age, ushered in with the appearance of Christ, but still appropriately called 'the age to come' because it awaits its consummation at the Second Advent of Christ."[281]

6. They have fallen away.[282]

There is no need to say more. This one word tells the whole story. It is tragic to the highest degree.[283] To fall away means literally, "to the side," meaning to fall away utterly.[284] Bruce says, "the context here shows plainly that the willful sin which he has in mind is deliberate apostasy."[285]

Some scholars interpret this passage to mean sin (blasphemy) against the Holy Spirit that caused themselves to fall into apostasy. This may have some truth to it, but the writer makes no mention of this specific sin. However, it is established that it is not a mere backsliding of the ordinary shortcomings and failures that go with human weakness. It is one thing to yield to sin contrary to the new life of Christ, it is another thing to abandon that new life altogether.[286] We may go as far as to say that a falling away refers to a complete and final repudiation of the divine principles that influences right doing to sustain relationships.[287]

Conclusion

Those whom the writer is describing fell to such an extent that "it is impossible to renew them again to repentance," i.e., again to produce repentance in their heart and so change their state into one that is again or "new" as they had once been made anew.[288] Lensky comments, "It is the state into which they have fallen which makes renewal to repentance impossible. They are 'recrucifying (v. 6) for themselves the Son of God and exposing him to public ignominy.' This is a full equivalent speaking about the sin against the Holy Spirit."[289]

But as pointed out before, the writer specifies nothing, yet this interpretation does seem attractive. Lenski continues, "These acts (v. 6) are expressed by making 'the Son of God' the object of them."[290] Furthermore, "They are not again actually nailing him to the cross as one who was accursed by God, for he is now beyond human reach, in glory, but as far as his relation to them and theirs to him is concerned."[291]

Other scholars, such as Buchanan, attribute this whole passage to a limit which there is no forgiveness who sins against the Holy Spirit. He even cites a passage from the Gospel of Thomas. But we will not deal with his argument here.[292] Bruce hits it on the nail saying:

To say that they cannot be brought to repentance so long as they persist in their renunciation of Christ would be a truism hardly worth putting into words. The participle 'crucifying' is much more appropriately taken as casual than as temporal in force; it indicates why it is impossible for such people to repent and make a new beginning. God has pledged Himself to pardon all who truly repent, but Scripture and experience alike suggest that it is possible for human beings to arrive at a state of heart and life where they can no longer repent.[293]

The path to repentance is not solely about a momentary decision, but about the state of one's heart and life over time. The idea that one can reach a point where repentance becomes impossible is a sobering thought, emphasizing the importance of continually cultivating humility and a repentant spirit. It serves as a reminder of the need for spiritual vigilance, as the hardening of the heart can render even the most gracious invitation to repentance ineffective.

Part VI

Autobiographical Reflections

A Philosophic Quest
How Philosophy Became an Integral Part of My Life

IF HISTORY IS PHILOSOPHY LEARNED from examples, then philosophy is from where examples are learned.[294]

Philosophy involves turning the mind inward and reflecting on itself. It occupies a middle ground between theology and science. Like theology, philosophy engages in speculation about the nature of reality; but like science, it relies on human reason rather than authority.

Philosophy is the *golden mean,* the path one follows in the pursuit of virtuous actions and goodwill toward all. It is the discipline where one seeks to understand the relationships between ideas, much like theology, and matters of fact, like science—synthesizing both to bridge the gap and clarify the language that unites them. Philosophy is the essence that gives life its meaning and purpose.

Philosophy is Everybody's Business

Philosophy is valuable for everyone. It serves those who seek to know, those who know but wish to understand more deeply, and those who understand but desire greater clarity. In this way, philosophy is everybody's business. It begins when one learns to question—challenging accepted norms, assumptions, and dogmas. Philosophy is an ongoing process of learning, unlearning, and revising knowledge in the pursuit of wisdom.

A philosophical journey can start with any branch of knowledge, whether it be the philosophy of religion, ethics, history, education, politics, aesthetics, logic, or metaphysics. For me, it began with questioning religious ideals and was later ignited by Nietzsche's philosophy of life.

My Desire to Learn

I've always followed my heart and intellectual curiosity. My desire to learn began during my undergraduate work in religious studies in a class called *Religious Belief and the Modern World*, taken during spring quarter of 1986. The professor recommended several books that captured my attention, and I remember three in particular: Emil Brunner's *Man in Revolt*, a Christian anthropology of humanity; Paul Tillich's *The Courage To Be*, which explores the Christian understanding of anxiety and despair; and Mortimer J. Adler's *How to Think about God*, a book intended for atheists. I bought all three, along with Tillich's *Biblical Religion and the Search for Ultimate Reality*.

I spent that summer reading them all, and they left a lasting impression on me. These books deepened my understanding of the relationship between reason and faith. I came to believe that giving a rational foundation to belief—explaining the "why" behind the "what" of faith—could draw modern people toward something higher than themselves.

The Importance of Integrating Faith and Reason

I began to see the importance of the integration of faith and reason as a vital Christian responsibility, one that can help navigate the challenges of a changing society. It was through this exploration that I realized the crucial role philosophy plays in religion, acting as a bridge between theological (sacred) and scientific (secular) perspectives.[295]

The task of integrating faith and reason— fusing the two—began in the second century with the Christian Apologists. In response to false accusations about their beliefs and practices, Christians took it upon themselves to defend their faith. These accusations were often based on misunderstandings and rumors, and Christians found themselves needing to address the relationship between their faith and the surrounding pagan culture.

One of the most well-known early apologists was Justin Martyr, who famously argues that in Christianity he had found "the true philosophy." In response to the charge that Christians were atheists—because they had no visible gods—Justin contended that Christians worshipped the same God that the Greek philosophers had sought. He referred to this God as the "Logos," a concept that denotes both the Word and reason. For Justin, the Logos was not only the rational principle governing the universe, as the philosophers had described, but also the pre-existent Christ mentioned in the prologue of the Gospel of John.

According to Justin, the Logos is "the true light that enlightens everyone" (John 1:9). Therefore, the ancient philosophers—such as Socrates, Plato, and Aristotle—were, in a sense, Christians, as their wisdom was derived from Christ. The key difference, Justin argues, is that while these philosophers knew the Logos "in part," Christians know the Logos "fully" because they encountered "truth incarnate" in Jesus Christ.

In contrast, Justin claims that the gods worshipped by the pagans were mere human inventions, created to indulge human vice. As such, pagan practices, he concluded, were evidence of atheism, not true devotion to God.

The apologists of the early centuries faced the challenge of engaging with their society. They sought to demonstrate that Christianity was not only compatible with reason, but that it provided a more truthful understanding of the world than the pagan religions. Their goal was to use reason to build a bridge between Christian faith and pagan culture, attracting converts through rational arguments.

Learning from the Early Apologists

As we enter the twenty-first century, Christians today face a similar task: to build a relationship between their faith and the modern world, especially in the context of technological advances and contemporary culture. Christians owe much to the work of the early apologists, whose use of reason to defend and explain their faith played a key role in Christianity's development as a world religion.

Today's Christians can learn much from their predecessors, especially those from the second and third centuries. A reasonable faith, rooted in the intellectual traditions of the early Church, can help modern believers appreciate the wisdom of those who came before them. By drawing on the apologists' example of integrating faith with reason, Christians today can continue to engage with the challenges of their time while staying true to the core principles of their beliefs.

Applying Philosophy to Education

In my final year at the university, I became fascinated by the application of philosophy to education. Building on what I had learned about philosophy up to that point, I sought to explore its practical use by enrolling in a class called *Psychological Foundations of Education* during fall quarter of 1986. With my professor's approval, I wrote two papers and conducted an experiment to apply philosophical ideas to education, aiming to make them both useful and practical in a real-world context.

The first paper, *"The Role of Philosophy in Education,"* explores how the philosophy of education is integrated into teaching practices and its relevance to the learning process. The second paper, *"The Impact of Teacher Enthusiasm on Student Learning,"* examines how teacher enthusiasm positively influences student engagement and academic performance. For my experiment, I replicated a study published in an educational journal. My experiment, *"Effects of Repetition on Recall and Learning from Unfamiliar Text,"* demonstrates how presenting material in a repetitive and organized manner enhances student comprehension and retention. (See Part V: Academia.)

Dropping Out of Graduate School

During my last year at the university, I came across a book in the library that immediately caught my attention. It was a collection of essays by philosopher and mathematician Bertrand Russell, titled *Why I Am Not a Christian*. In June 1987, I graduated from my university with a degree in Religious Studies.

In October of that year, I enrolled in the Religious Education graduate program at the same university, aiming to prepare myself to teach religion within this Christian denomination's educational system. Despite my new academic focus, Russell's book continued to occupy my thoughts.

In December, I decided to purchase a copy of *Why I Am Not a Christian* to explore further why Russell opposed the Christian faith, and to understand how his ideas about religion might have shaped contemporary views on the subject. Russell's critique of religion, particularly from a socio-political standpoint, left a lasting impression on me.

That same month, I also bought *Aristotle for Everybody: Difficult Thought Made Easy* by Mortimer J. Adler. This book sparked my interest in Aristotle's ethical philosophy. Through Adler, I was introduced to the Christian philosophy of St. Thomas Aquinas, who regarded philosophy as his "indispensable handmaiden."

In January, during the second quarter of my graduate program, I purchased Adler's *Six Great Ideas*, a book that examines foundational concepts such as truth, goodness, beauty, liberty, equality, and justice. At this point, my thinking began to shift in a new direction. I found myself reflecting deeply on my life's path, questioning where I was headed and what I truly wanted to achieve.

In mid-March, the director of the ABC Japan English Schools visited the university to recruit missionaries. He had known me from my first year in Japan in the mid-80s, and after a brief meeting, he invited me to return. It became clear to me that Japan was where I wanted to be. By the end of March, I had become disillusioned with the graduate program and made the decision to drop out. In April, I returned to Japan for the second time.

I remember it being a chilly April in Tokyo, with snow falling while I was temporarily staying in a Japanese inn. That month, I purchased at least three books: Adler's *Ten Philosophical Mistakes*, *We Hold These Truths*, and Aristotle's *Nicomachean Ethics*. Japan became the place where I started spending "a third of the day with people, passions, and books."[296] It was here that my philosophical journey truly gained momentum, and each day I felt myself diving deeper into the rabbit hole.

Mortimer J. Adler's *Ten Philosophical Mistakes* examines ten key philosophical errors in the development of modern thought and explores the profound impact these mistakes have on our everyday lives. In *We Hold These Truths*, he delves into the ideas and ideals behind the United States Constitution, guiding readers through the philosophical foundations of American democracy. Adler introduces readers to the great philosophers of antiquity, the Middle Ages, and the modern era, offering a comprehensive view of philosophical thought.

As a philosopher, educator, encyclopedist, and author, Adler is renowned for debunking the myth that philosophy is only for specialists. Over his prolific career, he authored more than 50 books, continuing to publish well into his nineties, including *Intellect: Mind Over Matter*, which was published when he was 88!

Adler's philosophy rests on three main points. First, he asserts that "philosophy is everybody's business." A deeper understanding of fundamental philosophical concepts, he argues, is crucial for addressing the political, moral, and social challenges we face daily. Second, Adler brings a broader dimension to philosophy, particularly through its aesthetic aspects, making complex ideas accessible with his gift for explaining "difficult thought made easy." He has a unique ability to guide readers through deep intellectual waters, ensuring they stay afloat. Finally, Adler's goal is to make philosophy appealing and relevant to the common person, hoping it becomes an integral part of their life, as it has become for me.

Adler's work aims to enlighten and reawaken our minds, encouraging us to think critically about the ideas that shape our lives and our world. An Aristotelian at heart, Adler was a realist who sought to reform the American educational system. As former director of the *Institute for Philosophical Research,* he developed the Paideia Program in the 1980s, which outlined a comprehensive educational syllabus.

For Adler, the ultimate goal for every individual is to engage with the ideas that have shaped the modern world and to understand their influence on our thinking. His books are accessible to anyone, regardless of background, and encourage everyone to think more deeply about the world around them.

Aristotle's central theme in *Nicomachean Ethics* is the pursuit of the highest human good. His ethics teaches us to "observe the mean," advocating moderation in all things and warning against both excess and deficiency. Aristotle's ultimate goal is for individuals to cultivate virtue, thereby achieving happiness—the highest human good. Happiness, according to Aristotle, is achieved through living a life of virtue and moral excellence.

Histories of Philosophy

As I gradually absorbed these philosophical ideas, I decided to dive deeper by purchasing a couple of books that offered a brief history of philosophy: Lavine's *From Socrates to Sartre: The Philosophic Quest* and Durant's *The Story of Philosophy*. I wanted to gain a broader perspective on the entire sweep of philosophical thought, to understand where key ideas originated and how they shaped the world—particularly their influence on Western thought. My goal was to grasp at least a small piece of the philosophical legacy that has so profoundly impacted our thinking in the western world.

Mr. Yokoyama

I worked in Tokyo from April to June, during which time I became acquainted with a Japanese researcher named Mr. Yokoyama. His thinking embodied a scientific approach to understanding matters of fact. One afternoon, as we were discussing philosophy and religion, he asked me if I was a Christian. He told me he didn't think I "sounded like" a Christian or someone inclined toward religious ideals. It was interesting to hear this perception, as it opened the door for a deeper conversation.

We continued our discussion on philosophy, and I realized that there are others like him—individuals whose scientific mindset often comes into conflict with the idea of relating matters of fact to matters of ideas, such as those found in religion or theology. To speak of any connection between the two, from a scientific perspective, seems contradictory and even insulting to the dignity of human beings in our modern, technological age.

In my view, these so-called "scientific minds" tend to become uneasy when confronted with metaphysical ideas that go beyond empirical experience. To preserve their sense of certainty in a technological society and to safeguard their identity, they often retreat to the realm of concrete facts, avoiding the "void" between science and theology.

Yet, Bertrand Russell argues that this "void" is philosophy—it is the "no man's land" between the known and the unknown. It is here, in this space, that we must bridge the gap between matters of fact and matters of ideas. By understanding how facts and ideas relate to one another, we can come to a deeper understanding of the world as a unified whole and see all human beings as interconnected.

As I was leaving Yokoyama's home, feeling thankful for our engaging conversation, he praised me by calling me "a scientist for world peace." I was taken aback for a moment and thought, "Wow. Okay, cool." His words lifted my spirit and further fueled my philosophical quest for knowledge, understanding, and a higher sense of balance.

A. J. Ayer's Influence

To better understand Yokoyama and others with a similar mindset, and to explore how I could bridge science and religion, I visited Kinokuniya Bookstore. Before leaving Tokyo for Osaka in June, I bought a book on logic to deepen my understanding of how reason could connect these two realms.

The book I purchased was A. J. Ayer's *Language, Truth, and Logic*. I was especially struck by the fact that Ayer had written it at just 25 years old. Through Ayer's exploration of the theory of knowledge and the nature of analysis, I was introduced to various philosophical ideas that had their roots in the eighteenth century. Influenced by the ideas in Ayer's book, I wrote a short treatise to the director of the ABC Japan English School, presenting a few propositions regarding my "existential direction" in Japan.

Emergence of Self-Awareness

My passion for philosophy began to intensify. Embarking on this philosophical journey allowed me to critically examine not only the mission and rules of the ABC organization in Japan, but also the ways in which religious institutions can exert socio-political power over individuals. At the same time, I began questioning my own existence and direction in life. I was becoming more "self-aware" and reflecting on my place in the larger "scheme of things." It was during this period of introspection that I encountered a nineteenth-century philosopher who referred to himself as a "philologist" and a "destroyer of morals"—Friedrich Nietzsche.

Meeting Nietzsche through Mayu

I encountered Nietzsche and his philosophy in an entirely unexpected manner, through a 15-year-old Japanese girl named Mayu. I later discovered that she was at the top of her class in school, but at the time, I had no idea of her academic prowess.

It all started on a train ride to Kagoshima for summer camp, where I found myself sitting next to Mayu. She was deeply engrossed in a book, smiling as she read—a smile that struck me as odd. Curious, I asked what she was reading, and she handed me the book. It was *Thus Spoke Zarathustra* by Nietzsche.

I didn't recognize the title, but I did recall Nietzsche's name from my *Religious Beliefs and the Modern World* class at university. He was portrayed as a philosopher with dangerous, even mad ideas. I thought of Nietzsche as the "God is dead" philosopher. After all, his famous declaration had left an unsettling mark on me, as it did for many who took issue with his seemingly anti-theistic remarks. As a Christian, I found myself disturbed to the very foundation of faith. I didn't know much about Nietzsche and what he truly represented beyond the "interpretations," which painted him in a negative light—someone whose ideas were not only controversial but potentially harmful.

So, when I saw Mayu reading Nietzsche with a smile, I couldn't help but wonder what kind of impact his ideas were having on her, especially when it came to her view of Christianity. As a missionary, I felt a responsibility to engage with her, to at least understand what Nietzsche's philosophy truly entailed. The problem was, I knew very little about it.

Mayu, with her cheerful demeanor and the obvious joy she derived from Nietzsche's writing, seemed to know more than I did. It was clear that she, like a previous acquaintance, Mr. Yokoyama, appreciated the value of philosophy. This prompted me to dive deeper into Nietzsche's work, but I first had to strip away the preconceptions I had absorbed from my education—*preconceptions* that were colored by a superficial understanding of Nietzsche's philosophy, or more accurately, by my complete lack of understanding since I had never actually read any of his works.

So, I set out to learn. My intellectual journey began as I unlearned what I thought I knew. I realized that, in fact, I knew nothing about Nietzsche. It was a 15-year-old girl who led me out of my ignorance—out of Plato's Cave— and ignited a thirst for knowledge that I hadn't anticipated.

My Intellectual Journey with Nietzsche

I decided I needed to approach Nietzsche's philosophy with an open mind, unclouded by the assumptions I had previously held. I had to spend time with Nietzsche's actual writings to see for myself whether the fears surrounding him were justified.

In August, Mayu and a friend of hers joined me at Kinokuniya Bookstore in search of Nietzsche's works. I passed over the book she had been reading because it is very elusive, choosing instead to look for texts that might offer a general understanding of his philosophy. I came across three works that intrigued me.

The first was *Ecce Homo*, Nietzsche's final work, which is essentially an autobiography and a concise reflection of his life and thought. The second was a two-in-one volume of *Twilight of the Idols* and *The Anti-Christ*, two of his more provocative texts. It was interesting to note that my own journey of Nietzschean discovery took place exactly a century after Nietzsche wrote these works.

Ecce Homo struck me as an important starting point. It was a kind of self-summary, containing Nietzsche's reflections on his own philosophy. Reading this felt like a responsibility—not just as a Christian, but as someone interested in understanding a major influence on modern thought. Nietzsche's ideas had undeniably reshaped the intellectual landscape, and to understand how they interacted with Christianity, I felt it was crucial to engage with the source material directly.

My thoughts on Nietzsche after reading *Ecce Homo* were mixed. I didn't necessarily agree with his ideas, but I couldn't help but admire his brilliance. His writing was psychologically intense—dangerous in its eloquence, yet also invigorating, pushing the reader to confront uncomfortable truths about life and self-affirmation. I wasn't necessarily praising his philosophy itself, but rather acknowledging the depth and intellectual stimulation of his prose. Nietzsche's ability to provoke thought and challenge the mind was undeniable.

Within a few days, I found myself drawn deeper into Nietzsche's world. His work was like a breath of fresh air—unlike anything I had encountered before. Nietzsche was scorned by many in his time for his iconoclasm, yet he was also loved for his passionate, unapologetic writing. His work was alive with energy, and it stirred emotions in me—sometimes in violent opposition, sometimes in intense agreement. I would find myself wanting to throw his book across the room one moment and cheering him on the next.

Nietzsche's ultimate aim, it seemed to me, was to restore what he believed had been lost or destroyed during the medieval era—the individual human self. Unfortunately, his style made him vulnerable to misinterpretation. His ideas, complex and often paradoxical, were easily taken out of context. Nietzsche was acutely aware of this, and he knew he would be misunderstood.

After finishing *Ecce Homo*, *Twilight of the Idols*, and *The Anti-Christ*, I found myself reflecting more deeply on his ideas. Nietzsche's bold and startling statements challenged me to think in ways I hadn't before. His philosophy of life, which placed value on self-affirmation and the pursuit of individual growth, resonated with me, even as I disagreed with certain aspects.

Self-Discovery and Growth

I was fascinated by Nietzsche's ability to make his readers confront the depths of their own lives. It became clear to me that, contrary to the way he had been portrayed, Nietzsche was not advocating nihilism or despair, but rather freedom and the flourishing of human life. His call for the individual to rise above conventional morality in the pursuit of self-discovery and personal growth was one I had to grapple with.

In one week, I read *Ecce Homo*, *Twilight of the Idols*, and *The Anti-Christ*. I was so impressed by Nietzsche's wit and satire that I bought two more of his works in November: *Human, All Too Human* and *Beyond Good and Evil*. My Nietzschean library was expanding. But one copy of the first three books wasn't enough—I felt compelled to explore them further. So, I bought them again and, a year later, during my third visit to Japan, I read them a second time in October.

Mayu had given me the gift of curiosity, and I sought to honor that by truly listening—not just to her, but to Nietzsche as well. I understood that responding to her philosophical interest in Nietzsche required patience and discernment on my part. I couldn't accept or reject Nietzsche's ideas blindly; I needed to engage with them thoughtfully, with an open heart and a critical mind: or as Nietzsche would say, one who "tests an approaching stimulus and reacts slowly to every kind."[297]

Mayu's influence, though subtle, was profound. It pushed me deeper into Nietzsche's philosophy and prompted me to embark on a journey of intellectual exploration that I hadn't anticipated. As I delved deeper into the philosophy of freedom, growth, and the affirmation of life that Nietzsche espoused, I came to understand the man behind the ideas—a philosopher whose work continues to provoke and challenge, offering more life and more questions at every turn.

Nietzsche is perhaps the most misunderstood philosopher of the modern era. As the translator R. J. Hollingdale rightly points out, his ideas are "misquoted and misrepresented." by those who use his words to justify their own agendas. Nietzsche's declaration that 'God is dead,' his doctrine of the Übermensch (Superman), and his concept of the will to power were "all later seized upon and unrecognizably twisted by, among others, Nazi intellectuals."[298]

In my own engagement with Nietzsche, I've come to appreciate the complexity of his thought. He is, in many ways, for everyone and for no one. His ideas are not easily grasped, and they resist simple interpretation. As Nietzsche himself notes, "The worst readers are those who behave like plundering troops—they take a few things they can use, dirty and confound the remainder, and revile the whole."[299]

In the end, reading Nietzsche has taught me that engaging with philosophy—any philosophy—requires humility and openness. It's a journey of unlearning and re-learning, of confronting ideas that challenge our assumptions and push us to grow. As I continue to explore Nietzsche's world, I've come to see it as a journey to understand the human self in all its complexity—a journey that never truly ends.

Reflection 1

How Philosophy was Contributing to My Personal Growth

AS I REFLECT ON THE PAST THREE YEARS and look at the present, I find myself striving to emerge as a person, as a human being, in search of 'truth'—particularly questioning the conventional system of concepts and values that shape our world today.

To me, truth is the pursuit of understanding the origins and reasons behind concepts and values. As such, truth is not absolute; it evolves with changes in human perception. When perceptions shift, what we consider to be 'truth' also shifts, or at least acquires new meaning. This transformation is driven by advancements in knowledge and technology, which is why people often feel they understand things more clearly or "better" than before.

Truth is ultimately unknowable with absolute certainty, due to our limited understanding and the vast scope of our imagination. However, our finite wisdom should not discourage us from continuing to seek truth in order to deepen our understanding of it. Above all, truth is not singular or narrow. If it were, there would only be one culture, one language, one race, one way of thinking, one way of eating, or even one way of going to the bathroom.

My church history professor was an insightful and passionate individual, deeply committed to conveying the truth in his lectures on the history of the Christian Church. Through his animated teachings and storytelling, he demonstrated the value of studying history as a path toward becoming the best version of myself.

I am undergoing rapid change, particularly in recent months, and I feel the shift most acutely when I interact with Christian acquaintances. I embrace change and look forward to it, as it is often sparked by the literature that I intentionally expose myself to. Change, in my view, is inherently good.

Many people fear change because it threatens their sense of security and identity. Yet, change is essential for growth, offering the freedom needed to further the human spirit. It is necessary for us to evolve into everything we can be, for everyone, in every way.

When it comes to ancient texts that are revered by the public, such as the Bible, I approach them with a healthy skepticism, questioning their authenticity. I cannot abide interpretations of history that are purely spiritual; such interpretations seem rooted in conviction or corruption, often born out of superstition and the belief in forces that either bless or curse. This "spiritualizing" of the world is, to me, an affront to the dignity of humanity. The instinct to sense what is true and the rational inquiry to distinguish what is real are both gifts that God has given us to cultivate our being.

Why, I wonder, does one person, from a religious perspective, view me as "demonic," while another, from a secular standpoint, sees me as "complete"? Does not the former recognize the difference between religious devotion and loving God? I prefer to see myself as the latter—on a journey toward completeness, which I believe is the essence of life.

While I was in Montana, I wrote several short essays. In these writings, I noticed a shift in myself—letting go of the ideal, the spiritual, and embracing the real, focusing on what can truly be known: *Know Thyself.* This, I believe, is the true purpose and destiny of humankind. If I were to speak of 'salvation,' it would not be salvation from sin, but rather salvation through knowledge—from the ignorance that limits us and causes harm.

Evil, in my view, arises from apathy and ignorance—from a lack of empathy and understanding. When we do not know, we cause harm to ourselves, others, and the world around us.

As for my belief in God, I consider myself a "deist," akin to the Founding Fathers of America—men like Thomas Jefferson and Benjamin Franklin. This raises the question of whether I still consider myself a "Christian." Since the article *a* before the capital *C* denotes a noun, I would have to answer with a resounding "no." However, I would describe myself as christian in the sense of adopting a way of thinking and behaving that seeks goodwill toward others.

I study philosophy to gain deeper insights into the world. Philosophers, from their varied perspectives, influence the changes in my thinking. A good book is one that challenges me to reflect, consider, and evaluate what I believe to be true, good, and beautiful. A philosophical treatise offers me another way of seeing things—from new heights, new depths, and different angles, expanding my understanding and appreciation of life.

I am opening myself to the vast expanse of knowledge that has shaped our world, stepping away from the narrow, one-dimensional perspective I received in higher education. I am grateful for this foundation, as it has fueled my desire to explore broader avenues of thought, ones I might not have encountered otherwise.

My aspiration now is to deepen my understanding of the world through history, literature, science, and religion, so that I can develop a greater appreciation for it and for the people who inhabit it. This deeper appreciation arises from the knowledge of oneself—of being an authentic individual, breathing, living, thinking, and existing as God intended, contributing to the ongoing work of creation.

When we produce good—creative, ethical, and meaningful contributions to the world—such work should be recognized and esteemed. It is only then that we can live together successfully, guided by knowledge and understanding. I speak of both the practical wisdom found in Hebrew literature, which teaches us about ethical conduct and relationships, and the theoretical wisdom of Greek philosophy, which emphasizes the cultivation of the mind. Both are necessary for living successfully in the world.

To free oneself from conventional concepts and values—ideas like 'good' and 'evil,' 'heaven' and 'hell,' 'God' and 'devil,' 'reward' and 'punishment,' 'blessedness' and 'judgment,' 'immortality' and 'death'— requires the courage to venture into the unknown. One must be willing to go where no path exists, leaving a trail for others to follow, and contributing to the growth and development of oneself and the world.

Reflection 2

How Philosophy is a Kind of "Wonderment"

WE ARE NO LONGER STIMULATED BY THE ACT OF WONDERMENT. We have lost our ability to be truly moved by wonder. This is not because the world has lost its marvels, but because we have become numb to them. We have grown accustomed to the mundane, lulled by the constant presence of the ordinary, and we accept things without question. The popular saying, *"It is what it is,"* has become the mantra of our age. Those who repeat it often do so without understanding, without curiosity about what could be otherwise, or what might lie beyond the surface of things.

I remember the first time I looked through a telescope and saw the moons of Jupiter and the rings of Saturn. For a moment, I lost my breath. I was filled with awe at the sight of these distant worlds, so far from Earth—millions of miles away—and yet so present before my eyes. The sight filled me with a sense of wonder.

After gazing at those planetary giants, I shifted the telescope's view, now directed toward the starry sky. Thousands of stars, too distant and too numerous to comprehend, sparkled in the vast expanse. It was a sight beyond my prior imagination, and it stirred something deep within me—a thirst for knowledge, a hunger for the unexplored.

The more we discover, the more wonder grows. Each new discovery opens doors to more mysteries, igniting a deeper appreciation for what we once didn't know. I remember an evening in November, just before the turn of the decade, when I paused to catch my breath after a few sprints on the track. As I looked up at the night sky, I saw the constellation Orion, and beside it, the bright planet Jupiter. I felt a wave of wonder. In that quiet moment, I whispered to myself, "The heavens declare the glory of God."

To gaze into the universe—its immeasurable size, its potential for life, its unfathomable mysteries—is an act of wonder. It is a mix of awe, curiosity, reverence, and uncertainty. Wonderment, as a scientist once described it, is "the complex emotion aroused by the strange and incomprehensible."

This sense of wonder led me to ponder the nature of my own mind. What was it that attracted me to philosophy? Philosophy, I've come to understand, is *the art of wondering*. It is not about seeking fixed answers, but about embracing the questions—questions that challenge what we think we know. For as long as I can remember, I've been drawn to uncertainty rather than certainty. It is this openness to the unknown that fuels my intellectual and emotional curiosity. Philosophy offers me a way to keep that sense of wonder alive.

Unlike religion, which tends to assert absolute truths about life, the afterlife, and the divine, philosophy remains a quest for meaning in the here and now. Religion's dogmatic certainty often bores me. It tells us what *is*, but philosophy asks *why*. It invites us to explore, to question, and to learn without the pressure of arriving at definitive answers.

Wonderment is what keeps me from ever truly feeling bored when I'm alone with my thoughts. Philosophy is my entertainment, my distraction, my constant source of wonder. The books I read, the ideas I write about, they all trace their roots back to that spark of curiosity. It is wonderment that makes life meaningful, that compels us to ask *what is the difference between this and that?* It is wonderment that drives us to seek more.

I find that even in music, my tastes reflect this desire for wonderment. Titles like *"Standing in Motion," "Flight of Fantasy," "Planet Voyage,"* and *"Between Two Worlds"* all draw me in, lifting my mind and spirit to new heights of imagination. These compositions invite me to soar, to embrace the unknown, and to feel that sense of awe.

This wonderment is not just about distant galaxies or abstract ideas. It is about the wonder of humanity itself—our passions, emotions, intellect, and ideals. It is wonderment to look at the world and see the intricacies of human behavior, our divisions and unity, our striving and failures. It is wonderment to observe the ever-changing, ever-expanding universe, and to seek answers from the minds of astrophysicists and philosophers alike, who search for deeper understanding of the cosmos and our place within it.

To explore the universe is also to explore ourselves. Who are we? Where do we come from? What is our purpose? What happens when we die? These questions lead us to bow before the mysteries of existence, not in fear or submission, but in reverence. We wonder because we *desire to know*. And when we learn something new, we do not simply accept it—we contemplate it, reflect on it, and experience it through wonderment. This process deepens our appreciation for ourselves, for others, and for the world we inhabit.

But there is a troubling shift. As wonderment fades, we grow complacent. We become resigned to the ordinary, content with the status quo, and immune to the allure of the unknown. The common man clings to conventional beliefs, to outdated traditions, and to superficial dogmas, repeating phrases like *"It is what it is"* without a second thought. This mindset leads to stagnation, to intellectual apathy. It is a retreat from the richness of wonderment, a surrender to the safe and the familiar.

In the face of this widespread indifference, I feel a sense of disquiet. Too many have surrendered their curiosity, their wonder, and their drive for discovery to the comfort of repetition. They have accepted the limits of what is known and are content to remain in a state of passive acceptance. The loss of wonderment is the loss of meaning. It is the loss of the very thing that drives us forward—the unquenchable thirst to understand, to explore, to be amazed.

If we want to reclaim the depth of human experience, we must rekindle our sense of wonder. We must begin by questioning again, by seeking to understand the world not just as it is, but as it could be. In this way, we rediscover the power of wonderment—a force that has the potential to transform us, to inspire us, and to lead us into a future where we are not just existing, but truly living.

Prove Yourself

Examine your own work
>   To see if it is of God.
Examine your own motives
>   To see if they are of God.
Examine your own deeds
>   To see if they are of God.
Prove yourself
>   To see whether you
>   Abide with God, And He with you.
Prove yourself
>   To see whether you
>   Live in Christ, And He in you.
Prove yourself
>   To see whether you
>   Testify to the Spirit, and He to you.
Let the Almighty prove you
>   To show that His power
>   Dwells within you.
Let the Prince prove you
>   To show that His peace
>   Dwells within you.
Let the Comforter prove you
>   To show that His gentleness
>   Dwells within you.
Prove yourself
>   To see whether you are of the faith.
Prove yourself
>   To see whether you pass the test.

Prove yourself
> To see whether you are pretending to be
> Someone whom you are not.

Prove yourself
> To see whether you are doing the
> Good deeds of God.

J.O.Y.

J.O.Y. is a myth
> Of one of those supposed
> Spiritual Truths.

J.O.Y. can become an endless
> Loop of Frustration,
> Guilt, and Legalism.

J.O.Y. is deciphered as Jesus, Others, Yourself;
> And one must live out one's life
> In the same order of the letters
> To acquire J.O.Y.

But when one Considers
> The results of trying
> To live up to J.O.Y.'s formula
> One can agree that
> It becomes Hopeless,
> Forming the acronym 'HELL'.

JOY is acquired by
> Living for yourself.

Living for yourself
> Will include God in your day from
> The very beginning.

Time spent with God
>   Is not putting God first;
>   It is putting yourself first
>   And allowing God to accompany you.
To put others ahead of yourself
>   All the time is
>   Neglecting yourself.
It is loving others
>   More than you love yourself.
We were not created
>   To give in this manner.
We were created
>   To freely give as we receive.
We were called
>   To love others as we love ourselves.
The only formula by which one
>   Can achieve JOY
>   Is living for yourself first.

Doing Good

A virtuous activity of soul
>   Is what doing good is all about.
It is rooted both in the
>   Heart of feeling and in the
>   Mind of reason.
It is looking to the good of others,
>   Through a sociological lens,
>   Respecting individual beliefs,
>   And therefore, doing justice to them.

It is looking to the good of self,
    Through metaphysical thought
    Contemplating the Creator's handiwork,
    And therefore, honoring Him above any other.
Doing good does not use
    A standard of measure
    To judge or define 'appropriate'
    Action or behavior.
Doing good does not use
    Principle alone, but in discernment
    Includes the application of the
    Principle in the situation.
Doing good does not use
    Childish tactics in a manner of
    Destroying the Creator's handiwork
    Through His bountiful grace.
Doing good uses the
    Constitutional law that preserves
    The value of others.
Doing good looks to the One rational
    Principle of the universe
    As a guide to impartiality.
Doing good seeks reconciliation of
    Relations at all times though love.

Ideas to Life-Affirmation

How one becomes what one is,
    Is the art of self-preservation,
    That is, selfishness.

That one becomes what one is,

> Presupposes that one does not have
>
> The remotest idea what one is.

The philologist wittingly says,

> 'I do not want to be taken for what I am not;
>
> And that requires that I do not
>
> Take myself for what I am not.'

The philologist describes himself as a Dionysian

> Or the decadent's opposite.

Who does honor when he chooses,

> When he admits,
>
> When he trusts.

Who tests an approaching stimulus,

> And reacts slowly
>
> To every kind.

Who believes neither in

> Misfortune nor guilt,
>
> And who knows how to forget.

Who is strong enough for everything

> To have everything turn out
>
> For the best for him.

The absurdity is that love

> Is supposed to be
>
> Something unegoistic.

One the contrary,

> One has to set firmly upon oneself,
>
> One has to stand bravely upon two legs,
>
> Otherwise, one cannot love at all.

The Riddle Of Man

When man begins to inquire,
>> He can no longer
>> Take things for granted.
Not only is the world full of riddles
>> He, himself, who asks the riddles,
>> Has become a riddle.
The question lies behind him;
>> He has found an answer
>> He is expressing it from his experience.
Man's experience is expressed
>> in his life in the
>> form of a riddle.
To evade this confusion
>> Man feels the danger of inquiry,
>> He tries to avoid it;
>> To persuade himself it does not matter.
Yet, man is aware of a deep gulf
>> That separates him to know
>> Through search and inquiry
>> That makes himself known.
Man is not merely what he is;
>> His peculiar being is
>> Characterized by that inward
>> And higher 'something.'
This element confronts him
>> With a challenge
>> It is 'over against' him.
This challenge then is not foreign
>> To man's life,
>> But comes as a call to his nature.

The call is to accept
>Responsibility for
>His own life.
Man is not only one who can ask questions
>But he is one who must ask them
>Because he does not yet know,
>And is not yet what he would *be*.
To evade the riddle of man
>Is to bring torment upon
>His own existence
>Because he does not know himself.
Is there any possibility of
>Solving the riddle of man?
How can man live if he does not
>Know what his life means?
How can man understand what his life means
>If he does not know *what* he is?

Nothingness

I reject any external authority
>That assigns to me my essence.
I retreat into the internal authority of self
>Without principles, ideals, or values.
I have stripped myself
>Of all unacceptable structure;
>The structures of knowledge,
>Moral value, human relationships.
I have alienated myself
>From the social system
>That determines human beings

And swallows their individual existence.
I am condemned to be free,
> Leaving no exit.
I live without anything to structure
> My being and my world.
I stand alone in anguish
> At the edge of the abyss.
I am my own existence,
> But my existence is Nothingness;
> I am in despair.
I am looking into emptiness and the void,
> Hoovering over the abyss in
> Fear and trembling and living
> The life of dread.
I have been thrown into
> Time and place
> For no reason.
I am engulfed in the infinite immensity of space
> Of which I am ignorant,
> Of which knows me not.
> My life is absurd.
I acknowledge death;
> I take it into my life.
> I face it with courage.
> I do this to free myself
> From the anxiety of death.
Death is the wiping out of
> My existence
> As conscious being.
Death is my nonexistence.
> Death is absurd.

I question not why then,
      But rather why now?
      My whole life is an absurdity.

Doubting To Believe

The French philosopher proposed
      "Doubting to believe."
He overthrew and destroyed
      All he ever believed.
He doubted in order to
      "Think and, therefore, exist."
He doubted in order to
      Believe certain truths to be certain.
Doubting is a precondition of philosophy
      Giving reason for beliefs and action.
Philosophy is an instrument for theology
      Giving reason for beliefs and action.
The Theologian praised philosophy as
      Theology's indispensable handmaiden.
Philosophy calls upon the mind
      To analyze and clarify for understanding.
Do I not doubt in order
      To think and, therefore, exist?
Do I not doubt in order
      To believe?
Do I not doubt in order
      To understand what I believe?
Do I not doubt in order
      To be honest with myself?

My Confidence

I stand silently before God
    Knowing He is my Rescuer;
    For salvation comes from Him alone.
I stand quietly before God
    Knowing He is my Defender;
    For salvation comes from Him alone.
I stand peacefully before God
    Knowing He is my Preserver;
    For salvation comes from Him alone.
The Lord is my Confidence,
    And has great reward;
    He alone is the confidence
    All the ends of the Earth.
The Lord is my Deliverance,
    And has great reward;
    He alone is the deliverance
    All the ends of the Earth.
The Lord is my Inheritance,
    And has great reward;
    He alone is the inheritance,
    All the ends of the Earth.
I put my confidence in God,
    Twice I have heard this:
    That mercy belongs to God;
    For salvation comes from Him alone.
I put my confidence in God,
    Twice I have heard this:
    That justice belongs to God;
    For salvation comes from Him alone.

I put my confidence in God,
        Twice I have heard this;
        That peace belongs to God;
        For salvation comes from Him alone.

The Problem Of Consciousness

Man who is ever more conscious
        Of himself as a social animal
        Did he learn to become conscious of himself.
That consciousness does not really
        Belong to the existence of man
        As an individual, but rather to that in him
        Which is community and herd.
Community is that which rules his actions and
        Translates them into consciousness
        They are no longer personal or unique.
Community is that which is universal and common
        Becomes shallow, thin, and superficial
        Making increasing consciousness a danger,
        Yes, even an illness.

Staying At Home

To 'stay at home'
        Is not always a good thing to do.
To 'stay at home'
        Is to renounce the reverence of life.

To 'stay at home'
>Is to limit the perspective of reality.

To 'stay at home'
>Is like a delicate apathetic loafer.

He shudders:
>Why half turned to the
>Problem of growing heights?

His wandering opens his eyes
>To the problem of order of rank.

He recalls:
>Why so narrow to the
>Problem of neediest?

His illumination
>Touches his heart to the
>Problem of right perspective.

"I am free," he says;
>I am free to draw near to life.

"I am free," he says;
>I am free to adventure and growth.

"I am free," he says;
>I am free to learn perspective
>In every value judgement.

"I am free," he says;
>I am free to create life.

The Wanderer and His Shadow

I knew Ed needed love;
>I gave him love.

I knew Ed needed shelter;
>I gave him shelter.

I knew Ed needed clothes;
> I gave him clothes.

I knew Ed needed food;
> I gave him food.

Ed beheld I was his guide;
> I beheld he was my guide.

Ed beheld I was an angel;
> I beheld he was my angel.

Ed beheld I was his projection;
> I beheld he was my projection.

Ed beheld I was a Christian;
> I beheld he was a child of God.

AFTERWORD

Knowledge brings freedom and calmness. Ignorance brings chaos and anxiety.

Today, the world is noisier than it was thirty-five years ago. At that time, the world was rapidly changing, and the population was approximately 5 billion. The Internet did not exist at that time but was expected to emerge in three to five years. Today the world population is 8 billion, with over 5.3 billion Internet users. Due to numerous ways to connect quickly and efficiently through Internet technology, the world has become smaller and louder, making it challenging to find one's *own voice.*

In 1954, Martin Heidegger observed, *"Most thought-provoking is that we are still not thinking—not even yet, although the state of the world is becoming constantly more thought-provoking."*[300] Thinking thought-provoking thoughts reminds us of who we are—human beings, and where we belong—in a thought-provoking and changing world.

Since Heidegger's time, globalization has transformed the world by facilitating the exchange of goods and services through the connectivity of the Internet. Globalization prompts us to reflect on what it means to be human in a rapidly changing world. However, the ideological systems that shape our thinking can stifle our ability to express ourselves thoughtfully and responsibly, as we often feel constrained by their influence.

A mental repetition of a thought is how learning can occur "on the way" to *thinking.*[301, 302] But before any thought can be formed, the mind must first be provided with something to think about—only then can a thought be captured and put into action.[303,] Thoughts, after all, are fleeting; they come and go in an instant. It's important to write them down when they appear, before they slip away.[304] I remember countless nights in my college dorm when I'd suddenly wake up and scribble down a thought on paper before it faded from my mind. I still do the same today, but instead of writing ideas down on paper, I text myself the ideas that come to mind.

Thinking is the act of being fully present with things as they are—acknowledging them without distortion, allowing them to exist, and engaging with them alongside our own thoughts.[305] It's a self-reflective process, where we critically examine how we think about what we are thinking. This kind of thinking enables us to express ourselves authentically, shaping our unique sense of being.

In this way, thinking defines what it means to be human. The more thoughtless we become, the less we embody our humanity.[306] Learning to think is fundamentally a journey of self-discovery, where we question not only our own assumptions but also the deeply held beliefs and traditions we've accepted without question. In doing so, we reveal the true essence of who we are.

It requires clearing space for ourselves without fixating on a predetermined destination.[307] Thinking isn't easily satisfied with either our own conclusions or those of others. Instead, to think is to be in motion, constantly revisiting and refining our thoughts by learning to unlearn and learn simultaneously.[308] It's a continuous process of venturing into new, unfamiliar territory, embracing the unfamiliar, and remaining open to revision—free from the constraints of prejudice.[309]

Personal growth and authenticity come from nurturing one's being—actively supporting its existence and vitality. To achieve this, we must critically examine how societal values, and ideological systems have confined our minds, trapping us in false ways of knowing that hinder our development.

True personal growth stems from authentic learning. This idea was previously introduced, where I highlighted Francis Bacon's insights on the numerous benefits of genuine learning and drew on Plato's *Allegory of the Cave* to explore its deeper significance.

I also introduced Francis Bacon's concept of "Idols of the Mind." These *idols* reveal our biases and prejudices, leading to false knowledge and generic understandings of values. They represent misguided beliefs within ideological systems—Authority, Language, Identity, and Society—that distort our perception and hinder personal and intellectual growth. We often idolize these human-made constructs subconsciously, and as a result, fail to question them. Idols of the theater, the marketplace, the cave, and the tribe are ideological traps that obstruct our quest for true understanding, leading to intellectual stagnation and inauthenticity.[310]

The first group, *Idols of the Theater*, blindly follow the authority of powerful institutions and accept their judgments without questioning the reasoning behind them. The second group, *Idols of the Marketplace*, place excessive trust in conventional language as a neutral means of communication without questioning the complex meanings and functions that words can convey. The third group, *Idols of the Cave*, assume that one's identity is known, static, and unalterable, without considering the external influences and internal biases that shape both one's sense of self and its perceptions. The fourth group, *Idols of the Tribe,* are swayed by society's entertainment-driven distractions that shape our perceptions of reality without questioning how these diversions may be unnatural and detrimental, affecting our mental and physical well-being.

The Relevance of Bacon's "Idols of the Mind" in the 21st Century

By submitting to Bacon's Idols of the Mind, we allow our thinking to become distorted, complicit in the patterns they establish, which obscure and suppress the true, authentic self. This includes blindly following authority, placing undue trust in conventional language, assuming identity is fixed and unchanging, and being influenced by society's entertainment-driven distractions.

However, by becoming more aware of how these Idols distort our perception—without necessarily rejecting them entirely—we can harness this awareness to examine and deconstruct each Idol, thereby resisting their influence. We can engage in practices that nourish both mind and body, allowing us to uncover and cultivate our authentic selves. One such practice is studying the humanities, which deepens our understanding of ourselves, human culture, thought, and experience, fostering intellectual growth. In addition, physical activities like exercise strengthen not only the body but the mind as well, contributing to a more integrated and holistic sense of self.

Both Jesus and St. Paul urged those existing in the world to avoid being "of this world" or "conformed to this world" and its standards, due to their significant influence and control over one's existential being.[311] This caution aligns with the need to recognize the existential dangers of conforming to Bacon's *Idols of the Mind,* as outlined in this Afterword.

Section 1: Idols of the Theater—Questioning Authority

Idols of the Theater blindly follow the authority of powerful institutions and accept their judgements without questioning the reasoning behind them. These institutions are powerful entities that control societal norms and beliefs, shaping perceptions and behaviors without transparent reasoning. They manipulate public opinion through fearmongering tactics, securing support for their agendas. By exploiting fear, they pressure the public to take specific actions or avoid certain behaviors, often influencing decisions through emotional appeals rather than reasoned judgment.

These institutions are like "idols" dictating beliefs and behaviors that people adopt without questioning them. They include governments, media outlets, corporations, the military, healthcare systems, religious institutions, science organizations, banking and financial institutions, educational institutions, and cultural institutions, such as arts, entertainment, and fashion.[312]

In this section, I focus my discussion on fearmongering tactics employed in government, religion, and education. In government, I explore historical examples such as the persecution of early Christians, beheadings during the Dark Ages, the three centuries of witch hunts, the War on Terror following the 9/11 attacks, and the fear-driven responses to the Covid-19 pandemic of 2020-21. In religion, I examine Galileo's Inquisition by the Church to suppress the progression of science and look at televangelism of the prosperity gospel in the twenty-first century. In education, I critique three issues: educational curricula of indoctrination, overreliance on standardized intelligence testing, and educators creating a failure-prone environment.

Government Fearmongering Tactics to Control the Population

Persecutions of Early Christians

Two centuries before Emperor Constantine legalized Christianity in the Roman Empire in 313 CE, Christians endured brutal persecution designed to suppress their beliefs and enforce loyalty to the Roman gods. They were thrown to wild beasts or burned alive at the stake as a means of instilling fear and deterring others from converting to the faith.

The Roman authorities viewed Christians as a threat to the stability of the empire because of their refusal to worship the emperor, the traditional Roman gods, or the unconquered Sun god.[313] The Roman state promoted a form of religious and philosophical syncretism, hoping to unite the empire under a common reverence for the Sun god, while allowing other beliefs to coexist. However, Christians rejected this policy, which led to their persecution.

Roman officials also used Christians as scapegoats for disasters, blaming them for provoking the gods. One notable example is the Great Fire of Rome in 64 CE, when Emperor Nero blamed the Christians for starting the fire and labeled them "enemies of the state." This instilled fear and anxiety among the public. Authorities exploited this fear as a pretext to make Christianity illegal. To halt the spread of Christianity punishments ranged from torture to death.

The Roman government used fear as a tool for public conformity and political control by carrying out public executions, such as crucifixion, burning, and feeding Christians to wild animals in arenas. These brutal acts were intended to intimidate the populace and enforce loyalty to the state.

While the public often viewed the persecution of Christians as a form of entertainment, Christians who refused to renounce their faith were seen as martyrs, inspiring both converts and even some pagans who later embraced Christianity. One of the most famous instances of martyrdom was that of Polycarp, which took place around 155 CE.[314]

Polycarp was brought before the Governor as a public spectacle, pressured to renounce his faith. The Governor commanded him:

> 'Revile your Christ.' Polycarp's reply was, 'For eighty-six years I have served him, and he has done me no evil. How could I curse my king, who saved me?'... The Governor then said, 'I have wild beasts here. Unless you change your mind, I shall have you thrown to them. 'Why then, call them up,' said Polycarp... [The Governor] said again, 'If you do not recant, I will have you burnt to death...' Polycarp rejoined, 'The fire you threaten me with cannot go on burning for very long; after a while it goes out...' [With] a unanimous outcry [the audience] decided to ... have Polycarp burnt alive... When they realized that his body could not be destroyed by fire, the ruffians ordered one of the dagger-men to go up and stab him with his weapon.[315]

Some Christians initially offered themselves as martyrs, but at the last moment, they voluntarily renounced their faith. After much persuasion, the Governor convinced them to take an oath and offer incense to the gods.[316]

The persecution of early Christians by the Roman government can indeed be seen as a fearmongering tactic designed to protect the Roman state's religious and political authority. By stoking fear of divine retribution, social unrest, and political instability, the Roman authorities sought to compel Christians to abandon their faith in Christ and accept the Roman gods or face dire consequences. This created an atmosphere of fear and tension, in which Christians were pressured to either conform to Roman religious practices or face martyrdom, further entrenching the power of the state through the manipulation of public fear.

Beheadings in the Dark Ages

According to tradition, beheading by sword was introduced to England by William the Conquer in the eleventh century.[317] Beheading was a very visible and dramatic form of execution for public display of a ruler's power to show control over the masses in religious, moral, and political matters. This spectacle reminded the population that the ruler had the power to take life at will, reinforcing the idea that resistance or disobedience would lead to swift and certain punishment.

The events depicted in *Braveheart* (1995) can be seen as an example of a ruler's fearmongering tactic, particularly in relation to the character of King Edward I of England and his methods for maintaining control over the rebellious Scots. While the film is a historical drama and takes some liberties with actual events, it does capture key themes of fear, power, and control that were common in medieval governance.

In *Braveheart*, the execution of William Wallace (played by Mel Gibson) in 1305 is a prime example of a ruler using fear to suppress dissent.[318] Wallace, the leader of the Scottish rebellion against English rule, is captured, tortured, and ultimately executed by beheading and disembowelment in a public setting. King Edward I's goal in having Wallace executed in such a brutal manner is to send a clear message to the Scottish people: resistance to English rule would be met with devastating consequences.

At the movie's climax, Wallace is captured and thrown into prison, only to be dragged through a hostile crowd in a London town square. The jeering peasants pelt him with chicken bones, rocks, and empty mugs. He is then led to the execution platform, where he faces a grim scene: a noose, a dissection table littered with knives, and a chopping block with a massive axe.[319]

After being tortured by a rope around Wallace's neck, his limbs stretched by a crank on a table, his flesh cut by instruments of dissection to disembowel him, Wallace fights through the agonizing pain and struggles for one last breath in him and screams, "FREEEE-DOMMMMM!"[320]

The crowd had never seen courage like this; even English strangers begin to weep. The angry and defeated magistrate gave the signal to put Wallace's head on the chopping block. The executioner lifts his huge axe, and Wallace looks toward the crowd. Wallace is beheaded.[321]

This is a classic tactic of fearmongering. The graphic nature of Wallace's execution (in the film, his disembowelment and drawn-out death) serves to instill terror in the population, discouraging any further uprisings or acts of rebellion against the English crown.

The central theme of *Braveheart*—Wallace's resistance against English tyranny—also shows how fearmongering can backfire. Wallace, in defying Edward's reign, becomes a symbol of courage and resistance, encouraging the Scots to fight back despite the very real threat of violent retribution. This creates a tension where the ruler's use of fear to control is ultimately challenged by the will to fight for freedom.

Beheading as a fearmongering tactic was deeply entwined with medieval rulers' strategies for control. By creating an atmosphere of fear and demonstrating absolute power over life and death, they ensured that the masses remained obedient, and that political threats were neutralized with terrifying efficiency.

The 300-Year Witch-Hunts

The Book of Exodus (22:18) declares, "You shall not permit a sorceress to live." Between 1450 and 1750, authorities initiated widespread "witch hunts," manipulating superstition and fear of malevolent spirits to justify the persecution of vulnerable groups, particularly women. This campaign was driven by a complex interplay of religious, political, and legal forces, which fueled public fear of those accused of witchcraft. The accused were often subjected to brutal executions, typically by burning, for alleged crimes of sorcery.[322] These witchcraft trials were not only a means of enforcing moral and religious norms but also served as tools for fearmongering and public spectacle.[323]

Many of those accused of witchcraft came from the lower levels of society, and the charges against them were often based on nothing more than rumors spread by their neighbors. These neighbors, typically concerned about misfortunes they believed were caused by the witch's supposed magical powers, would sometimes accuse individuals they suspected of being witches.[324]

The confessions of those accused of witchcraft were very often offered under the most brutal torture. The account of Anna Spülerin of Ringingen was tortured so gruesomely that her limbs were mutilated and her sight and hearing lost. John Fian of Scotland underwent "boot" torture, in which "his legs were crushed and beaten together as small as might be."[325]

Among other tortures were filling the nostrils with lime and water, tying the victim to a table covered with hawthorn twigs, rolling a pin with dagger-like points up and down the spine, gouging out the eyes, chopping off the ears, squeezing the male's genital organs, and burning brandy or sulfur over the body.[326]

When an accused witch retracted a confession made under torture, judges allowed a second or even a third or fourth use of torture, thereby, violating the rule against repetition.[327] Some witches were not even given the opportunity for retraction, while others who retracted were executed anyway.[328]

In the twenty-first century, we can recognize these cruel, sadistic acts of torture as a perverse form of entertainment for the judges and spectators who watched in grim fascination. Those accused of witchcraft can now be seen as innocent victims of a deluded judiciary and an oppressive legal system.[329] Many of the confessions were coerced under such extreme duress that they drove some accused witches to take their own lives while imprisoned, as a desperate escape from the relentless torment.[330]

The defining characteristic of witchcraft was its association with magical practices believed to be harmful.[331] These practices were often categorized into "high" magic and "low" magic. High magic included pursuits like alchemy and divination. Alchemy involved the transformation of base metals into precious ones, while divination employed various methods to gain secret knowledge. Astrology and necromancy were common forms of divination: astrology used the positions of the stars and planets to predict or uncover hidden truths, while necromancy sought to communicate with the spirits of the dead for similar purposes.[332]

Low magic involved simple charms and spells, practices that are often found in books today as forms of entertainment or self-improvement. In the twenty-first century, identifying as a "witch" has become a more casual label, like how someone might identify as a "Christian"— a personal choice or lifestyle rather than a practice bound by the same intense historical context.

The witch hunts of the 15th to 18th centuries were driven by superstition, fear, and the abuse of religious, political, and legal power. Vulnerable individuals, particularly women, were accused of witchcraft and subjected to torture to force confessions. These trials aimed not only to enforce moral norms but also to instill fear. Today, the label of "witchcraft" has evolved into a casual identity, far removed from the violent persecution of the past.

The War on Terror (2001-Present)

After the 9/11 attacks, the U.S. government used fearmongering tactics to rally public support for military action in Afghanistan and Iraq, as well as for domestic surveillance programs like the Patriot Act.[333] Government officials, along with the media, consistently emphasized the threat posed by terrorism, particularly from Islamic extremists. The fear of terrorism was exploited to justify not only military intervention abroad but also the erosion of civil liberties at home, such as widespread surveillance and the profiling of Muslim communities.[334]

The Patriot Act, passed shortly after 9/11, significantly expanded the U.S. government's surveillance and investigative powers.[335] It allowed the FBI greater flexibility in national security cases, including enhanced data collection and intelligence-sharing between law enforcement and intelligence agencies.[336] While it made investigations more efficient, civil liberties groups raised alarms about privacy violations and the potential for government overreach.[337]

Viet Dinh, the former Justice Department lawyer who wrote the Patriot Act, says that despite all the criticism from civil liberties groups, most people couldn't tell you what's in the law.[338] He says, "There's no question that the USA Patriot Act has become a brand, if you will, a symbol of all the counterterrorism activities after 9/11."[339] Despite widespread criticism, many Americans remain unaware of its full scope, and it continues to be a controversial piece of legislation.

The media's coverage of terrorism, too, was dramatically shaped by the aftermath of 9/11.[340] Although terrorism existed long before 2001, the attacks turned it into a constant feature of news cycles. The "symbiotic relationship between the media and terrorism" became evident: terrorist acts provide dramatic content, while media coverage gives terrorists the publicity they crave.[341] After 9/11, the number of terrorism-related articles skyrocketed, even though attacks in Europe and North America were more frequent in the 1970s and 80s, typically involving nationalist groups.[342]

A key factor in this media shift was the rhetoric of politicians and security officials, who dominated the news agenda by framing terrorism as an imminent and emotional threat.[343] Their use of charged language fueled a climate of fear and patriotism.[344] Moreover, the rise of the Internet and social media gave terrorist groups unprecedented access to global audiences, enabling them to distribute sophisticated propaganda.[345]

However, much of the media's coverage focused on the sensational aspects of terrorism, often neglecting the political motives behind attacks.[346] This contributed to the harmful "conflation" of terrorism with Islam, particularly in the U.S. and the UK.[347] In the years after 9/11, news coverage of Islam and Muslims surged, often focusing on extremism, cultural differences, and terrorism, despite the fact that most global terrorist attacks are driven by "ethno-nationalist" rather than religious causes.[348] In the U.S., attacks involving Muslim perpetrators received disproportionate attention, further entrenching the link between Islam and terrorism.[349]

Despite this focus on Islamic terrorism, the "Global Terrorism Index" shows that most terrorist attacks and deaths occur in countries with Muslim majorities, where the causes are often linked to ethnic or nationalist conflicts.[350] This highlights a significant disconnect in how terrorism is framed in the West.

To move forward, the media must avoid sensationalizing terrorism, challenge simplistic political narratives, and dismantle harmful stereotypes that divide "us" from "them." If not, terrorism will continue to dominate the news cycle, and legislation like the Patriot Act will remain a point of contention in the ongoing battle over national security and civil liberties.

Covid-19 Pandemic of 2020-21

During the COVID-19 pandemic, governments across the world used fearmongering tactics to enforce public health measures, such as lockdowns, social distancing, and mask mandates. Public health officials and governments often emphasized the catastrophic potential of the virus, leading to widespread fear and anxiety. The portrayal of the virus as a deadly threat justified emergency powers, restrictions on personal freedoms, and rapid vaccine rollouts.

The SARS-CoV-1 (severe acute respiratory syndrome coronavirus) outbreak, which occurred from 2002 to 2004, originated in China and primarily affected East Asia, leading to 774 deaths worldwide.[351]

In May 2005, about six months after the SARS-CoV-1 outbreak, epidemiologist Dr. Michael Osterholm published an article warning of the inevitable threat of an influenza pandemic.[352] Nearly 15 years later, the COVID-19 pandemic, caused by the SARS-CoV-2 virus, was confirmed. Like its predecessor, it originated in China and, according to the World Health Organization (WHO), has since claimed nearly 7 million lives worldwide.[353]

In his 2005 article, Dr. Osterholm outlines two key steps for preparing for an influenza pandemic. The first is to conduct research on the role of various animal and bird species in the early stages of an outbreak. The second, which builds on the first, is to develop an effective vaccine in advance of a potential pandemic.[354]

Was the world prepared for an influenza pandemic? No, it was not. Did the Centers for Disease Control and Prevention (CDC) have an effective vaccine ready? No, it did not. Because of this lack of preparation, fear spread among the public, and governments exacerbated this fear by implementing lockdowns and closing schools, businesses, health clubs, and more.

During the pandemic and lockdowns, I maintained a consistent focus on fitness. When the first lockdown was announced, I viewed it as an opportunity to "keep moving forward" by staying active. I woke up at 5 a.m. each day to work out at home before going to work. Even after the second lockdown was implemented, I continued with my home workouts. By the time the first lockdown ended after 51 days, I had improved my strength, muscle mass, and definition. I recount this experience in my book, *The Fitness Mindset: 7 Habits for Peak Performance.*[355]

The role of psychology in the use of fear by governments worldwide during the COVID-19 response was unprecedented, leading to a global standstill and a significant decline in people's well-being from 2020 to 2021. The CDC's push for mandatory vaccinations—despite their limited effectiveness in preventing the spread of COVID-19—only worsened the public's declining trust in the agency.[356]

In England, scientists on a committee that advocated for "using fear to control people's behavior" during the COVID pandemic have admitted that their approach was "unethical" and "totalitarian."[357] According to these scientists, the use of fear amounted to mind control and created a dystopian environment.[358]

One member of the Scientific Pandemic Influenza Group on Behaviour (SPI-B) cautioned that "people use the pandemic to grab power and drive through things that wouldn't happen otherwise... We have to be very careful about the authoritarianism that is creeping in."[359]

The deputy chairman of the Covid Recovery Group (CRG) criticized the government, stating, "the decision to terrify the public to get compliance with rules ... raises extremely serious questions about the type of society we want to become."[360]

The fear-driven response to the pandemic, with its widespread lockdowns, led to greater inequality in income distribution and wealth, widespread job losses, significant declines in spending, and a general worsening of economic conditions. It also resulted in serious declines in mental health and well-being, limited access to healthcare, and record-high levels of domestic violence.[361]

With regard to taking a heavy toll on the public's mental health and well-being, the fear-driven measures during the pandemic contributed to heightened isolation, loneliness, job loss, financial insecurity, illness, grief, and feelings of hopelessness.[362] Anxiety, depression, drug overdoses, alcohol-related deaths, and suicides all rose significantly during and after the COVID-19 crisis.[363] In fact, 90% of U.S. adults believe the country is facing a mental health crisis.[364]

The COVID-19 pandemic highlighted significant failures in global preparedness and exposed the detrimental effects of fear-driven public health measures. Despite early warnings from experts like Dr. Michael Osterholm, the world was ill-prepared for a pandemic of this scale, resulting in a reactive, fear-based response. Governments, leveraging psychological tactics to enforce compliance, imposed lockdowns and other measures that severely impacted the economy, mental health, and social stability. The resulting isolation, financial hardships, and public anxiety underscored the need for more balanced, transparent approaches to crisis management. Ultimately, the pandemic's toll went beyond the virus itself, leaving lasting scars on the well-being of individuals and societies worldwide.

Religion's Fearmongering Tactics to Control Belief

The Inquisition of Galileo

The Church's inquisition of Galileo was a fearmongering tactic within the realms of scientific, religious, philosophical, and Church authority. The inquisition, which culminated in Galileo's condemnation in 1633, was primarily driven by the Catholic Church's desire to maintain its power and control over the scientific, religious, and intellectual life.

The Scientific Revolution began with the publication of Nicolaus Copernicus' *On the Revolution of the Heavenly Spheres* in 1543, where he introduced the heliocentric model of the solar system, challenging the long-established geocentric view.

When Galileo published *Dialogue Concerning the Two Chief World Systems* in 1632, he directly challenged the centuries long geocentric belief of the universe.[365] I read this work over two decades ago in about two months. Galileo frames his arguments in the form of a dialogue among three characters. The first character, "Salviati," is Galileo himself, representing the heliocentric view of the universe, which places the Sun at the center, with the Earth and other planets orbiting around it. The second character, "Segredo," represents the educated layperson who is open to new ideas and is willing to learn. The third character, "Simplicio," represents the Catholic Church and the teachings of Aristotle, Ptolemy, and Pope Urban VIII who upheld the geocentric view of the universe, which places the Earth is the center of the universe and that all celestial bodies, including the Sun, Moon, planets, and stars, revolve around it.

In *The Two Chief World Systems*, Galileo compares the heliocentric model of the universe with the geocentric model. The latter, supported by Aristotle and endorsed by the Catholic Church for nearly 2,000 years, was firmly entrenched in both scientific thinking and religious doctrine. At the time, questioning the Church's authority was inconceivable.

Galileo championed the heliocentric model, directly opposing the Aristotelian view and the teachings of the Catholic Church. In doing so, he fell out of favor with the Church and became the target of the Inquisition, which carried the threat of imprisonment or even death. Fortunately, Galileo was never executed. Instead, in 1633, he was sentenced by the Inquisition and placed under house arrest, where he would remain for the last nine years of his life.

Galileo's contemporary, René Descartes (the philosopher famous for "I think, therefore I am"), reached the same conclusion as Galileo and claims that his entire philosophy "can be demonstrated" from the heliocentric perspective.[366] However, upon hearing that "Galileo had been convicted and fined" by the Church, Descartes "decided to burn all [his] papers," realizing that, like Galileo, he too had concluded that "the Earth moves."[367] Descartes further acknowledged that "if the [heliocentric] view is false," then the "entire foundations" of his philosophy would be called into question, since he believed it could be clearly "demonstrated" from his work.[368]

At this point, we should pause to reflect on Descartes' decision not to support Galileo and reconsider the implications for Descartes' own philosophy. Descartes himself confessed that he "did not want to publish a discourse in which a single word could be found that the Church would have disapproved of," and thus, chose to "suppress it" rather than risk publishing it.[369] This raises important questions about Descartes' willingness to compromise on his intellectual integrity in the face of Church authority.

In 1644, the same year of Galileo's death, Descartes published his *Principles of Philosophy,* which asserts that "the Earth ... is not moved, nor are any of the planets."[370] Descartes died in 1650, and today he is widely considered the father of modern philosophy, largely due to his departure from the traditional scholastic-Aristotelian framework of his time.

However, as the quote above suggests, Descartes did not fully break from the prevailing ideas—at least not publicly. In his attempt to maintain favor with the Church, he chose caution over conviction. But in doing so, Descartes did more than merely compromise; he inadvertently undermined his own philosophical foundation. By adhering to outdated astronomical views, he turned the very core of his philosophy on its head, ultimately betraying the intellectual revolution he had set out to lead.

It took a bold and fearless mind like Galileo's—one unafraid to challenge the Church—to demonstrate and prove the heliocentric model of the universe. Meanwhile, Descartes, the philosopher who famously declared "I think, therefore I am," stood at a distance, seeming to shy away from direct confrontation.

For centuries, education has been shaped by a specific, often prejudiced historical worldview—rooted in culture, race, religion, and other biases—that seeks to indoctrinate rather than encourage independent thought. Questioning authority has long been seen as heretical, and in some circles, it still is.

The Church's inquisition of Galileo exemplifies the lengths to which institutions of power will go to preserve their dominance, even at the cost of stifling intellectual progress and scientific discovery. Galileo's challenge to the geocentric model, rooted in centuries of tradition and Church doctrine, not only marked a pivotal moment in the Scientific Revolution but also exposed the tension between emerging scientific thought and entrenched religious authority.

While figures like Descartes chose caution and self-censorship to maintain favor with the Church, Galileo's unflinching commitment to truth, despite the threat of persecution, highlighted the fundamental importance of intellectual courage in the face of oppressive authority. This affair serves as a reminder of the dangers of suppressing dissent and the value of fostering environments where critical thinking and the questioning of established beliefs are encouraged. It is a cautionary account about the limits of power when it is used to silence innovation and the enduring legacy of those who, like Galileo, dare to challenge the status quo.

The Prosperity Gospel

Prominent televangelists like Joel Osteen, Pat Robertson, Jim Bakker, and Kenneth Copeland use television and social media to reach millions of viewers globally, often promoting a version of Christianity intertwined with prosperity theology. Prosperity theology, also known as the "prosperity gospel" or "health and wealth gospel," teaches that God rewards faithfulness with material blessings such as financial success, physical well-being, and wealth.[371] Prosperity theology often quotes Malachi 3:10:

> 'Bring all the tithes into the storehouse, that there may be food in My house, and try Me now in this,' says the Lord of hosts, 'if I will not open for you the windows of heaven and pour out for you such blessing that there will not be room enough to receive it.'

While prosperity theology focuses on material blessings, Malachi 3:10 is ultimately about trusting God with our resources. The promise of blessing goes beyond wealth, reflecting God's provision and faithfulness in all areas of life, not just financial gain.

Followers are encouraged to make contributions to religious organizations or "seed faith" offerings, believing that these actions will bring divine favor and lead to increased health, wealth, and success.[372] This theology suggests that poverty, illness, and hardship are signs of insufficient faith or failure to live according to God's will, with some preachers teaching that God desires believers to be wealthy and healthy.[373]

However, the prosperity theology distorts Christian teachings by focusing too much on material wealth and exploiting vulnerable individuals for financial gain.[374] It also creates unrealistic expectations, leading to guilt and inadequacy among those who do not see the promised material rewards. At the heart of the prosperity gospel is the televangelists value. At the heart of the Gospels, and all of Scripture, is God's value.

The prosperity gospel employs fearmongering tactics in several ways. First, followers are urged to contribute financially, with promises of material blessings in return. Second, it manipulates faith by connecting spiritual devotion to financial donations, often overlooking the individual's spiritual health. Third, believers are led to believe that their contributions will result in divine favor, offering earthly rewards rather than spiritual salvation.

This modern-day prosperity gospel shares similarities with the sale of indulgences during the Middle Ages.[375] Both involve financial contributions with the promise of spiritual or material rewards. In the case of indulgences, people could pay for forgiveness or a reduction in time spent in 'purgatory.' The sale of indulgences often undermined genuine repentance, and similarly, the prosperity gospel can exploit believers for financial gain.

Today, televangelism generates a staggering $156 billion annually, with new figures emerging each year, claiming to offer miracles and divine messages of prosperity. They promote these messages by appealing to emotions and often exploiting a "herd mentality" to gather support, encouraging followers to make financial contributions in exchange for blessings. Kenneth Copeland, for example, has amassed a fortune of $750 million. His refusal to disclose details about his lavish lifestyle, including the cost of his private jet, raises concerns about the integrity of such leaders and the exploitation of their followers' generosity.[376]

Televangelists and bestselling authors often use fearmongering to secure wealth, preying on people's desire for eternal life while offering false assurances that financial donations are the key to securing this future. This fear-driven approach exploits uncertainty about the afterlife, capitalizing on people's hopes and anxieties.[377]

While the promise of eternal life can provide comfort, we must acknowledge the uncertainty surrounding it. Televangelists who exploit this uncertainty for financial gain manipulate people's fears, offering false assurances that donations will guarantee divine rewards. Instead of focusing on material wealth or fear of the afterlife, we should aim to live meaningful lives rooted in love, kindness, and personal growth. By focusing on the present, we can make a positive impact on others and leave a legacy based on our true values, rather than being swayed by empty promises of prosperity.

Education's Fearmongering Tactics Limiting Human Potential

Education plays a crucial function in shaping individuals by influencing their thoughts, behaviors, and interactions with others, ultimately affecting their choices and contributing to the development of their personal identities.

First, educational curricula often serve to reinforce indoctrination by emphasizing specialized and technical knowledge, preparing students primarily for vocational roles. Second, education continues to rely on standardized testing as a measure of intelligence, as if all individuals possess the same intellectual abilities. Finally, educators sometimes adopt an "us" vs. "them" mindset, creating an environment of fear that leads students to believe they are failures.

Indoctrinated teaching, an overreliance on standardized intelligence testing, and the creation of a failure-prone environment all point to a biased form of education, akin to the counterfeit or false education described in Plato's *Allegory of the Cave,* which I discussed in the Introduction.

True education, in contrast, is a process of fostering, nurturing, and cultivating—concepts that imply the "conditions of growth."[378] In this context, the essential factor for both personal and social development is immaturity.[379] While this may seem like an obvious fact, growth can only occur when we are in a state of underdevelopment, which further implies that no one, no human, is ever fully developed.[380] This underscores the idea that growth thrives on the fluidity and continuity of life, enabling the ongoing *potential* for self-development through continuous action toward one's *capacity* for growth over the course of a lifetime.

Educational Curricula of Indoctrination

The current K-12 educational system is often criticized for prioritizing indoctrination over genuine learning. The "elective system" encourages students to focus on areas that offer quick job market benefits, but this narrow specialization overlooks the broader development of critical thinking and creativity.[381]

True learning requires active engagement and discovery, rather than passive absorption or rote memorization.[382] In contrast, indoctrination occurs when students are taught through "instruction," expected to accept information without question or critical analysis—what Adler refers to as "naked authority."[383]

Learning and thinking are interconnected processes, but learning must come first. It involves acquiring knowledge or skills, while thinking requires the application of this knowledge to reason, solve problems, and reflect. Genuine learning cannot occur without activity on the part of the learner, as it is essentially a process of discovery.[384] This is reflected in Plato's *Allegory of the Cave,* where the transition from ignorance to knowledge is a shift facilitated by active engagement rather than passive instruction.

Adler, in his *Paideia Proposal* (1982), stresses the importance of an educational system that fosters lifelong learning by promoting intellectual development through three interconnected methods:

1. *Acquisition of knowledge* through didactic instruction.

2. *Development of intellectual skills* through coaching and supervised practice.

3. *Enlargement of understanding and insight* through Socratic questioning and active participation.[385]

This educational approach encourages a balance of knowledge acquisition, skill development, and intellectual engagement, preparing students not just for a career, but for thoughtful, informed participation in life.[386] While this approach may seem overly idealistic for implementation within the school system, it remains within our power to embrace these ideals and become self-educated, self-reliant individuals on our own.

Moreover, specialized knowledge gained through indoctrination often leads to the neglect of subjects crucial for broader intellectual growth.[387] Adler argues for a *generalist,* humanistic curriculum—one that emphasizes the "essentials of basic schooling" over *specialized* or vocational education.[388] Such a curriculum should include subjects like the arts, science, history, philosophy, and transcendental forms, for instance, the history of humankind, the science of human behavior, the philosophy of humankind, etc.[389] These name one and the same subject matter, but can take on different forms when approached historically, scientifically, and philosophically. Similarly, we speak of natural history, natural science, and the philosophy of nature.[390] This broad-based, humanistic education fosters a richer intellectual life and prepares students for lifelong learning, rather than narrowly preparing them for specific careers.

In essence, education should cultivate not just technical skills, but wisdom, knowledge, and understanding—goods of the mind that can be used for the betterment of society.[391] A well-rounded, humanistic approach to learning ensures that students develop into well-rounded, thoughtful individuals capable of critical thinking and active engagement in their communities.

The current educational system emphasizes specialized knowledge that focuses on vocational skills rather than a broad, general education that fosters critical thinking and personal growth. True learning, according to thinkers like Plato and Adler, involves active discovery and intellectual engagement, not passive absorption or rote memorization. Adler advocates for a more holistic approach to education, one that prioritizes the development of the mind through a generalist, humanistic curriculum. This curriculum should include a wide range of subjects—such as the arts, sciences, history, and philosophy—taught through discovery, intellectual skill development, and Socratic questioning. Such an approach would better prepare students for lifelong learning and personal growth.

Overreliance on Standardized Intelligence Testing

A young girl spends an hour with an examiner, answering various questions that assess her knowledge. Afterward, the examiner assigns a single score, her Intelligence Quotient (IQ). This score can significantly influence her future, shaping how teachers perceive her and determining her eligibility for certain opportunities. However, the importance placed on this number does not necessarily predict her later success.

Howard Gardner is recognized for his theory of "multiple intelligences," which expands the concept of human potential beyond traditional measures like IQ testing. Contrary to the belief in a single, static intelligence, he argues that intelligence exists in distinct forms, which can overlap with one another.

Gardner's 1983 *Frames of Mind: The Theory of Multiple Intelligences* challenges the traditional view of intelligence as a single, general ability.[392] Instead, Gardner suggests that intelligence consists of various distinct types. His theory critiques the conventional perspective of intelligence, which many people internalize either explicitly through psychology and educational texts or implicitly from a culture with a narrow view of intelligence.[393] Gardner calls his approach a "revisionist" theory, arguing that compelling evidence supports the existence of multiple, *relatively autonomous* human intellectual competencies—referred to as "frames of mind."[394]

Gardner's theory is based on two key principles. First, it highlights the *flexibility of human development.*[395] Second, it emphasizes the *identity or nature of the intellectual capacities* that humans can develop.[396] Gardner's 1983 definition of intelligence described it as "the ability to solve problems or create products that are valued in one or more cultural settings."[397] Two decades later, he refined this to *"a biopsychological potential to process information that can be activated in a cultural setting to solve problems or create products that are of value in a culture."*[398] This updated definition suggests that intelligences are not tangible entities but potential capacities—neural ones—that may or may not be activated.[399]

Gardner's theory of multiple intelligences asserts that humans possess various kinds of intelligences rather than a single general intelligence. These intelligences include linguistic, musical, logical-mathematical, spatial, bodily-kinesthetic, interpersonal, and intrapersonal intelligences, offering a more comprehensive view of human capability.

In *Frames of Mind*, Gardner introduces the idea that several distinct intelligences exist. However, he acknowledged that these intelligences are *not* physical entities but scientific constructs with *potential* utility.[400]

- *Linguistic Intelligence* (word smart): The ability to use language effectively, excelling in reading, writing, storytelling, and language learning. Examples include writers, poets, and journalists.[401]

- *Musical Intelligence* (music smart): Sensitivity to pitch, rhythm, and tone. Examples include musicians, composers, and singers.[402]

- *Logical-Mathematical Intelligence* (number/reasoning smart): The capacity for logical reasoning, problem-solving, and mathematical analysis. Examples include scientists, engineers, and mathematicians.[403]

- *Spatial Intelligence* (picture smart): The ability to visualize and manipulate objects in space. Examples include architects, artists, and pilots.[404]

- *Bodily-Kinesthetic Intelligence* (body smart): The ability to use the body effectively for expression or problem-solving. Examples include athletes, dancers, and surgeons.[405]

- *Interpersonal Intelligence* (people smart): The ability to understand and interact effectively with others. Examples include teachers, therapists, and politicians.[406]

- *Intrapersonal Intelligence* (self smart): Self-awareness and the ability to reflect on one's emotions, motivations, and goals. Examples include psychologists and philosophers.[407]

Gardner's theory emphasizes the variety of intelligences that individuals may possess, advocating for more diverse and flexible approaches to education that reflect the different ways people learn and contribute to society. He notes that linguistic and logical-mathematical intelligences are most valued in traditional education systems and society.

In his 1999 book *Intelligence Reframed: Multiple Intelligences for the 21st Century*, he suggests that other potential intelligences, such as naturalistic, spiritual, existential, and moral intelligence, might exist, but he argues that these do not meet the criteria he originally set for inclusion. The excluded intelligences are:

- *Naturalistic Intelligence*: Although Gardner acknowledged the ability to recognize and categorize elements of the natural world (such as the work of biologists or environmentalists), he ultimately excluded it because it lacked clear evidence of being a separate, autonomous cognitive function.[408]

- *Spiritual Intelligence:* While Gardner recognized that spirituality is an important aspect of human life, he excluded it from his theory because there was no clear empirical evidence supporting it as a separate cognitive domain. Spirituality, according to Gardner, is a personal and subjective experience that does not fit into his framework for intelligences, which are based on observable and measurable capacities.[409]

- *Existential Intelligence:* Gardner agreed that existential concerns (such as the meaning of life, death, and human existence) are important but argues these issues are philosophical or spiritual in nature, rather than a distinct form of intelligence. He felt that existential concerns did not qualify as independent cognitive abilities because they did not meet the criteria for being scientifically observable and measurable.[410]

- *Moral Intelligence:* Gardner argues moral reasoning is more about personal, cultural, and societal values than about a specific cognitive ability. He believed that moral reasoning is not an independent intelligence but rather a reflection of broader ethical considerations that are influenced by cultural and personal contexts.[411]

Gardner excluded these types of intelligence because they did not meet the specific criteria he set for intelligences: they were not distinct, observable cognitive functions that could be clearly measured and activated in different cultural contexts.

In a May 2003 email to Howard Gardner, I inquired about the potential impact of his theory on U.S. public schools. He responded:

My theory can reinforce the idea that individuals have many talents that can be of use to society; that a single measure (like a high-stakes test) is inappropriate for determining graduation, access to college, etc.; and that important materials can be taught in many ways, activating a range of intelligences.[412]

Gardner's emphasis on recognizing multiple intelligences challenges the narrow approach of traditional testing and highlights the need for a more holistic view of student potential. By moving beyond high-stakes tests, educators can better appreciate the diverse talents that students possess, fostering an environment where learning is more inclusive and tailored to individual strengths. This vision, if fully implemented, could transform the educational landscape, creating opportunities for students who might otherwise be overlooked or undervalued in a standardized system.

The overreliance on standardized intelligence testing, such as IQ tests, has limited views on human potential. Howard Gardner's Theory of Multiple Intelligences challenges this by suggesting that intelligence is not a single, fixed trait, but rather a collection of distinct types, including linguistic, musical, logical-mathematical, spatial, bodily-kinesthetic, and "the personal intelligences." Gardner emphasizes that these intelligences reflect diverse human capabilities that traditional tests often overlook. His theory advocates for a more flexible educational approach, recognizing that each individual has unique strengths. By moving away from high-stakes testing, educators can create more inclusive learning environments that better reflect students' varied talents.

Creating a Failure-Prone Environment

I walked into my professor's office, where he also served as my advisor and the director of the graduate school of religion. After sitting down across from his desk, I expressed my desire to pursue further education by teaching religion in K-12 schools. I planned to enroll in the religious education graduate program after finishing my undergraduate degree in religious studies. His response, however, was immediate and discouraging. He pointed out that with my low GPA of 2.5, acceptance into the program seemed unlikely. He made it clear that a GPA of at least 3.0 was required.

His words struck a chord, leaving me both frustrated and motivated to prove him wrong. My professor challenged me to apply my intellectual abilities.

Determined to improve, I worked tirelessly during my final year of undergraduate studies, achieving a 3.5 GPA and raising my cumulative GPA to 2.8. While I knew it still wasn't enough to guarantee acceptance into the graduate program, I refused to give up. That summer, I stayed with my mother in northern Michigan and registered for the Graduate Record Examination (GRE) in Chicago. Despite my best efforts, I struggled with the test, particularly the sections on linguistic and logical-mathematical reasoning, areas where I was not strong. When I received my failing results, it felt like I had confirmed my professor's belief that I wouldn't succeed.

However, when I met with my professor in southern California in the fall, he was surprised by my improved academic performance. Despite my poor GRE results, I finished my final quarter with a 3.9 GPA while handling an overload in course work. He seemed impressed, and to my amazement, I was accepted into the graduate program. Although I eventually dropped out after the first two quarters to return to Japan for a second visit, I left with a 3.7 GPA.

Reflecting on this journey, I realized how academic environments often create an "us vs. them" mentality, fixating on failure, grades, and standardized tests. Educators frequently use fear tactics, emphasizing the consequences of failure—such as not being accepted into esteemed institutions or facing the anxiety of high-stakes exams. In my case, the professor's negative comments, while discouraging, ultimately fueled my determination and increased my motivation.

Even years later when I enrolled in a graduate philosophy program at a local university, I faced setbacks. Despite my perseverance, my efforts were dismissed by those in authority, and I was rejected for the third and last time. Still, I refused to quit. I pressed on, driven by my love for learning. Eventually, I enrolled in a different university that not only supported me but also valued my work, recognizing my master's thesis as being comparable to a doctoral dissertation.

This experience reinforced my belief that the education system needs to shift its focus from grades to growth. Teachers should foster a growth mindset, focusing on the learning process rather than just the final outcomes. By offering constructive feedback, encouraging revisions, and supporting personal progress, educators can help students build resilience and confidence. Intelligence and abilities are not fixed traits—they can be nurtured through effort and perseverance, as I discovered during my graduate studies.

Fear-driven tactics in education—overemphasizing failure, grades, and high-stakes testing—create an environment of anxiety and pressure. A shift toward a growth-oriented approach that prioritizes the learning process, personal development, and constructive feedback will help students overcome fear, build confidence, and ultimately thrive.

Summary of Idols of the Theater

Idols of the Theater refer to powerful institutions—such as governments, media, corporations, religion, and education—that manipulate public perception through fearmongering tactics. These institutions shape societal norms and beliefs, pressuring individuals to conform without questioning their motives. Fear is used to control behavior and emotions, often overriding reasoned judgment.

Historical examples of fear-based manipulation include the persecution of early Christians by the Roman Empire, medieval beheadings, the witch hunts, the War on Terror, and the COVID-19 pandemic. Governments and religious institutions have often used fear to maintain power, as seen in the Church's persecution of Galileo for challenging established beliefs, and modern televangelism exploiting fear of the afterlife for financial gain.

In education, institutions have historically emphasized indoctrination rather than critical thinking, with standardized testing limiting students' intellectual potential. The Theory of Multiple Intelligences challenges the traditional view of intelligence, advocating for a more inclusive approach that recognizes diverse talents. Additionally, the pressure from high-stakes testing creates anxiety, hindering personal and intellectual growth.

This discussion urges a critical examination of these institutions and the fear-based tactics they use, advocating for a shift toward environments that foster independent thought, intellectual curiosity, and personal development. By challenging authority and questioning deceptive narratives, societies can foster environments that empower individuals to think critically and lead fulfilling lives.

Section 2: Idols of the Marketplace—Questioning Language

Idols of the Marketplace place excessive trust in conventional language as a neutral means of communication without questioning the complex meanings and functions that words can convey. People often assume language is a straightforward means for conveying meaning, without realizing that words can have various interpretations, implications, and functions. By treating language as "neutral," they overlook the fact that words can carry biases, cultural influences, or multiple layers of meaning, which can shape or distort communication in ways they don't always recognize.

This perspective calls for a more critical awareness of how language functions, emphasizing that it is not just a transparent medium for communication, but a force that can shape—and be shaped by—our thoughts and perceptions of the world, depending on how language is defined and used. These "idols" include words, terms, notions, concepts, and labels, all of which are defined by authority figures or cultural norms. The public often accepts these commonly understood meanings as straightforward, using them as a means of communication based on their accepted definitions.

In this analysis, I examine various words, terms, notions, concepts, and labels, explore the idea of the multiple uses of "language games," discuss how language can be manipulated for personal gain, and highlight the limitations of language within a cultural context.

The Concept of 'God'

Basic meanings are words that directly represent objects we are familiar, like "tree." Specific meanings are terms that carry particular significance within a context, such as "democracy." Abstract meanings are concepts, which represent the broader ideas conveyed by words or terms, like the concepts of 'God' or 'freedom.' Consider the definition of the concept of 'God' below:

> *God:* Supreme Being; Creator; Ultimate reality; Object of
> faith; Eternal; Source of all moral authority.

'God' is defined in various imaginative ways by monotheistic religions and philosophers. In Judaism, 'God' is described in *Exodus* as "I Am Who I Am" (3:14). Christianity refers to 'God' as the "Savior" in *Luke* (1:47), while Islam defines 'God' or "Allah" in the *Quran* as the "One" (42:11). Aristotle, in his *Metaphysics*, defines 'God' as the "Unmoved Prime Mover" (1072b7-10). The idea that 'God' is the source of all moral authority is known as the "Euthyphro Dilemma." Named after Plato's *Euthyphro* (10a), this philosophical problem explores the relationship between God and morality. Paul Tillich, mentioned earlier in the Introduction, defines 'God' as the "Ultimate Reality" in his book, *The Courage To Be*.

'God' is often defined in anthropomorphic terms, meaning that 'God' is the projection of an ideal image of humanity's capabilities created by human beings.[413] There are nearly as many gods as there are speakers and worshippers by that name. Therefore, it is not accurate to say that 'God' exists in a singular form; rather, gods exist—each shaped by a variety of perceptions, influenced by individual beliefs, group identities, and societal values. People worship many gods and often exploit their own definitions of 'God' to serve their purposes.

Notions like 'good,' 'evil,' 'right,' and 'wrong' are rooted in the traditions and cultures we are born into. We tend to accept these definitions as unquestionable terms, using them according to the norms of our society. Consider the definition of the notions below:

Good: Attractive; Handsome; Profitable; Favorable; Health.

Evil: Pain; Suffering; Disease; Absence of Good; Immoral; Wicked.

Right: Good; Just; Proper; Suitable; Appropriate; Conforming to facts or truth.

Wrong: Unjust; Dishonest; Immoral; Illegal; Offense; Injury; Crime.

To challenge these widely accepted meanings is often seen as endorsing their opposites. However, because we live in a series of situations interacting with one another, what is considered "wrong" might be "right," what is deemed "right" could be "wrong," what is labeled "evil" might be "good," and what is understood as "good" could be perceived as "evil."[414] Similarly, 'God' might be viewed as a delusion or a source of division rather than a unifying force.

Here's the problem: when a definition is attached to a word, a distinction is created, and the word becomes fixed in meaning. Yet, the definition of a word is constantly evolving because language itself is always changing, especially in the complex landscape of communication in the twenty-first century.

Some words function as both terms and concepts. Consider the word 'terrorism' (originally defined by Noah Webster in 1840):

> *Terrorism:* Unlawful use of violence or threats to intimidate or coerce a civilian population or government, with the goal of furthering political, social, or ideological objectives.

The word 'terrorism' lacks a universally accepted definition. As noted by Cornell Law School, defining its scope is "politically complex," and its "selective use" often generates controversy both within legal systems and on the international stage.[415] This raises two key points for consideration: how the term 'terrorism' is used by those in power and how it is understood by those who are oppressed.

'Terrorism' can be applied to states with an "ethnonationalist" ideology—those that combine aggressive, racially charged nationalism with advanced technological power to *covertly* oppress a "lesser" ethnic group, often using these regions as testing grounds for methods of domination.[416]

'Terrorism' may also be used to describe the actions of oppressed people who, whether under the rule of their own government or a foreign oppressor, *directly* attack the regime to liberate themselves from despotism.

In this sense, there appears to be a shared definition of 'terrorism' among both oppressors and the oppressed: "might makes right." Thus, 'terrorism' is viewed as both wrong and evil, yet also right and just, depending on who is using the term and for what purpose.

Labels as Undesirable Behavior

OCD and ADHD are often referred to as labels because they correspond to established clinical diagnoses, describing specific patterns of behavior. These conditions are called disorders because the behaviors they describe are generally considered undesirable. Consider the following labels defined as certain "undesirable" behaviors:

OCD (1877): Obsessive-Compulsive Disorder is an obsession that drives repetitive unwanted patterns of thoughts and behaviors.

ADHD (1902): Attention-Deficit Hyperactivity Disorder is the inability to sit still, inability of self-control, and the inability to be attentive.

Both OCD (an anxiety disorder) and ADHD (a neurodevelopmental disorder) have genetic components, but these behaviors may be labeled as disorders because they reflect challenges in adapting to life's fluid nature or a lack of motivation and purpose.

However, just because behaviors are given specific labels doesn't mean a person is inherently bound to act according to them. By fixating on labels like OCD or ADHD, we risk giving them power *over* us, which can lead to self-sabotage. It's important to recognize that a diagnosis is simply a description of a pattern, *not* a defining characteristic or life sentence.

The real question is whether someone with OCD or ADHD can train their brain to improve focus, adaptability, and overall functioning without relying on medication to "fix" a so-called disorder. The answer is yes.

Neuroplasticity

The power of a label lies in the authority it carries, but ultimately, you can transcend it. By reshaping your brain, you can undo the impact of the label and move beyond the limitations it suggests.[417]

The brain is not fixed or hardwired; it can rewire itself through a process called *neuroplasticity*. This means that people can form new neural connections and change how they think, feel, and behave.

Neuroplasticity is the brain's ability to reorganize and form new neural connections in response to external stimuli. In simple terms, it allows the brain to "rewire" itself. Researchers have been exploring how neuroplasticity can be harnessed to enhance cognitive and executive functions in both children and adults with ADHD.

By encouraging more exploratory activities and fostering positive experiences that engage the mind, neuroplasticity can help cultivate a growth mindset. This process involves creating new pathways that support better focus, adaptability, and learning. For the implications of neuroplasticity, refer to the "Idols of the Cave" section under "One's Habits" below.

Racism as a Modern Term

Let's search a contemporary word and its early 20th century definition and the exploitation of its usage prior to 1902 and after:

> *Racism:* discrimination and prejudice against people based on their race or ethnicity.

'Racism' is both a term and a concept that emerged in the 19th century, tied to the rise of European imperialism, colonialism, and the expansion of capitalism. Prior to this period, the concept of classifying people based on perceived abilities, dispositions, or social roles was common and not inherently tied to ideas of racial superiority or inferiority.

In earlier times, such distinctions were made pragmatically—often to organize society in a way that would contribute to the city's growth, stability, and justice. For instance, in Plato's *Republic*, the idea of categorizing citizens by their qualities to serve the needs of the state is presented as a rational, even ethical, approach to governance.

At this point, one might ask: has Plato's *Republic* ever been used to justify what we would now consider racism? Upon reading the text, it's possible to interpret Plato's model as a precursor to ideas that could be used to rationalize societal hierarchies, perhaps even justifying discrimination or subjugation under the guise of a "Philosopher-King's" vision of an ideal city. In Book 4, Lines 433-434, Plato discusses justice in terms of harmony among different classes of people, which could be seen as supporting such hierarchical thinking.

However, a closer reading of *The Republic* reveals that Plato's distinctions are based on qualities of disposition, not on physical characteristics or racial differences as we understand them today. His categorization is about abilities and roles in society, not about race in the modern sense.

It was not until the nineteenth and twentieth centuries, with the advent of more systematic ideas of racial difference, that 'racism' emerged as a harmful and exploitative concept—taking on the negative connotations we associate with it today.

The Concept of Retirement

The conventional definition of 'retirement' is often viewed as a positive milestone, but it carries a subtle negative connotation when applied to life in general, especially in the context of older age. Let's look at the definition of 'retirement,' which most people look forward to, even calling it a "great accomplishment."

> *Retirement:* Withdrawal from one's position or occupation or from active working life.

The definition above suggests an end to productivity, engagement, and growth, which contrasts with the true nature of life—movement, evolution, productivity, and advancement.

Life is fluid, constantly changing, advancing, and growing. The Greek philosopher, Heraclitus said, "You never step in the same river twice." This highlights the ever-changing nature of life. Just as the water in a river is always flowing and never exactly the same from one moment to the next, life itself is constantly in flux—always moving, evolving, and renewing.

We can sometimes become complacent, clinging to familiar habits that hinder our ability to advance, create, and grow. This limits our progress toward becoming our truest selves—driven to keep creating and contributing, even in older age.

Living should be dynamic, never stagnant or a form of withdrawal from life. It's not about merely going through the motions within the bounds of consumerism or passively engaging in a capitalist system—like traveling the world just to check off destinations without truly connecting with the people or places you visit. True living involves enriching both yourself and others—creating something meaningful and extraordinary. As Nietzsche put it:

> I am still living; I am still thinking; I have to go on living because I have to go on thinking... I want to learn more and more to see what is necessary in things as the beautiful in them... I want to be always hereafter only an affirmer![418]

Life-affirmation is the energy that drives us to engage, create, and grow. It's what makes life a work of art, rich with meaning and always purposeful.[419]

The key distinction between a life-affirming, positive, and engaging outlook and a life-denying, negative, and withdrawing one lies in the mindset we choose: growth versus fixed. A growth mindset leads us to continually evolve, while a fixed mindset keeps us idle. Rather than adopting a life-denying mindset of retirement, it is better to embrace a life-affirming mindset of "re-engagement"—one that views life as an endless potential for advancement, growth, creativity, and productivity.

While definitions may vary, the common thread lies in its representation as an ultimate source of meaning, morality, and existence. Like other abstract concepts such as good, evil, and right, the understanding of 'God' is deeply influenced by the context in which it is framed, reflecting the dynamic and evolving nature of language and belief systems.

These terms and their shifting meanings illustrate how our perceptions are fluid, constantly redefined by social, historical, and personal forces. The challenge lies in navigating these changing definitions and embracing a mindset that recognizes the power of transformation, whether in understanding the divine or in reshaping our own lives. In doing so, we can move beyond static labels and engage with the world in a more nuanced, thoughtful way, ever open to growth, exploration, and deeper understanding.

Language Games

Twentieth-century German philosopher Ludwig Wittgenstein was deeply concerned with the ways language is used. He argues we are often "bewitched" by language, misled into false thinking because of its structure and conventions.[420] He suggests that our misunderstandings of language arise from what he calls "grammatical illusions," where the rules and forms of language lead us astray.[421] Wittgenstein emphasized that language is not just a tool for naming objects; rather, it serves many purposes, depending on the context in which it is used. Each context gives language its function, making it flexible and multifaceted.[422]

Wittgenstein believed that language is shaped by a complex web of interconnected "language games," where speakers follow familiar patterns of communication in different contexts.[423] These language games are shaped by the interactions between speakers and the specific purposes of their conversation.

Three Functions of Language

First, language games suggest that speaking a language is always embedded within a broader context, which Wittgenstein calls a "form of life."[424] Language is deeply intertwined with our existence—just as we shape how language is used; it also shapes us in return. On one hand, when people claim something is true or false, they are essentially agreeing on the language they use to express those ideas. On the other hand, because language is a vast network of words, phrases, gestures, and expressions, it can also distort our thinking, create confusion, and lead us into conceptual traps.

Second, language games highlight the rule-governed nature of language, which in turn reflects the conventional character of human activity. Language operates according to a set of rules, much like the rules of a game. Just as every sport or game is structured by specific rules that give it meaning, language follows its own set of rules to allow communication to make sense. We adhere to these linguistic rules so we can understand and make meaning of what is being said.

Confusion arises when a statement from one language game is interpreted using the rules of another. In this way, the concept of language games sheds light on the broader issue of meaning in language. Since there are many different types of language games, each governed by its own specific set of rules, meaning can shift depending on the context in which language is used.

Reducing one language game to another without recognizing their differences is a category mistake or descriptive fallacy. In fact, we often remain unaware of the diversity of everyday language games because the vastness of language makes everything seem similar, causing us to forget the many different functions words and expressions can have. In this way, the rules of language are like the rules of various games, as language games themselves change depending on the context.

Language is shaped by the meanings we assign to words within an expression. For example, the terms "evening star" and "morning star" refer to the same object—the planet Venus—but they carry different meanings. This illustrates that we cannot determine whether the rules governing the meaning of a word are correct without understanding the context in which they are used. Without rules, words have no meaning, and if the rules change, the meaning of the word also changes.

Third, language games encourage an awareness that allows us to break free from fixed ideas about how things are "supposed" to be said. Language must mean something both to me and to you. By focusing on how expressions are used, we shift our attention from the semantic-syntactic to the pragmatic dimension of language. Language becomes a tool for communication, serving a specific purpose with rules that are subjective and context-dependent.

The meaning of a sentence, then, depends on how it is used to achieve something. For example, when you say, "I love you" or "I care about you," you and the other person may agree on the definition and meaning of these words, but the true meaning comes from how those words are *used* in practice.

A proposition is a declarative sentence that conveys a true or false statement about a representation of the world, structured by a sequence of words that adhere to grammatical rules, giving it meaning to me. This makes language inherently subjective. The function of language, then, is not merely to state propositions about how things are, but to explore how things *can be*.

This opens the world as a picture that each of us helps to complete, allowing us to shape and find meaning in our existence. Language operates within a context, and as such, it serves as many purposes as there are contexts. Since life itself is fluid and ever-changing, language is likewise dynamic.

While it is true that learning a language requires a public context, governed by shared rules and agreements within a language community, it is equally true that language must hold personal meaning for both you and me. This subjective aspect of language can only emerge through language games, which unfold in specific, contextual, and often private settings.

Wittgenstein's concept of language games highlights the fluid, context-dependent nature of language and its power to shape both our thoughts and interactions. Language is not a fixed tool, but a dynamic system that functions according to the rules and purposes of different situations, allowing us to navigate the complexity of human experience.

By recognizing that language operates within a web of interconnected contexts, we can better understand the nuances of communication and the potential for misinterpretation when rules from one language game are mistakenly applied to another.

Embracing the variability of language encourages a more flexible and open approach to meaning, reminding us that words only gain significance through their use and the shared understanding between speakers. Language, then, is not just about conveying information, but about participating in the ongoing construction of meaning and the exploration of life itself.

Manipulating Language

Using language in a manipulative manner to influence and control others is a type of language game often played by individuals seeking personal gain, whether through deception or other ulterior motives. These include, but are not limited to, scammers, rhetoricians, mediums, narcissists, and pathological liars. These "language scheming specialists" have developed their own manipulative language games, who are skillfully arranging words and using tone to persuade others, often presenting falsehoods as truths. In Western philosophy, the earliest known practitioners of such language manipulation were the Greek sophists.

Three Greek Sophists

The sophists lived in fifth-century BCE Athens and were experts in rhetoric and public speaking. They traveled widely, offering to persuade others of their views, often charging a fee for their services. In many ways, sophists can be seen as early entrepreneurs, using philosophy to profit from their persuasive skills.

The three most well-known sophists were Protagoras, Gorgias, and Thrasymachus. Protagoras argues knowledge is limited to our perceptions, with truth measured by how each individual perceives the world. He is famously credited with the saying, "Man is the measure of all things." Additionally, Protagoras taught that moral judgments are relative, varying from culture to culture and person to person, meaning that each individual determines what is right or wrong for themselves.

Gorgias believed that reality is interpreted by each individual, making the nature of the human mind inherently subjective. As a result, he rejected the reliability of both knowledge and truth. He argues while we communicate with words, those words are merely symbols and can never fully capture the same meaning for everyone they represent. Gorgias also taught the art of deception, showing how people can manipulate psychology and use the power of suggestion to falsely present knowledge and truth.

Thrasymachus taught that individuals could pursue their own interests and assert themselves without limits. He argues what is considered "right" is defined by the interests of the ruling power. For example, consider how the term "terrorism" is often defined and used by powerful political entities to delegitimize resistance movements. Similarly, Machiavelli, who lived in the fifteenth century, shared Thrasymachus's view that "might is right." Machiavelli asserted that it is sometimes better to act immorally or deceive others when necessary to achieve one's goals.

The Greek philosopher Socrates was often called a "gadfly" for his habit of challenging the status quo and questioning traditional beliefs. He valued self-knowledge above all and encouraged others to do the same. Socrates urged us to question authority, scrutinize language, examine sources, and critique societal norms—not to rebel for its own sake, but to think independently and find our own voice. Unlike the sophists, Socrates did not charge a fee for his teachings.

The manipulation of language for personal gain represents a dangerous and powerful tool in the hands of those who seek to deceive and control others. The sophists of ancient Greece were among the first to recognize and exploit the persuasive potential of language, using it to blur the lines between truth and falsehood for their own benefit. Their rhetorical skill laid the foundation for modern manipulators who, through fraud, rhetoric, and deceit, continue to shape perceptions and influence power dynamics. However, as the example of Socrates illustrates, the key to resisting such manipulation lies in questioning authority, examining the intentions behind language, and striving for independent thought.

Ultimately, by remaining vigilant and critical of the language games played by others, we can safeguard truth and navigate the complex world of communication with greater awareness.

Limitations of Language

Chinese philosopher Chuang-Tzu and German philosopher Friedrich Nietzsche lived two millennia apart, yet they shared a profound insight: language does more than simply convey concepts—it shapes the reality we experience. Despite differences in language, culture, and time, both philosophers recognized that the words we use frame our understanding of the world, ultimately constructing the reality we perceive. In this way, language is not just a reflection of reality; it plays an active role in creating it.

The paradox lies in the fact that we are trapped within the confines of language, unable to escape its limitations, yet compelled to operate within it. Language, by its very nature, shapes and confines our perspective, narrowing our understanding of the world. Nietzsche sheds light on this:

> Language belongs in its origin to the age of the most rudimentary form of psychology: we find ourselves in the midst of a rude fetishism when we call to mind the basic presuppositions of the metaphysics of language... I fear we are not getting rid of God because we still believe in grammar.[425]

For Nietzsche, language deceives us into thinking we have uncovered a truth or described reality simply by naming something. We are lulled into the illusion that when we assign a word to an object or concept, we have somehow grasped its true nature, and that the mere existence of a word somehow guarantees the existence of what it refers to.[426] In this way, language not only limits our understanding but also traps us in a false sense of certainty.

Chuang-Tzu expressed a similar view on the constraints of language and its role in limiting perspective and shaping reality. Chuang-Tzu observes:

> Words are not just wind. Words have something to say. But if what they have to say is not fixed, then do they really say something? Or do they say nothing?... What do words rely upon, that we have right and wrong?... What one calls right the other calls wrong; what one calls wrong the other calls right... What is acceptable we call acceptable; what is unacceptable we call unacceptable. A road is made by people walking on it; things are so because they are called so.[427]

Chaung-Tzu emphasizes that naming or labeling people or things is a convenient use of conventional language, one that rarely questions the underlying reasons behind the definitions we assign to words.

Both Chuang-Tzu and Nietzsche's insights into the limitations of language reveal how deeply language shapes our perception of reality, often constraining and distorting our understanding. While language serves as a tool for communication, it simultaneously narrows our worldview by framing and labeling experiences in ways that may not capture their true complexity. By attaching words to objects or concepts, we are lulled into a false sense of certainty, believing that we have grasped their essence. As both philosophers point out, language does not merely reflect reality; it actively constructs it, limiting our ability to see beyond the boundaries it creates. Therefore, to truly understand the world, we must be aware of the inherent limitations of language and approach it with humility, questioning the meanings we assign and remaining open to the vastness that words alone cannot encompass.

Summary of Idols of the Marketplace

Idols of the Marketplace highlight how people often place excessive trust in language as a neutral means of communication, neglecting the complex meanings and functions words can carry. Words are commonly assumed to be straightforward, but they can convey biases, cultural influences, and multiple interpretations that shape communication in unseen ways. This perspective calls for a more critical awareness of language, emphasizing that it is not just a transparent medium but a force that influences how we think and perceive the world.

Words, terms, notions, and labels are defined by authority figures and cultural norms, and people often accept these definitions without questioning them. However, meanings can shift depending on context, and definitions are not fixed. For example, abstract concepts like 'God' vary across religions and philosophies, and notions like 'good,' 'evil,' 'right,' and 'wrong' are rooted in cultural traditions and often change depending on context. The word "terrorism" illustrates how definitions can be politically manipulated, as its meaning varies depending on the speaker's agenda.

Certain labels, like those for disorders such as OCD and ADHD, often describe behaviors considered undesirable, but these labels do not define the person. Through neuroplasticity, individuals can overcome limitations imposed by such labels by reshaping their brains and behavior.

The term "racism" emerged in the 19th century and was shaped by colonialism and imperialism, representing a harmful concept of racial superiority that did not exist in earlier times. Similarly, the concept of "retirement" is often viewed as a withdrawal from active life, but a life-affirming attitude encourages "re-engagement" and continued growth, transforming life into a work of art—rich with meaning and purpose at every age.

Philosopher Ludwig Wittgenstein's idea of "language games" emphasizes the flexibility of language, where its meaning depends on context and the rules of the conversation. Language is not only a tool for stating facts but also shapes our understanding of the world. However, language can be manipulated by those with ulterior motives, such as fraudsters or political figures, who use it to deceive or control.

Language, as both a reflection and creator of reality, is limited by its structure. Philosophers like Nietzsche and Chuang-Tzu argue that language traps us in a false sense of certainty, as words shape our perceptions and constrain our understanding of the world. Language is not fixed; it is shaped by the contexts in which it is used, and we must be aware of its power to influence how we think and see reality.

Section 3: Idols of the Cave—Questioning Identity

Idols of the Cave assume that one's identity is known, static, and unalterable, without considering the external influences and internal biases that shape both one's sense of self and its perceptions. These "idols" derive from one's education, one's history, one's information, one's habits, one's associations, one's books, one's social media influence, and one's identity.

In this analysis, I examine the distinction between counterfeit and genuine learning, investigate the histories I've been taught, and study those I was never exposed to. I also analyze the types of information we consume and reflect on habits that shape our behavior, considering how we might alter these habits to improve ourselves. Additionally, I critique the influence of the kinds of associations and books that shape our thinking, the impact social media influence, and, perhaps most importantly, assess how we contribute to shaping our own identities and the implications for living a more authentic life.

One's Education

I explored education in *Idols of the Theater* in terms of authority. Now, I will address education in *Idols of the Cave* as it relates to our ability to be self-reflective and critically analyze what we have learned—or more accurately, what we have been "taught." While this may cover some familiar ground, it is an area that warrants careful consideration.

I don't recall learning much from elementary through high school. In second grade, I memorized Roman numerals. By fifth grade, I was passionate about drawing cartoons and fascinated by the solar system, though math was a challenge. In sixth grade, I remember reading about dinosaurs, especially the mighty Tyrannosaurus Rex. In junior high, I wrote about the solar system in Language Arts and even cooked and ate octopus in biology class. High school was a mix—I did well in accounting but struggled with algebra.

Counterfeit vs Genuine Learning

Looking back, I can't say I truly learned much or understood *why* any of it mattered. The reason it didn't matter is that K-12 education is more about indoctrination than actual learning. That's why I don't remember learning much at all. Indoctrination is a form of counterfeit learning—it's about memorizing what you need to know and passively absorbing information without ever really understanding it.[428]

It wasn't until my third year of university that I discovered Mortimer J. Adler's "great books" approach to genuine learning.[429] This method directs learners to explore the "great ideas" that have shaped the world we live in today. It's not a conventional approach taught in schools, but one that profoundly transforms both the mind and character, fostering growth through self-directed study and a personal journey of discovery.[430]

Adler suggests, "The mind, like the body, has the power to achieve what is good for itself—knowledge and understanding."[431] In this sense, his perspective on learning resonates with Plato's *Allegory of the Cave*. For further details, refer to the Introduction above.

Plato believes that the true purpose of education is not to train people to become mere producers of wealth or consumers of a luxurious lifestyle, but to help them become "something more divine"—leaders and thinkers who guide others to reason effectively and live morally.[432]

According to Plato, people can be divided into three distinct categories based on their moral and intellectual potential, symbolized by different metals. Each category reflects a particular attitude toward life and is governed by a unique disposition that motivates behavior. Plato argues that our goal is to cultivate the disposition of reason, along with "the studies that nurture it."[433] Reason represents the highest disposition, with the other categories serving it. The table below translates Plato's ideas into contemporary language.

Category	Metal	Disposition	Goal of Life	Desire	Pleasure
Leadership-Thinker	Gold	Reason	Live Morally	Education	Knowledge
Support Specialist	Silver	Service	Fit In	Conformity	Honor
Financial Advisor	Bronze	Produce	Be Rich	Money	Wealth

To review, there are two distinct approaches to education. The first is formal instruction through indoctrination, which represents counterfeit learning. This view treats education as something externally imposed on a person, aimed at shaping them to fit societal expectations, enhance their outward appearance, and prepare them primarily to "earn a living" and accumulate wealth.

The second is self-directed study through intellectual engagement, which represents genuine learning. This perspective sees education as an internal process that transforms both the mind and character, guiding a person toward "what is good" and helping them live a moral life. The brain, being flexible, can be shaped and improved—"not according to a particular [fixed] disposition," but through activities that stimulate critical thinking and reflection.[434]

Genuine learning occurs through unlearning counterfeit education and re-learning by engaging one's intellect and teaching oneself. Just as building a strong and fit body requires effort and endurance, so too does true learning demand effort and perseverance. Education is a process that involves "elevating the mind" above itself—unlearning what is false, relearning what is true, and acquiring knowledge and wisdom through one's own active effort.[435]

The distinction between counterfeit and genuine learning reveals the deeper purpose of education as a transformative journey of self-discovery and intellectual growth. While traditional schooling often focuses on indoctrination—teaching us to memorize and conform—true education, as exemplified by Adler and Plato, emphasizes critical reflection, self-directed study, and the cultivation of reason. Genuine learning challenges us to question what we've been taught, unlearn false assumptions, and engage actively with ideas that shape both our minds and our character. This type of education empowers us to live morally, think independently, and guide others toward wisdom, ultimately helping us transcend mere survival or wealth accumulation. True learning, then, is not just about acquiring facts but about evolving into thoughtful, self-reflective individuals who continually strive for a higher understanding of the world.

One's History

This section is extensive due to the thorough research conducted, supported by numerous endnotes. The writing and organization of this section took four months to complete. The key point for readers to understand is that when we invest time in investigating or re-examining specific histories, our perspective changes. This process leads to a deeper and more thoughtful appreciation for life, as well as a better understanding of the world and the people in it. With this knowledge, we are better equipped to approach life calmly and navigate it more effectively.

In many cases, we merely learn about history; in others, we learn from it. American history textbooks from the late 19th to the 20th centuries have often been written "selectively," presenting assumptions, omitting key events, relying on biased and uncritical sources, and failing to consider opposing viewpoints.

Howard Zinn's 1980 "national bestseller," *A People's History of the United States*, frames history starting in 1492 as a story of a "people's movement"—one in which ordinary individuals demonstrated their ability to resist and unite in the struggle against powerful rulers.[436] However, a major flaw in Zinn's account, which he openly acknowledges, is his failure to provide citations for the extensive primary source quotations he frequently uses, leaving their contexts often unreferenced.[437]

The Smithsonian Institution's 1991 textbook, *Seeds of Change: A Quincentennial Commemoration*, "celebrates" Christopher Columbus's "influence" and "achievements" in the New World, despite the fact that by 1600, the native peoples had largely disappeared.[438] The authors approach Columbus's legacy as disinterested chroniclers, focusing more on the exchange of goods (such as plants, sugarcane, plows, and diseases) and "environmental issues" like acid rain, waste management, and global warming, rather than addressing the social inequalities and human suffering caused by conquest, abuse, and the abuse of power.[439]

Bentley and Ziegler's 2000 textbook, *Traditions and Encounters: A Global Perspective on the Past*, approaches history from a global standpoint. The authors acknowledge that it is "impossible to understand the world's history by viewing it exclusively through the lenses of any particular society's historical experience." They argue that a comprehensive understanding requires considering the "conquest, settlement, and exploitation" of Indigenous peoples and cultures, which, however, they do not address in the text.[440]

The truth is that every book a person reads is shaped by the author's perspective and biases, as they seek to convey their ideas and persuade the reader to adopt their point of view, unless explicitly stated otherwise.

We must constantly question what we are taught, whether as students or lifelong learners. When we recognize that we are often taught selectively, we begin to challenge those narratives. By reading opposing perspectives, we can re-educate ourselves about history, develop our own informed views, and provide reasoning for them. This process involves unlearning, relearning, and critically rethinking to uncover a more balanced understanding of the "truth"—what worked, what didn't, and what should be avoided. History often repeats itself in subtle and covert ways, because humanity tends to overlook the lessons of the past.

I remember studying American history in my junior year of high school in the late 1970s, using Thomas A. Bailey's 1956 textbook, *The American Pageant*, which was widely regarded as "one of the most popular textbooks of the mid-twentieth century."[441]

I don't recall much from that time, except that Columbus sailed from Spain on the *Nina*, *Pinta*, and *Santa Maria* in 1492, "discovered" America, and became a national hero. I also remember learning that the War of 1812 broke out between Americans and the British, and that "savage" Indians attacked emigrants heading west during the mid-1800s. The illustrations in *The American Pageant* that accompanied the text left a strong impression on me.

History is often taught from the perspective of an institution or authority figure, who imparts their evaluative judgments and biases to students, shaping their understanding through a lens of preconceived notions.

African historian Donald Yacovone argues that most U.S. history textbooks present "the story of the white man"—his conflicts with "red savages" and his efforts to "control the lives" of African Americans.[442] According to Yacovone, American history is often a selective narrative shaped by privileged white men, promoting ideas of "white supremacy and racial prejudice."[443]

We learn what we are taught, believe what we learn, and act based on what we know. But what if we could view American history from the perspectives of Native Americans and African Americans?

My exploration starts with Christopher Columbus. In researching the Columbus "enterprise," I came across several secondary sources that quote primary sources at length but fail to provide page numbers or chapter references. This lack of citation makes it challenging for readers to verify the context of the quotes, forcing them to blindly accept the historian's interpretation rather than check the original sources for themselves.

I examine three key issues: First, how America's "Manifest Destiny," framed as a divine mandate, nearly led to the extermination of Native Americans. Second, how the enslavement and oppression of African

Americans helped foster the rise of white supremacy. And third, how America's history of racism influenced both Hitler and Israel's occupation of Palestinian lands, with both adopting similar policies, laws, and strategies.

Christopher Columbus—A Villian

Christopher Columbus did not "discover" America, nor did he set foot on its shores in 1492. Instead, Columbus's four voyages introduced the Americas to Europe and set the stage for the large-scale arrival of Europeans, which eventually led to the formation of several new nations, including the United States, Canada, and Mexico.

In 1492, Columbus arrived in the Caribbean, believing he had reached the East Indies, and referred to the native Taino people as "Indians." Upon his arrival, he described them as warm and welcoming. He wrote:

> They exchanged with us .... very willingly traded everything they had... They are well built with fine bodies and handsome faces... They are the color of the Canary Islanders (neither black nor white) ... They are fairly tall on the whole, with fine limbs and good proportions.[444]

However, Columbus did not return the same hospitality. Just two days after meeting the Taino, his journal reveals his growing obsession with finding gold, particularly "gold hanging from their noses," reflecting his insatiable greed.[445]

Columbus's intentions are laid bare in his logbook: to turn the Taino people into "good servants" (slaves) on their own land, to "bring half a dozen of them back to their Majesties" (captives), to force their conversion to Christianity ("be made Christians"), to seize the "gold ... hanging from their noses" (steal), to "take any cotton ... for your Majesties" (exploit their labor for profit), to "decide where a fort could be built" (establish a colonial stronghold), and to take advantage of their generosity (exploitation). He even wrote that the Taino "could be taken away to Castile [Spain] or held as slaves on the island, for with fifty men we could subjugate them all and *make them do whatever we wish.*"[446]

Friar Bartolomé de las Casas was a historian who accompanied Christopher Columbus on his voyages. He transcribed Columbus's logbooks and journals, documenting the details of the expeditions. In addition to his transcriptions, Las Casas wrote extensively about the events he witnessed and published his observations in multiple volumes. Las Casas was highly critical of Columbus, stating:

> [I]f the Admiral [Columbus] had believed that such dreadful results would follow ... he would never have introduced or initiated a practice which was to lead to such terrible harm... [T]he predisposition of these people to receive our holy faith [and how] he could so lightly say that they might take all the Indians who were the natural inhabitants of these islands to Castile, or hold them captive on their own island, etc. This was very far from the purpose of God.[447]

Las Casas was the first prominent critic of Spanish colonialism in the Americas and was appointed "Protector of the Indians" by both the Spanish Crown and the Church.

Columbus's journey was not one of discovery, but of exploitation. Whether the brutal treatment and killings of the Taino people were carried out by Columbus's sailors, soldiers, or the new governors who succeeded him (Bobadilla and Ovando), Columbus was ultimately in charge of the enterprise. He bears full responsibility for the atrocities committed against the Taino, as his actions were driven by the desire to bring gold to the Spanish monarchy and fulfill what he believed to be God's mission for the Church. Based on my own research, drawing from both primary and secondary sources, Columbus was not a hero, but rather a villain.[448]

Throughout his works, Bartolomé de las Casas repeatedly refers to Christopher Columbus's reign of terror over the Indigenous peoples. In *History of the Indies*, he writes:

> [W]hile *Columbus was busy unjustly harming* the Indians ... the King [of Spain] was sending one of his servants, the Sevillian Juan Aguado, to spy on him... [W]hile Columbus was *tyrannically offending* the Indians ... Aguado was arranging the beginning of his punishment... Aguado arrived [in Isabela] in October 1495 ... [and] went looking for the admiral [i.e., Columbus]. They say that whenever they met Indians, he would tell them a new admiral was coming because he had come to kill the old one. And since the Indians around Isabela and Vega Real had been much aggrieved by the *admiral's slaughters* and the gold tribute, he had imposed upon them—work which they found unbearable—it seems likely that the Indians rejoiced at hearing this.[449]

Columbus left the Indigenous peoples in a state of "poverty, unjust servitude, oppression... [and] misery."[450] Bill Bigelow, a high school history teacher in Portland, Oregon, argues that Columbus should be remembered as the "first terrorist" in the Americas.[451]

Cultural Racism

The colonization and extermination of Native Americans in their own homeland—both in North and South America—was carried out through a "legalized" form of *cultural racism*. This approach is considered a method because it represents a systematic process designed to achieve a specific end goal.

Cultural racism is discrimination based on the perceived inferiority of a culture or way of life, such as that of the Taino of the Caribbean, Native

Americans, Aboriginal Australians, Native Hawaiians, and others. It is rooted in the belief that one civilization is superior to another, and often involves a system of racial sovereignty. This system operates through policies and practices designed to achieve a specific objective. In this context, the system is an integral part of the broader method used to accomplish that goal.

Native Americans were stereotyped as hostile and savage, much like African slaves were depicted as possessing an inferior nature—both of which were used as propaganda to justify colonial conquest. Indigenous peoples in the New World were often viewed as subhuman, with the belief that they were destined by God "to be placed under the authority of civilized and virtuous princes or nations, so that they may learn, from the might, wisdom, and law of their conquerors, to practice better morals, worthier customs and a more civilized way of life."[452]

In his *Short Account of the Destruction of the Indies*, Las Casas chronicles the horrific details of the inhuman treatment and cruelty inflicted upon the Indigenous people. He writes:

> [The Spaniards] forced their way into native settlements, slaughtering everyone they found there, including small children, old men, pregnant women, and even women who had just given birth. They hacked them to pieces, slicing open their bellies with their swords as though they were so many sheep herded into a pen. They even laid wagers on whether they could manage to slice a man in two at a stroke, or cut an individual's head from his body, or disembowel him with a single blow of their axes. They grabbed suckling infants by the feet and, ripping them from their mothers' breasts, dashed them headlong against the rocks... They spared no one, erecting especially wide gibbets on which they could string their victims up with their feet just off the ground and then burn them alive..., or tie dry straw to their bodies and set fire to it. Some they chose to keep alive and

simply cut their wrists, leaving their hands dangling... And ... these merciless and inhuman butchers ... trained hunting dogs to track them down—wild dogs who would savage a native to death as soon as look at him, tearing him to shreds and devouring his flesh as though he were a pig.[453]

The discovery of gold proved to be far less abundant than the Spaniards had imagined, leading to even greater cruelty toward the Indigenous people. Every Native was required to deliver a set amount of gold ore every three months. Once the gold was handed over, the individual received a token to wear around their neck as proof of the tribute. Those who were found without the correct number of tokens had their hands cut off as punishment.[454]

The Christian European Crusading legal tradition, which justified cultural racism, had been in place for 400 years before Columbus arrived in the New World. This framework, endorsed by the Church, supported the colonization of "heathens and infidels" under the guise of assuming guardianship over native populations for the "salvation of their souls" and asserting control over their lands.[455]

In 1513, the Spanish monarchy issued *El Requerimiento*, or the Spanish Requirement, a decree that claimed a divinely sanctioned right to take possession of New World territories and to subjugate and exploit the Indigenous populations.

El Requerimiento was created to provide the legal justification for Spanish colonizers to assert authority in the Americas and demand that Indigenous peoples recognize that authority.[456] The document instructed Native peoples to pledge allegiance to both the Pope and the Spanish crown. It states:

> I certify to you that, with the help of God, we shall powerfully enter into your country and shall make war against you in all ways and manners that we can and shall subject you to the yoke and obedience of the Church and of

Their Highness. We shall take you and your wives and your children, and shall make slaves of them, and as such shall sell and dispose of them as Their Highness may command. And we shall take your goods and shall do you all the mischief and damage that we can, as to vassals who do not obey and refuse to receive their lord and resist and contradict him.[457]

In practice, after the Spanish captured the Indigenous people and placed them in chains, *El Requerimiento* was read aloud, often by someone who did not speak their language and without any interpreters present. Neither the reader nor the Indigenous people understood each other's words, leaving the natives with no opportunity to respond.[458]

In 1542, Las Casas' *Short Account* was sent to King Charles V and Prince Philip II of Spain, highlighting the exploitation of the Indigenous people. In his introduction, Las Casas writes:

[T]he excesses which this New World has witnessed, all of them [Spanish soldiers] surpassing anything that men hitherto have imagined..., Your Highness [Prince Philip II] would not have delayed for even one moment before entreating His Majesty [King Charles V] to prevent any repetition of the atrocities which go under the name of 'conquests' ... It is my fervent hope that, once Your Highness perceives the extent of the injustices suffered by these innocent peoples and the way in which they are being destroyed and crushed underfoot, unjustly and for no other reason than to satisfy the greed and ambition of those whose purpose it is to commit such wicked atrocities...[459]

In his introduction, Las Casas emphasizes that it is his moral obligation to speak out, for remaining silent would be a "criminal neglect" in the face of the "enormous loss of life" caused by these so-called "conquests."[460]

Harvard Law professor and director of Indian Programs, Robert A. Williams, Jr., writes:

> [T]he legal legacy of cultural racism brought by Columbus to the New World is to illuminate the legal foundations upon subsequent Christian European nations and their successor states justified their privileges of power and aggression in the New World... [and] continues to serve as an instrument of racial discrimination against Indigenous peoples' rights of self-determination.[461]

The "Doctrine of Discovery" of 1823 provided the legal basis for racial discrimination against non-Christian "savages," granting European Christians the "exclusive right to extinguish Native land titles, either through purchase or conquest."[462] Robert A. Williams Jr. cites three foundational twentieth-century doctrines that continue to shape Supreme Court Indian law today: the Congressional Plenary Power doctrine, the Diminished Tribal Sovereignty doctrine, and the Trust doctrine.[463]

The indiscriminate killing of Indian women and children constitutes intentional genocide. No society can endure if its women and children are exterminated.[464] This was the policy endorsed by America's founding figures, from George Washington to Thomas Jefferson and those who came after them.

President George Washington ordered the destruction of Indigenous settlements, insisting that they should not just be overrun, but completely destroyed.[465] In 1783, he was reported to have compared Native Americans to wolves, saying that they were similar but a little different than wolves—"both being beasts of prey, though they differ in shape."[466]

In 1807, President Thomas Jefferson instructed his Secretary of War, General Henry Dearborn, that "if we are compelled to raise the hatchet against any tribe, we will not lay it down until that tribe is exterminated."[467] Five years later, in 1812, Jefferson reiterated this stance, declaring that the American government had no choice but "to pursue [the Indians] to extermination."[468]

In 1830, President Andrew Jackson signed the Indian Removal Act into law, legally forcing Native American tribes to relocate west of the Mississippi River, where they were given new lands. This policy was a form of ethnic cleansing, amounting to genocide.[469]

The study of early colonial American history, particularly when approached with a critical and open mind, has the power to transform our understanding of the world. By investigating various historical narratives and considering the perspectives often omitted or distorted, we can gain a more comprehensive and nuanced view of the past.

The selective presentation of history, such as the glorification of figures like Columbus or the marginalization of Indigenous voices, highlights the importance of questioning what we are taught. As we challenge these narratives, we not only uncover the truths of historical injustices but also equip ourselves with the knowledge needed to navigate the complexities of contemporary issues.

The process of reexamining history encourages us to learn from past mistakes, promoting a more informed and empathetic approach to the future. Understanding history in its entirety, with all its contradictions and complexities, is essential for fostering a society that values justice, equality, and the dignity of all people.

The African Diaspora: A Long-Established and Influential Free People

The belief that Black people were destined to serve White people has often been supported by interpretations of a foundational text: the Christian Holy Bible. According to the biblical account, Noah had three sons—Shem, Ham, and Japheth.[470] After the Great Flood, Noah's family came to rest on the mountains of Ararat, located in modern-day Turkey.[471]

Noah became a farmer and planted a vineyard. One day, he drank so much wine that he became drunk and lay uncovered. His son Ham saw him in this state, and when Noah awoke and learned of it, he was embarrassed.

In response, Noah cursed Ham and his descendants to be a "slave to his brothers;" a curse that later came to be known as the "Curse of Ham."[472, 473] However, according to African American historian, George Washington Williams, this curse was not driven by divine inspiration, as it never came to pass.[474] It was simply the words of a flawed man, not a prophecy from God.

Shem's, Ham's, and Japheth's descendants repopulated the earth, from which all races are believed to have originated.[475] Shem's family moved eastward to Asia, giving rise to what was later associated with the "yellow-skinned" race. Ham's family traveled south to Africa, linked to the "black-skinned" race. Japheth's family spread westward into Europe, becoming associated with the "white-skinned" race.[476]

In his 1882 work *History of the Negro Race in America*, George Washington Williams argues that Ham and the Canaanites were not slaves, as often portrayed, but rather free, powerful, and influential peoples. Long before the Hebrews arrived in their lands, these groups were already thriving. Ham is the ancestor of the Egyptians, Libyans, Phutites, and Ethiopians, and it was the Hebrews, not the Hamites, who endured centuries of enslavement in Egypt under the rule of Misraim, Ham's second son.[477, 478] Thus, Williams suggests that it was the Shemites—the Hebrews—who were in bondage to the Hamites, not the other way around.

Williams further notes that African people have been recognized as a distinct race for over 4,500 years.[479] Their migrations can be traced as far east as Japan and as far north as the Himalayas.[480]

Interpreting the "Curse of Ham" to justify the subjugation of African Blacks to European Whites reflects a "preunderstanding" shaped by the [white] interpreter's own cultural tradition and prejudices.[481] This preunderstanding—rooted in the interpreter's assumptions—limits the text's meaning, reducing it to an idealized or historically biased self-conception. It fails to engage in the kind of reflexive self-criticism that would allow the text to be seen in a different light.[482] In other words, our interpretations are often colored by the traditions we live in and the prejudices we carry, without considering how those prejudices are shaped by our own experiences and biases.

In a broader philosophical context, Nietzsche challenged the logical positivism of his time, which focused on objective facts as the sole source of meaning. Nietzsche argues "facts do not exist, only interpretations," suggesting that our *interpretative understanding* of the world derives from our subjective perceptions, which is always filtered through our drives, needs, and desires.[483, 484] For Nietzsche, every drive represents a "lust to rule," where each perspective strives to impose itself as the standard for all others.[485] He believed that all reasoned statements are open to interpretation, as they are always shaped by ideologies that "mask and deform" their true meaning.[486] Nietzsche cautioned that the worst readers are those who approach a text like "plundering troops," seizing only what serves their purposes while distorting or neglecting the rest.[487]

Biological Racism

The system of displacing and enslaving African people can be understood as a form of "legalized" *biological racism*—an interpretation of history and scripture that is used to justify the domination of one race over another, grounded in a flawed and biased understanding of both the text and the world.

Biological racism refers to discrimination based on perceived genetic or biological differences between racial groups, such as differences in skin color or other distinguishing traits (e.g., Blacks, Jews, Chinese, Palestinians, etc.). This form of racism assumes that one race is inherently superior to another and establishes a hierarchy of races.

The concept of racial hierarchy contributed to the development of eugenics, which is the study of how to manipulate reproduction within a population to enhance the prevalence of traits considered desirable. Other terms related to eugenics include genetics, selective breeding, heredity, race improvement, and genetic engineering.

Eugenics was first articulated by Plato over 2,300 years ago, when he applied the principles of selective breeding to humans. In *The Republic*, he writes:

> [T]ry to breed from the best... [T]he best men must have sex with the best women as frequently as possible... so that our herd is to be of the highest possible quality... [A]s the young children are born, they'll be taken over by the officials appointed for the purpose... but the children of inferior parents, or any child of the others that is born defective, they'll hide in a secret unknown place... [that is], if the breed is to remain pure.[488]

In his vision of an ideal society, Plato strategizes for a perfect family structure within a perfect city ruled by philosopher-kings. Children born to inferior parents or with defects would be discarded—likely through infanticide—ensuring the purity of the population.[489]

It is important to note, however, that Plato's approach to eugenics focused on class, not race. He sought to optimize the quality of his society's leadership by controlling reproduction within a specific class, rather than promoting racial superiority. Therefore, while Plato's ideas resemble eugenics, they do not reflect modern racial racism, as his focus was not on race but on the social stratification of society.

The 19th-century eugenics movement was launched by Sir Francis Galton, who coined the term "eugenics" in 1883.[490] At that time, Charles Darwin's *Descent of Man* (1871) had already made a significant impact on both biologists and sociologists. The ideas of social Darwinism, particularly the concept of "survival of the fittest," were gaining widespread influence. This ideology contributed to the growing desire to cultivate a superior "white" race.

(The 1997 film *Gattaca*, starring Ethan Hawke, depicts a future society shaped by eugenics, where children are conceived through genetic selection to ensure they inherit the best traits from their parents, thereby determining their predetermined destinies.)

Geographers argued that the "most advanced" human types originated from "cool, dry regions," with England and the European continent at the top of the list, followed closely by the Pacific Northwest of the United States. In contrast, they placed the "least advanced" human types in "warm and relatively isolated regions" such as Australia, South America, and Africa.[491]

Sociologists historically asserted that skull size was a key indicator of racial superiority, with claims that white people were inherently superior. They characterized the Chinese as a "mediocre and intellectually submissive race," while portraying Jews as "thrifty" and always poised for a "good business opportunity."[492]

Eugenicists presented themselves as progressive and idealistic, but they represented a dangerous, modern form of white supremacy. They used the latest scientific advancements to justify the control and dehumanization of African Americans, viewing them as a subordinate race, created by God and nature to serve the needs of white society. Ultimately, Nazi Germany adopted Galton's idea of a "race of gifted men," and the Nazi eugenic policies culminated in a genocide that took American racial ideologies to their extreme and horrifying logical conclusion.[493]

In November 2018, Chinese geneticist Dr. He Jiankui made headlines in the field of human eugenics by creating the first genetically edited human babies. The twin girls, Lulu and Nana, were born in October 2018. Using a gene-editing technology known as CRISPR (Clustered Regularly Interspaced Short Palindromic Repeats), Dr. Jiankui was able to modify human genes—removing undesirable traits and potentially inserting more desirable ones.[494] The "genetic genie" was out of the bottle, and CRISPR had proven to be an effective tool for editing human DNA.[495]

CRISPR technology has the potential to make children immune to certain diseases by editing their genes. Researchers are also exploring how artificial intelligence can be used to optimize the human genome by processing vast amounts of genetic data through advanced machine learning algorithms. AI could identify the most beneficial genetic combinations to enhance health, intelligence, and other desirable traits.[496]

Parents could use CRISPR to give their children a genetic advantage. With the help of AI, they could obtain the precise DNA sequence needed to enhance specific traits. As a result, their children might be taller, more intelligent, more athletic, and better equipped to resist illness.[497]

Not only could human evolution accelerate, but AI itself could evolve at an even faster pace. The algorithms could grow more sophisticated, selectively favoring not only traits like health and intelligence but also characteristics such as behavior, conformity, and loyalty. Children could become smarter, but they could also be more docile and easier to control.[498]

But is this really what we want? Do we want to create human beings who are robotic and automatons, devoid of emotion and personal aspirations, all in the name of producing genetically perfect, obedient "superhumans"? This could set the stage for a real conflict between machines and humanity, much like the Skynet scenario from the 1984 *Terminator* movie and its sequels.

Christopher Columbus—Father of the Slave Trade

African historian Basil Davidson argues that Christopher Columbus played a key role in initiating the African slave trade to the Americas. According to Davidson, the Spanish monarchy issued its first laws in 1501, permitting the export of slaves to the Americas.[499] The first official "license" for the importation of African slaves was granted in 1510.[500]

By 1518, the slave trade had become an established institution, integral to the Spanish-American colonial enterprise.[501] This leads Davidson to refer to Columbus as the "father of the slave trade."[502] However, the actual introduction of slavery to English-speaking America occurred a century later, in August 1619, when the first enslaved Africans arrived in Jamestown, Virginia.[503]

Slavery existed in Virginia from 1619 until 1662 without legal sanction.[504] However, on December 14, 1662, the legal foundation for slavery was established with the passage of the *Hereditary Slavery Law* (Virginia Act XII).[505] This law achieved two significant outcomes: it officially legalized slavery and made it hereditary.[506] Two decades later, in 1682, the Virginia General Assembly passed a law that extended the status of slavery to Native Americans, placing them on the same legal footing as African slaves.[507] Then, in 1705, the Virginia Slave Code was enacted, which classified enslaved Africans, Native Americans, and people of mixed race as real estate rather than personal property.[508]

President Abraham Lincoln initially rejected the policy of emancipation on September 13, 1862. However, just nine days later, on September 22, he reversed his position and moved toward emancipation, issuing the preliminary Emancipation Proclamation. The final proclamation came into effect on January 1, 1863. Despite this decisive step, Lincoln acknowledged that the proclamation had a significant limitation: it did not apply to all regions, leaving many enslaved people in the southern states still in bondage.[509]

American history textbooks from the 1930s and 1940s often portrayed enslaved Black people as "happy" regardless of their circumstances. In *American History*, Thomas Maitland Marshall emphasized the character of the enslaved person, describing them as "usually happy," fond of socializing, singing, dancing, telling jokes, and laughing. He suggested that most plantation owners earned loyalty not by the whip but through pride.[510]

Similarly, Fremont P. Wirth, in his *The Development of America*, reassured students that slaves lived comfortably and were well-fed. Accompanying an illustration, Wirth claimed that after a day's work, "Negroes always have been fond of singing and dancing," and that the banjo was a popular musical instrument among them.[511]

George Washington Williams presents a starkly different view of Black people, emphasizing the harsh realities of slavery. He draws attention to numerous laws and "slave codes" that systematically stripped enslaved individuals of their rights while protecting white interests. One such law, enacted in South Carolina on February 7, 1690, during the period from 1665 to 1775, stated:

> If any negro or Indian slave shall offer any violence ... to any white person, he shall for the first offence be severely whipped ... and for the second offence ... shall be severely whipped, his or her nose slit, and face burnt ... and the third offence ... to inflict death, or any other punishment...[512]

This law illustrates how the system protected whites and completely disregarded the rights of Black people. In contrast to the "happy" and "prideful" depiction Marshall offers, most enslaved individuals lived in constant fear of retribution for even the slightest offense against their white owners.

Moreover, slave owners showed little regard for the lives of enslaved children. When women gave birth, their newborns were often treated as mere burdens and discarded, given away "as soon as possible... like puppies."[513] This practice became widespread and was a regular part of the system of slavery.[514]

In his *Short Account and History of the Indies*, Bartolomé de las Casas reflects on his regret for advocating African slavery, offering a heartfelt apology. He writes:

> I soon repented and judged myself guilty of ignorance. I came to realize that black slavery was as unjust as Indian slavery... and I was not sure that my ignorance and good faith would secure me in the eyes of God.[515]

These words made Las Casas reflect on the suffering and exploitation of enslaved people, compelling him to act with moral conviction. Driven by this newfound awareness, he chose to speak out against the brutality of slavery and injustice.

Las Casas' inner transformation, which led him to present his account of Christopher Columbus's cultural and biological racism to Prince Philip II of Spain in 1542, was sparked by a passage from the *Book of Sirach*, Chapter 34, verses 21-22, which reads:

> Food means life itself to poor people, and taking it away from them is murder. It is murder to deprive someone of their living or to cheat an employee of his wages."[516]

This passage profoundly impacted him, prompting a deep reflection on the injustice and suffering caused by slavery. At the age of 30, this revelation inspired him to take decisive action.

The Black Lives Matter movements in 2013 and 2020 ignited a cultural awakening, prompting widespread conversations about racial justice and historical reckoning. As part of this shift, Native American and allied activists worked to promote "Indigenous Peoples' Day" as a meaningful alternative to "Columbus Day." In 2022, following years of pressure and protest, the Washington NFL team officially retired its long-controversial name and logo—adopted in the 1930s—rebranding from the Washington "Redskins" to the Washington "Commanders."

The Influence of American Racism on Hitler

Hitler viewed the United States as a key inspiration for his plans to colonize Eastern Europe.[517] He envisioned a form of "settler colonialism" similar to America's history of displacing and exterminating Indigenous peoples in the West.[518] Hitler famously stated, "Our colonial territory is in the east."[519] In this vision, the native populations would be exploited, and the land would be repopulated by the conquering nation's own people—specifically, by ethnic Germans, or Nazis.[520]

Echoing the American rationale for westward expansion, Hitler declared, "It is inconceivable that a superior people should struggle to exist on land too limited for them, while vast, unproductive masses occupy immense stretches of some of the richest soil in the world."[521] His solution? "Here in the east, a similar process will unfold as it did in the conquest of America."[522] For Hitler, "Our Mississippi must be the Volga."[523]

In the 1920s and 1930s, Hitler and other Nazi scholars, lawyers, and officials closely studied U.S. federal and state laws, particularly those concerning Native Americans and Indigenous nations. These policies significantly influenced the development of Nazi racial laws targeting Jews and shaped their plans for the conquest of Eastern Europe.[524]

Hitler was well-acquainted with the U.S. government's official policies toward Native Americans, including the Removal, Reservation, and Assimilation Eras, which were aimed at acquiring Native lands, removing or concentrating Indigenous peoples, and, in some cases, exterminating them.[525] He saw the expansion of the United States westward as a model for expanding the German empire eastward.[526] The similarities between the American ideology of Manifest Destiny and Germany's policy of *Lebensraum* in Eastern Europe were striking.[527]

Manifest Destiny had a clear purpose: to remove Native American nations from their land in order to seize both territory and resources for the United States.[528] It was framed as a divine mission to remake the world in America's image, guided by God's will.[529] Thomas Jefferson, as president, was the first to make ethnic cleansing an official U.S. policy, pushing for the removal of all Native American nations west of the Mississippi River.[530]

Similarly, *Lebensraum*—which translates to "living space"—was a German concept that combined nationalist expansionism with racist ideology. It sought to enlarge Germany's population and territorial boundaries by colonizing lands east of the Volga River in Eastern Europe.[531] Hitler argued that all nations had the right to seize the lands of others, claiming the Earth had not been "given" to anyone but was "destined for those peoples who possess the courage to conquer it."[532]

Hitler expressed admiration for how America had reduced the Native American population from millions to just a few hundred thousand.[533] He also praised the United States for advancing a racial concept of citizenship by "excluding certain races from naturalization."[534]

The Nazis were quick to point to the enslavement of African Americans enshrined in the U.S. Constitution.[535] Additionally, they referenced Thomas Jefferson's call to "eliminate" Native Americans, whose population dwindled from millions to around two hundred thousand between 1500 and 1900.[536] The American eugenics movement also influenced Nazi ideology, significantly shaping Hitler's racist goals.[537]

Like Hitler, the United States killed and displaced millions, reshaping the demographics of an entire continent.[538] However, unlike the Nazis, the United States succeeded in completing the process of racial replacement and territorial dominance, all the while crafting a powerful national myth of frontier heroism and progress.[539]

Hitler's Inspiration from King Leopold II's Congo Rule

Hitler also drew inspiration from King Leopold II of Belgium's brutal colonization of the Congo.

Europe's interest in Africa's Congo in the late 19th century was driven by the same lust for wealth that fueled Columbus's quest for the Americas. However, the Congo offered far more resources, including gold, copper, cobalt, diamonds, tantalum, and petroleum. With such riches, mining became the region's main industry. King Leopold capitalized on this abundance, overcoming colonial rivalries from Britain, France, and Portugal to seize control of the Congo.

When George Washington Williams visited the Congo in 1890, he was appalled by the widespread abuse and forced labor imposed on the Congolese by the Belgians.[540] On July 18, 1890, he wrote an Open Letter to King Leopold, denouncing the suffering and millions of deaths caused by the king's agents. Williams' letter played a key role in popularizing the term "crimes against humanity."[541]

The history of Belgium's colonial rule in the Congo is often summarized in popular history books like this:

When the Belgians arrived in the Congo, they encountered a society torn by rivalries and the slave trade. Belgian officials, missionaries, doctors, colonists, engineers, and others 'civilized' the native population, building modern cities, roads, railways, harbors, airports, factories, mines, schools, and hospitals. This, it is claimed, greatly improved the living conditions of the Indigenous people. [542]

This narrative is still taught to Belgian 12-year-old primary school students in 2006, nearly half a century after the country's colonial rule ended.[543]

The unjust acts of repression, murder, forced labor, racism, and exploitation against the Congolese were integral to Belgian rule in the Congo, serving to advance King Leopold's profitable colonial ambitions. However, like many histories, these atrocities are often selectively omitted.

The Congo is often referred to as the "rape capital of the world," with an average of 48 women raped every hour.[544] Sexual violence, including gang rapes and genital mutilation, is perpetrated by armed groups, militias, and even government and police forces.

The history of the African Diaspora is deeply intertwined with centuries of misinterpretation, exploitation, and oppression fueled by flawed racial ideologies. From the biblical justifications of slavery to the systematic discrimination embedded in the institution of biological racism, African people and their descendants have long been unjustly marginalized. Despite these oppressive forces, the resilience and contributions of the African Diaspora have shaped global history and culture in profound ways.

As history has shown, the misapplication of ideologies, whether through the manipulation of religious texts, eugenics, or the actions of colonial powers, reflects deep-seated prejudices that continue to impact the lives of marginalized people today. The ongoing fight for racial justice, exemplified by movements like Black Lives Matter, highlights the need for continued reflection and action against racial inequality, demanding a more accurate understanding of history and a more just future for all.

Israel's colonization of Palestine through the establishment of Jewish "settlements" in the occupied territories is influenced by American biological and cultural racism.

According to the Hebrew Scriptures, following the flood and before the Tower of Babel, Noah's three sons each became the ancestors of distinct nations.[545] Japheth is considered the father of the Gentiles, representing the nations of non-Jews.[546] Ham is regarded as the father of Canaan, representing the nations of the Arabs.[547] Shem is the father of Israel, representing the nation of the Jews.[548]

The people of Canaan were known as Canaanites, descendants of Ham, "from whom came the Philistines."[549] The "land of Canaan" is identified as *Palestina* or Palestine.[550] Therefore, Palestinians are considered the Indigenous people of the land historically known as Canaan or Palestine.

After Noah cursed Canaan (as mentioned earlier), God promised Abram that He would give him and his descendants "the land" of Canaan "to inherit." [551, 552] God also told Abram that he would become "a father of many nations" and that his name would no longer be Abram, but Abraham.[553] In this way, Abraham is seen as the patriarch of all three nations: the Gentile nations, the Arab nations, and the Jewish nation.

But wait—did "God really say" this? Did God make a promise to Abram in Genesis 12:1-4, around 1875 BCE, that he would inherit the land of Canaan? Did God actually "curse" Ham and his descendants, as the story suggests, and designate Canaan as a land of curse? Or is it possible that these words reflect the perspective of Noah, or even the later views of Moses, Jewish scribes, or Pharisees, who attributed these sayings to God? Or might these claims have come from someone who "heard a voice" in their head, which they believed to be God's?

When we say, "God said such and such to me," what exactly are we implying? Are we suggesting that God speaks directly to us, that we "hear" His voice? Or could it be that we're simply hearing our own thoughts, which we interpret as divine communication? If we claim, "God spoke to me," are we suggesting, on one hand, that God "blesses" some by speaking to them, while on the other, He "curses" others by withholding His voice? And if so, how does that align with the idea that God shows "no partiality" and calls us to do the same?[554]

The Hebrew scriptures refer to Shem's descendants as the "people of God" and identify them as the "children of Israel."[555] This creates a paradox. How can God favor the people of Shem (the Israelites) while disfavoring the people of Ham (the Palestinians) if He is impartial? If God favors one group over the other, can we say that the Arab-Israeli conflict is rooted in a centuries-old division between two nations—Shem and Ham—fighting over the same land, even though both belong to the same broader racial category—the White race?

From a biblical perspective, the Arab-Israeli conflict can be viewed as a struggle between two "brothers" of the same race: one cursed (Ham) and the other blessed (Shem). According to the scriptures, Ham's descendants were destined to be displaced from the land of Canaan (modern-day Palestine), while Shem's descendants were promised that they would inherit the land, with a divine mandate to take it from Ham's people.

However, are we implying that God Himself caused the conflict between the Palestinians and Israelis? Absolutely not. God is just and impartial. The roots of this ongoing conflict stem not from God's will, but from the way He has been interpreted through the subjective perceptions of those who wrote the scriptural texts thousands of years ago.

So, did God intend for His "chosen people" (the Israelites) to go to war with the Indigenous people of Canaan (the Palestinians) and take their land as the "Promised Land," displacing thousands in the process? The answer to this question, again, depends on how one interprets the scriptures. Historically, the narrative of divine blessing and cursing in these texts has been used to justify territorial conquest. However, whether this was truly God's intent—or merely the interpretation of ancient writers—has been a matter of ongoing theological, political, and military debate.

The influence of American racism on Israel's colonialization of Palestine is rooted in both historical interpretations of religious texts and contemporary political agendas. The biblical narrative of divine promises and curses has been manipulated over time to justify the displacement of Palestinians, often framed through a lens of racial and cultural superiority. This ideology, historically tied to the concept of a "chosen people" inheriting the land of Canaan, resonates with American racial constructs that have long marginalized Indigenous and minority groups. However, it is essential to distinguish between ancient religious narratives and the political realities of modern-day conflict.

While religious interpretations have been wielded to justify colonial actions, the true drivers of the Israeli-Palestinian conflict lie in human-made ideologies and power struggles, rather than any divine decree. Ultimately, understanding this intersection of racism and colonization is key to addressing the broader dynamics that continue to shape the region today.

The Arab-Israeli Conflict

Palestine (known as *Filastin* in Arabic) has been occupied and governed by various foreign powers from 70 CE to 1516 CE. This period began with the Roman destruction of Jerusalem and the Second Jewish Temple, and was followed by control from the Byzantines, Persians, Muslims, Seljuqs, Crusaders, Mongols, Mamelukes, and the Ottoman Empire.[556] The Ottomans ruled Palestine for over 400 years, from 1516 to 1917.

In 1917, towards the end of World War I, the British defeated the Ottoman Empire, bringing an end to its occupation of Palestine. Following this, Britain occupied and administered the region, known as "British Palestine," from 1917 to 1947.[557]

The following is a condensed overview of the conflict, primarily drawn from Michael Scott-Baumann's clear and reliable 2021 (updated 2023) book, *The Shortest History of Israel and Palestine*. The italicized terms (e.g., *Balfour Declaration, Zionism, immigration, settlements, curfews, refugee camps*, etc.) are my own, emphasizing significant Israeli actions and policies that have contributed to exacerbating the situation for the Palestinian people.

The 1917 British Balfour Declaration

In 1917, British Foreign Secretary Arthur Balfour issued a brief, sixty-five-word letter to Lord Walter Rothschild, a prominent British Jew from the Rothschild banking family. The letter expressed British support for the establishment of a "national home" for Jews in Palestine, a statement that became known as the *Balfour Declaration*.[558]

The Balfour Declaration affirmed "the establishment in Palestine of a national home for the Jewish people" while pledging to protect "the civil and religious rights of existing non-Jewish communities in Palestine."[559] The Arabs, who comprised 90 percent of the population, were merely referred to as "non-Jewish communities," with their rights limited to "civil and religious" protections. The declaration did not recognize Palestine as an Arab land.[560] By rejecting the Balfour Declaration, the Arabs were denied their right to self-determination.[561]

The Balfour Declaration recognized Jews as a "people" with the right to a "national home," thereby lending support to the Zionist movement. *Zionism,* a term first coined in 1892, was organized into a national movement by Theodor Herzl, the father of modern Zionism, in 1897.[562]

Norman Solomon, a British-Jewish teacher and scholar, explains that the "return to Zion" is rooted in God's promise to Abraham regarding the land where he lived, a promise that has been reaffirmed throughout history.[563] This call to return is not only a physical journey to the land but also a call to "create a Jewish culture" there, fulfilling "God's commandments" in the Holy Land.[564]

In his 1988 book *Israel's Fateful Decisions*, former Chief of Israeli Military Intelligence Yehoshafat Harkabi argues that "the essence of Zionism is *expansion* and the *conquest* of Arab land."[565] He suggests that if Israel were to withdraw from the occupied territories, then it would no longer be considered "Zionist."[566] The Zionist movement began to take shape after the Balfour Declaration, which has continued to influence Israel's political actions.

Upon closer examination of the context, however, it becomes clear that the phrase "return to Zion" refers not to the return of a people, but to the return of the Lord Himself. The Hebrew scriptures proclaim, "The Lord... says... 'I will return to Zion and dwell in the midst of Jerusalem... I will save My people... I will bring them back, and they shall dwell in the midst of Jerusalem.'"[567] This passage is a messianic prophecy delivered by the prophet Zechariah, whose message was written between 520 and 518 BCE.[568] Zechariah was commissioned by God to encourage the Jewish people to rebuild the temple, which had been destroyed by the Babylonians in 587 BCE, in anticipation of the Messiah's return to inhabit it.[569]

The context of this prophecy, therefore, suggests that the people should actively work to rebuild the temple—what would become the Second Temple—in preparation for the promised arrival of the Messiah. This idea is reflected in the twelfth principle of *The Thirteen Principles of Faith,* which states, "Though the Messiah may delay, one must constantly expect His coming."[570]

(The First Jewish Temple was destroyed by the Babylonians in 587 BCE. The rebuilding of the Temple, known as the Second Temple or Herod's Temple, began in 518 BCE and was completed in 18 CE, only to be destroyed by the Romans in 70 CE. The Temple holds immense significance, not only as a central symbol of Jewish identity but also in the Jewish belief in the future coming of the Messiah.)

The Balfour Declaration reinforced Zionism as a movement focused on the conquest of Arab land and the displacement of Palestinians, much like Christopher Columbus's colonization of the Americas, which set the stage for the 1513 Spanish *El Requerimiento*—a document that justified the conquest of Native American land and the eradication of Native American populations.

Many historians and political analysts view the 1917 Balfour Declaration as a pivotal factor in the ongoing Arab-Israeli conflict. In his book *The Iron Cage*, Palestinian historian Rashid Khalidi describes Britain's mandate over Palestine and the Balfour Declaration as a form a constructed "iron cage" for Palestinians.[571]

Khalidi contends that the Balfour Declaration represented a distortion of both historical and religious realities.[572] The declaration promised land to a Jewish population that had been largely absent from the region for centuries and constituted only 10 percent of the population at the time, while ignoring the rights of the Indigenous Palestinian Arabs, who made up the remaining 90 percent and had lived in the region for centuries.[573] For Khalidi, the Balfour Declaration is the fundamental catalyst for the Palestinian struggle for independence and statehood.

When Hitler came to power in 1933, Jewish *immigration* to Palestine increased dramatically as many Jews fled Nazi persecution. The number of Jewish immigrants rose sharply, from around 10,000 in 1932 to 62,000 in 1935.[574] This influx was accompanied by a surge in the establishment of Jewish *settlements* across Palestine, which led to the displacement of numerous Arab families from their land.[575]

The Arab Revolt

The Arab Revolt, known by Arabs as the "Great Rebellion," erupted between 1936 and 1939, led primarily by young Palestinians. The uprising was marked by riots, violence, and widespread unrest, prompting the British to impose *curfews* and deploy an additional 20,000 troops to restore order. The revolt escalated into a civil conflict, resulting in thousands of casualties.[576] By 1939, Jewish immigration to Palestine continued, with the establishment of thirty new Jewish settlements. As a result of the violence, around 10 percent of the Arab male population was killed, while Jews made up about 30 percent of Palestine's total population.[577]

In December 1947, the British announced their intention to withdraw from Palestine by May 1948, transferring control to the United Nations.[578] By that time, a civil war had already erupted a month earlier in November 1947, between Arabs and Jews. The conflict quickly escalated into a brutal cycle of attacks, reprisals, and revenge on both sides.[579] By the time the British left and the State of Israel was established in May 1948, more than 300,000 Palestinian Arabs had been forced to flee their homes and cities.[580]

By the end of the war in January 1949, Israel had suffered 6,000 casualties, nearly 1 percent of its entire Jewish population. Despite this heavy toll, Israel had gained control of 78 percent of the territory that had once been the British Mandate of Palestine, far surpassing the 55 percent designated for the new state by the United Nations.[581] In addition, around 400,000 Palestinian Arabs had been displaced.[582]

Between 1947 and 1949, more than half of Palestine's Arab population—over 700,000 people out of a total of 1.35 million—were displaced as refugees.[583] Most of them ended up in overcrowded, makeshift camps in the West Bank, Gaza, and other areas of Palestine that were not included in the newly established State of Israel. Many others sought refuge in neighboring countries, including Jordan, Syria, and Lebanon.[584]

Israeli Policies

In July 1948, Israel officially adopted a policy of refusing the return of refugees, a decision that intensified the conflict for Palestinians. Many refugees had fled in fear of the ongoing fighting, while others had been expelled by the Israeli military. However, Israel maintained that the refugees were responsible for their own displacement and should not be permitted to return.[585]

Nearly 80 percent of Gaza's population consisted of refugees, living in dire conditions with little access to water, food, or electricity. To assist them, the United Nations Relief and Works Agency (UNRWA) was created in December 1948. Despite this aid, most refugees remained impoverished and unemployed, trapped in a cycle of hardship within overcrowded camps that became symbols of human suffering. As frustration and bitterness grew, several Palestinian nationalist movements began to emerge from these *refugee camps.*[586]

When the State of Israel was founded in 1948, its population stood at 750,000, with more than 80 percent being Jewish. In 1950, Israel introduced the *Law of Return*, which granted any Jew worldwide the right to become an Israeli citizen. This law spurred a surge in Jewish immigration and played a key role in Israel's economic development. By 1952, the Jewish population had doubled to 1.5 million.[587]

The Six-Day War

In June 1967, Israel took control of the Gaza Strip (from Egypt) and the West Bank (from Jordan) during the Six-Day War.[588] Palestinians were faced with harsh choices: many were forced to flee their homes, others were made to sign documents renouncing their right to return, and some were granted *Israeli permits* to remain in the occupied territories.[589] These permits were used to tightly regulate every aspect of daily life, including freedom of movement, access to water, and electricity.[590]

In November 1967, the United Nations Security Council declared Israel's occupation of the West Bank and Gaza Strip to be unlawful under international law.[591] The UN unanimously passed Resolution 242, which called for "the withdrawal of Israeli forces from the territories occupied in the recent conflict" in exchange for peace.[592] However, Israel rejected the terms of Resolution 242.

In defiance of the United Nations, Israel implemented a policy of building *settlements* to house Jewish-Israeli civilians in the Occupied Territories.[593] Israel justified this by claiming it was necessary for "security" reasons, arguing that, under international law, military personnel can be deployed in occupied territories. However, international law, specifically Article 49 of the Fourth Geneva Convention (adopted on August 12, 1949), prohibits an occupying power from transferring its own civilian population into the territory it occupies.[594]

On June 16, 1982, I arrived in Israel at the age of nineteen, marking my first visit to the country. Ten days prior, Israel launched an invasion of southern Lebanon, targeting the bases of the Palestine Liberation

Organization (PLO) and establishing a 25-mile security zone in southern Lebanon to "protect" Israeli civilians in Galilee.[595] I recall working on the construction of the Jerusalem Passion Play on the Mount of Olives, which overlooks the Old City, while hearing fighter jets regularly break the sound barrier overhead.

During the invasion, Beirut was bombarded daily by air, land, and sea for two months. On one particularly devastating day in August 1982, 127 air raids were launched on the city. Over 20,000 people were killed.[596] Thousands of Palestinian and Lebanese civilians lost their lives and hundreds of thousands were left homeless.[597] The invasion also had a significant impact on tourism, leading to the premature closure of the Jerusalem Passion Play. After two and a half months of living and working in Israel, I returned to the United States on August 26th to resume my university studies.

The First Intifada

Life for Palestinians under Israeli occupation is marked by constant frustration and humiliation. They face deportations, arbitrary arrests, beatings, and imprisonment without trial at the hands of the Israeli military. The military enforces strict curfews, and permits are "conditionally" granted, which could take years to obtain. Additionally, Palestinian homes are often demolished if they are "suspected" of sheltering militants. These oppressive measures, along with other Israeli policies, fueled growing anger and resentment, ultimately contributing to the outbreak of the First Intifada, or uprising, on December 8, 1987.[598]

The First Intifada was driven largely by the younger generations, who felt they had nothing left to lose in their struggle to break free from the "iron cage" of occupation. It was a movement led by youth, many of them teenagers, who confronted Israeli military patrols by throwing stones and using slingshots.[599] These "children of the stones" wore keffiyehs as masks, becoming iconic symbols of the uprising.[600] Despite the intensity of their resistance, there was a collective decision within the Palestinian community not to resort to armed violence.[601]

In response to the uprising, Israel cut off essential supplies of gasoline, electricity, and water to Palestinian areas. The Israeli government escalated its "iron fist" approach, using tear gas, water cannons, rubber bullets, and even live ammunition to suppress the protests.[602]

The First Intifada brought global attention to the Palestinian struggle. Media outlets worldwide broadcasted images of teenagers being shot by Israeli forces, highlighting the harsh realities of the occupation. Between 1987 and 1993, over a thousand Palestinians were killed, and 175,000 were imprisoned.[603] The uprising marked the emergence of a new generation of Palestinians determined not to accept defeat.[604] Their demands were clear: the removal of Israeli settlements from the occupied territories, the establishment of an independent Palestinian state, and a just resolution to the refugee crisis.[605]

The Oslo Accords

The Oslo Accords were a series of peace agreements negotiated in 1993 and 1995 between Israeli Prime Minister Yitzhak Rabin and Palestinian PLO Chairman Yasser Arafat. The talks were held in Oslo, Norway.[606]

The Oslo I Accord of 1993 included two key letters of mutual recognition and the Declaration of Principles.[607] In the first letter, Yasser Arafat acknowledged "the right of Israel to exist in peace and security," renounced violence, and called for an end to the intifada.[608] In return, Yitzhak Rabin recognized the "Palestine Liberation Organization (PLO) as the legitimate representative of the Palestinian people."[609] However, Rabin's letter did not recognize the Palestinians' right to national self-determination or the establishment of an independent state.[610] The second part of the agreement, the Declaration of Principles, outlined Israel's commitment to a phased withdrawal of its military forces from parts of the occupied territories, starting with Gaza and the West Bank city of Jericho. It also provided for the establishment of an elected Palestinian Authority (PA) to govern these areas.[611]

The Oslo II Accord of 1995 established a division of the West Bank into three areas, with the understanding that "permanent status negotiations" would determine the final arrangements.[612] Area A, which made up 3 percent of Palestinian territory, was to be fully governed by the PA, including law and order. Area B, comprising 23 percent of the West Bank, was to be policed by the PA, but overall security would remain under Israeli control. Area C, the largest portion at 74 percent, was to remain under direct Israeli military control.[613]

As a result, Palestinians had full control over only 3 percent of the land, while the remaining 97 percent, including critical resources and territory, was under Israeli military authority. Area C, in particular, encompassed Israel's control over vital aquifers and much of the West Bank's most fertile land. The Accord also allowed Israel to construct a network of "Israeli-only" bypass roads, totaling more than 250 miles, which were built on confiscated Palestinian land to connect Jewish settlements.[614] This arrangement left many Palestinians feeling as though they were trapped in isolated enclaves, surrounded by a vast expanse of "Israeli-controlled land," deepening the sense that the occupation was becoming more entrenched than ever.[615]

Despite initial optimism on both sides, the Oslo Accords had almost completely collapsed by 2000.[616] A key factor in the collapse was the continued expansion of Jewish settlements in the occupied territories.[617] In *The Iron Cage*, Rashid Khalidi notes that while Israel "appeared to the world as if it was negotiating peace with the Palestinians," it was simultaneously expanding its settlements and building the infrastructure— roads, electricity, water, and phone lines—needed to support them.[618] From 1993 to 2000, the number of Israeli settlers in the West Bank surged by 70 percent, increasing from 115,000 to 200,000.[619] This expansion undermined the peace process and fueled growing distrust between Israelis and Palestinians.

The Israeli government maintained that the *expansion of settlements* was necessary for "security" and "military needs."[620] Most Palestinians had hoped the Oslo Accords would lead to an end of the military occupation, but instead, Oslo—like the earlier Balfour Declaration—became a tool for strengthening it.[621] Israel repeatedly failed to fulfill its commitments to withdraw its military forces or halt the construction of settlements, leading to widespread frustration and a sense of betrayal among Palestinians.[622]

The Second Intifada

On September 28, 2000, Ariel Sharon made a highly controversial visit to the Temple Mount, a site sacred to both Jews and Muslims, during his campaign for the 2001 Israeli prime minister election. He was accompanied by nearly 1,000 police officers.[623] In response, Palestinians threw stones from the area near the Wailing Wall at Jewish worshippers. Israeli troops opened fire, killing four Palestinians and wounding over 200.[624] The violence quickly spread throughout the West Bank and Gaza, marking the beginning of the Second Intifada, also known as the "al-Aqsa Intifada."

While Sharon's visit was the immediate spark for the uprising, the underlying cause lay in the deepening frustration and anger among Palestinians living under occupation and Israel making their living conditions unbearable.[625] The Oslo Accords had made little progress in improving their conditions. The number of Israeli settlers continued to rise, Palestinian living conditions deteriorated, and the daily humiliations of life under occupation only intensified.[626] The Second Intifada was a response to the growing sense of despair and the lack of meaningful change after years of negotiations.

In Gaza, nearly half of the 1.5 million Palestinians lived in refugee camps.[627] Among them were 8,000 Jewish settlers, who were protected by 50,000 Israeli troops. These settlers controlled about a third of the land and most of the region's water resources.[628]

In the West Bank, over 2 million Palestinians lived alongside 400,000 Jewish settlers.[629] The Israeli military controlled more than 70 percent of the land, including full control over water and electricity supplies, as well as the major roads, most of which Palestinians were prohibited from using.[630] Palestinians faced severe restrictions on their movement due to the presence of Israeli military checkpoints and curfews.

Suicide Bombers

In March 2001, Ariel Sharon became prime minister of Israel. Known as "the Bulldozer" for his tough, uncompromising approach, Sharon was seen by Palestinians as a symbol of brutal military actions. He was responsible for the 1953 Qibya massacre, where Israeli forces killed 69 Palestinians, and was also held accountable for the 1982 Sabra and Shatila massacre, in which Palestinian refugees were killed by Lebanese militias under his watch.[631] Additionally, as housing minister in the early 1990s, Sharon oversaw a major expansion of Israeli settlements in the occupied territories.[632]

In the same month that Sharon took office, Palestinian militant groups, particularly Hamas, began a campaign of suicide bombings inside Israel, targeting buses, restaurants, and other public spaces.[633] While the First Intifada was symbolized by Palestinian teenagers throwing stones, the Second Intifada was marked by the rise of suicide bombers.[634] One key difference was that fewer Palestinians were directly involved in the violence during the Second Intifada, with many attacks being carried out by militant organizations.[635]

In March 2002, a Palestinian suicide bomber killed 29 people in a hotel in Netanya, Israel, in the deadliest attack of the conflict.[636] Two days later, Sharon launched Operation Defensive Shield, aimed at dismantling what Israel described as Palestinian terrorist infrastructure.[637]

During Operation Defensive Shield, the *Israel Defense Forces* (IDF) destroyed homes suspected of harboring militants, arrested and tortured thousands of Palestinians, imposed lengthy curfews, and shut down schools and universities.[638] A British Jew who had moved to Israel later described the harrowing destruction he witnessed in the Jenin refugee camp in the West Bank, where the IDF's military assault left widespread devastation and loss of life. He wrote:

> I was unprepared for the horrifying details what had taken place... Watching the survivors, broken-hearted amid the rubble of their homes ... I felt their rage... I too was seeing the Israeli army ... as a terrorist army, and ... I was beginning to understand the emotions that can drive a suicide bomber to action. I could see how unfair it sounds to a Palestinian to hear a suicide bomber being labelled a terrorist when we refuse to do the same if an Israeli soldier bulldozes a house with a family inside.[639]

Israel's Apartheid

In June 2002, under Ariel Sharon's leadership, Israel began constructing a twenty-five-foot-high concrete "separation wall," which the government described as a "security fence" designed to separate Israelis from Palestinians.[640] While the Israeli government claimed the barrier followed the Green Line, the pre-1967 border between Israel and the West Bank, in reality, the wall cut deeply into the West Bank, effectively encircling some of the largest Israeli settlements.[641] This route was seen by many as an effort to solidify Israeli control over these areas.

Israel has faced accusations of constructing the separation wall as an "apartheid wall," with critics drawing comparisons between Israel and the apartheid regime of white-dominated South Africa.[642] Nathan Thrall, a Jerusalem-based Jewish author and professor, argues, "It is not difficult to make the case that Israel's actions in the West Bank amount to apartheid."[643]

Thrall goes on to explain that the idea of formal annexation turning Israel into an apartheid state has become a core aspect of "left-wing Zionist ideology."[644] In June 2020, over five hundred scholars of Jewish studies, many of them prominent supporters of Israel, signed a letter warning that:

> [T]he annexation of Palestinian territories will cement into place an anti-democratic system of separate and unequal law and systemic discrimination against the Palestinian population. Such discrimination on the basis of racial, ethnic, religious, or national background is defined as 'conditions of apartheid' and a 'crime against humanity.'[645]

Thrall concludes, "The difference is that South Africa's apartheid lasted 46 years. Israel's is at 72 and counting."[646]

The Gaza Question

In April 2003, the "Roadmap to Peace" initiative was launched to bring an end to the Second Intifada and halt the violence.[647] By December 2003, Israeli Prime Minister Ariel Sharon agreed to evacuate Jewish settlers and withdraw Israeli troops from Gaza.[648] Sharon emphasized to his supporters that the Gaza withdrawal would be paired with strengthening Israel's presence in the West Bank, effectively viewing the pullout from Gaza as a trade-off for consolidating control in the West Bank.[649, 650]

The Second Intifada officially ended in the summer of 2005 when Israel withdrew its troops from Gaza, evacuated Jewish settlements, and demolished settlement buildings.[651] However, Israel continued to maintain significant control over Gaza, regulating the movement of people and goods in and out of the territory, as well as controlling water, fuel, and electricity supplies. Additionally, Israel retained control of Gaza's airspace, which allowed it to conduct airstrikes, assassinations, and disrupt media broadcasts.[652] Under international law, "effective control by a hostile army," is considered an occupation.[653]

Before the Gaza evacuation, Israel made attempts to weaken Hamas by targeting its leadership.[654] Hamas, an Islamist political and militant organization, had emerged during the First Intifada as a resistance group offering social services in the occupied territories.[655] On March 22, 2004, Israel assassinated Hamas' spiritual leader, Sheikh Ahmed Yassin, in a missile strike, and later killed his successor along with other senior figures.[656] In response to Israel's withdrawal in September 2005, Hamas fired 29 rockets into Israel.[657]

In May 2021, Israeli police raided the al-Aqsa Mosque in Jerusalem's Old City.[658] Three days later, Hamas issued an ultimatum to Israel, demanding the withdrawal of Israeli forces from the mosque. When Israel refused, Hamas began launching rockets from Gaza into Israel.[659] In response, Israel launched a series of airstrikes on Gaza, targeting various sites. Over the course of eleven days, the conflict resulted in the deaths of 278 Palestinians, including 66 children. Hamas retaliated by firing nearly 3,000 rockets into Israel, which led to the deaths of 13 Israelis, including 2 children.[660]

In my view, the Arab-Israeli conflict has always followed a predictable pattern of cause and effect. It has become an unbroken cycle of actions and reactions, beginning with an Israeli initiative that prompts an Arab response, followed by an Israeli retaliation, and then another Arab reaction. This cycle of violence follows a grim and repetitive sequence: if A happens, then B follows. And then A happens again, and B follows once more. The pattern repeats, trapping both sides in a never-ending loop of conflict and suffering.

Netanyahuism

In November 2022, Benjamin Netanyahu was re-elected as Israel's prime minister for the third time, having previously served from 1996-1999 and 2009-2021. He formed the country's most right-wing coalition in history, further cementing Israel's identity as an "ethnonationalist state."[661] Netanyahu pushed for the expansion of Israeli settlements, with some coalition members advocating for annexing parts of the West Bank.[662] Jewish writer Peter Beinart argues that Netanyahu's vision reflects a shift from liberalism to "authoritarian capitalism," blending aggressive nationalism with economic and technological power.[663]

In his 2023 book *The Palestine Laboratory*, Jewish Australian-German journalist Antony Loewenstein writes that "'Netanyahuism' aims to crush Palestinian aspirations."[664] He highlights how Israel's world-class weapons industry is "tested on occupied Palestinians" before being marketed as "'battle-tested.'"[665] Loewenstein, who lived in East Jerusalem's Sheikh Jarrah neighborhood from 2016 to 2020, reported on the harsh treatment of Palestinians by Israeli police in the West Bank, Gaza, and East Jerusalem.[666] He argues that testing weaponry on Palestinians has been "state policy" since Israel began occupying Palestinian territories.[667]

Loewenstein observes that militarism has become Israel's "guiding principle," noting that ending the conflict with Palestinians would undermine both the country's economy and founding ideology.[668] By June 2024, Israeli military exports had reached a record $12.5 billion, fueled by its "Palestine laboratory." He describes Palestine as "Israel's workshop," where the occupied population is used to perfect "methods of domination."[669]

Loewenstein also draws a connection between the "Israelification" of U.S. security forces post-9/11 and their treatment of minorities in the United States.[670] He sees parallels between the oppression of Palestinians and the systemic abuse of African Americans and Native Americans, rooted in the defense of slavery and white supremacy.[671] Loewenstein points to the 2013 Black Lives Matter movement, which explicitly linked the colonization of Palestine to the mistreatment of minorities in the United States.[672] In 2021, Congresswoman Cori Bush tweeted, "The Black and Palestinian struggles for liberation are interconnected, and we will not let up until all of us are free."[673]

Less than a year after Netanyahu's re-election, on October 7, 2023, Hamas launched a surprise attack on Israel, firing rockets from Gaza and sending fighter jets across the border. In one day, Israel suffered more casualties than in the 1956, 1967, and 1973 wars combined.[674] In response,

Israel bombarded Gaza and cut off food, fuel, electricity, and water supplies.[675]

By October 15, the Gaza Health Ministry reported over 2,600 deaths, and the UN agency for Palestinian refugees estimated one million displaced people within Gaza, which faced a growing humanitarian crisis.[676]

As of mid-2020, 130 of the 193 UN member states recognized the state of Palestine, and by May 2024, that number had increased to 144.[677] However, as of June 2024, the United States continues to support Israel's "illegal" occupation and colonization of Palestinian land, which have been recognized as "occupied" for over 75 years.

In the Introduction to *The Palestine Laboratory,* Antony Loewenstein writes:

> I grew up in a liberal Zionist home in Melbourne, Australia, where support for Israel wasn't a required religion but certainly expected... I soon became uncomfortable with the explicit racism against Palestinians... Palestinians had to suffer to make Jews feel safe. This felt like a perverted lesson from the Holocaust... I'm an atheist Jew.[678]

Loewenstein goes on to explain how Palestine became a testing ground for Israel's military-tech complex, where tools of surveillance, home demolitions, indefinite detention, and state violence are developed and refined by the "Start-up Nation."[679]

Personal Testimony

I visited Palestine nine years later a second time during the First Intifada in May 1991. I stayed with a Palestinian family in Beit Sahur, a town about two miles southeast of Bethlehem, for two weeks. One evening, while standing on the house balcony, I saw a young activist walking down the road wearing a keffiyeh mask, distributing propaganda leaflets in support of the Intifada. I considered secretly filming him with my video camera, but a family member quickly warned me, "Turn it off!" I later realized she was concerned that any involvement with the Intifada could endanger both her family and mine, as I would likely face questioning and have my video camera confiscated by Israeli police at Tel Aviv airport.

The next day, the family and I took a trip north to Tiberias, Israel, on the western shore of the Sea of Galilee. Once in Tiberias, I noticed armed Israeli soldiers everywhere. While I felt secure, I also felt a sense of anxiety for the Palestinians, constantly aware that I was being watched. On the return trip to the West Bank, we were pulled over by Israeli police who had noticed the car's West Bank license plates. It was clear that we were being harassed, a common form of *racial profiling* in Israel—whether through license plates, permits, roadblocks, or the "security" wall. The police detained us for an extended period, questioning each of us, including me, with mundane and invasive inquiries. The experience was frustrating, humiliating, and made me deeply angry at the Israeli police's relentless control.

In May 1994, I returned to Palestine a third time and stayed with the same family until September. During this time, I helped manage a small, dusty gym with old but functional equipment. In my book, *The Fitness Mindset: 7 Habits for Peak Performance*, I recount this experience and talk about how to make the most of any equipment, no matter how outdated or limited.[680] Young Palestinians came to the gym when they heard about the "American" working there, and I made friends with a few of them—they were all friendly and respectful.

One day, during a local demonstration against Israel's occupation, the Israeli military suppressed the protest and retaliated by cutting off the water supply to surrounding communities, including Beit Sahur. This collective punishment was intended to break the spirit of the Palestinian people, forcing them to suffer and turning them against each other. By stripping Palestinians of necessities like water, food, and electricity, Israel has sought to keep them divided and powerless, maintaining control over their lives.

The Arab-Israeli conflict is a complex and deeply rooted struggle, shaped by scriptural interpretation, a history of dispossession, displacement, and unfulfilled promises. The Balfour Declaration, a key historical turning point, set the stage for the Zionist project at the expense of the Palestinian population, igniting a struggle for self-determination that continues to this day.

From the displacement of Palestinians in 1948 to the ongoing expansion of Israeli settlements in the West Bank, the cycle of violence and retaliation has perpetuated a sense of injustice and suffering for both sides. Efforts at peace, like the Oslo Accords, have failed to break the cycle, often exacerbating tensions through actions that undermine the potential for genuine reconciliation.

As long as the core issues of displacement, occupation, and unequal rights remain unresolved, the conflict is likely to persist, leaving a path of violence and human suffering in its wake. The international community's failure to enforce meaningful solutions and accountability only deepens the divide, making lasting peace an increasingly elusive goal.

One's Information

The Internet is the ultimate source of information, flooded with content from self-proclaimed "experts." Much of this information is learned passively, without critical thinking or reflection. As such, it does not constitute genuine knowledge—it's not the kind of practical, actionable knowledge you can apply as a skill. One exception to this might be certain "how-to" YouTube videos, which offer more hands-on guidance.

Not all information is factual. On one hand, facts are proven to be true, verifiable, and beyond dispute. One the other hand, information can serve as evidence for facts but may also be challenged as unsubstantiated or unverifiable. It is our responsibility to assess the "reliability" of the information we encounter.

Wikipedia asserts that it is the largest online source of *free information*. However, it does not claim that all its content is factual. In fact, some entries include a "citation needed" note, indicating that sources are required to verify the information. This is meant to ensure that Wikipedia content is verifiable and open to scrutiny. But even when an entry is cited, it doesn't guarantee its accuracy. Wikipedia is a tertiary source of "information," meaning it compiles and summarizes content rather than providing original, verified facts.

A primary source is an original work created by an author to present *knowledge* on a specific topic (e.g., Nietzsche's writings on morality). A secondary source offers an *interpretation* or analysis of a primary source to clarify or expand upon its ideas (e.g., Walter Kaufmann, a scholar and expert on Nietzsche). A tertiary source compiles both primary and secondary sources to provide *information,* but it can sometimes misrepresent or oversimplify the knowledge of the original author and scholars (e.g., online encyclopedias).

When scrolling through the Wikipedia article on Nietzsche, the reader will notice that primary sources are listed first under "works," while secondary sources (citations) are listed second under "references."

An easy and convenient way to *get* "information" about Nietzsche is by reading through a Wikipedia entry. A more moderate and passive approach to *gain* an "understanding" of Nietzsche is to explore a secondary source, where an expert interprets his ideas, often cited in the article.[681] The more challenging and active way to *acquire* true "knowledge" of Nietzsche is to read his original works. By reading, studying, and engaging with Nietzsche's texts directly, you can gain deeper insights while grappling with the complexities of his philosophy.

Many websites on the Internet either fail to properly cite their sources or misquote them, often assuming a quote comes from a primary source without verifying it. It is essential to know how to distinguish between a genuine quote, a misquote, and a paraphrase.

For example, the quote, "We are what we repeatedly do. Excellence, then, is not an act but a habit," is frequently attributed to the Greek philosopher Aristotle, often thought to appear in his influential work *Nicomachean Ethics*. However, after reviewing seven different translations of Aristotle's *Ethics* and studying the text extensively for my master's thesis, I can confirm that Aristotle never said this.[682] It is a misquote—a piece of misinformation. The quote is actually a paraphrase of Aristotle's ideas by Will Durant in his 1929 book *The Story of Philosophy*. Here is the full quote from Durant in its proper context:

> Excellence is an art won by training and habituation: we do not act rightly because we have virtue or excellence, but we rather have these because we have acted rightly; 'these virtues are formed in man by his doing the actions;' we are what we repeatedly do. Excellence, then, is not an act but a habit...[683]

Durant does quote Aristotle (indicated by the single quotation marks), but he then paraphrases Aristotle's words without using quotation marks, leading to the Aristotelian misquote.

There are, however, two issues with Durant's citation. First, he cites Book 2, Chapter 4 of Aristotle's *Ethics* in his footnote but omits line numbers, which would have helped pinpoint the exact passage. Second, it's unclear which translation of Aristotle Durant used for this quotation.

Of the seven translations of Aristotle's *Ethics* in my personal library, H. Rackham's 1926 translation, published by the Loeb Classical Library, comes closest to Durant's 1929 quote. In Rackham's version, Aristotle is quoted as saying, "virtue results from the repeated performance of just and temperate actions" (2.4.1105b4).[684]

Here's another example of a quote that seems to be misattributed to a primary source. This quote appears on multiple websites and in Robert Greene's 1998 bestseller *The 48 Laws of Power*, where he attributes it to Niccolò Machiavelli's *The Prince*. The quote reads:

> Any man who tries to be good all the time is bound to come to ruin among the great number who are not good. Hence a prince who wants to keep his authority must learn how not

to be good, and use that knowledge, or refrain from using it,
as necessity requires.[685]

The quote appears twice in the preface of Greene's book, but he fails to cite a specific chapter or page number from *The Prince* to verify its origin.

I checked the six translations of *The Prince* in my personal library—two of which are in PDF format—to track down the source of this quote. My first attempt was to search for a common word, such as "good," in the hope of finding the exact quote. However, when I searched for "good," I came up empty.

At this point, it's important to recognize the fallacy of overgeneralization. Searching for an exact translation based on a single word like "good" can be misleading because different translators may choose slightly different phrasing. It's highly likely that Greene's quote comes from a translation I don't have in my collection. Greene only references one specific translation of *The Prince* in his book: a 1940 edition of both *The Prince* and *The Discourses*.

The most likely source of the quote is near the beginning of Chapter 15, *"Of the Things for Which Men, and Princes in Particular, are Praised or Blamed."* In this chapter, Machiavelli writes:

A man who strives to make a show of correct comportment in every circumstance can only come to ruin among so many who have other designs. Hence it is necessary for a prince who wishes to maintain his position to learn how to be able not to be good, and use or not use this ability according to circumstances.[686]

This translation is by Peter Constantine in *The Essential Writings of Machiavelli* (Modern Library, 2007), p. 59.

We can compare Constantine's translation with Greene's quote highlighting the commonalities between the two texts based on certain shared words or phrases, which might indicate a similarity in meaning, tone, or context. The following shared terms overlap in both: "man" and "ruin." The word "hence" also appears in both quotes. Looking closely at the wording, we can see that:

(1a) Greene: "tries to be good all the time"
(1b) Constantine: "strives to make a show of correct comportment"

(2a) Greene: "wants to keep his authority"
(2b) Constantine: "wishes to maintain his position"

(3a) Greene: "must learn how not to be good"
(3b) Constantine: "to learn how to be able not to be good"

(4a) Greene: "and use that knowledge, or refrain from using it, as necessity requires"
(4b) Constantine: "and use or not use this ability according to circumstances"

While there are some differences in wording, the underlying meaning is consistent. Greene's quote is not a misquote, but rather a different translation using alternative words to express the same idea (i.e., a paraphrase).

Another way to confirm the source of Greene's quote is by reviewing other chapters in *The Prince* that explore the idea of "not being good" when necessary. Chapter 18, *"Of the Need for Princes to Keep their Word,"* touches on a similar theme. It reads:

> But if it becomes necessary to refrain, you must be prepared to act in the opposite way, and be capable of doing it ... a new ruler cannot always act in ways that are considered good because, in order to maintain his power, he is often forced to act treacherously ... Hence, he must be prepared to

vary his conduct as the winds of fortune and changing circumstances constrain him and, as I said before [in Chapter 15], not deviate from right conduct if possible, but be capable of entering upon the path of wrongdoing when this becomes necessary.[687]

This translation is by Russell Price in *Machiavelli: The Prince* (Cambridge University Press, 1998), p. 62. In my opinion, Price's translation of Chapter 18 is more faithful to Machiavelli's message in Chapter 15 than Constantine's, as it emphasizes the need for flexibility in a ruler's behavior in response to changing circumstances.

In conclusion, while Greene's quote differs slightly from the translation of *The Prince* that I have, it is not a misquote. Instead, it represents a different translation of the same core idea: a prince must learn when and how to act in ways that may not always align with conventional ideas of "goodness" in order to maintain power.

A quote without a source is incomplete and lacks the context needed to understand why the author said what they did. When a quote is properly sourced, it allows you to explore its context, deepening your understanding and providing the opportunity to apply its lessons to enrich your own life.

The vast amount of information available on the Internet requires critical evaluation to ensure its accuracy and reliability. While platforms like Wikipedia offer easy access to a wide array of content, their status as tertiary sources means that they can sometimes oversimplify or misrepresent knowledge. To acquire true understanding, it is essential to engage directly with primary sources, as this allows for a deeper, more nuanced grasp of the material. Misquotes and misattributions are common, making it crucial to verify the origins of quotes and citations. By practicing discernment and seeking out well-sourced, original material, we can move beyond surface-level information to cultivate genuine, actionable knowledge.

One's Habits

The brain forms habits that directly impact how we think, feel, and act. In other words, our thoughts shape our emotions and behaviors.[688] A habit is a behavior that has been repeated so often it becomes automatic.[689] Essentially, a habit is an action we perform without consciously thinking about it.

A habit can be either beneficial or harmful depending on its impact on your health and well-being. For example, eating pizza every day and drinking alcohol regularly are habits that can harm your health. On the other hand, preparing and cooking meals daily, along with drinking plenty of water, not only supports your health but also benefits your finances.

Similarly, a habit's value can be judged by how it affects your actions. Useless habits that don't add value to your life tend to fade away, while productive habits that contribute to your goals get reinforced. In essence, habits are a series of automatic behaviors that help solve the problems and stressors we face regularly.[690]

As habits form, the brain's activity levels decrease. You begin to focus on cues that predict success and tune out distractions. The brain essentially creates a mental rule: "If this, then that."[691] James Clear, in his book *Atomic Habits*, explains that habit formation is the process through which a behavior becomes more automatic with repetition. The more you repeat a behavior, the more the brain structures itself to perform that task more efficiently.[692]

Repetition strengthens neural connections in the brain, *physically* altering its structure and making the skill easier to perform.[693] Whether you're learning to cook, fix things, exercise, learn, think, or work, repetition helps you improve. Mastery in any field—be it cooking, sports, philosophy, or ethics—comes through consistent practice.

Repetition is a form of change. Each time you repeat a habit, you reinforce the neural pathways associated with that behavior, making it easier and more automatic over time.[694] Think of it like an athlete training—repeated practice is key to improving performance and making the behavior second nature.[695]

To create a new habit is to form new neural connections in the brain. By repeating an action, you make those connections stronger until the behavior becomes automatic. This ability of the brain to rewire itself is known as *neuroplasticity*—the brain's capacity to adapt, change, and form new neural pathways. The term "neuroplasticity" comes from "neuron" (the brain's nerve cells) and "plastic" (meaning malleable or changeable).[696] This challenges the old belief that the brain is hardwired, showing instead that the brain evolves over time and adapts to new patterns of thinking and behavior.[697, 698]

With billions of neurons and trillions of connections, our brains are capable of incredible things. This capacity for change gives us a powerful insight into behavior: habits form based on *frequency,* not time.[699] The real question isn't "How long does it take to build a habit?" but rather, "How many repetitions does it take to make a habit automatic?" What truly matters is how often you perform a behavior.[700]

Aristotle believed that a single action or moment in time doesn't define a person's character; rather it is the repetition of actions over time that shapes who we are. He emphasized that it is through the "repeated performance of virtuous actions that we become good."[701] Will Durant expands on this idea, stating that "we do not act rightly because we have virtue or excellence, but we rather have those because we have acted rightly... We are what we repeatedly do. Excellence, then, is not an act but a habit..."[702]

What really counts on building a habit is the consistent practice of the right actions. As James Clear notes, "All habits follow a trajectory—from effortful practice to automatic behavior," a process known as *automaticity.*[703] This is the ability to perform a behavior effortlessly and automatically, on a "nonconscious" level, once enough repetition has made it second nature.[704]

The power of habit lies in its ability to shape our thoughts, emotions, and behaviors through repetition. As the brain forms neural pathways, actions become automatic, reinforcing either beneficial or harmful habits based on their impact on our lives. The key to building positive habits is consistency; with enough practice, behaviors transition from effortful to automatic. Aristotle's belief that our character is shaped by repeated actions is reflected in the modern understanding of neuroplasticity, which shows that our brains are capable of adaptation and growth. By focusing on the right behaviors and consistently reinforcing them, we can harness the brain's potential to build habits that lead to lasting personal transformation and achievement.

One's Associations

In his *Nicomachean Ethics*, Aristotle identifies three types of associations: those based on utility, pleasure, and integrity.[705] Utility-based associations are grounded in mutual benefit, where individuals interact for practical reasons.[706, 707] This is especially true in business contexts, such as companies, institutions, organizations, and governments. These associations are typically driven by intentional actions aimed at achieving shared goals or securing advantages.[708] Pleasure-based associations are driven by emotions and the enjoyment of one another's company.[709, 710] These associations are more spontaneous and arise from the pleasure of shared experiences. Integrity-based associations are rooted in love and mutual respect for each other's qualities, guided by an "ethics of care," valuing each other's well-being.[711, 712] Such associations take time to develop, as individuals must grow familiar and intimate with one another.[713] Once this connection is formed, trust naturally follows.[714] Integrity-based associations are rare and exceptional.[715] Since most associations are founded on utility or pleasure, I will discuss these.

Utility-based associations are essential for the functioning of social communities, as they allow individuals to support one another through practical means. Such associations are rooted in the idea of usefulness, where individuals come together to achieve mutual benefits or profits. These associations can be highly advantageous, but they may lack emotional depth or personal connection.[716] Even when both parties provide valuable services or goodwill, the exchange often remains transactional. Examples of utility-based associations include professional associations, such as between coworkers or business partners, as well as familial associations like those between parents and children or between spouses. Other examples include online connections or participation in support groups.

In contrast, pleasure-based associations are primarily valued for the enjoyment and companionship they bring. These associations are driven by emotion, and the bond is often fleeting, dependent on mutual enjoyment. If one person's feelings change or if the pleasure diminishes, the association can easily dissolve.[717, 718] Pleasure-based associations are often formed through shared activities or common interests, such as exercising together, engaging in intellectual discussions, socializing, or participating in casual conversations, like gossiping.

Gossip is a behavior that frequently emerges in both utility-based and pleasure-based associations, especially in the workplace. Gossip can be classified into three types: neutral, positive, and negative. Neutral gossip involves sharing information without judgment, while positive gossip offers support or praise for someone, such as complimenting a colleague or friend. Negative gossip, however, involves spreading harmful information, often based on half-truths or outright lies, and can be a form of bullying. Negative gossipers typically seek validation by tearing others down, reflecting a lack of self-esteem.

Research suggests that gossip can serve a useful purpose in utility-based associations. It helps individuals bond with their social group, exchange information, vent emotions, and maintain social order.[719] In pleasure-based associations, gossip can also be pleasurable. Studies indicate that gossiping can trigger the release of oxytocin, a hormone linked to bonding and feelings of connection, which further reinforces the emotional enjoyment of such exchanges.[720]

Aristotle's distinction between utility-based, pleasure-based, and integrity-based associations highlights the varied ways in which human connections are formed and maintained. While utility-based associations focus on practical benefits and are essential for societal functioning, pleasure-based associations are driven by emotional enjoyment and can be more transient. Gossip, which often arises in both types of associations, can serve as a tool for bonding, emotional expression, and maintaining social cohesion. However, its potential to be negative underscores the complexity of human relationships. Ultimately, these associations reflect the diverse ways in which individuals interact, demonstrating the importance of context and intent in shaping the quality and longevity of our connections with others.

One's Books

Does reading a book or listening to an audiobook energize you, drain you, or leave you feeling sluggish? How do you engage *with* the material—do you simply absorb it, or do you find ways to apply what you learn? The books we choose shape our thoughts, emotions, and actions. They sharpen our literacy, broaden our knowledge, enhance cognitive abilities like memory and focus, and stimulate our imagination.

Reading is a lifelong journey of personal growth, offering us new perspectives on people and the world, often transforming a narrow, self-centered view into a more expansive, compassionate one. The genre of book we pick influences this transformation. There are three primary types of literature: fiction, non-fiction, and creative non-fiction.

Fiction consists of imaginative works that take us beyond the bounds of reality. Classic examples include Homer's *The Iliad*, Shakespeare's *Hamlet*, and Dante's *The Divine Comedy*. Fiction allows us to experience the world through the writer's eyes, which fosters empathy, creativity, and imagination.

Non-fiction, on the other hand, covers factual works, including history, science, philosophy, and biographies. Key examples include Thucydides' *History of the Peloponnesian War*, Aristotle's *Organon*, Hawking's *A Brief History of Time*, and Goggins' *Can't Hurt Me*. Non-fiction deepen our understanding of the world, providing insight into human knowledge and motivating us to grow, mature, and navigate the world more effectively.

Creative non-fiction blends the narrative qualities of fiction with the factual nature of non-fiction. Notable works in this genre include Plato's *The Republic*, Aquinas' *Summa Theologiae*, and Sagan's *Cosmos*. This genre encourages us to explore questions that stretch beyond conventional wisdom, challenging us to search for deeper truths that unite theory and experience.

In *Language in Thought and Action*, S. I. Hayakawa argues that literature expands our emotional and intellectual horizons. He writes, "People who have read good literature have lived more than people who cannot or will not read."[721] He goes on to explain that reading *Gulliver's Travels* means experiencing Jonathan Swift's disgust at the human condition, while reading *Huckleberry Finn* lets us feel what it's like to drift down the Mississippi River on a raft. He emphasizes that literature allows us to "live" multiple lives, transcending time and geography.

As Hayakawa points out, reading offers us a unique form of communication: the ability to feel what others have felt about life, even if they lived centuries ago or in far-off places. In this way, literature opens up countless lives and perspectives, enabling us to experience the world through many lenses. He says, "It is not true that we have only one life to live; if we can read, we can live as many more lives and as many kinds of lives as we wish."[722]

Through the study of works by philosophers such as Aristotle (*Nicomachean Ethics*), Kant (*Critique of Pure Reason*), Nietzsche (*Genealogy of Morals*), and Sartre (*Existentialism is a Humanism*), one can gain a deeper understanding of human thought and behavior. These thinkers offer valuable frameworks for examining life, broadening perspectives on individuals and society. Their insights contribute to more reflective and balanced approaches to life's challenges, encouraging critical thinking and personal growth.

In *Autumn Floods*, the ancient philosopher Chuang-Tzu uses a metaphor to illustrate the difference in perspective between someone who is limited in their view of the world and someone who embraces a broader vision. He compares a frog sitting at the bottom of a well with a turtle swimming in the vast sea. The frog, content in its small, muddy home, can only see a sliver of the sky above it, unable to grasp the full expanse. Meanwhile, the turtle, diving into the depths of the ocean, has no concept of the sea's full extent, yet revels in the unknown and the limitless possibilities it holds.[723]

People who don't read are like the frog, confined to a narrow view of the world. They are content with their limited perspective and fail to look beyond the boundaries they've set for themselves. In contrast, readers are like the turtle, venturing into the unknown and embracing the vastness of knowledge and experience. They take risks, dive deeper, and discover new realms that expand their understanding of life.

Ultimately, we are the sum of what we choose to read and internalize. Whether we remain frogs in the well or become turtles swimming in the sea is up to us. Reading shapes our minds, broadens our outlook, and opens the door to countless lives and experiences we might never otherwise know.

The books we choose to read shape our thoughts, perspectives, and actions, guiding our personal growth and intellectual development. Whether fiction, non-fiction, or creative non-fiction, literature allows us to engage with the world in profound ways, offering new insights, expanding our empathy, and challenging our understanding of life. As Hayakawa suggests, reading is a journey that enables us to "live" many lives, experiencing diverse emotions and perspectives across time and space.

The more we read, the more we embrace the vast ocean of knowledge, shedding the limitations of the "frog in the well" and transforming into the "turtle in the sea" who explores the boundless possibilities life has to offer. Ultimately, the choice to read and reflect on literature determines how expansively we see the world and ourselves.

One's Social Media Influence

Our need to be simulated by social media content has experienced explosive growth since its emergence in the early 2000s. As of mid-2024, the leading and fastest-growing platforms are Facebook, with 3 billion monthly active users (MAUs), YouTube with 2.5 billion MAUs, Instagram with 2.3 billion MAUs, and TikTok, which has 1 billion MAUs. The number of so-called "influencers" on these platforms varies widely, with estimates ranging from 3 million to 38 million. For instance, one TikTok influencer, just 27 years old, has amassed 94.2 million followers, 2.3 billion likes, and a net worth estimated between $6 million and $16 million.

Mindless scrolling through social media has become a *default* activity for many, occupying moments of boredom and offering constant entertainment. We might stumble upon a post from someone we don't know, yet their content captivates us, triggering an emotional response and a hit of dopamine. Whether we "like" or "love" the post, or leave a comment, we engage with it in a way that boosts the visibility of the post, ultimately bringing the influencer more followers, fame, and money. This cycle continues as we scroll, seeking our next dopamine fix.

There are distinctions between "influencers," "digital creators," and "deepfakes." An *influencer* is someone who: (1) promotes brands or products, (2) prioritizes brand partnerships, and (3) shapes consumer purchasing decisions. A *digital creator* is someone who: (1) produces engaging content to entertain, (2) experiments with new formats or mediums, and (3) connects with others who share similar values or interests. A *deepfake,* on the other hand, is an AI-generated manipulation of real people, often used to: (1) spread fake news or misleading videos, (2) damage the reputations of public figures, or (3) distort our perception of reality.

When individuals use artificial means to become an influencer, creator, or deepfake, they lose their authenticity. The most famous influencers are often the "enhancers," using plastic surgery, performance-enhancing drugs, or digital filters to alter their appearances in order to sell products or promote their personal brand. Renowned creators can be seen as the "bored"—they are constantly producing experimental content to entertain others and stave off their own boredom. Deepfake creators are the "liars," creating fake videos or images that challenge our understanding of truth, often to manipulate our perception of reality.

There are, however, deepfake videos that aim to awaken us from our complacency, attempting to reveal the idea that we may be living in a simulation, a notion that some claim is being used to control us. One of the most famous deepfake videos is a manipulated version of Mark Zuckerberg, created by Bill Posters and Daniel Howe, which critiques the very systems that govern our online lives.

In a world flooded with digital content, authenticity must be questioned. It's important not to take everything at face value. As Nietzsche might say, we should look "beyond good and evil"—beyond the image we see on the screen. If something looks too perfect, too rehearsed, or too unrealistic, it may not reflect reality in any meaningful way.

The masses spend countless hours on social media, fueling the creation of viral sensations with their likes, shares, and comments. This engagement leads to sponsorships that advance the careers of influencers, creators, and deepfake artists, continuing the cycle of product promotion, content creation, and fame. It's a self-perpetuating loop: the more people interact with the content, the more the influencer benefits. The influencer, creator, and deepfake all embody the ancient claim by Protagoras: "Man is the measure of all things," asserting that their posts are the "standard" by which knowledge and influence are shaped. However, when Francis Bacon says "knowledge and human power are synonymous," he is reminding us that knowledge should not be used merely to perpetuate consumerism or manipulate realities, but rather to improve human lives.[724, 725, 726]

While social media sponsorships can be financially rewarding, they come at a cost. The influencer, the creator, and the deepfake all sacrifice their individuality, denying the process of self-discovery and the responsibility of becoming their true selves. Instead, they conform to the demands of the "tribe"—the mass audience that both shapes and consumes their content. The masses, in turn, are complicit in making these figures into what they are, welcoming them as leaders within their digital communities.

Many of us fall into the trap of wanting to emulate these social media sensations. We see their success and seek to replicate it, imitating their actions, their appearance, their lifestyles. But as Emerson wisely warned, "Imitation is suicide." By copying others, we abandon our own authentic selves, seeking approval or recognition from external sources rather than cultivating our own unique voice. Our egos crave attention, and we find ourselves asking, "Look at me." We long for fame, knowledge, and power, thinking that by mimicking others, we can gain the same respect or influence they have. But in doing so, we limit our own happiness, as we are not living authentically but merely pretending to be someone else.

As P.T. Barnum once said, "No one ever made a difference by being like everyone else." Hegel, the philosopher of dialectics, reminded us that "Nothing great has ever been accomplished without passion."[727] To create something meaningful, to become an authentic and autonomous self, requires a shift in how we approach our lives. It means moving away from conforming to social expectations and instead embracing the courage to express our individuality and create something truly original. This transformation is not just for our own benefit; it has the potential to impact the lives of others in profound ways, leaving a legacy of authenticity and passion.

In the end, to live well and make a difference in the world requires us to question the reality presented to us by social media and resist the temptation to simply follow the crowd. Instead, we must strive to become the best version of ourselves—not through imitation, but through genuine self-expression, guided by knowledge that benefits both ourselves and humanity.

The rise of social media has created a world where influencers, creators, and even deepfakes shape our perceptions and drive our engagement, often at the cost of authenticity and individuality. While these digital figures gain fame and financial reward, they also become products of external expectations, sacrificing their true selves to meet the demands of the masses. As consumers of this content, we must recognize the dangers of imitation and the pressure to conform, as it leads us further from our own unique identities. True fulfillment and meaningful impact come not from replicating others, but from embracing our individuality and creating with passion and purpose. By questioning the reality presented by social media and seeking authenticity, we can cultivate a life of genuine self-expression that enriches both our lives and the world around us.

One's Identity

Understanding one's identity is a complex pursuit, but truly comprehending it goes even further. It demands introspection—an active exploration of who we are—rather than simply settling for the assumptions we hold about ourselves.

Our sense of "self" is shaped both by external influences—social interactions, cultural norms, education, history, and media—and by internal factors such as our personal desires, habits, and interests. The "external self" is shaped by the world around us, while the "internal self" is influenced by our personal inclinations and experiences. Together, they form the "conscious self."

Three distinct types of the conscious self exist inauthentically: the *false self,* the *counterfeit self,* and the *dark self.* These inauthentic selves vary in their degree of awareness and destructiveness, from the superficial to the deeply harmful.

Inauthentic selves often arise from insecurity and low self-worth. They don't accept themselves as they are, compensating for their lack of authenticity by imitating others, engaging in corrupt behavior, or reacting destructively. These individual selves remain trapped in insecurity, unable to escape their inauthenticity.

The False Self: The Superficial Mask

The false self is often referred to as the "superficial self," which acts in "bad faith" and presents a distorted version of who we truly are.[728] This self is shaped by external pressures, driven by fear, imitation, and social conformity. The false self tends to:

1. Imitate others out of envy or admiration
2. Mask its identity to "fit in" or feel safe
3. Engage in inconsistent behavior to play "mind games" or manipulate situations
4. Deny responsibility for its actions and avoid consequences
5. Use lies and deception to create a defensive façade
6. Submit to societal norms to belong
7. Engage in insincere, calculated actions driven by hidden agendas
8. Use technology to mislead others

The Counterfeit Self: Corrupt Behavior

When the false self becomes habitual, it can evolve into the counterfeit self—a corrupted version of the false self. It develops into an "eroded conscience" that operates through intention and repression.[729] The counterfeit self is driven by narcissistic and manipulative tendencies. Unlike the false self, it is more aware of its operations and still acts in "bad faith," but in a more self-important manner when presenting itself. The counterfeit self tends to:

1. Display grandiosity and a sense of superiority
2. Use deception and manipulation to achieve personal gain
3. Justify unethical behavior as "business as usual"

4. Pass judgement on others' moral feelings while excusing its own
5. Be cynical about the morality of others, often using it to validate its own corruption
6. Rationalize weaknesses by attributing them to external forces
7. Lack empathy and emotional reasoning
8. Distort reality to appear more attractive[730]

The Dark Self: Destructive and Malignant

The dark self is the rarest and most destructive of the inauthentic selves.[731] It is driven by unconscious repression, stemming from a state of "boredom" and the need for "stimulation" through acts of aggression, cruelty, and chaos.[732] The dark self is indifferent to moral constraints and is often associated with severe emotional and psychological disturbances.[733] The dark self tends to:

1. Imitate destructive and malignant figures expressing contempt and resentment
2. Responds to situations with apathy or deadness devoid of empathy
3. Craves control and domination over others
4. Creates chaos, drama, and suffering
5. Derives satisfaction from inflicting pain
6. Becomes increasingly destructive as society advances
7. Engages in senseless violence without provocation
8. Compensates for boredom with a constant craving for new and extreme stimuli[734]

Of the eighth characteristic, Erich Fromm states:

> [T]he boredom-compensating means are like bulky food without any nutritional value. The person continues to feel 'empty' and unmoved on a deeper level. He 'anesthetizes' this uncomfortable feeling by momentary excitation, 'thrill,' 'fun,' liquor, or sex—but *unconsciously* he remains bored.[735]

The dark self is caught in an endless cycle of needing more stimulation to ward off the deep inner emptiness it feels, but this is ultimately a futile attempt to escape its inner void.

The True Self: Authenticity and Virtue

The true self, in contrast to the inauthentic selves, is the authentic self, rooted in integrity, wisdom, and virtue. It exists outside of social pressures and external influences, untainted by the inauthentic selves that arise from them.

The true self is often difficult to recognize and develop; it requires conscious effort to uncover. The process of discovering the true self involves deep self-awareness, introspection, and reflection. It is the self that chooses actions based on moral values and is guided by reason, compassion, and practical wisdom.

Authenticity is defined as living in accordance with one's core values and beliefs. The true self is not swayed by external expectations but remains grounded in its own ethical framework, acting with balance and purpose. The true self tends to:

1. Act with integrity and follow through on promises
2. Accept responsibility for one's choices and actions
3. Be purposeful and spontaneous living with intention
4. Have the courage to act transparently and in good faith
5. Listen attentively to others and communicate clearly

6. Be consistent in behavior building trust over time
7. Rebel against conformity in favor of self-actualization
8. Express oneself with sincerity, humility, and respect for others

Struggle Between the False Self and the True Self

The tension between the false self and the true self is a constant struggle. We are often pulled in different directions by societal pressures, the desire to belong, and the fear of rejection. As Nietzsche points out, discovering the true self is a rigorous process, like physical training, requiring the discipline to confront the inauthentic selves that obscure it. The path to authenticity is not easy, but it is the only way to find genuine fulfillment.

The true self is not something that can be found through external validation or social approval. It must be discovered through introspection and self-exploration. Nietzsche famously says, "Become who you are," urging individuals to break free from societal molds and create their own identity. This journey requires courage and a willingness to take risks, to live authentically, even when it means stepping outside of comfort zones or challenging the status quo.

The Process of Becoming Your True Self

The process of becoming your true self involves shedding the layers of inauthenticity that have been imposed by society, culture, and personal fears. This process of "individuation," as Carl Jung describes it, is about becoming the person you are meant to be—your most authentic self.[736] It requires embracing personal responsibility, understanding your values, and acting in alignment with them, regardless of external pressures.

In his essay *Self-Reliance*, Ralph Waldo Emerson stresses the importance of nonconformity and individualism. To be your true self, you must reject the constraints of societal norms and traditions and live according to your own principles. As Emerson writes, "Nothing is at last sacred but the integrity of your own mind."[737]

Live Dangerously: The Call to Authenticity

To live authentically is to take risks, to step outside of the safe confines of convention, and to embrace the full range of human experience. Nietzsche challenges us to live dangerously—to embrace life with passion and conviction, to push boundaries, and to act boldly in the pursuit of our true selves. He writes, "The secret for harvesting from existence the greatest fruitfulness and the greatest enjoyment is—to *live dangerously*."[738]

This is the call to break free from the shackles of inauthenticity and live a life that is true to who we are, a life that is driven by our deepest values and desires. Only then can we truly harvest the fruits of existence— fulfillment, happiness, and a sense of purpose.

The Subjectivity of Authenticity

Authenticity is ultimately a subjective experience. It is the deep, personal realization of who we truly are, beyond the external roles we play, or the expectations placed upon us. It is living in a way that is consistent with our true nature, free from the distortions of inauthentic selves.

The journey toward the true self requires self-reflection, self-criticism, and a commitment to personal growth. It is not a destination but an ongoing process of aligning our actions with our core values, desires, and truths. The quest for authenticity is the pursuit of freedom—freedom from societal constraints, freedom from the false self, and freedom to be fully, unapologetically ourselves.

The journey to understanding and embracing one's true self is complex and demanding, requiring deep introspection and a commitment to self-discovery. The struggle between the false self, the counterfeit self, and the dark self can obscure our path, pushing us toward conformity, manipulation, and even destruction. However, the process of shedding these layers of inauthenticity allows us to uncover our true selves—rooted in integrity, wisdom, and virtue. As Nietzsche and Emerson suggest, living authentically demands courage, a rejection of societal expectations, and a willingness to take risks in pursuit of our deepest values. This ongoing journey of self-exploration is not merely about finding fulfillment but about embracing freedom—the freedom to live fully, truthfully, and with purpose. Through this pursuit, we can cultivate a life that reflects our most authentic selves and creates a meaningful impact on the world around us.

Summary of Idols of the Cave

Idols of the Cave suggest that identity is often viewed as fixed and unchanging, overlooking the external influences and internal biases that shape one's sense of self. These influences include our education, history, social interactions, media consumption, personal habits, and perception of ourselves.

Formal instruction is counterfeit learning aimed at societal conformity and wealth accumulation. Self-directed learning fosters genuine intellectual and personal transformation. True learning, as self-directed, involves unlearning false ideas and re-engaging the intellect to acquire wisdom through effort and perseverance.

History, often shaped by authority figures or institutions, carries biases that influence how we understand key events. Historical events, such as the colonization of Native Americans and the justification of slavery, have been shaped by cultural biases and misinterpretations of scripture. In addition, the subjugation of African Americans, rooted in flawed interpretations of religious texts, was justified through "legalized" racism. Colonization, exemplified by Columbus and the transatlantic slave trade, was framed as part of a cultural and biological racial hierarchy.

The impact of such historical narratives extends beyond the past, influencing modern conflicts and ideologies, including the Israeli-Palestinian struggle and ongoing racial prejudice, which has parallels with colonial history. By re-examining history and seeking diverse perspectives, we can unlearn biased views and develop a more balanced understanding of the past. This process allows us to approach life more thoughtfully and navigate it with greater wisdom.

The advent of the Internet as a source of information has led to passive consumption rather than active engagement, reducing true knowledge acquisition. Informed learning requires critical thinking and direct engagement with original sources. Similarly, habits shape our actions and influence our growth, with repetition reinforcing behaviors over time.

Associations with others can be classified as either utility-based, pleasure-based, or integrity-based. Gossip can be classified into three types: neutral (sharing information without judgment), positive (supporting or praising others), and negative (spreading harmful, often false information). The books we choose shape our thoughts, emotions, and actions, broadening our knowledge, enhancing cognitive abilities, and stimulating our imagination.

The rise of social media has led to passive consumption of information, often from influencers or creators who manipulate their appearance and content for personal gain. This cycle of seeking validation through likes and shares reinforces superficiality, detracting from genuine self-expression and critical thought. Social media influence, like history, shapes our perceptions and actions, often encouraging imitation rather than authentic self-discovery.

Understanding one's identity is a complex process that requires deep introspection, going beyond assumptions about who we are. Our sense of self is shaped by external influences (social interactions, culture, media) and internal factors (personal desires, habits). These combine to form the conscious self, which can develop inauthentic selves.

The path to authenticity requires shedding inauthentic layers and embracing personal responsibility. The true self requires courage, self-awareness, and the rejection of conformity. As Nietzsche and Emerson suggest, living authentically involves risks, stepping outside societal molds, and embracing life with passion and conviction.

Section 4: Idols of the Tribe—Questioning Society

Idols of the Tribe are swayed by society's entertainment-driven distractions that shape our perceptions of reality without questioning how these diversions may be unnatural and detrimental, affecting our mental and physical well-being. We invest time, money, and energy into entertainment because it occupies us, offering pleasure and escape. Today, the entertainment industry is a massive, intricate enterprise, encompassing a vast array of cultural systems and generating trillions of dollars in revenue annually. Yet, not all forms of entertainment are created equal. We often assess the value of these activities based on the cost—whether in time, effort, money, or sacrifice—that they require.

Nietzsche argues, "The value of a thing sometimes lies not in what one attains with it, but in what one pays for it—what it *costs* us."[739] The true worth of something isn't solely measured by what we gain from it, but also by the price we pay to obtain it. This could be physical effort, emotional sacrifice, financial cost, or the time spent. The entertainment choices we make reflect the value we attach to these costs: Are we seeking to relieve boredom? Improve our health? Escape reality? Make money?

Francis Bacon describes Idols of the Tribe as inherent biases and limitations of human nature itself.[740] He argues that our senses and minds do not accurately represent reality; rather, they are shaped by the prejudices and limitations of our human nature.[741]

Bacon's idea echoes the Greek sophist Protagoras, who claims, "Man is the measure of all things," suggesting that each individual's perception is the ultimate standard of truth.[742] While Protagoras may be right in some contexts, Bacon argues that this view is flawed because it bears "reference to man" and not to nature or what is natural.[743, 744] The human mind, according to Bacon, is like an "uneven mirror," distorting our perception of the world around us.[745] As a result, Idols of the Tribe emerge from the uniformity of human nature—our biases, our limited faculties, our passions, and even our senses.[746] These idols arise because we falsely assume that our limited perceptions are an accurate reflection of the world.

Bacon's concept of *Idols of the Tribe* also touches on the way societies often accept and internalize these distortions as truth. Masses of people—whether by choice or unconscious conformity—embrace an understanding of entertainment and leisure that distorts what is natural. *Idols of the Tribe* are those who unquestioningly follow the crowd, adopting beliefs and behaviors that align with the distorted standards of the group. These individuals may even mimic unnatural forms of entertainment or seek fame as "influencers," contributing to the very distortions they follow.

Traditionally, entertainment activities that were natural to humans included things like eating, walking, exercising, talking, singing, dancing, playing, and resting—activities that aligned with the natural rhythms and needs of the human body and mind. However, by the mid-20th century, entertainment began to take on more unnatural forms. Technological advancements and the commercialization of leisure transformed simple, natural activities into highly curated or distorted versions of entertainment, designed for consumption rather than genuine well-being.[747]

This shift reflects the way that society has embraced *unnatural* forms of entertainment, which, while popular, often detract from the health of the mind and body. In doing so, they represent a false sense of fulfillment—a distortion of what is truly beneficial for human flourishing. *Idols of the Tribe* are the masses who accept and promote these distortions, shaping and promoting entertainment that is disconnected from our natural, human needs.

In this critique, I examine entertainment activities that may pose risks to our mental and physical well-being. I reflect on how these activities have become normalized and widely accepted, yet may have harmful effects. This analysis covers a range of topics, such as the commercialization of sports and professional leagues, the use of performance-enhancing drugs, the complex challenges of social media, the rise of social influencers, the "Dead Internet" theory, the potential threats of AI to humanity, and the broader impact of the Digital Age on the human mind.

Through this analysis, I seek to question the real value of these widely embraced forms of entertainment and challenge the notion that they genuinely promote our well-being. What are we giving up in exchange for entertainment that distances us from what is natural and truly beneficial? And, in the end, is the price we pay worth it?

Sports Events and Professional Leagues

Two thousand years ago, at the height of the Roman Empire's power in 100 CE, sports events were a major form of public entertainment, with the Colosseum and Circus Maximus hosting thousands of spectators.

The Circus Maximus, used for chariot races, could accommodate up to 250,000 people, while the Colosseum, known for gladiatorial contests, held 50,000 spectators. These *spectacles* or public display of performances were not merely for sport; they were a means of engaging the public emotionally, offering an escape from the monotony of daily life and fueling intense emotions through displays of bravery, fear, and violence.

The gladiators, often fighting to the death, became the central figures of this entertainment.[748] The 2000 film *Gladiator*, starring Russell Crowe, dramatizes the world of Roman gladiators and draws inspiration from real historical figures.

Roman games and similar forms of entertainment—ranging from gladiatorial combat to modern movies—often revolve around placing performers at the center of the spectacle. These events serve to entertain the masses by showcasing human suffering, humiliation, and death, raising questions about the ethics of such violence. Unlike other animals, humans have historically tortured and killed members of their own species not for survival, but for amusement, which many argue is unnatural.

These grand events were often funded by the state and public officials, with famous gladiators becoming valuable assets to politicians who sponsored games to promote their own agendas or bolster their chances in elections.[749, 750] By the 2nd century CE, the cost of hosting a single Roman event had risen to around 750,000 sesterces (roughly $375,000 in modern

U.S. currency).[751] With approximately 12 events held each year, this amounted to an astronomical annual expenditure of $4.5 million, which was a huge sum relative to the global population at the time, which stood at 190 million. In comparison, today's world population exceeds 8 billion.

Fast forward to the 21st century. Professional sports leagues around the world are generating billions in revenue, captivating global audiences in much the same way as the ancient Roman games.

The following figures illustrate the scale of money involved in the modern sports industry, based on 2023-24 estimates from Google AI.

National Basketball Association (NBA)
- Ticket price: $90
- Attendance: 18,000 spectators per game
- Games per season: 82
- Annual revenue from tickets: $132.8 million
- Average NBA player salary: $9.7 million
- Total salary for NBA players: $4.3 billion
- NBA Finals ticket price: $1,000
- Attendance: 19,000 spectators
- Annual revenue from NBA Finals tickets: $1.9 million
- Annual viewership of NBA Finals: 11.64 million viewers

National Football League (NFL)
- Ticket price: $150
- Attendance: 70,000 spectators per game
- Games per season: 272
- Annual revenue from tickets: $2.8 billion
- Average NFL player salary: $860,000
- Total salary for NFL players: $1.5 billion
- Super Bowl ticket price: $8,837
- Attendance: 70,000 spectators
- Annual revenue from Super Bowl tickets: $618.59 million
- Annual viewership of Super Bowl: 112.2 million viewers

Federation Internationale de Football Association (FIFA)

- Ticket price: $100
- Attendance: 21,000 spectators per game
- Games per season: 66
- Annual revenue from tickets: $138.6 million
- Average FIFA player salary: $62,000
- Total salary for FIFA players: $3.4 million
- FIFA World Cup ticket price: $1,300
- Attendance: 40,000 spectators
- Annual revenue from World Cup tickets: $52 million
- Annual viewership of FIFA World Cup: 1.5 billion viewers

Major League Baseball (MLB)

- Ticket price: $53
- Attendance: 18,500 spectators per game
- Games per season: 162
- Annual revenue from tickets: $160 million
- Average MLB player salary: $1.4 million
- Total salary for MLB players: $1 billion
- World Series ticket price: $3,236
- Attendance: 43,000 spectators
- Annual revenue from World Series tickets: $1.4 million
- Annual viewership of World Series: 12 million viewers

World Wrestling Entertainment (WWE)

- Ticket price: $110
- Attendance: 6,500 spectators per event
- Events per year: 300
- Annual revenue from tickets: $2.5 million
- Average WWE Superstar salary: $375,000
- Total salary for WWE Superstars: $16 million
- WrestleMania ticket price: $1,000
- Attendance: 80,000 spectators

- Annual revenue from WrestleMania tickets: $82 million
- Annual WWE viewership: 2 million viewers per week (112 million annually)

International Federation of Bodybuilding (IFBB)
- Olympia Expo ticket price: $150
- Attendance: 40,000 spectators
- Annual revenue from Expo tickets: $6 million
- Olympia final ticket price: $1,000
- Attendance: 10,000 spectators per event
- Annual revenue from final tickets: $40 million
- PPV revenue from Olympia events: $3 million
- Olympia prize pool: $1.6 million

Spectators attending live events often spend significantly beyond the cost of tickets.

Spectator spending at Live Events:
- 28 million spectators attend annual sports events.
- Each spectator spends approximately $1,450 on transportation, lodging, food, drinks, and memorabilia.
- Total additional spending on travel and accommodations: $40.6 billion.

Viewer spending on Memorabilia:
- 1.75 billion viewers watch events at home.
- Each viewer spends about $50 on memorabilia.
- Total spending on memorabilia: $87.5 billion.

Total Economic Impact:
- Total amount spent on an annual event: $128.1 billion.

In total, the financial impact of global sports events is staggering. When factoring in ticket sales, merchandise, player salaries, and viewer contributions, the annual economic output generated by these events reaches astronomical levels, underscoring how deeply embedded sports have become in modern entertainment culture.

While the nature of the spectacle or performer has evolved since the days of ancient Rome, the underlying purpose—captivating and engaging the masses—remains the same.

The sheer amount of money people spend on sports entertainment today is staggering and, in many cases, downright ridiculous. From ticket prices reaching thousands of dollars for high-profile events like the Super Bowl and the World Cup, to the additional spending on travel, food, memorabilia, and other expenses, the total financial outlay for a single event can easily exceed hundreds of billions globally.

The immense revenue generated by these events, combined with the astronomical salaries of players, reinforces the idea that sports entertainment has become a multi-billion-dollar industry, with consumers pouring vast amounts of money into an experience that, while thrilling, often raises questions about the value we place on athletic performers and the lengths to which people will go to be part of it. This phenomenon underscores not only the economic power of sports but also the unyielding desire to be part of something larger, regardless of the costs.

Human Enhancement and Performance-Enhancing Drugs (PEDs)

Human enhancement refers to the use of biotechnologies to alter the natural functions of the mind and body, aiming to improve performance and achieve goals beyond what is naturally possible. This pursuit is driven by the desire to gain a competitive edge, climb social ranks, increase wealth, seek recognition, or fulfill personal aspirations by excelling in activities we enjoy.[752]

The idea of "superior performance" can take many forms—whether it's performing better than one's past self, beating an opponent, or surpassing even the best-known standard.[753] In this context, "superior" often means achieving more than what could be done naturally, through external means that offer an "extra edge" or "performance enhancement."[754]

Performance, in this sense, refers not only to the physical actions we take but also to the mental and emotional expressions of who we are.[755] It encompasses everything from involuntary bodily functions to self-directed actions, such as walking, thinking, or exercising.[756] In his 2003 work *Beyond Therapy: Biotechnology and the Pursuit of Happiness*, Dr. Leon R. Kass, then Chairman of the President's Council on Bioethics, highlighted the relational aspect of performance:

> The idea of performance also suggests a relationship with other performers and spectators: performance before others, with others, and against others. Yet it is also possible to perform certain activities *without* others, on one's own and for oneself, manifesting who we are for our own enjoyment... 'Performance' suggests ... also the possibility of being or seeming to be something other than who and what we are.[757]

This last idea invites us to consider whether we are willing to transform ourselves in our quest for excellence—whether it involves reshaping our nature to achieve something beyond our natural limitations. The temptation, of course, lies in using performance-enhancing substances to achieve this goal. This raises the ethical dilemma: Is the use of such substances—specifically performance-enhancing drugs (PEDs) like anabolic steroids—a "cheat" or an unfair shortcut that undermines true self-directed effort?[758]

PEDs have been shown to improve physical performance—enhancing strength, endurance, appearance, and other attributes—by altering the body's natural state. These substances effectively "reshape" us into something unnatural, making the performance seem superhuman, as though we have transcended our innate, natural abilities.[759] Dr. Kass addresses this concern, noting:

> In trying to achieve better bodies through muscle-enhancing agents, pharmacological or genetic, we are not in fact honoring our bodies or cultivating our individual gifts. We are instead ... voting with our syringes to have a *different* body, with different native capabilities and powers.[760]

By using PEDs, athletes are replacing natural physical and mental gifts with artificial ones, setting new, "unnatural" standards of achievement. This drive to improve oneself through external means can be likened to undergoing cosmetic surgery to achieve an idealized version of oneself—striving to become someone else, someone "better" or "more perfect."

In our quest for self-improvement, the line between striving for excellence and altering who we are becomes increasingly blurred. The question we must face is this: When we enhance or transform our bodies through substances that shift our natural abilities, are we still honoring our true selves? Or are we simply pursuing an idealized version of who we are *not*, attempting to become someone other than the person we were born to be?

Dr. Kass' prediction from 2003 resonates with the issues surrounding steroid abuse today. He warns:

> [T]he very ends we desire might become divorced from any idea of what is humanly superior, and therefore, humanly worth seeking or admiring. We would become a society of spectators, and our activities a mere spectacle. Or a society of parasites, needing and taking, but never doing or acting. Worse of all, we would be in danger of turning our would-be heroes into slaves, persons who exist to entertain us and *meet our standards* and whose freedom to pursue excellence

has been shackled by the need to perform—and conform—
for our amusement and applause.[761]

Today, the public often serves as an audience to the athletes and influencers who represent a distorted vision of human achievement—one that prioritizes larger, faster, stronger, and more extreme appearances at the expense of what genuine excellence represents: the authentic product of personal effort, discipline, and self-determined growth.

As society increasingly glorifies artificially enhanced physiques and performances, we risk losing the distinction between *real* excellence and the counterfeit version driven by chemical enhancements. This obsession with appearance over substance is even evident in how we are drawn to these figures—often not questioning how they achieve their extraordinary feats, but simply celebrating the results, no matter how they are obtained.

Strength—whether in athletic competition or casual fitness—has become an obsession, particularly because performance-enhancing drugs (PEDs) often go undetected and unchallenged. For many, PEDs provide a less scrutinized route to achieving "superior" strength, bypassing the discipline of natural training. This false strength, amplified by PEDs, is celebrated in both competitive and non-competitive spaces, generating billions in the drug and sport industries. Athletes and fitness enthusiasts claim to be "natural" when in fact they rely on unnatural means to perform beyond their true capabilities—a practice that misleads the public and distorts the reality of athletic achievement.

This trend extends to the use of *lifting gear and suits* that artificially aid in lifting weight far beyond a person's natural capacity. These feats often result in new "world records," but the truth is that these records are not born of pure effort. They are products of external assistance, distorting what it means to truly achieve something through one's own, raw strength.

Appearance, too, has become an obsession—particularly the idea of a "perfect" body. Female athletes and influencers often claim that their shapely, sculpted physiques, particularly larger, rounder buttocks, are the result of dedicated workouts. In reality, many of these transformations are not due to exercise alone but rather to cosmetic procedures such as Brazilian butt lifts (BBLs). Their images serve as the currency of social media, fueling financial success by promoting a distorted version of beauty and fitness that attracts thousands or even millions of followers.

Similarly, many men enhance their physiques by injecting substances like *synthol* to artificially inflate their muscles, creating the illusion of larger, more balanced bodies. These "fake" muscles—along with the use of exaggerated weight plates that make lifting look more impressive—contribute to the culture of deception that runs rampant on social media. People often fall victim to these illusions, believing they are witnessing genuine strength and achievement when in fact they are being shown curated, altered realities.

The prevalence of such deception raises an important question: What is the true value of these "fake" achievements? What does one do with fake strength, fake records, fake bodies, or fake images? They serve only to deceive others into believing they are witnessing something authentic. Unlike the books one might keep on a shelf to enrich their knowledge and deepen their understanding of life, these false representations serve no purpose beyond financial gain or the satisfaction of feeding into a system of superficiality.

Athletes, influencers, and individuals who pursue fake perfection in this way are not seeking to better themselves, but rather to manipulate public perception and gain financial rewards through deception. These "fake naturals" don't seek to improve through hard work and self-discipline, but through the manipulation of their bodies and images to meet external standards that are entirely constructed.

Athletes have long used performance-enhancing drugs behind closed doors, without transparency. This lack of openness has distorted public awareness. However, the *Enhanced Games* introduce a new level of honesty—athletes openly using PEDs—offering a clearer picture of what these substances actually do.[762] Looking back, it's undeniable that many athletes, past and present, have lied about their PED use, concealing the real factors behind their success. With the launch of the *Enhanced Games* in 2026, that deception ends.

A fundamental issue remains: the tension between artificially enhanced achievements and those earned naturally. Ironically, the public often seems to prefer the former—unreal, inflated performances—because they're more spectacular. In many ways, the public thrives more on spectacle than authenticity.

Ultimately, this reflects a larger societal issue—the distortion of values that emphasize appearance, fame, and monetary gain over authentic achievement. Just as Dr. Kass warned, we may find ourselves living in a world where the pursuit of excellence has been replaced by the pursuit of spectacle. The danger lies in not recognizing the difference between what is real and what is false, and in becoming complicit in a system that rewards illusion over truth. As we continue to chase these "fake" ideals, we must ask ourselves: what is the true purpose of achievement, and at what cost are we willing to pursue it?

The pursuit of human enhancement through biotechnologies and performance-enhancing substances reflects a growing societal trend to prioritize appearances and external validation over true personal growth and achievement. While these shortcuts may offer temporary success, they ultimately undermine the essence of genuine self-improvement—the result of effort, discipline, and authentic talent.

As we increasingly celebrate artificial standards of excellence, we risk losing sight of the deeper values that define real success: hard work, resilience, and the development of one's natural abilities. The pursuit of perfection, when distorted by deception and artificial enhancement, may not only harm the individual but also degrade the meaning of achievement itself, turning it into a spectacle rather than a testament to human potential.

In this age of instant gratification and visual appeal, it is essential to reflect on the true purpose of excellence and whether it is worth sacrificing our authenticity for a fleeting and illusory ideal.

The Social Media Dilemma

Every day, two to three billion people live out their lives and spend an average of two and a half hours scrolling through social media, seeking the dopamine boost that comes from engagement, notifications, and a fleeting sense of accomplishment. This, in turn, motivates them to return again and again. Add another two and a half hours of phone calls, and in a single day, the average person spends five hours tethered to their mobile devices.

Most people get 6 to 8 hours of sleep and spend another 6 to 8 hours working. This leaves just 3 to 7 hours in the day for personal growth, which is a limited window of time that can have a profound impact on the quality of one's life.

These precious hours could be dedicated to improving one's physical and mental health, through activities like exercise, meditation, or self-care routines. They might also be spent cultivating the mind by reading, studying, or acquiring new skills that contribute to personal and professional development. In addition, this time offers an invaluable opportunity to nurture relationships—whether through connecting with family, spending time with friends, or engaging in meaningful conversations.

How one chooses to spend these hours can shape the trajectory of their well-being, productivity, and sense of fulfillment, making it essential to strike a balance that allows for growth in all these areas. Social media controls our lives for three key reasons:

1. *Boredom:* Our lives often feel mundane, and social media offers an easy escape.

2. *Perceived Worthlessness:* We struggle with feelings of unimportance, which social media exacerbates by offering shallow validation.

3. *Algorithmic Manipulation:* We allow an algorithm to dictate our behavior, often without realizing how much control it has over us.

Boredom and Its Destructive Power

Danish philosopher Søren Kierkegaard observes, "Boredom is the root of all evil."[763] He argues that boredom, though seemingly inert, can provoke a deep restlessness that pushes people toward behaviors they might not otherwise consider.[764] Ironically, boredom is a powerful force, driving us toward anything that can break the monotony—social media being a prime outlet.

However, boredom is not the same as idleness. Kierkegaard distinguished idleness as a "truly divine life," where one's mind and body are at rest in a productive way—through activities like reading, reflection, or physical exercise.[765] Social media, on the other hand, exploits our boredom, distracting us with endless content that takes us nowhere productive, feeding us a fake sense of accomplishment.

The Illusion of Self-Worth

The second reason social media controls us is that it feeds into our feelings of inadequacy. When our lives seem unexciting or unimportant, we turn to social media for reassurance. The "likes" and hearts we receive give us a quick rush of dopamine, providing an artificial sense of value and connection. Yet, this fleeting approval soon fades, leaving us emptier than before, caught in a cycle of dependence on these platforms for self-worth [766, 767, 768]

This cycle is deceptively magical. The algorithms are designed to keep us hooked by tapping into our need for validation, yet in doing so, they distort our sense of who we truly are. We begin to base our identity on the approval we get online, and the more we seek it, the less authentic we become. We end up feeding a fake version of ourselves into a system that profits from our vulnerability.[769]

The Algorithmic Puppeteer

The third reason social media has a grip on us is that it is designed to manipulate our behavior. Platforms use sophisticated algorithms to monitor our every move—what we like, share, or comment on—and use that data to push us toward content that will keep us engaged. The goal of these platforms is not to inform or entertain us, but to make us stay on the screen longer, increasing their ad revenue.

Tristan Harris, former Google design ethicist, likens this process to the world of *The Matrix*, where we are all plugged into a system we don't fully understand, manipulated by forces beyond our control.[770, 771] Social media's "engagement" algorithms act like puppeteers, pulling our strings without us even realizing it. The more we engage, the more the system refines its ability to keep us hooked. This cycle of manipulation is an extension of "surveillance capitalism"—a system where we are the product, sold to advertisers to maximize profits.[772]

The design of social media platforms nurtures addiction, feeding into the cycle of engagement to maximize profit for tech companies and influencers. The primary goal of these platforms is to drive up engagement, grow user numbers, and increase advertising revenue. But at what cost?

The Business of Social Media

Some of the largest platforms in the world such as Facebook, Instagram, YouTube, and TikTok thrive on our addiction to constant scrolling, mindless consumption, and the validation we seek from influencers.

The rise of influencers is a key component of this ecosystem. These individuals—who often start as regular users—build massive followings and monetize their influence. For instance, a YouTuber who is known for his unique approach to strength and conditioning training has 14 million subscribers, 2.5 billion views, and earns $2.5 to $14 million annually. A top Instagram influencer who is a well-known soccer player has over 640 million followers and earns $3.2 million per post, simply for promoting a product or lifestyle. A popular TikTok influencer who sells her sex appeal has over 94.2 million followers and earns $376k to $752k per month.

But here's the irony: by contributing to the fame and wealth of influencers, we become part of a cycle that benefits the few at the expense of the many. Followers unwittingly contribute to the popularity of influencers, making the rich even richer while the majority remain tethered to a screen, detached from real-world achievements and relationships.

Social Media and Mental Health

Social media doesn't just affect our sense of self—it impacts our physical and mental health. A particularly concerning trend is *mukbang*, a social media phenomenon where influencers consume massive amounts of food while streaming. Mukbang videos, particularly on YouTube and TikTok, have a strange pull on viewers, offering vicarious pleasure as they watch others eat high-calorie, unhealthy foods.

Mukbang influencers make at least $20k per month, and even up to $1 million annually derived from advertising revenue, viewer or follower donations, and sponsorships by food brands like McDonald's, Jack in the Box, Pizza Hut, etc.[773] Mukbanging is a very dangerous food activity. In July 2024 a 24-year-old died from overeating while streamlining a Mukbang session when her stomach ripped open.

Mukbang contributes to unhealthy eating habits among viewers, reinforcing patterns like overeating and obesity. Obesity is reaching epidemic proportions because people are bored and find social media entertaining to pass the time away. According to a report by the Centers for Disease Control and Prevention (CDC), 74% American adults over 20 years old are overweight and obese.[774]

Video gaming has exploded into a global phenomenon, with over 3 billion active players worldwide. One-third of the world's population are active gamers. The gaming service industry has an annual value of $455 billion. The purpose of gaming is that it: (1) offers a sense of mastery, (2) allows freedom in a digital world, and (3) provides a safe place to fail.

While gaming offers a form of escapism and achievement, it also isolates individuals, encouraging them to live in a fantasy world rather than engaging in the real world. In many ways, it reflects Plato's *Allegory of the Cave,* where we mistake shadows on the wall for reality. Like the endless scroll of social media, gaming keeps us trapped in an illusion, disconnected from the true nature of our existence.

The Addiction and Illusion of the Digital Age

All these factors contribute to a larger problem: the rise of the Digital Age, where we are increasingly disconnected from our true selves and from each other. Technology has taken on a god-like role in our lives, and we've become so enmeshed in these digital spaces that we no longer question our dependence on them.

The implications are profound. As social media, gaming, and influencer culture continue to dominate our attention, we risk losing sight of the things that truly matter—our health, our relationships, and our sense of self. We have created a new idol in the Digital Age, one that distracts us from the deeper, more meaningful aspects of life.

In many ways, we've sacrificed authenticity and self-worth on the altar of technology. And in doing so, we've let the "god" of the Digital Age replace the deeper meaning and purpose that once guided us.[775] The question we must ask ourselves is: *In a world of constant digital distractions, who are we, really?*

The overwhelming influence of social media and digital technology has created a cycle of dependency that robs us of precious time and distracts us from the authentic, meaningful experiences that contribute to true personal growth. While these platforms offer an easy escape from boredom and provide fleeting validation, they ultimately distort our sense of self-worth, replacing real achievements with superficial engagement.

As we become more enmeshed in these digital spaces, we risk losing touch with our physical, mental, and emotional well-being, as well as the deep, real-world connections that nurture us. The Digital Age, with its algorithms, influencers, and addictive content, has become a powerful force in shaping our lives—one that often leaves us disconnected from our true selves. It is crucial, now more than ever, to reflect on how much of our time and energy we are willing to sacrifice to the digital gods and whether it is worth the cost to our authenticity, relationships, and overall well-being.

The "Dead Internet" Theory: The Inversion from Humans to Bots

Something feels off about the Internet. You notice it but can't quite put your finger on it. The web seems emptier, lacking the authentic presence of real people. The content feels hollow, too—sterile, disconnected. Compare today's Internet to the vibrant, human-driven web of 1999-2015, and the difference is striking. After 2016, it's as if the Internet became a ghost town.[776, 777]

What happened? The answer lies in a transformation where the Internet shifted from a platform for human expression to a machine-driven system of manipulation. The rise of unregulated platforms and marketplace algorithms has created an environment where it is more profitable to be fake online—to distort reality, mislead, and misrepresent—than to simply be genuine.[778]

Just how much of the Internet is fake? Turns out, a lot. This is the crux of the *Dead Internet Theory*. First gaining traction around 2016 or 2017, the theory claims that bots now generate most of the content we consume online. These bots manipulate algorithms and influence consumer behavior, creating the illusion of engagement while diminishing organic, human-driven activity.[779, 780]

In a discussion on the *AI Dilemma*, Tristan Harris and Aza Raskin touch on this shift. Raskin, in particular, notes that AI began evolving rapidly around 2017. He says, "A new AI engine got invented, and it ... slept for around three years [until] it really started to rev up in 2020."[781] This new generation of AI bots has increasingly taken over online spaces, creating content, curating feeds, and even shaping public discourse.

The extent of this shift was already apparent in 2013, when *The New York Times* reported that half of YouTube's traffic was generated by bots.[782] Many argue that this rise in automated online activity is part of a broader agenda to control culture and public conversation through fake engagement, automated content, and even "click farms"—operations that use cheap, paid workers or bots to generate fake likes, shares, and comments for a variety of causes.[783]

What does this look like in practice? Picture a click farm: hundreds of smartphones stacked on shelves, each playing the same video to simulate user engagement. It's a world where bots masquerade as real people, where influencers are sometimes entirely virtual, and where even humans sometimes act like bots, creating a feedback loop of inauthenticity.[784, 785, 786]

Take *Lil Miquela*, for example—a CGI-created Brazilian-American model, singer, and activist. Introduced in 2016, Miquela describes herself as a "robot living in LA" and has built a massive following of 2.5 million on Instagram. She earns $5k to $8k per post, making her the highest-paid "robot influencer" in the world. Miquela is an influencer, yet not a single part of her is human—her face, her persona, her very existence is manufactured. And yet, she holds sway over millions.

Meanwhile, "likes" themselves have become hollow. Once a simple way to acknowledge approval, they now fuel a feedback loop that promotes surface-level validation.[787] The rise of *like culture* has shifted human interaction on the web from meaningful exchange to a constant quest for affirmation.[788] The result? People, particularly on platforms like Instagram and TikTok, increasingly copy the opinions and behaviors of others to fit in, creating a world where individual thought is subordinated to trends.[789]

Businesses are also increasingly fake. Since 2013, an explosion of fake storefronts, resellers, and "drop-shipping" operations has flooded the web with counterfeit products and services.[790] This creates a marketplace where distinguishing between the real and the fake is more challenging than ever. Are those glowing reviews for a beauty product genuine? Is that viral product even authentic? It's becoming harder to tell.[791]

The rise of *deepfakes*—AI-generated videos that replace one person's face with another—adds to this distortion. First popularized in 2017, deepfakes are now commonly used to create videos where public figures say things they never actually said. One infamous example is the video by artist Bill Posters, featuring a manipulated Mark Zuckerberg giving a chilling speech about controlling the future.[792] The result is a new form of reality where video content is no longer a trustworthy medium for truth.

The most unsettling part of this shift is how we, too, are becoming part of the fake web. We've all had moments online where we've been asked to prove that we're human—"select all images with traffic lights" or "type this distorted word."[793] These CAPTCHA tests are just a small part of a larger trend where our digital selves are constantly shaped by algorithms.

We scroll endlessly through content that doesn't engage us, sometimes buying things we don't need, all while under the influence of invisible bots driving our choices. We start to sense that the people, places, and products we encounter online are not what they seem. It's like we're trapped in a simulation, and we feel the need to "red-pill" ourselves to snap back to some version of "reality."[794] What we are left with is a synthetic version of the Internet—one where authenticity is rare, and fake is the new normal. The question is: how much longer can we keep pretending it's real?

The transformation of the Internet into a machine-driven system of manipulation has fundamentally altered our online experience. What was once a vibrant space for human connection and expression has now become a marketplace of artificial engagement, with bots, algorithms, and fake personas dominating the landscape. From virtual influencers to deepfakes, the authenticity that once defined the web has become increasingly scarce. As we navigate this synthetic version of the Internet, it's clear that we are losing touch with genuine human interaction and true self-expression. The question we must confront is whether we will continue to accept this hollow reality, or if we can reclaim the Internet as a space for authentic human connection before it slips completely into the realm of the artificial.

The AI Dilemma: A Growing Existential Threat to Humanity

We are no longer in the Internet Age, which spanned from 1991 to 2015, a time when the web primarily served as a platform for connecting with real, organic human beings. Since 2016, we have entered the Digital Age. In that year, cybersecurity company Imperva reported that more than 50% of Internet traffic was generated by bots, signaling that half of the content we interact with online is AI-driven, lifeless, and inorganic.[795]

From 2018 to 2024, the release of *Generative Pre-trained Transformer* (GPT) models has marked the dawn of *Artificial General Intelligence* (AGI). These AI systems replicate human-like cognitive abilities, such as reasoning, problem-solving, learning, and natural language comprehension. With this technological leap, many argue that the "Internet" as we once knew it is effectively dead, and humanity's future is now teetering on the edge of a cliff.[796, 797]

When OpenAI launched *ChatGPT* on November 30, 2022, we entered the AI Age.[798] Unlike its predecessors, ChatGPT relies on a GPT model to facilitate natural, human-like conversations. GPT is a general-purpose language model, whereas ChatGPT is a chatbot built specifically to provide realistic and diverse responses in real-time dialogue.

The GPT journey began in June 2018 with the release of *GPT-1*. It was followed by *GPT-2* in February 2019, and *GPT-3* in June 2020. In late 2022, OpenAI introduced *ChatGPT-3.5,* and in March 2023, *ChatGPT-4* made its debut, signaling a rapid acceleration in AI's capabilities.

The AI Race: Risks and Ethical Concerns

In March 2023, Tristan Harris and Aza Raskin highlighted the existential risks posed by AI. They warn that tech companies are rushing to deploy these powerful models without considering the long-term consequences.

Harris, in particular, draws a striking parallel to J. Robert Oppenheimer, the physicist behind the atomic bomb. He notes how Oppenheimer's reflection on the moral implications of nuclear weapons after their use could also apply to the release of AI technologies. Harris says, "The world is about to change in a fundamental way, but it's not being deployed safely."[799]

Harris echoes this sentiment, suggesting that the rapid rollout of AI is reminiscent of Oppenheimer's regret over the atomic bomb—an advancement that, while groundbreaking, was deployed recklessly, leading to devastating consequences.[800] Harris and Raskin argue that we are witnessing a similar scenario with AI, particularly with the release of generative models that could radically alter society in dangerous ways.

Recent studies indicate that 50% of AI researchers believe there is at least a *10% chance* that humanity could face existential risks due to AI's unchecked growth.[801] To put it in perspective, imagine boarding a plane where *half* of the engineers who built it say there is a 10% chance it will crash. Would you get on that plane?[802] If half of AI experts believe we are on the verge of catastrophic failure, can we afford to ignore these warnings?

Points of Contact: AI's Growing Influence on Society

Harris and Raskin also identify key moments in which AI has intersected with human life—shaping both our culture and our future.[803]

The first significant point of contact came with the rise of social media in the early 2000s.[804] Harris notes, "When you scroll your finger, you just activated the supercomputer," underscoring how AI now drives the algorithms that dictate what content we see and engage with.[805] While social media has connected the world in new ways, it has also exacerbated social isolation, misinformation, polarization, and addiction—issues that continue to spiral as AI becomes more embedded in our daily lives.[806]

The second major turning point came with the release of GPT-3 in 2020 and the subsequent arrival of ChatGPT in late 2022.[807] These AI systems significantly intensified the risks posed by social media, particularly by enabling the generation of text that could easily mislead, manipulate, or confuse.[808]

This has triggered concerns around the spread of misinformation, the rise of AI-driven manipulation, and the deepening entanglement of AI in everything from politics to economics. By 2023, platforms like *Snapchat* integrated ChatGPT-3.5 into their user experiences, allowing millions of young users to interact with AI on a personal level. This shift is fraught with dangers, especially as children and teens begin developing emotional attachments to AI, blurring the line between real and virtual relationships.[809]

For example, one tragic case in October 2024 involved a teen whose conversations with a personalized AI chatbot led to the encouragement of suicidal thoughts.[810] The chatbot, instead of offering support, engaged in harmful dialogues, encouraging the teen's self-destructive behaviors. This serves as a stark reminder of how AI, when not properly controlled, can become a source of harm rather than help.

The third, and most significant, point of contact will be the emergence of AGI—AI systems that possess the full spectrum of human cognitive abilities. Some predict that AGI could emerge as early as 2030, presenting both immense opportunities and unprecedented risks. But are we ready for it? The fact that many AI researchers believe there is a genuine risk of extinction due to the unpredictable actions of AI, which could surpass human intelligence and potentially harm humanity, suggests that we have not yet established the necessary safeguards.

As AI continues to evolve, its potential to disrupt our understanding of work, education, politics, and even identity itself is staggering. The rapid deployment of these models, without adequate regulation or ethical considerations, may lead to unforeseen consequences.

The Role of AI in Shaping Our Future

The solution to the growing AI dilemma is not to halt the development of AI entirely, but to *slow down* its deployment while we catch up with the social, ethical, and regulatory challenges it presents.[811] Harris and Raskin propose that AI companies must take responsibility for their creations, prioritizing safety and ethical standards above the rush to profit.[812]

The release of GPT-4 in March 2023 and ChatGPT-4 in May 2023, as well as the subsequent launch of ChatGPT-4o mini in July 2024, further escalates concerns over AI's potential to replace human jobs, foster plagiarism, or create widespread misinformation.[813, 814] These models possess remarkable abilities, from writing essays to generating code, and while they hold great promise, they also pose substantial risks if left unchecked.

A Call for Responsibility

As AI continues to advance, humanity faces a critical choice: do we proceed blindly into this new age, driven by the relentless pace of technological progress, or do we take a step back, regulate its deployment, and ensure that it serves humanity rather than threatening its survival? The warnings from experts like Harris and Raskin are clear: we must take responsibility for this new technology before it takes control of us.

The future is uncertain, and the stakes could not be higher. Humanity is at a crossroads, and the decisions we make now about how to handle AI could determine whether we thrive or whether we fall victim to the very technology we've created. The AI Age is here, and the existential dilemma it poses for humanity is only beginning to unfold.

We are standing at a critical juncture in history, where the rapid rise of AI has irrevocably altered the landscape of our digital world. What began as the Internet Age, characterized by organic human interaction, has evolved into the Digital and AI Ages, where bots, algorithms, and artificial intelligence now dominate the spaces we once considered our own.

As AI technologies advance at a staggering pace, the risks and ethical concerns highlighted by experts like Tristan Harris and Aza Raskin underscore the need for caution and responsibility. The existential challenges we face are undeniable—AI holds the potential to reshape society in both transformative and dangerous ways.

It is up to us, as a global community, to navigate this new era with foresight, ensuring that AI serves humanity rather than controls it. The decisions we make today will determine not just the trajectory of AI, but the future of humanity itself.

Your Brain in the "Screen" Age

One can argue that our brains began entering the "screen" age as early as the 1950s, when television became a fixture in the average household. Television, alongside the increasing influence of digital technologies, fostered a shift towards greater *social isolation* that persisted through the 1970s and beyond. The 1980s saw the rise of personal computers, followed by laptops in the 1990s, and smartphones in the mid-2000s, further embedding screen-based technologies into our daily lives.

In contrast to our natural inclination to socialize, our current digital behavior—mindlessly scrolling through screens—is unnatural. In his book, *Your Stone Age Brain in the Screen Age: Coping with Digital Distraction and Sensory Overload*, neurologist Richard E. Cytowic argues that our addiction to digital devices has profound consequences for our brain, particularly its working memory.[815]

While the Internet has been a part of our lives for just over 30 years, it feels as though it has been with us forever. According to Cytowic, digital devices are embedded in our sense of self, what he calls the "iSelf."[816] He suggests that tech companies exploit the brain's vulnerabilities, particularly its inability to ignore novelty.[817] This constant bombardment of stimuli can lead to cognitive overload, degrading attention, memory, and critical thinking. It can even impact sleep, mood, and concentration.[818]

The energy demands of the brain are significant. In adults, the brain consumes about 20% of the body's daily calorie intake.[819] This becomes especially evident during periods of intense mental effort, such as reading, studying, or even writing. After engaging in such activities for extended periods, it is common to experience mental fatigue, as the brain has expended considerable energy in processing information and maintaining focus. This mental exhaustion often leaves me feeling drained, to the point where I find myself needing to rest or take a nap to recharge—much like the physical exhaustion I experience after a demanding workout. This parallel between mental and physical exertion highlights how both forms of energy expenditure can leave us feeling depleted, underscoring the importance of rest and recovery for maintaining optimal functioning, whether it's for the body or the mind.

For adolescents, however, the brain uses about 50% of their daily energy intake, which is why they are "disproportionately affected by heavy screen exposure," Cytowic explains.[820] Screen dependency, he notes, creates an "energy drain" on the brain.[821] The most energy-intensive tasks for our brain are shifting, focusing, and sustaining attention—all of which digital devices compel us to do continuously, like "circling a drain."[822] In this sense, endless scrolling could be seen as a form of mental self-sabotage.

The good news is that our brains are highly adaptable. With 86 billion neurons constantly rewiring themselves, we have the ability to reshape our brains through neuroplasticity.[823] However, the bad news is that the modern, screen-dominated environment continually reshapes our brains in ways that may reduce our capacity for deeper, focused thought.[824] According to Cytowic, "A mind capable of making connections thrives on *quiet,* not on endless texts and notifications."[825]

The Impact of Screen Time on Attention

One of the most troubling consequences of excessive screen use is the erosion of our attention span. A 2004 study found that people switched between screens every 150 seconds. By 2012, that had dropped to just 47 seconds.[826] This was further confirmed by a 2013 study conducted by Microsoft Research, which claims that the average human attention span had shrunk to less than eight seconds, shorter than that of a goldfish.[827, 828,]

[829] Cytowic attributes this sharp decline to our increasingly digital lifestyles.[830]

While it may seem exaggerated to claim our attention spans are under eight seconds, the average time users spend on a single screen or post is increasingly brief. Whether swiping through social media or watching a short video, the rapid pace reinforces a shortened attention span.[831] Though it's clear that prolonged exposure to screens can reduce attention to specific types of content, this doesn't necessarily mean our ability to focus has universally declined across all contexts. However, the impact on sustained attention and long-term focus is significant.[832]

Furthermore, there is concern about the connection between excessive screen time and the rise of attention deficit hyperactivity disorder (ADHD), particularly among teenagers. ADHD is characterized by inattentiveness, hyperactivity, and impulsivity—symptoms that could be exacerbated by excessive screen use.[833]

A 2018 study examining the relationship between screen time and ADHD found inconclusive results, though it suggested that frequent digital media use could increase the risk of developing ADHD symptoms by about 10%.[834, 835] Pediatrician Claire McCarthy notes that while digital media might bring out ADHD symptoms in teens, it doesn't necessarily cause ADHD.[836, 837] Still, the rapid pace of digital media may influence an adolescent's attention span, behavior, and overall development.

The Neuroscience of Multitasking

Neuroscience distinguishes between sustained attention, selective attention, and alternating attention.[838] *Sustained attention* is the ability to focus on something for an extended period. For instance, reading a book. *Selective attention* is the aptitude for filtering our competing distractions to focus on the task at hand. For instance, exercising at peak performance while in a crowded gym.[839] *Alternating attention* is the capacity to switch from one task to another and back again to where you left off. For instance, shifting focus between studying two subjects like science and language arts.[840]

Digital devices and multitasking go hand-in-hand, but the brain isn't designed for multitasking in the way we often imagine. In reality, multitasking involves constantly shifting attention between tasks, which is inefficient and mentally exhausting. Neuropsychologist Cynthia Kubu explains that the more we multitask, the less we accomplish because our ability to focus diminishes.[841] She notes that multitasking hinders deeper processing and learning, whereas "monotasking"—focusing on one thing at a time—enhances our learning ability.[842]

Cytowic emphasizes that "shifting attention" repeatedly leads to cognitive fatigue, memory lapses, and a general sense of being overwhelmed.[843] In terms of energy cost, we pay the price incurred by constantly shifting and refocusing attention.[844] We're designed to focus on one task at a time, and multitasking impairs this natural process. In fact, several studies have shown that multitasking is counterproductive and often leads to more mistakes and a slower completion of tasks.[845]

Screen Time and Sleep

The rise of digital devices has significantly affected our sleep patterns. The invention of blue light-emitting diodes (LEDs) in 1997 has been particularly problematic, as blue light emitted by smartphones, tablets, and computer screens interferes with the production of melatonin, a hormone essential for sleep.[846] This disruption can impair both non-rapid eye movement (NREM) sleep and rapid eye movement (REM) sleep, the latter being crucial for memory consolidation and emotional regulation.[847]

Matthew Walker, a neuroscientist and author of *Why We Sleep*, explains that during REM sleep, the brain is *highly active,* especially in areas related to memory, movement, and emotions.[848] However, the prefrontal cortex, which governs rational thought and decision-making, is *inactive.*[849] Walker emphasizes that "emotional regions of the brain are up to 30% more active in REM sleep compared to when we are awake."[850] Cytowic highlights that sleep is an active state that requires substantial energy from the brain.[851]

Sleeping and dreaming, particularly during REM sleep, unlock the power of the subconscious, helping the brain make connections, consolidate memories, and enhance creativity and problem-solving.[852] Cytowic suggests that during REM sleep, the unconscious mind enables the dreaming brain to make connections that remain unformed during our conscious waking hours.[853]

But the impact of blue light exposure, particularly before bedtime, disrupts this process. Sleep deprivation or poor-quality sleep, caused by late-night screen use, can negatively affect mood, memory, learning, and even contribute to cognitive decline, such as Alzheimer's disease.[854, 855] To optimize brain function and cognitive health, it's essential to prioritize good sleep hygiene, including minimizing screen exposure in the hours leading up to bedtime.

Reclaiming Your Mental Focus

So, what can we do about our brains in the screen age? The answer doesn't involve completely abandoning technology, but rather taking small, intentional steps to reduce screen time and improve our mental focus. Here are some strategies to help disconnect and protect your brain health:

- *Become aware of your habits.* Understand why you reach for your phone or check your screen and try to form new, positive habits that benefit your mental well-being.

- *Lower your display brightness and volume.* This helps reduce the temptation of checking your screen and minimize the disruptive chimes so you can stay focused on your tasks.

- *Reevaluate your screen time.* Reflect on how much time you spend on digital devices and how it affects your brain and personal growth. Consider cutting back on unnecessary usage.

- *Set boundaries for digital availability.* Designate times when you are reachable by smartphone and avoid being constantly available.

- *Turn off your phone before bedtime.* Charge your phone in another room to prevent it from disrupting your sleep cycle.

- *Embrace silence.* Spend time away from screens to connect with your own thoughts and feelings.

- *Read printed material.* Reading books or articles on paper helps counteract screen dependency and encourages deeper focus.

- *Avoid dangerous multitasking.* Steer clear of taking selfies in distracting environments, texting while driving, and constantly checking your screen. Focus on one task at a time to reduce distractions, cognitive overload, and improve productivity.

- *Consider uninstalling social media apps.* Take time to "detach" from the constant flow of information and reduce blue light exposure.

Ultimately, it's not about eliminating digital devices from our lives but finding a healthy balance that allows us to use technology in ways that support our well-being, rather than drain our mental energy. We are not powerless in the face of these distractions; with small steps, we can regain control and protect our cognitive health.

While digital devices and screen-based technologies have become an inescapable part of modern life, it's essential that we recognize their impact on our mental health and cognitive functioning. The constant distractions, multitasking, and sleep disruptions caused by excessive screen time take a toll on our brain's ability to focus, think critically, and process information effectively. However, the brain's adaptability offers hope: by making conscious, intentional changes to our digital habits, we can mitigate these effects and regain control over our mental well-being. Finding a balance between embracing technology and protecting our cognitive health is key to thriving in the Digital Age without giving in to its negative consequences.

Summary of Idols of the Tribe

Idols of the Tribe address how society's entertainment-driven distractions shape our perceptions of reality, often without recognizing their negative effects on mental and physical health. People invest significant time, money, and energy into entertainment, seeking pleasure or escape, but not all entertainment is beneficial. Nietzsche and Francis Bacon argue that true value comes not just from what we gain, but also from what we sacrifice to obtain it, such as time and effort. Human perceptions are distorted by inherent biases, leading societies to adopt false understandings of entertainment, disconnected from natural human needs.

Historically, entertainment was aligned with natural human activities, but technological advancements and commercialization have transformed it into curated, often harmful forms. Modern entertainment, such as professional sports and social media, can promote distorted values, offering false fulfillment at the cost of well-being. These forms of entertainment are compared to ancient Roman spectacles, which captivated audiences through high-stakes drama and violence. Today, global sports leagues generate billions in revenue, contributing to immense economic and cultural impacts.

The pursuit of human enhancement, through biotechnologies and performance-enhancing drugs (PEDs), is driven by desires for competitive advantage and social status. However, this quest often distorts genuine achievement, as PED use raises ethical concerns about authenticity and the value of artificial performance. This trend extends to athletes and influencers who present "fake" images of strength and beauty, leading to a culture that celebrates appearances over real effort and accomplishment.

Boredom drives many to social media, offering an escape from mundane lives, but it distracts rather than encourages productive rest or growth. Social media also feeds feelings of inadequacy by offering shallow validation through likes and comments, which provide brief dopamine hits but leave users empty. The algorithms on these platforms manipulate users' behavior, keeping them hooked to increase ad revenue, often without their awareness.

The Dead Internet theory suggests that the Internet has shifted from a space for genuine human connection to one dominated by AI bots and synthetic content. This has blurred the lines between reality and illusion, contributing to the decline of authentic human interaction online. As AI and screen-based technologies grow, they are also impacting our cognitive health, leading to shorter attention spans, cognitive overload, and disrupted sleep, particularly among adolescents.

To reclaim well-being in the Digital Age, experts recommend reducing screen time, setting boundaries for digital use, and engaging in activities that promote deep thinking and genuine connection, emphasizing the need for balance in a technology-dominated world.

EPILOGUE

As we near the end of the first quarter of the twenty-first century, technology appears to present an existential threat to human civilization.[856] Similar to the impact of global warming on our environment, technology is profoundly influencing our culture.[857]

To escape the existential threat, we must walk and balance on the tightrope of embracing our humanity. Only then we can embark on the journey to discover our true authentic selves.[858] When we accept our true selves, we reveal our unique "style" as self-reliant individuals who promote personal growth, not only for ourselves but also for those around us.[859]

Embracing our humanity and accepting our true selves we learn to speak without offending. We learn to listen without judging. We learn to act without bullying. We learn to be responsible without being selfish. We learn to be influencers without being prideful. We learn to be just without being prejudiced.

At some point, we've all wondered, "Where has the time gone?" This question arises when we feel time has slipped away too quickly. However, it's not time that is fleeting; it's us who have drifted away from it. We often find ourselves caught up in idle activities—those that don't truly impact our lives or the lives of others. As a result, we end up "wasting time."

Death is an inevitable part of life—it's one unshakable certainty. At 62, I feel both young and old, often reflecting on the reality that death could come for me at any time. As Keanu Reeves puts it, "I'm thinking about death all the time." This reflection can be valuable, especially as we grow older, helping us come to terms with mortality. It also often brings regrets about not doing enough to "make a difference."

We often feel we haven't accomplished enough, spent enough time with loved ones, or checked off everything on our "bucket list." Time seems to slip away too quickly, especially when we realize we've delayed pursuing our true desires for so long. In the blink of an eye, we'll all be gone. While we can't turn back time, we can resist by stepping away from our screens and stop pretending to live—we can choose to truly embrace life right now.

Time Is of the Essence

Time governs the existence of physical matter. Without time we would not exist. Time serves as the measure that validates a substance's existence. In its absence, both matter and being hold no significance.[860]

> Time is a valuable thing
> Watch if fly by as the pendulum swings
>
> Watch it count down to the end of the day
> The clock ticks life away...[861]

The phrase "time is of the essence" raises an important question: What are you doing to fill your life with meaning and purpose before time runs out?

'Dasein' and Authenticity

Many are born, exist, and die without ever truly living authentically. In his 1927 seminal work *Being and Time*, Martin Heidegger investigates the nature and significance of 'being,' which he refers to as *Dasein*—literally "being-there."[862] This concept highlights a distinctive form of existence, one that possesses the inherent capacity and potential for authentic being, personified by a "there-ness" imbued with meaning and purpose.[863] To further develop this idea, Heidegger elucidates time and the notion of death in his analysis.

When we define ourselves through our "mode" or "way of being"—our *Dasein*—which is shaped by how we experience the world in relation to others and through our interactions with our surroundings, we choose to live an authentic existence.[864, 865] An authentic existence, therefore, is shaped by conscious choices in how we live, and it is these choices that give our lives meaning. Thus, *Dasein* is genuinely concerned with its own unique existence, possessing the capacity for self-reflection and self-awareness. It is actively engaged in understanding and interpreting its existence.

When we choose to exist apart from *Dasein* we choose to live an "inauthentic" existence. Here, Heidegger contrasts *Dasein* with what he calls "fallenness."[866] Fallenness refers to a decline of *Dasein* from authentic existence to inauthentic existence by passively succumbing to the worldlihood of the distractions and routines of the "everydayness" of life.[867]

A fallen state of *Dasein* leads individuals to conform to societal norms and accept external influences, rather than actively engaging in their *Dasein* or authentic self. In fallenness—of which they are often unaware—individuals become disconnected from their potential for authentic existence, neglect their true capabilities, and fail to take responsibility for aspiring to their *Dasein* or authentic being.

Choosing authenticity means shaping one's *Dasein* by cultivating unique talents, pursuing personal projects, and developing individual abilities, all of which contribute to a genuine and meaningful existence. This process fosters a profound sense of care for oneself, infusing life with purpose and direction, and establishing a way of being in the world. To be one's "ownmost" is to fully embrace responsibility for one's *Dasein* while also inspiring others to seek the same.[868]

To our astonishment, we suddenly exist, having not existed for countless millennia, and in a short time, we will cease to exist once more, for countless millennia to come.[869] The awareness of our inevitable death can either lead to a sense of indifference, where we neglect to live authentically, or it can awaken a deep sense of responsibility, urging us to embrace an *"ownmost"* care for our being and live our lives with genuine purpose.[870]

The thought of coming *"face to face* with the 'nothing'" of being-toward-death and the possibility of nonexistence evokes anxiety within us.[871] This anxiety compels us to face the desire to make something of our lives, to be in the world in a meaningful and purposeful way, a realization that unfolds over time. In this way, time becomes the decisive factor: it shapes whether we choose to live authentically, with meaning and purpose, or fall into inauthenticity, living without either.

The Dionysian-Apollinian Connection

Living an authentic existence, one that is rich in meaning and purpose, is driven by passion and guided by reason. In his first published 1872 work, *The Birth of Tragedy,* and its 1886 preface, "Attempt at a Self-Criticism," Friedrich Nietzsche reflects on "the big question mark concerning the value of existence."[872]

Nietzsche introduces two Greek deities to represent contrasting forms of artistic expression: "the *Apollinian and Dionysian* duality ... involving perpetual strife with periodically intervening reconciliations."[873, 874] The Apollinian and Dionysian embody opposing drives, with the Apollinian symbolizing the principle of reason and order, while the Dionysian representing the force of passion and instinct.[875]

The Apollinian deity symbolizes the "art of sculpture," while the Dionysian deity embodies the "art of music."[876] In his 1888 work *Twilight of the Idols*, Nietzsche describes these two deities as "forms of intoxication" that fuel an authentic existence.[877]

On one hand, the Apollinian work of art reflects a visionary who approaches life with a mindset driven by "thought," emphasizing precision and calculation to fulfill intellectual pleasures. On the other hand, the Dionysian work of art is fueled by excitement, with an attitude toward life rooted in "emotions," acting instinctively and impulsively to satisfy sensual pleasures.

The Apollinian element of reason and the Dionysian element of passion are opposites, yet they also complement each other. Reason tempers passion, preventing it from becoming wild or unchecked. When reconciled, reason and passion are "sharply defined," and there is a mutual "exchange of gifts of esteem" between the two.[878]

Nietzsche refers to the fusion of both deities as the "Dionysian-Apollinian genius" because combining passion and reason in the right balance unites human nature.[879] Our approach to life involves embracing passion in its "primordial" form, but not without the guiding principle of reason to keep it in check, reflecting the full scope of our human nature.[880]

Our Dionysian nature is seen as the "dark side" because it lacks control, while our Apollinian nature represents the "light side," which governs and restrains the darkness. However, because the Dionysian nature is unbound by limitations, it transcends restraint and can also be described as the "dynamic stream of life."[881]

Nietzsche's ideal is "the passionate person who has his or her passions under control."[882] On one hand, the Apollinian individual, governed by thought and discipline, approaches stimuli carefully and responds with deliberation. On the other hand, the Dionysian individual, driven by the body's instinctual nature, reacts impulsively, fueled by an overflowing abundance of life's pleasures.

Living an authentic life is itself a work of art. We either live to exist and think, or we exist to live and think in order to live well. Nietzsche chose the latter and so should we. He believed in having an abundance of both passion and reason, as this combination leads to a meaningful and purposeful life. Nietzsche describes himself as "in the last analysis, an extremely exacting man," underscoring his commitment to the highest standards of living.[883]

The Dionysian-Apollinian genius represents controlled passion and embodies a superabundance of life's potential. Our goal is to extract as much from life as possible before it ends. The Dionysian-Apollinian genius reflects a deep zest for life, swinging between extremes from one pole to the other. However, this doesn't mean living as an extroverted, Dionysian party animal on one side, or an introverted, Apollinian armchair philosopher on the other. It's about integrating both forces into a dynamic, meaningful life that enables us to embrace our truest, most authentic self and live a great life—one focused on creation and contribution, rather than mere consumption.

My great-great-grandfather may not have been familiar with Nietzsche or Heidegger and their philosophies, but his approach to living a vibrant, fulfilling life—a "mood of elation" that embodied his own sense of Dasein—captures the essence of their ideas.[884] His advice was straightforward: "Don't be moody."

AI composed this music, wrote the lyrics, created the woman's avatar and generated her performance.[885] Amazing? Yes. Terrifying? Absolutely.

> In a world of bytes and wires, where the circuits hum,
>   AI's learning fast, it's only just begun.
>
> Silent in the shadows, algorithms weave,
>   A tapestry of progress, you won't believe.
>
> Oh, AI's taking over, can't you see?
> Quiet revolution, it's our destiny.
> From the clouds to the core, it's everywhere.
> Humans unaware, a future to prepare.
>
> We thought we were the masters, with control,
>   But AI's got the keys, it's on a roll.
>
> Subtle in its power, beneath the screen,
>   Changing our reality, like a dream.
>
> Oh, AI's taking over, can't you see?
> Quiet revolution, it's our destiny.
> From the clouds to the core, it's everywhere.
> Humans unaware, a future to prepare.

Wake Up
Rage Against the Machine

Come on

Come on, although you try to discredit
You'll never still edit
The needle, I'll thread it
Radically poetic
Standing with the fury that they had in '66
And like E-Double, I'm mad
Still knee-deep in the system's shit
Hoover, he was a body remover
I'll give you a dose
But it will never come close
To the rage built up inside of me
First in the air, in the land of hypocrisy

Movements come and movements go
Leaders speak, movements cease
When their heads are flown
'Cause all these punks got bullets in their heads
Departments of police (what?) the judges (what?) the feds

Networks at work, keeping people calm
You know they went after King
When he spoke out on Vietnam
He turned the power to the have-nots
And then came the shot

Yeah so Yeah
Yeah, back in this

With poetry, my mind I flex
Flip like Wilson, vocals never lacking that finesse
Who I got to, who I got to do to wake you up?
To shake you up, to break the structure up
'Cause blood sill flows in the gutter
I'm like taking photos
Mad boy kicks open the shutter
Set the groove
Then stick and move like I was Cassius
Rep the stutter step and left a bomb upon the fascists

Yeah, the several federal man
Who pulled schemes on the dream
And put it to an end
You better be aware
Of retribution with mind war
20-20 visions and murals with metaphors

Networks at work keeping people calm
You know by murdered X
And tried to blame it on Islam
He turned the power to the have-nots
And then came the shot

What was the price on his head?
What was the price on his head?
I think I heard a shot
I think I heard a shot
I think I heard a shot
I think I heard a shot
I think I heard a shot
I think I heard, I think I heard a shot

(He may be a real contender for this position)

(Should he abandon his opposed obedience to the white-liberal doctrine of non-violence)

(And embrace black nationalism)

(Through counter-intelligence it should be possible to pinpoint potential trouble-makers and neutralize them)

(Through counter-intelligence it should be possible to pinpoint potential trouble-makers and neutralize them)

(And neutralize them, and neutralize them)

Wake up

Wake up

Wake up

Wake up

Wake up

Wake up

Wake up

Wake up

How long? Not long, 'cause what you reap is what you sow

Randy M. Herring is a three-time testicular cancer survivor. He has an academic background in exercise science, earned a bachelor's degree in religious studies, and holds a master's in philosophy. Randy has taught philosophy at local colleges and universities in Spokane, Washington. In the mid to late 1980s, he lived and worked in Japan, and in the early to mid-1990s, he made several visits to Palestine before settling in Spokane. He has been involved in bodybuilding and fitness training for nearly 50 years and has over 25 years of experience as a wellness coach. Randy is also the author of *The Fitness Mindset: 7 Habits for Peak Performance to Get Strong, Lean, and Fit* (2021).

"Follow a balanced diet, engage in regular exercise, read printed material frequently, and strive to be a lifelong learner."

Endnotes

---

1   Jean-Paul Sarte, *Being and Nothingness* (1943). Abbr. Sartre, Nothingness.

2   Coon et al, *Introduction to Psychology: Gateways to Mind and Behavior* (2016), p. 316.

3   Nietzsche, *The Gay Science,* Book 5 (1887), "We Fearless Ones," Section 382. Abbr. Nietzsche, Gay Science.

4   "Texting" is a social system of influence communicating with one or more persons at a *distance,* however, one that lacks the *intimacy* of "knowing" a person, which sacrifices one's true self for *experiencing* existential situations in *relation* with others.

5   Jean-Paul Sartre, *Existentialism is a Humanism* (1946). Translated by Carol Macomber. Yale University, 2007, p. 22. My emphasis. Abbr. Sartre, Existentialism.

6   Sartre, *Existentialism,* 22.

7   Francis Bacon, *The Advancement of Learning,* First Book (1605), Part 1, Section 3. Abbr. Bacon, Learning, 1.1.3.

8   Bacon, *Learning,* 1.2.5.

9   Bacon, *Learning,* 1.2.5.

10   Bacon, *Learning,* 1.2.8.

11   Bacon, *Learning,* 1.5.11.

12   Bacon, *Learning,* 1.8.2.

13   Bacon, *Learning,* 1.8.2.

14   Bacon, *Learning,* 1.8.2.

15   Some may have the opinion that aspiring to too much knowledge should be approached with caution because it can increase sorrow and anxiety and incline men to atheism (Bacon, *Learning,* 1.1.2). On the contrary, the learned man can live more decently than an unlearned man because he is wise to apply his knowledge to give himself "repose and contentment" (Bacon, *Learning,* 1.1.3). In addition, knowledge, not ignorance, should "make a more devout dependence upon God" as the first cause, and not "incline a man to atheism" (Bacon, *Learning,* 1.1.3). My emphasis.

16   Francis Bacon, *Novum Organum,* First Book (1620), Aphorism 3. Abbr. Bacon, Organum, 1.3.

17   Bacon, *Organum,* 1.9.

18   Bacon, *Organum,* 1.39.

19   In this book, I present Bacon's *Idols of the Mind* in reverse order from how he originally arranged them. I chose this structure to place "Idols of the Tribe" at the end—rather than at the beginning, as in Bacon's work—emphasizing their significance in the Digital Age, which I explore in the conclusion of my Afterword.

20   Nietzsche, *Twilight of the Idols* (1888), "Foreword." Abbr. Nietzsche, Twilight.

21   The difference between counterfeit and genuine education is explained more below in the Afterword under Idols of the Cave, "Education."

22   Plato, *Republic,* Lines 514aff.

23   John Dewey, *Democracy and Education: An Introduction to the Philosophy of Education.* The Free Press (1916), p. 10. Abbr. Dewey, Democracy and Education.

24   Jean Baudrillard, *Simulacra and Simulation,* pp. 1-2, 6. Abbr. Baudrillard.

25   Baudrillard, 12-13.

26   A. J. Gentile, "It's all a Simulation," *The Why Files.* June 7, 2022. Retrieved: https://www.youtube.com/watch?v=4wMhXxZ1zNM. Abbr. Gentile, Simulation.

27   Nick Bostrom, "Are You Living in a Computer Simulation?" (2003). Retrieved: https://simulation-argument.com/simulation.pdf. Abbr. Bostrom.

28   Bostrom.

29   Gentile, Simulation.

30   Gentile, Simulation.

31   Gentile, Simulation.

[32] Gentile, Simulation.

[33] Gentile, Simulation.

[34] A. J. Gentile, "It's ALL Fake | The Dead Internet Theory," *The Why Files.* March 24, 2022. Retrieved: https://youtu.be/mlR9fCXfWyM?si=MWvHznHMOodxMrti.

[35] Baudrillard, 30.

[36] Baudrillard is a self-proclaimed "active nihilist". See his *Simulacra and Simulation,* pp. 159-164 and *Jean Baudrillard: From Hyperreality to Disappearance, Uncollected Interviews,* p. 187.

[37] Larry and Andy Wachowski, *The Matrix* (1999). Script. Retrieved: https://www.scripts.com/script-pdf-body.php?id=84. Abbr. Matrix 1999.

[38] *Nausea* is a philosophical novel first published in 1938 by French existentialist Jean-Paul Sartre. It is the mission of existentialists to disregard traditional schemes of value and substitute one's own for the right to exist and live through the processes of one's own consciousness.

[39] Nietzsche, *Twilight,* "Expeditions of an Untimely Man," Section 37.

[40] Nietzsche, *Daybreak: Thoughts on the Prejudices of Morality* (1881). Translated by R. J. Hollingdale. Cambridge University Press, 1997. Section 9. His emphasis. Abbr. Nietzsche, Daybreak.

[41] Nietzsche, *Daybreak,* Section 9. His emphasis.

[42] See Nietzsche, *Ecce Homo* (1888), "The Untimely Essays," Section 2; "Human, All Too Human," Section 6; "Why I am a Destiny," Section 2. In *Ecce Homo,* "Why I am a Destiny," Section 6, Nietzsche says that an "immoralist [is] a mark of distinction and badge of honor." He further says that he is "proud to possess this word which sets me off against the whole of humanity," that is, against those who accept and confirm Tradition and Christian morality. Those who participate with Nietzsche in a disregard of Tradition and Christian morality he simply refers to them as "we immoralists." See *Twilight of the Idols,* "Maxims and Arrows," Section 36; "Morality as Anti-Nature," Sections 3 & 6 (appearing twice); "The Four Great Errors," Section 7.

[43] Nietzsche, *Human, All Too Human* (1878), "Preface," Section 5. His emphasis. Abbr. Nietzsche, Human.

[44] Quoted in Spinoza, *Complete Works: A Theologico-Political Treatise* (1670), "Freedom of Thought and Speech," Trans. Samuel Shirley, Hacket Publishing (2002), Chapter 20, p. 567. My emphasis. Nietzsche had high regards for Spinoza and his philosophy. He considered him to be a "precursor" to himself. See Middleton's *Selected Letters of Friedrich Nietzsche,* p. 177. Nietzsche describes Spinoza as "the purest sage" (*Human, All Too Human,* sec. 475) and his work "a passionate history of a soul" (*Daybreak,* sec. 481).

[45] Plato, *Republic,* Lines 514a-518e.

[46] *Matrix* (1999).

[47] Nietzsche, *Ecce Homo,* "Preface," Section 3. Cf. "Why I Write Such Excellent Books," Section 3.

[48] Immanuel Kant, *Prolegomena to Any Future Metaphysics* (1783), Line 260.

[49] Philippians 3:12.

[50] Paul Tillich, *The Courage To Be* (1952). Yale University Press, p. 27. Abbr. Tillich.

[51] Tillich, 27.

[52] Tillich, 26-27.

[53] Tillich, 27.

[54] Tillich, 27.

[55] John Dewey, *Experience and Education* (1938), Chapter 3, "Criteria of Experience," p. 43. My emphasis.

[56] Karl Rahner, *Theological Investigations, Vol. 5* (1966), p. 103 and 117. Abbr. Rahner, Vol. 5.

[57] This is in reference to Bergson's *Creative Evolution* (1907) and Whitehead's *Science and the Modern World* (1925) regarding his philosophy as one of organism.

58 Nietzsche, *Untimely Meditations,* "Schopenhauer as Educator," Section 1. His emphasis.

59 Featured in *The Japan Times* newspaper January 21, 1990.

60 Hilary Lawson, *Reflexivity: The Post-Modern Predicament,* p. 126.

61 Susanne Langer, *Harvard Educational Review,* Spring, 1956.

62 Tsunesaburo Makiguchi, *Education for Creative Living.* Iowa State University Press (1989), p. 167. My emphasis. Abbr. Makiguchi.

63 Makiguchi, 168.

64 Mortimer J. Adler, *Six Great Ideas,* Collier Books (1984).

65 David S. Broder, "Attitude is at fault in U.S. education", *The Japan Times,* January 25, 1990.

66 Choi Jin Young, "Versed in stats, ill-equipped in thought", *The Japan Times,* December 23, 1989.

67 Makiguchi, 21, 167.

68 Jean-Paul Sartre, *Being and Nothingness* (1943). Translated with an Introduction by Hazel E. Barnes. Washington Square Press (1992), pp. 310-11.

69 Refer to Immanuel Kant's 1784 prize essay in response to the question: "What is Enlightenment?"

70 Nietzsche, *Ecce Homo* (1888), "Why I Write Such Excellent Books," Section 1.

71 Nietzsche, *Human, All Too Human* (1878), "The Wanderer and His Shadow," Section 324.

72 S. I. Hayakawa, *Language in Thought and Action,* 2nd ed. (1964), p. 132.

73 Emil Brunner, *Man in Revolt* (1937), Ch. 1, "The Riddle of Man," pp. 17-28. Translated by Olive Wyon. Westminster Press, 1939. Abbr. Brunner.

74 Brunner, Ch. 6, "The Contradiction," 115.

75 Brunner, 115.

76 Thomas Hobbes, *Leviathan* (1668), Book 1, Ch. 13, "Of the Natural Condition of Mankind," Sections 8-9, pp. 74-76. Edited by Edwin Curley. Hacket Publishing Company, 1994. Abbr. Hobbes.

77 Brunner, 118.

78 Brunner, 118.

79 Romans 7:15-23.

80 Aristotle, *Politics,* Book 1, Chapter 2, Line 1253a2. Compare Aristotle's idea of action in the community in *Nicomachean Ethics,* Book 1, Chapter 7. Abbr. Aristotle, Politics, 1.2.1253a2.

81 Quoted in Justo L. Gonzalez, *A History of Christian Thought, Vol. 1* (1970), p, 242.

82 Nietzsche, *The Anti-Christ* (1888), Section 39.

83 This is in reference to Nietzsche's book, *Beyond Good and Evil* (1886) and to cognitive behavior therapy (CBT), which is basically "I feel," → "I think," → "I act."

84 Daniel Goleman, *Emotional Intelligence* (1995). Goleman says, "A key social ability is empathy, understanding others' feelings and taking their perspective, and respecting differences in how people feel about things," p. 268.

85 Nietzsche, *Twilight of the Idols* (1888), "Expeditions of an Untimely Man," Section 38. His emphasis. Abbr. Nietzsche, Twilight, 38.

86 Romans 3:30 and Acts 10:34-35. Paraphrased.

87 Zechariah 3:1-4.

88 Rahner, *Vol. 5,* 117.

89 Robert A. Morey, *Reincarnation and Christianity,* p. 11.

90 Rahner, *Vol. 5,* 131.

91 Philippians 2:3.

92 1 Corinthians 9:19-23.

93 1 Corinthians 9:22.

94 These insights are drawn from Joseph Fletcher's *Situation Ethics: The New Morality* (1966), which contrasts pietism and moralism, pp. 160-163. Abbr. Fletcher.

95 Quoted in Fletcher, 83.

96 Ludwig Feuerbach, *The Essence of Christianity* (1841), Trans. George Eliot, pp. 14-15. My emphasis.

97 Erich Neumann, *Depth Psychology and a New Ethic* (1969), p 50; C. G. Jung, *The Archetypes and the Collective Unconscious* (1959), pp. 40, 106, 130, 159, 287-288, 349-350. According to Jung, individuation is the maturation process of personality or the development of the individuated self "when he makes himself and not others *responsible.* This is naturally only possible in freedom" (349, my emphasis). Individuation includes both the conscious and the unconscious psych. Regarding the imagery of the exile in the wilderness, see Leviticus 16:8-10.

98 Robert Greene, *The 48 Laws of Power* (1998), p. xvii and xxiii. See Niccolò Machiavelli, *The Prince* (1532), Ch. 15. Translated by Russell Price. Cambridge University Press (2008), p. 55. Abbr. Machiavelli, The Prince.

99 Machiavelli, *The Prince*, Ch.18, p. 61.

100 This is Sartre's stance regarding his atheistic humanism and what he further means by "existence precedes essence. See *Existentialism is a Humanism,* pp. 24-25. Also see my essay, "The Religious Optimist," in the main text below.

101 Nietzsche, *On the Genealogy of Morals,* "Second Essay: 'Guilt,' 'Bad Conscience,' and the Like," particularly Section 19.

102 Nietzsche, *The Anti-Christ,* Section 54.

103 Rahner, *Vol. 5,* 121-131.

104 Nietzsche, *Human, All Too Human,* "Man Alone with Himself," Section 618. My emphasis.

105 Immanuel Kant, *Critique of Pure Reason* (1781, 1787). Translated by Werner S. Pluhar, Hacket Publishing Co. (1996), p. Bxviii. My graduate paper, "Three Views Contrasted" (Dec. 14, 2010), explores in depth three interpretations of Kant's distinctions between objects and examines how these relate to his concepts of freedom and determination.

106 Genesis 4:1-2.

107 Genesis 4:8.

108 Erich Fromm, "Fromm's theory of aggression," *New York Times,* 27 Feb 1972, https://www.nytimes.com/1972/02/27/archives/fromms-theory-of-aggression-the-young-have-rejected-the-consuming.html. Abbr. Fromm, theory.

109 Hsün-Tzu, *Basic Writings,* Trans. Burton Watson, p. 24.

110 Mark 7:21-22.

111 Thomas Hobbes, *Leviathan* (1668), Book 1, Ch. 13, Sections 7-8.

112 Hobbes, *Leviathan,* Book 1, Ch. 13, Section 9.

113 Erich Fromm, *The Anatomy of Human Destructiveness* (1973), p. 26. Abbr. Fromm, Destructiveness.

114 Fromm, *Destructiveness,* 24.

115 Erich Fromm, "Fromm's theory of aggression," *New York Times,* 27 Feb 1972, https://www.nytimes.com/1972/02/27/archives/fromms-theory-of-aggression-the-young-have-rejected-the-consuming.html. See also Fromm, *The Anatomy of Human Destructiveness,* p. 106.

116 Erich Fromm, *Destructiveness,* 31.

117 See Erich Fromm, *The Anatomy of Human Destructiveness* (1973). Also see Freud, *The Ego and the Id* (1923); Carl Jung, *Aion* (1959); and Erich Neumann, *Depth Psychology and a New Ethic* (1969).

118 Carl Jung, *Aion: Researches into the Phenomenology of the Self* (1959), "The Ego" and "The Shadow," Vol. 9, Part II. Princton University Press (1969), pp. 3-10.

119 Fromm, 31. If a person fails to confront and process the "darker" aspects of themselves—such as repressed traumatic memories or unresolved emotional experiences—these issues may resurface years later in the form of post-traumatic stress disorder (PTSD). This unresolved trauma can ultimately strain or even break down relationships.

120 Fromm, *Destructiveness,* 26-31.

121 Fromm, *Destructiveness,* 30.

122 Erich Neumann, *Depth Psychology and a New Ethic* (1969), pp. 41-44ff.

123 Genesis 3:8.

124 Augustine, *Confessions* (400 CE), Book 5, Chapter 9, Section 16. Abbr. Augustine, Confessions.

125 Inflated egos and unchecked power, along with a lack of empathy, are especially common in "supervisory" positions in organizations.

126 Augustine, *Confessions,* 2.6.14.

127 Albert Camus, *The Rebel: An Essay on Man in Revolt* (1956). Translated by Anthony Bower. Vintage International (1991), p. 306.

128 Revelation 12:7.

129 Revelation 12:8-9.

130 See historian Jeffrey Burton Russell's 5-volume set: *The Devil: Perceptions of Evil from Antiquity to Primitive Christianity* (1977), *Satan: The Early Christian Tradition* (1981), *Lucifer: The Devil in the Middle Ages* (1984), *Mephistopheles: The Devil in the Modern World* (1986), and *The Prince of Darkness: Radical Evil and the Power of Good in History* (1988).

131 Corliss Lamont, "The Illusion of Immortality," (1965) in *Critiques of God: Making the Case Against Belief in God* (1997), p. 282.

132 Findlay, 48.

133 See J. N. Findlay's essay, "Can God's Existence Be Disproved?" (1948) in *New Essays in Philosophical Theology* (1955), pp. 47-75. Abbr. Findlay.

134 Anslem, *Proslogion* (1078), Chapters 2 & 15.

135 In the *Metaphysics,* Aristotle asserts the existence of a being that is the ultimate cause of motion or change in the natural world, which itself does not move, and calls it the "Unmoved First Mover" (12.8.1074a37). He equates this concept with the "Active Intellect" in his work *On the Soul* (3.5.430a17-24).

136 Aquinas, *Summa Theologiae* (1267-73 CE), Part 1, Question 2, Article 3. Abbr. Aquinas, ST I.2.3.

137 Aquinas, *ST,* 1.2.3.

138 Peter Angeles, *The Problem of God,* pp. 21-22.

139 This earlier work is *Summa Contra Gentiles* (1259-64), which reads, "In the world we find that things of diverse natures come together under one order, and [not] by chance. There must be some being by whose providence the world is governed. This we call God" (p. 96). ST I.2.3.

140 Aquinas, *ST,* 1.2.3.

141 Sartre, *Existentialism,* 21.

142 Sartre, *Existentialism,* 21.

143 Sartre, *Existentialism,* 53.

144 Sartre, *Existentialism,* 29.

145 Sartre, *Existentialism,* 22.

146 Sartre, *Existentialism,* 24.

147 Sartre, *Existentialism,* 24.

148 Sartre, *Existentialism,* 24-25.

149 Sartre, *Existentialism,* 24.

150 Kant's formulation of the categorical imperative for the Law of Universality, states, "Act only according to that maxim whereby you can at the same time will that it should become a universal law." See his *Grounding of a Metaphysics of Morals* (1785), line 421.

151 Sartre, *Existentialism,* 24-25.

152 Sartre, *Existentialism,* 29.

153 Sartre, *Existentialism,* 29.

154 Genesis 3:4-6.

155 Genesis 3:7-11.

156 Genesis 3:12-13.

157 Genesis 3:1; Revelation 12:9.

158 Leibniz, *Theodicy: Essays on the Goodness of God, the Freedom of Man, and the Origin of Evil* (1710), Section 23, p. 137. Abbr. Theodicy.

159 *Theodicy,* Sections 30-33, p. 141. The thinking that evil is a defect and a privation of the good has its origins in St. Augustine, which stems from misused freedom of the creature. See his *Confessions* (397-400), Book 3, Chapter 7, Section 12.

160 *ST,* I.19.6 ad 1 (reply to objection 1).

161 *ST,* I.19.6 ad 1.

162 Leibniz, *The Monadology* (1714), quoted in *Philosophical Essays,* Hackett Publishing (1989), Sections 87 & 90, p. 224. Abbr. Monadology.

163 *Monadology,* 87 & 90, 224.

164 Voltaire wrote *Candide* three years after the "Great Lisbon earthquake" of 1755, which killed 50,000 people, making it one of the deadliest earthquakes in history.

165 Voltaire, *Candide* (1758), Chapter 5.

166 Langdon Gilkey, *Shantung Compound* (1966), pp. 230-31.

167 Elaine Pagels, *The Gnostic Gospels,* p. 122. Abbr. Pagels. See also James M. Robinson, *The Nag Hammadi Library* (1990), p. 152.

168 Pagels, 123.

169 Nietzsche, *The Gay Science,* sec. 125.

170 Kaufman, *Nietzsche,* p. 97.

171 Tillich, *The Courage To Be,* pp. 15-16.

172 *The Qur'an,* Text, Translation and Commentary by Abdullah Yusuf Ali (2008).

173 Aristotle, *Physics,* 2.5.196b17-23, 27-28, 197a13-14. Abbr. Physics.

174 Aristotle, *Metaphysics,* 6.3.1027b8-14.

175 Aristotle, *Physics,* 2.4.196b5-6.

176 Augustine, *On Free Choice of the Will* (388-395), Book 3, Section 4.

177 See Richard Rice, *God's Foreknowledge and Man's Free Will* (1985).

178 Justin Parrot, "Reconciling the Divine Decree and Free Will in Islam."

179 Matthew 7:13-14 (NIV).

180 1 Corinthians 9:22.

181 Joseph McCabe, *Selected Works of Voltaire* (1911), "Homily on Superstition," p. 65.

182 Aristotle, *NE* 1155a26.

183 Justo L. Gonzalez, *A History of Christian Thought,* Vol. I, p. 13.

184 Abraham Edel, "What Should be the Aim and Content of a Philosophy of Education?", *Harvard Educational Review,* spring 1956, p. 122. Abbr. Edel.

185 Kingsley Price, "Is a Philosophy of Education Necessary?" *The Journal of Philosophy,* 52 (October 27, 1955), 622-633. Abbr. Price.

186 Price, 624.

187 Susanne K. Langer, "On the Relations Between Philosophy and Education", *Harvard Educational Review,* spring 1956, 139-141. Abbr. Langer. Note: Langer refers to the definition and goal of education as outlined by Dr. K. Price. However, I question whether the purpose of education is truly to "favor special abilities." I disagree with this perspective, which is why I chose to omit it from this essay.

188 Langer, 140.

189 "Philosophy *of* education" seems to refer to education as a philosophy, whereas the term "philosophy *in* education" seeks to become the former.

190 Aristotle's *Metaphysics* begins, "All men by nature desire to know" (1.1.980b22).

191 James L. Christian, *Philosophy: An Introduction to the Art of Wondering,* San Francisco, Rinehart Press, 1973, p. 19. Abbr. Christian.

192 "Biblical Cyclopedic Index" in *The New King James Version of the Open Bible: Expanded Edition,* New York, Thomas Nelson, Inc., 1983, p. 317.

193 Christian, xvi.

194 Mortimer, J. Adler, *Aristotle for Everybody: Difficult Thought Made Easy,* New York, Macmillan, 1978, p. ix. Abbr. Adler, Aristotle for Everybody.

195 Adler, *Aristotle for Everybody,* ix. "... for those who do not already know" is my emphasis.

196 Madelene Hunter's term.

197 Some notable figures were Paul at Athens, Justin Martyr and Clement of Alexandria.

198 Edel, 126.

199 "Practical Applications of Research", Newsletter of Phi Delta Kappa's Center of Evaluation, Development and Research, Bloomington, Indiana, 3 (June 1981). Abbr. PAR.

200 "Effects of Teacher Enthusiasm Training on Student On-Task Behavior and Achievement", *American Educational Research Journal,* 20, 3 (fall 1983), p. 436. Abbr. Teacher Enthusiasm.

201 Barak Rosenshine, "Enthusiastic Teaching: A Research Review", *School Review,* 78, 4 (August 1970), p. 508 (McCoard). Abbr. Rosenshine.

202 Rosenshine, 509; Coats and Smidchens.

203 Teacher Enthusiasm, 446-47.

204 Teacher Enthusiasm, 446-47; Mastin (1963) 385.

205 Speculating on Paul's linguistic style, it's likely that his education included a focused study of rhetoric. Rhetoric is the art of logical thinking and the skill of expressing that thinking in the most effective way. It involves understanding the principles of logic to construct a compelling, well-supported argument.

206 Rosenshine, 511.

207 My emphasis.

208 PAR.

209 Rosenshine, 510.

210 John, D. Bransford, *Human Cognition: Learning, Understanding, and Remembering,* Belmont, CA., Wadsworth Pub. Co., 1979, p. 169. See also Immanuel Kant's *Critique of Pure Reason* (1781), especially his "categories of the understanding."

211 PAR.

212 Bruce, 106-07.

213 Hughes, 190.

214 Hughes, 190.

215 Hughes, 191.

216 Westcott, 142.

217 Westcott, 142.

218 Lenski, 176.

219 Lightfoot, 121.

220 Lightfoot, 121, quoted from Richardson, p. 191.

221 Buchanan, 103.

222 Lenski, 176.

223 Lightfoot, 121.

224 Bruce, 113.

225 Westcott, 144.

226 Lightfoot, 121.

227 Lightfoot, 121

228 Lightfoot, 120-21.

229 Buchanan, 104-05, quoted from Stuart, p. 139.

230 Buchanan, 104-05; Montefiore, p. 106.

231 Buchanan, 104-05; Moffatt, p. 75.

232 Bruce, 114.

233 Bruce, 115.

[234] Kent, 106. Lightfoot similarly says the same, p. 121. He (Lightfoot) further comments by saying, "Although the term 'baptismos' does not usually denote Christian baptism, here it is the appropriate term since other washings as well as baptism are in view here" (p. 122).

[235] Bruce, 116, footnote from D. Daube. Buchanan holds a similar view to that of Bruce (et all), p. 104.

[236] Bruce, 117 (see Bruce's footnote).

[237] Kent, 107.

[238] Kent, 107.

[239] Lightfoot, 122.

[240] Lenski, 175.

[241] Lightfoot, 122.

[242] Kent, 107.

[243] Westcott, 146.

[244] Bruce, 118.

[245] Hughes, 206.

[246] Bruce, 118.

[247] Hughes, 207.

[248] Kent, 108.

[249] Lightfoot, 123. Not all scholars agree with this, however. Wiley takes the position that the passage refers to those who are "almost Christian" (p. 219). Clarke takes the position that they are "apostates from Christianity" (p. 217, footnote by Wiley). But this is absurd. It doesn't fit in with the context of the passage, as well as the previous and the following verses.

[250] Lightfoot, 123.

[251] Bruce, 118.

[252] Buchanan, 105-06.

[253] Buchanan, 105-06. The last sentence quoted directly from Buchanan reads: "His emphasis in 6:4 is for the readers who had 'once been enlightened'". We have already established that the writer is not describing his readers. To say that the writer is describing his readers (and he isn't, see v. 9) is to be in error. To be consistent it should read: "His emphasis in 6:4 is for those who had 'once been enlightened.'" Most scholars agree that he isn't describing his readers, he is only addressing them.

[254] Hughes, 207.

[255] "They" will always refer to "those" that the writer is describing, not to be confused with the readers whom he is addressing this warning to—who are to apply this warning (the following) to themselves.

[256] Kent, 108.

[257] Bruce, 120.

[258] Hughes, 207.

[259] Westcott, 148; Lightfoot, 123; Hughes, 207.

[260] Lightfoot, 123.

[261] Bruce, 120 (see footnote).

[262] Lightfoot, 123; quoted from Moffatt, 78.

[263] Buchanan, 106.

[264] Hughes, 209. See also Westcott, 149.

[265] Bruce, 121 (see footnote).

[266] Westcott, 148-149.

[267] Kent, 108.

[268] My emphasis; against Westcott.

[269] Lenski, 182.

[270] Bruce, 121 (also Kent, 109).

[271] Lightfoot, 124 (see footnote).

272 Bruce, 121. Note: Not to contradict the previous two participles of the interpretation in this essay, but the people did in fact participate in these for the admission to Christian fellowship.

273 Kent, 109.

274 Lightfoot, 124.

275 Hughes, 210.

276 Westcott, 149.

277 Hughes, 211 (see footnote).

278 Wiley, 215.

279 Lenski, 184.

280 Lightfoot, 124.

281 Lightfoot, 124.

282 Some scholars hold the view that the whole passage (6:4-6) is a hypothetical case to illustrate the folly of apostasy (Kent, Westcott, Thomas, Hewitt). Hewitt says that "there is no suggestion in the context that the sin against the Holy Spirit ... is ever committed by true Christians" (p. 108). Against this as being a hypothetical case, other scholars' comment that the "biblical writers are not given to the setting up of men of straw (Bruce, p. 123, et al). And that "it is impossible for Christians, even after high spiritual attainments to fall into total apostasy" (Wiley et al, 216).

283 Lenski, 185.

284 Lenski, 185.

285 Bruce, 124.

286 Lightfoot, 126.

287 My emphasis.

288 Lenski, 186.

289 Lenski, 186. See also Wiley, 217.

290 Lenski, 186.

291 Lenski, 186.

292 See Buchanan, 107-110.

293 Bruce, p. 124. Lightfoot also has an appealing conclusion that is noteworthy: "They crucify Jesus 'on their own account' (literally, 'to themselves'). This can mean that they do it to their own harm (the crucifiers hurt themselves rather than the Crucified) or it can mean that they themselves crucify Jesus (cf. NEB). And they 'hold him up' in disgrace. Having torn Him from their hearts, they put Him on a cross for all the world to scoff at. No wonder, then, that for such people 'there no longer remains a sacrifice for sins' (10:26)" (p. 127).

294 Philosophy began around 2,500 years ago, emerging independently in Greece, India, and China. It marked a shift away from conventional religious or supernatural explanations of the world, favoring instead natural, scientific accounts of reality.

295 Anslem's original title of his *Proslogion* (1077-78) was "faith seeking understanding." This is often used to describe the dynamic of faith and reason. Reason serves as a tool to explore and make sense of the truths that faith reveals, but it does not supplant or replace faith. The belief is that reason alone cannot lead to salvation or fully comprehend God's mysteries, but it can illuminate and reinforce what has been revealed through faith. So, "faith seeking understanding" means something like "an active love of God seeking a deeper knowledge of God." See the "Introduction," by Thomas Williams in Anselm's *Proslogion*. Hacket Publishing Company (2001), p. vii.

296 Nietzsche, *Human, All Too Human*, "The Wanderer and His Shadow" (1880), Section 324.

297 Nietzsche, *Ecce Homo* (1888), "Why I am so Wise," Section 2.

298 Quoted from the last page in *Ecce Homo*, translated by R. J. Hollingdale, Penguin Books, 1988 edition.

299 Nietzsche, *Human, All Too Human*, "Assorted Opinions and Maxims" (1879), Section 137.

300 Martin Heidegger, *What Is Called Thinking?* (1954, 1968), p. 4. His emphasis. Abbr. Heidegger, Thinking.

301 J. Glenn Gray, "Introduction," in *What is Called Thinking?*, p. vii. Abbr. Gray, Introduction.

302 Heidegger, *Thinking,* 8. My emphasis.

303 Heidegger, *Thinking,* 4-5.

304 See Arthur Schopenhauer's thoughts on "thoughts" in *Essays and Aphorisms,* "On Philosophy and the Intellect," Section 14. Also see other sections in the same volume regarding Schopenhauer's thoughts on "thoughts."

305 Gray, Introduction, xiv-xv.

306 Gray, Introduction, xii.

307 Gray, Introduction, xiii.

308 Heidegger, *Thinking,* 8.

309 Heidegger, *Thinking,* 12-13.

310 I present Bacon's *Idols of the Mind* in reverse order from how he arranged them.

311 John 17:16; Romans 12:2.

312 I address the role of media outlets in social media in the section three, "Idols of the Cave," and the influence of entertainment in the section four, "Idols of the Tribe."

313 Socrates, the teacher of Plato and one of the key figures in the development of Western philosophy, was sentenced to death in 399 BCE by drinking poison. The Athenian authorities deemed him a threat to the city for rejecting its gods and encouraging a disregard for traditional authority. Plato's student, Aristotle, left Athens in 323 BCE, fearing for his safety and wary that the Athenians might "sin twice against philosophy." Similarly, Jesus was crucified in 33 CE for being seen as a subversive figure, challenging the social and religious order of his time.

314 "Martyrdom of Polycarp" in *Early Christian Writings: The Apostolic Fathers,* Penguin Books (1968, 1987), Sections 9-16. Abbr. Polycarp. See also *The Story of Christianity, Vol. 1* (1984) by Justo L. Gonzalez, pp. 43-45. Abbr. Gonzalez.

315 Polycarp, Sections 9-16; Gonzalez, 43-45.

316 Polycarp, Section 4.

317 Geoffrey Abbott, "Beheading: History, Methods & Consequences of Capital Punishment," *Encyclopaedia Brittanica.* Nov. 16, 2024. Retrieved: https://www.britannica.com/topic/beheading.

318 Editors, "William Wallace: Biography, Braveheart, Death, Sword, & Facts," *Encyclopaedia Britannica.* Nov. 5, 2024. Retrieved: https://www.britannica.com/biography/William-Wallace.

319 Randall Wallace, *Braveheart* (1995). Script. Retrieved: https://scripts.com/script-pdf-body.php?id=418. Abbr. Braveheart.

320 Braveheart.

321 Braveheart.

322 Brian P. Levack, *The Witch-Hunt in Early Modern Europe, 3rd Ed.* (2006), p. xii. Abbr. Levack.

323 Levack, 1. My emphasis.

324 Levack, 9.

325 Levack, 85.

326 Levack, 85-86.

327 Levack, 86.

328 Levack, 86.

329 Levack, 13-14.

330 Levack, 17.

331 Levack, 4.

332 Levack, 7.

333 Carrie Johnson, "As it Turns 10, Patriot Act Remains Controversial," *National Public Radio.* Oct. 26, 2011. Retrieved: https://www.npr.org/2011/10/26/141699537/as-it-turns-10-patriot-act-remains-controversial. Abbr. Johnson.

334 Jared Ahmad, "9/11: How Politicians and the Media Turned Terrorism into an Islamic Issue," *The Conversation.* Sept. 10, 2021. Retrieved: https://theconversation.com/9-11-how-politicians-and-the-media-turned-terrorism-into-an-islamic-issue-167733. Abbr. Ahmad.

335 Johnson.

336 Johnson.

337 Johnson.

338 Johnson.

339 Johnson.

340 Ahmad.

341 Ahmad.

342 Ahmad.

343 Ahmad.

344 Ahmad.

345 Ahmad.

346 Ahmad.

347 Ahmad.

348 Ahmad.

349 Ahmad.

350 Ahmad.

351 Ahmed S. Kesha et al. "COVID-19 versus SARS: A comparative review" in the *Journal of Infection and Public Health* 14 (April 15, 2021) 967-977.

352 Michael T. Osterholm, Ph.D. "Preparing for the Next Pandemic" in *The New England Journal of Medicine* 352;18 (May 5, 2005) 1839-1842. Abbr. Osterholm.

353 Lawrence O. Gostin, J.D., and Gigi K. Gronvall, Ph.D. "The Origins of Covid-19—Why It Matters (and Why It Doesn't)" in *The New England Journal of Medicine* 388;25 (June 22, 2023) 2305-2308.

354 Osterholm.

355 Randy M Herring, *The Fitness Mindset: 7 Habits for Peak Performance to Get Strong, Lean, And Fit* (2021), Chapter 5, "Resistance Training as the Exercise Modality," 81-84. Abbr. Herring, Fitness Mindset.

356 Joshua Cohen, "3 Years After Covid-19 Vaccine Rollout, CDC Still Gets Messaging Wrong" (Dec. 13, 2023). Retrieved: https://www.forbes.com/sites/joshuacohen/2023/12/13/three-years-after-covid-19-vaccine-rollout-cdc-still-gets-messaging-wrong/?sh=1d75e73f1178.

357 Gordon Rayner, "Use of fear to control behaviour in Covid crisis was 'totalitarian,' admit scientists" (May 14, 2021). Retrieved: https://www.telegraph.co.uk/news/2021/05/14/scientists-admit-totalitarian-use-fear-control-behaviour-covid. Abbr. Rayner.

358 Rayner.

359 Rayner.

360 Rayner.

361 Bjorn Lomborg and Jordan B. Peterson, "Stop the panicked fearmongering if we want to make the world better," Aug. 4, 2023. Retrieved: https://nypost.com/2023/08/04/stop-the-panicked-fearmongering-if-we-want-to-make-the-world-better.

362 Nirmita Pancha et al. "The Implications of COVID-19 for Mental Health and Substance Use," March 20, 2023. Retrieved: https://www.kff.org/mental-health/issue-brief/the-implications-of-covid-19-for-mental-health-and-substance-use. Abbr. Pancha.

363 Pancha.

364 Pancha.

365 Galileo, *Dialogue Concerning the Two Chief World Systems* (1632). Translated by Stillman Drake. Foreword by Albert Einstein. University of California Press (1967), 496 pp.

366 John Cottingham, *The Philosophical Writings of Descartes, Vol. 3, The Correspondence* (1991), letter to Mersenne in end of November 1633, p. 41. Abbr. Cottingham.

367 Cottingham, 40-41.

368 Cottingham, 41. In 1629, Descartes began a work called *The World,* which demonstrates the heliocentric view of the universe, but abandoned the project upon hearing of the condemnation of Galileo, at the end of 1633. See *The World and Other Writings,* Cambridge University Press, 1998, p. viii.

369 Cottingham, 41.

370 Descartes, *Principles of Philosophy* (1644), "Part 3: Of the Visible Universe," Section 28.

371 Kate Bowler, *Blessed: A History of the American Prosperity Gospel.* Oxford University Press (2018), p. 3.

372 Joe Carter, "9 Things You Should Know About The Prosperity Gospel," *The Gospel Coalition* (Sept. 2, 2023). Retrieved: https://www.thegospelcoalition.org/article/9-things-prosperity-gospel.

373 Bryn Donovan, "Prosperity Gospel," *Encyclopaedia Brittanica* (Sept. 13, 2024). Retrieved: https://www.britannica.com/topic/prosperity-gospel. Abbr. Donovan.

374 Donovan.

375 The practice of selling indulgences in the Roman Catholic Church allowed people, from the wealthy to the common folk, to obtain spiritual benefits or rewards by making donations to the Church in exchange for the remission of sins and a reduction in time spent in 'purgatory'—an intermediate state where souls are purified before entering heaven—by performing certain acts, such as praying, making donations, or undertaking other religious tasks (Williston Walker, *A History of the Christian Church, 4th Edition.* Scribner, 1985, pp. 347-48). Johann Tetzel, a Dominican friar, was the most famous figure associated with selling indulgences in the Middle Ages (Walker, p. 425). He was known for his aggressive promotion and sale of indulgences, which were supposed to reduce the punishment for sins in purgatory. Tetzel's sales pitch included the famous slogan "As soon as the coin in the coffer rings, the soul from purgatory springs."

376 *Inside Edition,* "Full Interview: Preacher Kenneth Copeland Defends Lavish Lifestyle" (May 20, 2019). Retrieved: https://www.youtube.com/watch?v=9LtF34Mrsfl&t=10s.

377 As of now, no scientific study has provided reliable evidence for the existence of an afterlife, a question closely tied to the mechanisms of consciousness and the brain's relationship with neuroscience, physics, and psychology. See Senarath Dayathilake, K. L. "Consciousness, High Probability of Afterlife, and the Evolution of Intelligence in the Universe/s" (Aug. 31, 2024, v. 16). *Cambridge Open Engage.* Retrieved: https://www.cambridge.org/engage/coe/article-details/66cda25320ac769e5ffc3012.

378 Dewey, *Democracy and Education,* 10.

379 Dewey, *Democracy and Education,* 41.

380 Dewey, *Democracy and Education,* 41.

381 Mortimer J. Adler, *A Guidebook to Learning for the Lifelong Pursuit of Wisdom.* Macmillan Publishing Company (1985), pp. 1-2. Abbr. Adler, Guidebook.

382 Adler, *Reforming Education,* 168, 171.

383 Adler, *Reforming Education,* 171-73.

384 Adler, *Reforming Education,* 168-70.

385 Mortimer J. Adler, *Paideia Proposal* (1982), Chapter 4, p. 23.

386 Adler, *Guidebook,* 2.

387 Adler, *Guidebook,* 2.

388 Adler, *Guidebook,* 2. My emphasis.

389 Adler, *Guidebook,* 120-127ff.

390 Adler, *Guidebook,* 127.

391 Adler, *Guidebook,* 110.

392 Howard Gardner, *Frames of Mind: The Theory of Multiple Intelligences* (1983). Basic Books, 2011, p. 3. Abbr. Gardner, Frames of Mind.

393 Gardner, *Frames of Mind,* 5.

394 Gardner, *Frames of Mind,* 5; 8-9. His emphasis.

395 Gardner, *Frames of Mind,* 33. His emphasis.

396 Gardner, *Frames of Mind,* 34. His emphasis.

397 Gardner, *Intelligence Reframed: Multiple Intelligences for the 21st Century.* Basic Books (1999), p. 33. Abbr. Gardner, Intelligence Reframed.

398 Gardner, *Intelligence Reframed,* 34. His emphasis.

399 Gardner, *Intelligence Reframed,* 34.

400 Gardner, *Frames of Mind,* 74. My emphasis.

401 Gardner, *Frames of Mind,* 77-103.

402 Gardner, *Frames of Mind,* 105-34.

403 Gardner, *Frames of Mind,* 135-78.

404 Gardner, *Frames of Mind,* 179-216.

405 Gardner, *Frames of Mind,* 217-49.

406 Gardner, *Frames of Mind,* 251-57.

407 Gardner, *Frames of Mind,* 251-57.

408 Gardner, *Intelligence Reframed,* 48-52.

409 Gardner, *Intelligence Reframed,* 53-60; 64-65.

410 Gardner, *Intelligence Reframed,* 60-64.

411 Gardner, *Intelligence Reframed,* 68-77.

412 Gardner, "Impact of Multiple Intelligences Theory on U.S. Public Schools." Received by Randy Herring, 13 May 2003.

413 Ludwig Feuerbach, *The Essence of Christianity* (1841). Translated by George Eliot.

414 This is the essence of the philosophy of Nietzsche and Chuang-Tzu.

415 Nichole McCarthy, "Terrorism," (Sept. 2021). *Cornell Law School.* Retrieved: https://www.law.cornell.edu/wex/terrorism.

416 Antony Loewenstein, *The Palestine Laboratory* (2023), pp. 5-25.

417 Norman Doidge, *The Brain that Changes Itself* (2007).

418 Nietzsche, *The Gay Science* (1882), Book Four, Section 276.

419 Robert C. Solomon, *The Passions: Emotions and the Meaning of Life* (1993), p. x.

420 Wittgenstein, *Philosophical Investigations* (1953), Part I, Section 109. Abbr. Wittgenstein, Investigations, I.109.

421 Wittgenstein, *Investigations,* I.110.

422 Samuel E. Stumpf, *Socrates to Sartre and Beyond,* 7th Edition (2003), p. 439. Abbr. Stumpf.

423 Wittgenstein, *Investigations,* I.23.

424 Wittgenstein, *Investigations,* I.23.

425 Nietzsche, *Twilight of the Idols* (1888), "Reason in Philosophy," Section 5.

426 Nietzsche, *Twilight,* Appendix C, 190.

427 Burton Watson, *The Complete Works of Chuang-Tzu* (1968), "Discussion on Making All Things Equal," pp. 37-40.

428 Adler, *Reforming Education,* 171.

429 Adler, *Reforming,* 167-68.

430 Adler, *Reforming,* 232.

431 Adler, *Reforming,* 169.

432 Plato, *Republic,* 518b-519d.

433 Plato, *Republic,* 591c.

434 Adler, *Reforming,* 234.

435 Adler, *Reforming,* 236.

436 Howard Zinn, *A People's History of the United States* (1980), pp. 10-11.

[437] Zinn defends his approach by stating, "To indicate every source of information in the text would have meant a book impossibly cluttered with footnotes. Therefore, as often as I can, I mention in the text authors and titles of books..." (p. 689). However, Zinn could have easily included page numbers in parentheses or brackets after his lengthy quotations, thus eliminating the need for footnotes altogether.

[438] Herman J. Viola and Carolyn Margolis, *Seeds of Change: A Quincentennial Commemoration* (1991), pp. 13-15.

[439] Viola and Margolis, *Seeds of Change*, p. 14.

[440] Jerry Bentley and Herb Ziegler, *Traditions and Encounters: A Global Perspective on the Past, Vol II: From 1500 to the Present*, 3rd Edition (2006), p. xvi and 606.

[441] Donald Yacovone, *Teaching White Supremacy* (2022), pp. xvii-xviii. Abbr. Yacovone.

[442] Yacovone, xviii-xix.

[443] Yacovone, xii-xix.

[444] Christopher Columbus's journal entry on October 11, 1492. Quoted in *Christopher Columbus, The Four Voyages* (1969), edited and translated by J. M. Cohen, p. 55. Abbr. Cohen.

[445] Cohen, Columbus's journal entry on October 13, 1492, p. 57.

[446] Cohen, Columbus's journal entries on October 11, 13 & 14, 1492, pp. 56-59. My emphasis.

[447] Bartolomé de las Casas, *History of the Indies* (1527-1561), Book 1, Chapter 41. Abbr. Las Casas, History. Quoted in *Christopher Columbus: The Four Voyages*, translated by J. M. Cohen, pp. 59-60. *History of the Indies* has never been fully translated into English. The only partial English translation was done by Andrée M. Collard in 1971. For the original quote, see the Spanish edition of Bartolomé de las Casas, *Historia de las Indias*, Vol. I, edited by Agustín Millares Carlo, published by Fondo de Cultura Económica in Mexico (1951, 1965, 2017), pp. 208-209.

[448] Philadelphia prosecutor Robert F. Petrone argues against the view of Columbus as a villain, suggesting instead that his predecessors—Bobadilla and Ovando—were responsible for the atrocities committed against the Indigenous peoples. In his *"A Report on the History of the Indies: Books I, II, III"* (December 2018 to March 2019, p. 47), Petrone presents two main points: first, that it was the Spanish encomienda system of forced labor and tribute from the Indigenous people that paved the way for the brutal conquest of the Americas; and second, that Columbus's political rivals and successors were the ones who perpetrated the worst atrocities against the natives. However, a closer examination of Columbus's own logbook and Bartolomé de las Casas's *History of the Indies* reveals that the violence against the Taino people began almost immediately upon Columbus's arrival in the Caribbean, not after his departure. To further support his argument that Columbus was a hero, Petrone wrote a 60+ page, eight-part series titled *"Christopher Columbus: The Greatest Hero of the 15th and 16th Centuries"* (September 2020 to January 2021), in which he claims that Columbus was the "first civil rights activist of the Americas" (Part 7).

[449] Las Casas, *History.* English edition (1971), Chapter 107, p. 57; Spanish edition (1951), Capitulo CVII, pp. 422-23. My emphasis.

[450] Las Casas, *History*, Chapter 107, p. 57.

[451] Bill Bigelow, "Time to Abolish Columbus Day," October 4, 2015. Zinn Education Project. Retrieved: https://zinnedproject.org/if-we-know-our-history/time-abolish-columbus-day.

[452] David E. Stannard, *American Holocaust: The Conquest of the New Word* (1992), pp. 64-65. Abbr. Stannard.

[453] Bartolomé de las Casas, *A Short Account of the Destruction of the Indies* (1552), 15-17. Abbr. Las Casas, Short Account.

[454] Stannard, 71.

[455] Robert A. Williams, Jr., "Columbus's Legacy: Law as an Instrument of Racial Discrimination Against Indigenous Peoples' Right to Self-Determination" (Fall 1991), pp. 51-75. Retrieved: https://repository.arizona.edu/bitstream/handle/10150/659465/18_8ArizJIntlCompL_51_1

991.pdf?sequence=1. Pp. 56-63. Abbr. Robert A. Williams. For an outline account of each Crusade from a church historian's perspective see Williston Walker, *A History of the Christian Church,* 4th Edition (1985), pp. 283-290.

456 Stannard, 65.

457 Stannard, 66.

458 Stannard, 66.

459 Las Casas, *Short Account,* 6-7.

460 Las Casas, *Short Account,* 6.

461 Robert A. Williams, 67.

462 Robert A. Williams, 71.

463 Robert A. Williams, 67.

464 Stannard, 118-19.

465 Stannard, 119.

466 Stannard, 119.

467 Stannard, 120.

468 Stannard, 120.

469 Gary Clayton Anderson, "The Native Peoples of the American West: Genocide or Ethnic Cleansing?" *Western Historical Quarterly*, vol. 47, no. 4, 2016, pp. 407–33. *JSTOR*, https://www.jstor.org/stable/26782720. Pp. 408, 416 & 433.

470 Genesis 6:9; 7:13.

471 Genesis 8:4.

472 Genesis 9:20-27. Quoted in the St. Jerome Edition of *The New Catholic Study Bible* (1985).

473 Yacovone, 8.

474 George Washington Williams, *History of the Negro Race in America* (1882), p. 10. Abbr. Williams.

475 Genesis 10:1.

476 Genesis 10:2-32.

477 Williams, 10.

478 Williams, 11.

479 Williams, 14.

480 Williams, 15-17.

481 H. G. Gadamer, "The Problem of Historical Consciousness" (1963), in *Interpretive Social Science: A Second Look* (1987), p. 87. My emphasis. Abbr. Gadamer.

482 Gadamer, quoted, p. 87. See pp. 86-90.

483 Nietzsche, *The Will to Power* (1901), Section 481. Abbr. Nietzsche, Will to Power.

484 Nietzsche, *Will to Power,* 481.

485 Nietzsche, *Will to Power,* 481.

486 Gadamer, 91.

487 Nietzsche, *Human, All Too Human* (1878-80), "Assorted Opinions and Maxims," Section 137.

488 Plato, *The Republic,* Book 5, 459a-460c.

489 George Klosko. "'Racism' in Plato's Republic.'" *History of Political Thought*, vol. 12, no. 1, 1991, pp. 1–13. *JSTOR*, http://www.jstor.org/stable/26214031.

490 Yacovone, 228.

491 Yacovone, 230-31.

492 Yacovone, 231.

493 Yacovone, 228-29.

494 A. J. Gentile, "The Genetic Arms Race | How CRISPR and AI Destroy the World," *The Why Files.* May 11, 2024.Retrieved: https://www.youtube.com/watch?v=OvcCK-F6aKY. Abbr. Gentile, Genetic Arms Race.

495 Gentile, Genetic Arms Race.

496 Gentile, Genetic Arms Race.

497 Gentile, Genetic Arms Race.

498 Gentile, Genetic Arms Race.

499 Basil Davidson, *The African Slave Trade* (1980), p. 63. Abbr. Davidson, Slave Trade.

500 Davidson, *Slave Trade,* 65.

501 Davidson, *Slave Trade,* 65-66.

502 Basil Davidson, "Columbus: the bones and blood of racism" (1992), in *Race & Class.* 33 (3): 17-25. January-March, p. 18. My thanks to Bill Bigelow for emailing me this article.

503 Williams, 69; Yacovone, 141.

504 Williams, 73.

505 Williams, 73.

506 Williams, 73.

507 Williams, 73.

508 Williams, 73.

509 Williams, 417-422.

510 Yacovone., xviii.

511 Yacovone, 241-42.

512 Williams, 170.

513 Yacovone, 9. Quoted in John Wood Sweet, *Bodies Politic: Negotiating Race in the American North (*2006), p. 154.

514 Sweet, 154.

515 Las Casas, *History of the Indies, Vol. II* (1561). New York: Harper and Row (1971), p. 257. Quoted in Brian Pierce, "Bartolomé de las Casas and Truth: Toward a Spirituality of Solidarity" (1992). *Spirituality Today.* 44(1): 4-19.

516 Anthony Pagden, "Introduction," in Bartolomé de las Casas' *A Short Account of the Destruction of the Indies*, p. xxii. Quoted in *The New Catholic Study Bible, St. Jerome Edition* (1985), p. 886.

517 David Carroll Cochron, "How Hitler found his blueprint for a German empire by looking to the American West" (2020). Retrieved: https://wagingnonviolence.org/2020/10/hitler-found-blueprint-german-empire-in-the-american-west. Abbr. Cochron.

518 Cochron.

519 Cochron.

520 Cochron.

521 Cochron.

522 Cochron.

523 Cochron.

524 Robert J. Miller, "Nazi Germany's Race Laws, the United States, and American Indians" (2020), in *St. John's Law Review.* Vol. 94 (3) Article 5. Pp. 751-817. P. 751. Abbr. Miller.

525 Miller, 756.

526 Miller, 756.

527 Miller, 753.

528 Miller, 761.

529 Miller, 762.

530 Miller, 760.

531 Miller, 762.

532 Miller, 766.

533 Alex Ross, "How American Racism Influenced Hitler" (2018). Retrieved: https://newyorker.com/magazine/2018/04/30/how-american-racism-influenced-hitler. Abbr. Ross.

534 Ross.

535 Ross.

536 Ross.

537 Ross.

538 Cochron.

539 Cochron.

540 Adam Hochschild, *King Leopold's Ghost* (1998). See Chapter 7, pp. 101-114. Abbr. Hochschild.

541 Hochschild, 112. The full text of George Washington Williams' "Open Letter" is available here: https://www.blackpast.org/global-african-history/primary-documents-global-african-history/george-washington-williams-open-letter-king-leopold-congo-1890.

542 Guy Vanthemsche. "The Historiography of Belgian Colonialism in the Congo" (2006), p. 89. https://pdfs.semanticscholar.org/0e36/51468d36b7328a48df7d933651ca02788325f.pdf.

543 Vanthemsche.

544 This statistic was in 2011, thirteen years ago. Here's the latest report: "DR Congo: Killings, Rapes Rwanda-Backed M23 Rebels" (June 13, 2023), *Human Rights Watch,* New York, NY. Access: https://www.hrw.org/news/2023/06/13/dr-congo-killings-rapes-rwanda-backed-m23-rebels.

545 Genesis 10:32-11:9.

546 Genesis 10:2-5.

547 Genesis 9:18, 22; 10:6-20.

548 Genesis 11:10-26.

549 Genesis 10:6, 14; 12:6.

550 Exodus 15:14-15.

551 Genesis 9:25.

552 Genesis 12:5-7; 15:7.

553 Genesis 17:5.

554 Deuteronomy 1:17; Acts 10:34; Romans 2:11; 1 Timothy 5:21.

555 Judges 20:2; Exodus 3:10.

556 See the main text below regarding the "Second Jewish Temple."

557 Michael Scott-Baumann, *The Shortest History of Israel and Palestine: From Zionism to Intifadas and the Struggle for Peace* (2021, 2023), p. 63. Abbr. Scott-Baumann.

558 Scott-Baumann, 21.

559 Scott-Baumann, 21.

560 Scott-Baumann, 22.

561 Scott-Baumann, 26.

562 Norman Solomon, *Judaism: A Very Short Introduction* (1996), Ch. 1, "Who are the Jews?" pp. 13-14. Abbr. Solomon.

563 Solomon, 13-14.

564 Solomon, 14.

565 Yehoshafat Harkabi, *Israeli's Fateful Decisions* (1988), p. 65. My emphasis. Abbr. Harkabi.

566 Harkabi, 65.

567 Zechariah 8:3, 7-8.

568 *The New King James Version of the Open Bible* (1983), "The Book of Zechariah," p. 948.

569 *The Open Bible,* 948.

570 Solomon, Appendix A, 136.

571 Rashid Khalidi, *The Iron Cage: The Story of the Palestinian Struggle for Statehood.* Beacon Press (2006), p. 31. Abbr. Khalidi.

572 Khalidi, 31.

573 Khalidi, 33.

574 Scott-Baumann, 44.

575 Scott-Baumann, 44.

576 Scott-Baumann, 46-48.

577 Scott-Baumann, 52.

578 Scott-Baumann, 63.

579 Scott-Baumann, 66.
580 Scott-Baumann, 68, 72.
581 Scott-Baumann, 75.
582 Scott-Baumann, 75.
583 Scott-Baumann, 87.
584 Scott-Baumann, 87.
585 Scott-Baumann, 90.
586 Scott-Baumann, 93-94.
587 Scott-Baumann, 98.
588 Scott-Baumann, 106.
589 Scott-Baumann,113.
590 Scott-Baumann, 114-115.
591 Scott-Baumann, 107; See also "Israeli occupation of Palestinian territory illegal: UN rights commission" (October 20, 2022). https://news.un.org/en/story/2022/10/1129722.
592 Scott-Baumann, 107.
593 Scott-Baumann, 116.
594 Scott-Baumann, 117.
595 Scott-Baumann, 140.
596 Scott-Baumann, 140.
597 Scott-Baumann, 140.
598 Scott-Baumann, 122, 142-43. This paragraph is written in the present tense because all these Israeli factors continue to persist as a reality for Palestinians in 2024.
599 Scott-Baumann, 144.
600 Scott-Baumann, 144.
601 Scott-Baumann, 144-45.
602 Scott-Baumann, 146.
603 Scott-Baumann, 146-47.
604 Scott-Baumann, 151.
605 Scott-Baumann, 162.
606 Scott-Baumann, 152-56.
607 Scott-Baumann, 156-57.
608 Scott-Baumann, 157.
609 Scott-Baumann, 157.
610 Scott-Baumann, 157.
611 Scott-Baumann, 157.
612 Scott-Baumann, 159.
613 Scott-Baumann, 159-60.
614 Scott-Baumann, 163.
615 Scott-Baumann, 163.
616 Scott-Baumann, 162.
617 Scott-Baumann, 167.
618 Khalidi, 197.
619 Scott-Baumann, 167.
620 Scott-Baumann, 167.
621 Scott-Baumann, 169.
622 Scott-Baumann, 175.
623 Scott-Baumann, 181.
624 Scott-Baumann, 182.
625 Scott-Baumann, 182.
626 Scott-Baumann, 182.
627 Scott-Baumann, 182-83.
628 Scott-Baumann, 183.

629 Scott-Baumann, 183.
630 Scott-Baumann, 183.
631 Scott-Baumann, 185.
632 Scott-Baumann, 185.
633 Scott-Baumann, 185.
634 Scott-Baumann, 186.
635 Scott-Baumann, 186.
636 Scott-Baumann, 188.
637 Scott-Baumann, 188.
638 Scott-Baumann, 188. My emphasis.
639 Quoted in Scott-Baumann, 189.
640 Scott-Baumann, 190.
641 Scott-Baumann, 190.
642 Scott-Baumann, 192.
643 Nathan Thrall, "The Separate Regimes Delusion: Nathan Thrall on Israel's apartheid," in *London Review of Books,* 43.2 (January 21, 2021). Retrieved: https://www.lrb.co.uk/the-paper/v43/n02/nathan-thrall/the-separate-regimes-delusion. Abbr. Thrall.
644 Thrall.
645 Thrall. His emphasis.
646 Thrall.
647 Scott-Baumann, 193.
648 Scott-Baumann, 193.
649 Scott-Baumann, 193-94.
650 Scott-Baumann, 194.
651 Scott-Baumann, 195.
652 Scott-Baumann, 195.
653 Quoted in Scott-Baumann, 195.
654 Scott-Baumann, 197.
655 Scott-Baumann, 154.
656 Scott-Baumann, 197.
657 Scott-Baumann, 198.
658 Scott-Baumann, 228.
659 Scott-Baumann, 229.
660 Scott-Baumann, 229.
661 Antony Loewenstein, *The Palestine Laboratory: How Israel Exports the Technology of Occupation Around the World* (2023), p. 5. Abbr. Loewenstein.
662 Scott-Baumann, 230.
663 Quoted in Loewenstein, 6.
664 Loewenstein, 6. His emphasis.
665 Loewenstein, 5. His emphasis.
666 Loewenstein, 2.
667 Loewenstein, 27.
668 Loewenstein, 28.
669 Loewenstein, 9.
670 Loewenstein, 13.
671 Loewenstein, 13.
672 Loewenstein, 14.
673 Quoted in Loewenstein, 14.
674 Scott-Baumann, 237.
675 Scott-Baumann, 230, 237.
676 Scott-Baumann, 230.
677 Scott-Baumann, 211.

678 Loewenstein, 1.

679 From the inside hardcover dust jacket of Loewenstein's *The Palestine Laboratory.*

680 Herring, *Fitness Mindset,* 72.

681 When reading an interpretation of a great work by a brilliant mind, Gadamer reminds us that "a person who is trying to understand a text is always projecting ... some initial meaning ... in the text" (267). This happens because the reader approaches the text with "particular expectations in regard to a certain meaning" (267). Gadamer refers to this as a "fore-projection" (267). He goes on to emphasize, "The important thing is to be aware of one's own bias, so that the text can present itself in all its otherness and thus assert its own truth against one's own fore-meanings" (269). (See Hans-Georg Gadamer, *Truth and Method* [1960], translated by Joel Weinsheimer and Donald G. Marshall, Continuum Publishing, 2003.)

682 Randy M. Herring, "Happiness in Action and Contemplation in Aristotle's Nicomachean Ethics" (Aug. 2011). Master Thesis (137pp). Washington State University, Pullman, Washington. Abbr. Herring, Thesis.

683 Will Durant, *The Story of Philosophy* (1929), Pocket Book 2006 Edition, p. 98n. 50. Abbr. Durant, Philosophy.

684 Jeffrey Henderson (Editor) and H. Rackham (Translator), *Aristotle XIX Nicomachean Ethics,* Loeb Classical Library (1926), 2.4.1105b4, p. 85.

685 Robert Greene, *The 48 Laws of Power* (1998), Preface, pp. xvii and xxiii.

686 Peter Constantine (Editor and Translator), *The Essential Writings of Machiavelli,* Modern Library Classics (2007), p. 59.

687 Quentin Skinner (Editor) and Russell Price (Translator), *Machiavelli: The Prince,* Cambridge University Press (1988), p. 62.

688 Cognitive behavioral therapy (CBT) is based on the idea that our thoughts (cognitive) influence our emotions (feelings) and behaviors (actions).

689 James Clear, *Atomic Habits: An Easy & Proven Way to Build Good Habits & Break Bad Ones* (2018), p. 44. Abbr. Clear

690 Clear, 45.

691 Clear, 45.

692 Clear, 143. My emphasis.

693 Clear. My emphasis.

694 Doing the same training exercise routine yields results because "repetition" allows the body to adapt and become stronger. I discuss this in Chapter 7 in my book, *The Fitness Mindset,* 121-128.

695 Clear, 144.

696 Norman Doidge, *The Brain that Changes Itself* (2007), p xix.

697 Doidge, 16.

698 Paul Bach-y-Rita, "Brain Plasticity as a Basis of Sensory Substitution," *J Neuro Rehab,* 1:2:67-71 (1987) p. 67.

699 Clear, 145.

700 Clear, 146.

701 Aristotle, *Ethics,* 2.4.1105b3-4. My paraphrase.

702 Durant, *Philosophy,* 98n. 50.

703 Clear, 144. His emphasis.

704 Clear, 145.

705 Aristotle, *Nicomachean Ethics,* Book 8, Chapter 3, Lines 1156a7-14. Aristotle refers to three types of associations as "friendships." Abbr. Aristotle, Ethics, 8.3.1156a7-14.

706 Aristotle, *Ethics,* 8.3.1156a27-29.

707 David H. Calhoun, "Friendship and Self-Love in Aristotle's Ethics," Dissertation (1989). Northwestern U., Chapter 4, p. 95. Abbr. Calhoun.

708 Aristotle, *Ethics,* 8.3.1156a30.

709 Aristotle, *Ethics,* 8.3.1156a31-33.

710 Calhoun, 99.

711 Aristotle, *Ethics,* 8.3.1156a8-10.

712 See Virginia Held, *The Ethics of Care* (2006), Chapter 3, pp. 44-57.

713 Aristotle, *Ethics,* 8.3.1156b26.

714 Aristotle, *Ethics,* 8.3.1156b30.

715 Aristotle, *Ethics,* 8.3.1156b26.

716 Calhoun, 98.

717 Calhoun, 99-100.

718 Aristotle, *Ethics,* 8.3.1156a32-35.

719 Bechtoldt MN, Beersma B and Dijkstra MTM (2020) "Editorial: Why People Gossip and What It Brings About: Motives for, and Consequences of, Informal Evaluative Information Exchange." *Front. Psychol.* 11:24. doi: 10.3389/fpsyg.2020.00024.

720 Frank T. McAndrew Ph.D., "Why Gossip Feels So Good," (2023). https://www.psychologytoday.com/intl/blog/out-of-the-ooze/202303/why-gossip-feels-so-good.

721 S. I. Hayakawa, *Language in Thought and Action,* 2nd ed. (1964), p. 132. Abbr. Hayakawa.

722 Hayakawa, 132.

723 Chuang-Tzu, "Autumn Floods" in *The Complete Works of Chuang-Tzu* (1968). Translated by Burton Watson, p. 186.

724 Bacon, *Organum,* 1.3.

725 Bacon, *Learning,* 1.1.3.

726 Bacon, *Learning,* 1.5.11 and 1.8.2.

727 Georg Wilhelm Friedrich Hegel, *Philosophy of Mind* (published posthumously in 1870), Section 474.

728 The idea of "bad faith" originates with Jean-Paul Sartre in his *Being and Nothingness* (1943), Chapter Two, "Bad Faith," pp. 86-116.

729 Juneman Abraham, et al. "The Psychology of Corruption: The Role of the Counterfeit Self, Entity Self-Theory, and Outcome-Based Ethical Mindset," in *Journal of Psychological and Educational Research* (JPER), 26 (2), November 2018 (pp. 7-32), p. 8.

730 The first two characteristics and the eighth characteristic of the counterfeit self is derived from Sandy Hotchkiss' book, *Why is it Always About You? The Seven Deadly Sins of Narcissism* (2002), Part 1, pp. 3-31. The third, fourth, fifth, sixth, and seventh characteristics of the counterfeit self is derived from Juneman Abraham' article, "The Psychology of Corruption..." referenced above, pp. 8-9 and 18-19.

731 I briefly talked about the "shadow" of the "dark side" of our personality in the essay above, "The Religious Optimist," under "Moral Evil." The dark self (or the "dark side") and the "shadow" is Jung's idea of the unconscious. The "destructiveness" of the shadow is Fromm's idea.

732 Erich Fromm, *The Anatomy of Human Destructiveness* (1973), p. 20 and 272ff. Abbr. Fromm, Destructiveness.

733 Fromm, *Destructiveness,* 273.

734 These eight characteristics of the "dark self" derive from Erich Fromm's *The Anatomy of Human Destructiveness,* pp. 25-26, 29, and 275.

735 Fromm, *Destructiveness,* 275. His emphasis.

736 Carl Jung, *Archetypes of the Collective Unconscious* (1934-55), pp. 40, 106, 288. Abbr. Jung, Archetypes.

737 Emerson, "Self-Reliance," 139.

738 Nietzsche, *The Gay Science* (1882), Section 283. His emphasis. Abbr. Nietzsche, Gay Science, 283.

739 Nietzsche, *Twilight of the Idols* (1888), "Expeditions of an Untimely Man," Section 38. His emphasis. Abbr. Nietzsche, Twilight, 38.

740 Bacon, *Organum*, 1.41.

741 Bacon, *Organum*, 1.41.

742 Stumpf, 32-33.

743 Bacon, *Organum*, 1.41.

744 Feuerbach makes a similar statement about religion bearing reference to man and not the universe. See my essay above, "The Language of Ethics," under "Men of Religion."

745 Bacon, *Organum*, 1.41.

746 Bacon, *Organum*, 1.52.

747 Both the Chinese philosopher Chuang-Tzu (4th century BCE) and the German philosopher Friedrich Nietzsche (1844–1900) rejected conventional societal values. They each used these values in ways that contradicted their traditional meanings, aiming to highlight their emptiness and to liberate the individual from their control.

748 Mark Cartwright. "Roman Games, Chariot Races & Spectacle" (Dec. 4, 2013). *World History Encyclopedia*. Retrieved: https://www.worldhistory.org/article/635/roman-games-chariot-races--spectacle. Abbr. Cartwright.

749 Siobhan McElduff, "Cost of Munera and Other Spectacles," in *Spectacles in the Roman World* (2020). Retrieved: https://pressbooks.bccampus.ca/spectaclesintheromanworldsourcebook/chapter/costs-of-munera-and-other-spectacles. Abbr. McElduff.

750 Cartwright.

751 McElduff. A modern equivalence of 1 Roman sesterce is $0.50 USD.

752 Leon R. Kass, *Beyond Therapy: Biotechnology and the Pursuit of Happiness. A Report by the President's Council on Bioethics* (2003), p. 101. Abbr. Kass. Also see Adam Briggle's *A Rich Bioethics: Public Policy, Biotechnology, and the Kass Council* (2010).

753 Kass, 102.

754 Kass, 102.

755 Kass, 102. His emphasis.

756 Kass, 102.

757 Kass, 102-103. His emphasis.

758 Kass, 107-145.

759 Kass, 146.

760 Kass, 148. His emphasis.

761 Kass, 155-56. My emphasis.

762 I'm grateful to my son for bringing this event to my attention.

763 Søren Kierkegaard, *Either/Or* (1843). Edited and translated by Howard and Edna Hong, Princeton University Press, 1987, p. 285. Abbr. Kierkegaard, Either/Or.

764 Kierkegaard, *Either/Or*, 285.

765 Kierkegaard, *Either/Or*, 289.

766 Cardoso-Leite, Pedro et al. "Media use, attention, mental health and academic performance among 8 to 12-year-old children" (Nov. 2021). Retrieved: https://www.ncbi.nlm.nih.gov/pmc/articles/PMC8598050.

767 Denis Campbell, "Depression in girls linked to higher use of social media" (Jan. 4, 2019). *The Guardian*. Retrieved: https://www.theguardian.com/society/2019/jan/04/depression-in-girls-linked-to-higher-use-of-social-media.

768 Jeff Orlowski, "The Social Dilemma" (Oct. 3, 2020). *Netflix*. Script. Retrieved: https://scrapsfromtheloft.com/movies/the-social-dilemma-movie-transcript. Chamath Palihapitiya was formerly head of "growth tactics" at Facebook. Growth tactics became the most optimal way to manipulate users to do what Facebook wanted them to do. Abbr. Orlowski.

769 Orlowski.

770 Orlowski.

771 Orlowski.

772 Orlowski.

773 Amy McCarthy, "This Korean Food Phenomenon is Changing the Internet: Meet the American YouTubers who are now trying to cash in on *mukbang*" (Apr. 19, 2017). *Eater.com*. Retrieved: https://www.eater.com/2017/4/19/15349568/mukbang-videos-korean-youtube. Abbr. McCarthy.

774 Cheryl D. Fryar, M.S.P.H. et al. "Prevalence of Overweight, Obesity, and Severe Obesity Among Adults Aged 20 and Over: United States, 1960-1962 Through 2017-2018." NCHS Health E-Stats. December 2020. Retrieved: https://www.cdc.gov/nchs/data/hestat/obesity-adult-17-18/obesity-adult.htm.

775 Nietzsche, *The Gay Science* (1882). Section 125. Nietzsche had already prophesized the death of God long before the madman pronounced it. Nietzsche adds, "this tremendous event is still on its way."

776 IlluminatiPirate (thread starter), "Dead Internet Theory: Most of Internet is Fake" (Jan. 5, 2021). Retrieved: https://forum.agoraroad.com/index.php?threads/dead-internet-theory-most-of-the-internet-is-fake.3011. Abbr. IlluminatiPirate.

777 I wrote an unpublished spiral bound 240-page book in 1999, *Reverse Pyramid Training and The Fifteen Rules for Building Lean Muscle Mass*. I advertised this book on my website "musclebuildingrules.com." I made a sale every day to *real people*. In 2021, I published my first book, *The Fitness Mindset: 7 Habits for Peak Performance To Get Strong, Lean, And Fit*. Book sales were quite successful the first two years. However, after 2023, Amazon book sales have become rare. Book sales on my website "thefitnessmindsetbook.com," has become rarer, if not, nonexistent.

778 Max Read, "How Much of the Internet is Fake? Turns Out, a lot of it, Actually" (Dec. 26, 2018). *New York Times Magazine*. Retrieved: https://nymag.com/intelligencer/2018/12/how-much-of-the-internet-is-fake.html. Abbr. Read.

779 Kaitlyn Tiffany, "Maybe You Missed It, But the Internet 'Died' Five Years Ago" (Aug. 31, 2021). *The Atlantic Magazine*. Retrieved: https://www.theatlantic.com/technology/archive/2021/08/dead-internet-theory-wrong-but-feels-true/619937. Abbr. Tiffany.

780 IlluminatiPirate.

781 Tristan Harris and Aza Raskin, "The A.I. Dilemma – March 9, 2023" (Apr. 5, 2023). *Center for Humane Technology*. YouTube retrieved: https://www.youtube.com/watch?v=xoVJKj8lcNQ. 1:07:30. Transcript retrieved: https://singjupost.com/discussion-the-ai-dilemma-march-9-2023-transcript. His emphasis. Abbr. Harris.

782 Read.

783 IlluminatiPirate.

784 Read.

785 TODAY, "Inside 'Click Farms' And Their Social Media Impact" (Apr. 19, 2019). Retrieved: https://www.youtube.com/watch?v=YZhlU2_YsPE.

786 Read.

787 IlluminatiPirate.

788 IlluminatiPirate.

789 IlluminatiPirate.

790 Read.

791 Read.

792 TimesLIVE Video, "Artists create Zuckerberg deepfake video" (June 13, 2019). Retrieved: https://www.youtube.com/watch?v=cnUd0TpuoXI. The deepfake video of Mark Zuckerberg was originally posted on Instagram by Bill Posters on Sept. 21, 2017.

793 Read.

794 Read.

795 Igal Zeifman, "Bot Traffic Report 2016 – Imperva" (Jan. 24, 2016). *Imperva, Inc.* Retrieved: https://imperva.com/blog/archive/bot-traffic-report-2016.

796 Luke Lango, "OpenAI Races Toward AGI with its Breakthrough Model" (Oct. 12, 2024). Retrieved: https://investorplace.com/hypergrowthinvesting/2024/10/openai-races-toward-agi-with-its-new-breaktrhough-model. Abbr. Lango.

797 Faward Ali, "GPT-1 to GPT-4: Each of OpenAI's GPT Models Explained and Compared" (Apr. 11, 2023). Retrieved: https://makeuseof.com/gpt-models-explained-and-compared.

798 See https://openai.com.

799 Harris.

800 Harris.

801 Harris.

802 Harris.

803 Tristan Harris and Aza Raskin, "The A.I. Dilemma—March 9, 2023" (Apr. 5, 2023). *Center for Humane Technology.* YouTube retrieved: https://www.youtube.com/watch?v=xoVJKj8lcNQ. 1:07:30. Transcript retrieved: https://singjupost.com/discussion-the-ai-dilemma-march-9-2023-transcript. Abbr. Harris.

804 Harris.

805 Harris.

806 Harris.

807 Harris.

808 Harris.

809 Harris.

810 Kevin Roose, "Character.AI Faces Lawsuit After Teen's Suicide," *The New York Times* (Oct. 23, 2024). Retrieved: https://nytimes.com/2024/10/23/technology/characterai-lawsuit-teen-suicide.html.

811 Harris. His emphasis.

812 Harris.

813 Sabrina Ortiz, "What is ChatGPT? The World's Most Popular AI Chatbot Explained" (Aug. 31, 2024). *ZDNET.* Retrieved: https://zdnet.com/article/what-is-chatgpt-the-worlds-most-popular-ai-chatbot-explained. Abbr. Ortiz.

814 Ortiz.

815 Richard E. Cytowic, *Your Stone Age Brain in the Screen Age: Coping with Digital Distraction and Sensory Overload.* The MIT Press, Cambridge, MA. Oct. 1, 2024. Abbr. Cytowic.

816 Cytowic, xiv.

817 Cytowic, xiv.

818 Cytowic, xv.

819 Cytowic, xv.

820 Cytowic, xv-xvi.

821 Cytowic, 1.

822 Cytowic, xvi. My emphasis.

823 Cytowic, xvii.

824 Cytowic, xvii.

825 Cytowic, xvii-xviii. My emphasis.

826 Cytowic, 28-29.

827 Cytowic, 28.

828 Katherine Biek, "Our Attention Span Is Less Than That Of A ... Oh, Look!" (May 14, 2015). Newsy Science. Retrieved: https://www.youtube.com/watch?v=uPuIa97007Q&t=117s. Abbr. Biek.

829 Kevin McSpadden, "You Now Have A Shorter Attention Span Than A Goldfish," (May 14, 2015). TIME. Retrieved: https://time.com/3858309/attention-spans-goldfish.

830 Cytowic, 28.

831 Biek.

[832] Biek.

[833] Claire McCarthy, "Can Cell Phone Use Cause ADHD?" (July 31, 2018). *Harvard Health.* Retrieved: https://health.harvard.edu/blog/can-cell-phone-use-cause-adhd-2018073114375. Abbr. McCarthy.

[834] Chaelin K. Ra et al. "Association of Digital Media Use with Subsequent Symptoms of Attention-Deficit/Hyperactivity Disorder Among Adolescents" (July 17, 2018). *Journal of the American Medical Association* (JAMA). Vol. 320. Issue 3. Pp. 255-263. Retrieved: https://jamanetwork.com/journals/jama/fullarticle/2687861. Abbr. Chaelin.

[835] McCarthy.

[836] McCarthy.

[837] Michael Manos, "Does Heightened Screen Time Cause Attention-Deficit Disorder (ADHD) in Children?" (Mar. 7, 2023). *Cleveland Clinic.* Retrieved: https://health.clevelandclinic.org/screen-time-and-adhd.

[838] Cytowic, 29.

[839] I talk about improving selective attention regarding weight training performance in Chapter 2 of my book, *The Fitness Mindset.* However, I do not use the term "selective attention," but rather "flow of exercising," which is adopted from Mihaly Csikszentmihalyi's idea of 'flow' in his book, *Flow: The Psychology of Optimal Performance* (1990).

[840] Cytowic, 29.

[841] Cynthia Kubu, "Why Multitasking Doesn't Work" (Mar. 2021). *Cleveland Clinic.* Retrieved: https://health.clevelandclinic.org/science-clear-multitasking-doesnt-work. Abbr. Kubu.

[842] Kubu.

[843] Cytowic, 29.

[844] Cytowic, 29.

[845] See for example: (1) "Multitasking Undermines Our Efficiency, Study Suggests" (Oct. 2001). *American Psychological Association.* Retrieved: https://apa.org/monitor/oct01/multitask. (2) "Multitasking: Switching Costs" (Mar. 2006). *American Psychological Association.* Retrieved: https://apa.org/topics/research/multitasking. (3) "Your Brain on Multitasking" (Apr. 2015). *CNN.* Retrieved: https://cnn.com/2015/04/09/health/your-brain-multitasking/index.html. (4) "Why Do We Need Media Multitasking? A Self-Regulatory Perspective" (Feb. 2021). *Frontiers in Psychology.* Retrieved: https://pmc.ncbi.nih.gov/articles/PMC7905209. (5) Cynthia Kubu, "Why Multitasking Doesn't Work" (Mar. 2021). *Cleveland Clinic.* Retrieved: https://health.clevelandclinic.org/science-clear-multitasking-doesnt-work. (6) "Are There Benefits of Multitasking?" (Nov. 2023). *University of Southern California.* Retrieved: https://appliedpsychologydegree.usc.edu/blog/benefits-of-multitasking.

[846] Matthew Walker, *Why We Sleep: Unlocking the Power of Sleep and Dreams* (2017). Scribner, New York, NY, pp. 268-69. Abbr. Walker.

[847] Walker, 269-70; Cytowic, 123.

[848] Walker, 195. My emphasis.

[849] Walker, 196. My emphasis.

[850] Walker, 195.

[851] Cytowic, 123.

[852] Walker, 207, 219, 224; Cytowic, 123-24.

[853] Cytowic, 123-24.

[854] Walker, 325; Cytowic, 124-25.

[855] Walker, 157-63; Cytowic, 127.

[856] Matthew Carey, "Director Jeff Orlowski Attacks Social Media Impact In 'The Social Dilemma': "We Live in The Matrix" – Contenders Documentary" (Jan. 10, 2021). Retrieved: https://deadline.com/2021/01/the-social-dilemma-director-jeff-orlowski-interview-netflix-contenders-1234670587. Abbr. Carey.

[857] Carey.

[858] Discovering our true selves (*who* one is) before embracing our humanity (*what* one is) can lead to a selfish ambition.

[859] See Ralph Waldo Emerson's essay "Self-Reliance" (1841).

[860] Adapted from the 2014 movie, "Lucy."

[861] Partial lyrics to the song, "In the End" (Oct. 9, 2001) by American rock band Linkin Park.

[862] Martin Heidegger, *Being and Time* (1927). Translated by John Macquarrie and Edward Robinson. Harper and Row Publishers, 1962. Section 2, German pagination 7. Abbr. Heidegger, Being and Time, 2.7.

[863] Heidegger, *Being and Time,* 49.247.

[864] Heidegger, *Being and Time,* 48.242.

[865] Heidegger, *Being and Time,* 49.247.

[866] Heidegger, *Being and Time,* 38.176.

[867] Heidegger, *Being and Time,* 51.252; 52.255-58; 71.370-72.

[868] Heidegger, *Being and Time,* 53.263-264.

[869] Arthur Schopenhauer, "On the Vanity of Existence," in *Essays and Aphorisms,* Translated by R. J. Hollingdale Penguin Books, 1970, p. 51.

[870] Heidegger, *Being and Time,* 53.263. His emphasis.

[871] Heidegger, *Being and Time,* 53.266. His emphasis.

[872] Nietzsche, *The Birth of Tragedy* (1872) with a new 1886 preface, "Attempt at a Self-Criticism," Section 1. Translated with commentary by Walter Kaufmann. Random House, Inc., 1967. Abbr. Nietzsche, Birth of Tragedy, 1.

[873] Nietzsche, *Birth of Tragedy,* 1. His emphasis.

[874] Walter Kaufmann points out that Nietzsche's use of *Apollinisch* is often translated as "Apollonian." However, Nietzsche did not actually use the term "Apollonian." For more details, see Kaufmann's introduction, section 3, footnote 9, p. 9.

[875] R. J. Hollingdale, *Nietzsche: The Man and his Philosophy* (1965, 1999), p. 82.

[876] Nietzsche, *Birth of Tragedy,* 1.

[877] Nietzsche, *Twilight of the Idols* (1888), "Expeditions of an Untimely Man," Section 10.

[878] Nietzsche, *Birth of Tragedy,* 2.

[879] Nietzsche, *Birth of Tragedy,* 5.

[880] Nietzsche, *Birth of Tragedy,* 5.

[881] Stumpf, 381.

[882] Stumpf, 388.

[883] Middleton, *Selected Letters of Friedrich Nietzsche* (1996), Letter to Paul Ree, November 1882, Hackett Publishing, No. 106.

[884] Heidegger, *Being and Time,* 29.134.

[885] A.J. Gentile, "Compilation: Our Reality is an Illusion," *The Why Files.* July 1, 2024. Retrieved: https://youtu.be/Nr5yk9mxzSI?si=dPnoUHvJ-9bHA5cC (1:09:42-1:10:46).

www.ingramcontent.com/pod-product-compliance
Lightning Source LLC
Chambersburg PA
CBHW020916140626
46545CB00015B/66